Grilling For Dumm...

D0599400

The IDG Books Worldwide logo is a registered trademark under exclusive license to IDG Books Worldwide, Inc., from International Data Group, Inc. The ...For Dummies logo is a trademark, and For Dummies and ...For Dummies are registered trademarks of IDG Books Worldwide, Inc. All other trademarks are the property of their respective owners.

The Ten Commandments of Grilling

- **Practice patience.** Wait for the fire to be ready before you begin grilling — be sure that the coals are uniformly ashy gray and use the handheld test to gauge the heat.

- **Be organized.** Set up a small table right next to the grill with all of your ingredients, utensils, serving platters, and so on.

- **Marinate, marinate, marinate.** Marinating adds moisture and flavor to almost all foods. (See Chapter 5.)

- **Don't skimp on fuel.** Build a fire that won't lose its heat before you finish grilling. Spread the coals about 2 inches beyond the edges of the food.

- **Police the fire!** A fire changes constantly and demands your attention. Stay vigilant.

- **Build a fire with different hot spots.** A fire with different heat areas allows you to shift food around to sear, cook through, and keep warm. Set gas burners to different temperatures to provide varying degrees of heat. Build an indirect fire in a charcoal or gas grill. (See Chapter 1.)

- **Understand the grilling variables.** Air temperature, wind, grill type, the kind of fuel used, the temperature of the food (whether or not it's been refrigerated) — all affect your grilling times. Use recipe cooking times only as a rough estimate.

- **Figure out when food is done.** Overcooked food doesn't have a reverse gear to take it back to rare. To test for doneness, make a small cut in the center of the food so that you can peek inside. Test frequently for doneness a few minutes before the estimated final cooking time. Use an instant-read thermometer (see Chapter 2) for thick chops, roasts, and whole poultry.

- **Sprint from the grill to the table.** Small, thin pieces of food rapidly lose their heat after taking them off the grill. Be sure to have diners ready and waiting at the table for finished platters.

- **Relax!** Grilling is carefree cooking. Enjoy the live fire, the fresh air, and the friends and family members who gather around to admire your burger-flipping techniques.

A Few of Our Favorite Recipes

- Lamb Burgers (Chapter 8)

- Satay with Peanut Dipping Sauce (Chapter 9)

- Just-Right Ribs (Chapter 10)

- Rotisserie-Grilled Chicken with Lemon-Herb Gravy (Chapter 11)

- Grilled Tenderloin Au Poivre (Chapter 12)

- Dale Curry's Hickory Smoked Whole Turkey (Chapter 15)

- Lemon-Cilantro Chicken with Garlic-Ginger Mayonnaise (Chapter 15)

- Asian-Style Salmon Fillets with Vegetables (Chapter 16)

- Smoked Salmon Fillet (Chapter 16)

- Whole Trout with Thyme and Almond Butter Sauce (Chapter 16)

- Baba Ghanoush (Chapter 17)

- Grilled Bananas with Caramel Sauce (Chapter 17)

- Roasted Sweet Pepper Salsa (Chapter 17)

- Stuffed Summer Squash (Chapter 17)

- Best-Ever Fajitas (Chapter 18)

- Sun-Dried Tomato and Mozzarella Pizza (Chapter 18)

- Hoisin Marinade and Basting Sauce (Chapter 5)

- Bow Ties with Peppers, Peas, and Saffron Mayonnaise (Chapter 7)

- Three-Bean Bake (Chapter 7)

Copyright © 1998 IDG Books Worldwide, Inc. All rights reserved.

Cheat Sheet $2.95 value. Item 5076-4.

For more information about IDG Books, call 1-800-762-2974.

IDG BOOKS WORLDWIDE

...For Dummies®: Bestselling Book Series for Beginners

Grilling For Dummies®

Great Grilling Secrets

- Allow about 10 to 15 minutes to preheat a gas grill and about 30 to 40 minutes to get a charcoal fire ready for cooking.

- Brush the grill with vegetable oil before heating it to keep food from sticking.

- Grill quick-cooking pieces of meat, fish, poultry, and vegetables on fresh, oiled herb sprigs or lemon slices for more flavor.

- Soak wooden skewers in water at least 30 minutes before threading food on them to prevent the skewers from burning.

- Use long-handled tongs rather than a fork to turn food. A fork pierces the food, which releases juices.

- Use sweet basting sauces made with sugar, honey, or ketchup only during the final 10 to 15 minutes of cooking, to prevent surface charring.

- Place larger and thicker pieces of food closest to the center (the hottest area) of the grill. Shift cooked pieces to the edges to keep them warm.

- Use the grill cover to increase the heat, give food more smoky flavor, and to extinguish flare-ups.

- Open the vents on a covered grill to add oxygen and increase the intensity of the fire — close the vents to do the opposite.

- Flavored wood chips work best when used on foods that are slow-cooked for 20 minutes or more in a covered grill.

- Tap the coals with long tongs to knock off surface ash and instantly heat up the fire.

- Building an indirect fire (see Chapter 1) gives you two levels of heat — one to sear food directly and another to cook food slowly and thoroughly. An indirect fire is the best way to grill ribs, chicken on the bone, and pork tenderloins.

Quick Grilling Safety Tips

- Set the grill on level ground in a well-ventilated area, away from trees, branches, leaves, or anything that might easily catch fire.

- Keep small children and pets away from the grill and never place a grill near the backyard basketball hoop or other recreational area. Never leave a fire or hot grill unattended.

- Never use gasoline or kerosene as a liquid fire starter — it can cause an explosion or flare-up and envelop you in flames. Never add liquid fire starters to charcoal that is already warm.

- Keep a spray bottle handy for dousing flames and flare-ups and have a garden hose or a fire extinguisher available for emergencies.

- After grilling, cover the grill and close all the vents to cut off the oxygen supply and extinguish the coals. To be sure you've cooled the coals, douse them with water or with a layer of ash or sand. Be sure to remove wet coals as soon as they are cool to prevent the grill from rusting.

- Store spare or disconnected propane tanks in an open space, never in the garage, a shed, or in the house. Always transport tanks in an upright position. Never grill indoors or in a closed garage.

- If grilling on a wooden deck, use a hose to soak the area around the grill — burning embers that fall from the grill can set the wood on fire.

The Handheld Fire Test

Use the following simple technique to gauge the temperature of the coals. Place the palm of your hand just above the grid. If you can hold your hand in that position for two seconds (counting "one-thousand one, one-thousand two"), the coals are hot; a three-second hold tells you the coals are medium-hot; four seconds is medium; and five is low.

Praise for *Grilling For Dummies:*

"*Grilling For Dummies* will forever change the way you think about grilling. Here is a wealth of information for turning the great American cooking machine into a tool for creating contemporary, sophisticated dishes."

> — Alfred Portale, Chef-Author *Gotham Bar and Grill Cookbook*

"It's all here — from the hottest advice on buying a grill to the coolest ways to use it. Marie and John let you in on the secrets true grill-friends share."

> — Christine Smith Koury, Food Editor and Writer

"Even cooks who deem themselves 'grilling gurus' have much to learn from this concise volume of essential information, presented with sophistication and style. The complex tastes of the recipes come from a creative use of ingredients and belies how easy they are to prepare."

> — Ellen Brown, Author of *All Wrapped Up* and
> Former Food Editor of *USA Today*

"*Grilling For Dummies* is the perfect guide for all you aspiring backyard gourmets — with this book in one hand, your spatula in the other, and your "Kiss the Cook" apron around your neck, you're ready for grilling greatness."

> — Willard Scott, TV Personality

"An historic achievement — Rama and Mariani clearly have written the greatest book on barbecuing since Thomas Torquemada's 15th century classic *Spanish Inquisition Grilling Techniques.*"

> — A. Craig Copetas, *The Wall Street Journal*

"Marie Rama's and John Mariani's library of cooking knowledge unlocks for you the secrets of grilling over an open fire. Imagine learning to tame the flames for perfectly cooked juicy poultry and meats with that special, full, rich, grilled flavor that commands the attention of your guests — all from your simple grill. This book is a must for anyone with an appetite for the great grilled flavors of life."

> — Jimmy Schmidt, Chef/Owner of The Rattlesnake Club

More Praise for *Grilling For Dummies:*

"Invaluable reading for anyone who intends to put match to charcoal. Rama's and Mariani's advice will help transform the worst steak-arsonist into an accomplished grillmaster."

> — John Atwood, Editor in Chief, *Sports Afield*

"You, too, can master the art of outdoor grilling. Marie Rama and John Mariani take the mystery out of fire and smoke in this comprehensive but easy to follow guide, full of smart tips and tasty recipes."

> — Dotty Griffith, Dining Editor/Restaurant Critic,
> *Dallas Morning News*

"From the broad range of recipes to side dishes and condiments, *Grilling For Dummies* will become one of your most important tools for the grilling season. This book allows you to grasp the understanding of the various styles and techniques of grilling, and the use of your equipment. Most importantly, the recipes for grilled fare are not complicated, using a creative approach with ingredients that are in your everyday use. Enjoy your new Adventures in Grilling."

> — Chef Keith Famie, T.V. Host of *Famie's Adventures in Cooking*
> and Celebrated Chef

"Grilling has traditionally been a man's thing — Marie Rama and John Mariani have now made it everyone's art. I suggest that you flip open to the chapter called "All About Ribs" and break into some heavy fixin', mixin', rubbin', and grillin', only to accompany this action with some cold beer, wet-naps, and a side of Orange-Ginger Coleslaw!"

> — Gary Danko, Best Chef California, 1995,
> James Beard Foundation

"*Grilling For Dummies* is a comprehensive technical resource loaded with educational fun facts that every passionate grill enthusiast will enjoy!"

> — Clifford Pleau, Chef

 TM

References for the Rest of Us!™

BESTSELLING BOOK SERIES

Do you find that traditional reference books are overloaded with technical details and advice you'll never use? Do you postpone important life decisions because you just don't want to deal with them? Then our *...For Dummies*® business and general reference book series is for you.

...For Dummies business and general reference books are written for those frustrated and hard-working souls who know they aren't dumb, but find that the myriad of personal and business issues and the accompanying horror stories make them feel helpless. *...For Dummies* books use a lighthearted approach, a down-to-earth style, and even cartoons and humorous icons to dispel fears and build confidence. Lighthearted but not lightweight, these books are perfect survival guides to solve your everyday personal and business problems.

> *"More than a publishing phenomenon, 'Dummies' is a sign of the times."*
> — The New York Times

> *"...you won't go wrong buying them."*
> — Walter Mossberg, Wall Street Journal, on IDG Books' ...For Dummies books

> *"A world of detailed and authoritative information is packed into them..."*
> — U.S. News and World Report

Already, millions of satisfied readers agree. They have made *...For Dummies* the #1 introductory level computer book series and a best-selling business book series. They have written asking for more. So, if you're looking for the best and easiest way to learn about business and other general reference topics, look to *...For Dummies* to give you a helping hand.

GRILLING

FOR

DUMMIES®

GRILLING
FOR
DUMMIES®

by Marie Rama and John Mariani

IDG Books Worldwide, Inc.
An International Data Group Company

Foster City, CA ◆ Chicago, IL ◆ Indianapolis, IN ◆ New York, NY

Grilling For Dummies®

Published by
IDG Books Worldwide, Inc.
An International Data Group Company
919 E. Hillsdale Blvd.
Suite 400
Foster City, CA 94404
www.idgbooks.com (IDG Books Worldwide Web site)
www.dummies.com (Dummies Press Web site)

Copyright © 1998 IDG Books Worldwide, Inc. All rights reserved. No part of this book, including interior design, cover design, and icons, may be reproduced or transmitted in any form, by any means (electronic, photocopying, recording, or otherwise) without the prior written permission of the publisher.

Library of Congress Catalog Card No.: 98-84960

ISBN: 0-7645-5076-4

Printed in the United States of America

10 9 8 7 6 5

1B/SY/QW/ZZ/IN

Distributed in the United States by IDG Books Worldwide, Inc.

Distributed by CDG Books Canada Inc. for Canada; by Transworld Publishers Limited in the United Kingdom; by IDG Norge Books for Norway; by IDG Sweden Books for Sweden; by IDG Books Australia Publishing Corporation Pty. Ltd. for Australia and New Zealand; by TransQuest Publishers Pte Ltd. for Singapore, Malaysia, Thailand, Indonesia, and Hong Kong; by Gotop Information Inc. for Taiwan; by ICG Muse, Inc. for Japan; by Norma Comunicaciones S.A. for Colombia; by Intersoft for South Africa; by Eyrolles for France; by International Thomson Publishing for Germany, Austria and Switzerland; by Distribuidora Cuspide for Argentina; by Livraria Cultura for Brazil; by Ediciones ZETA S.C.R. Ltda. for Peru; by WS Computer Publishing Corporation, Inc., for the Philippines; by Contemporanea de Ediciones for Venezuela; by Express Computer Distributors for the Caribbean and West Indies; by Micronesia Media Distributor, Inc. for Micronesia; by Grupo Editorial Norma S.A. for Guatemala; by Chips Computadoras S.A. de C.V. for Mexico; by Editorial Norma de Panama S.A. for Panama; by American Bookshops for Finland. Authorized Sales Agent: Anthony Rudkin Associates for the Middle East and North Africa.

For general information on IDG Books Worldwide's books in the U.S., please call our Consumer Customer Service department at 800-762-2974. For reseller information, including discounts and premium sales, please call our Reseller Customer Service department at 800-434-3422.

For information on where to purchase IDG Books Worldwide's books outside the U.S., please contact our International Sales department at 317-596-5530 or fax 317-596-5692.

For consumer information on foreign language translations, please contact our Customer Service department at 1-800-434-3422, fax 317-596-5692, or e-mail rights@idgbooks.com.

For information on licensing foreign or domestic rights, please phone +1-650-655-3109.

For sales inquiries and special prices for bulk quantities, please contact our Sales department at 650-655-3200 or write to the address above.

For information on using IDG Books Worldwide's books in the classroom or for ordering examination copies, please contact our Educational Sales department at 800-434-2086 or fax 317-596-5499.

For press review copies, author interviews, or other publicity information, please contact our Public Relations department at 650-655-3000 or fax 650-655-3299.

For authorization to photocopy items for corporate, personal, or educational use, please contact Copyright Clearance Center, 222 Rosewood Drive, Danvers, MA 01923, or fax 978-750-4470.

LIMIT OF LIABILITY/DISCLAIMER OF WARRANTY: THE PUBLISHER AND AUTHOR HAVE USED THEIR BEST EFFORTS IN PREPARING THIS BOOK. THE PUBLISHER AND AUTHOR MAKE NO REPRESENTATIONS OR WARRANTIES WITH RESPECT TO THE ACCURACY OR COMPLETENESS OF THE CONTENTS OF THIS BOOK AND SPECIFICALLY DISCLAIM ANY IMPLIED WARRANTIES OF MERCHANTABILITY OR FITNESS FOR A PARTICULAR PURPOSE. THERE ARE NO WARRANTIES WHICH EXTEND BEYOND THE DESCRIPTIONS CONTAINED IN THIS PARAGRAPH. NO WARRANTY MAY BE CREATED OR EXTENDED BY SALES REPRESENTATIVES OR WRITTEN SALES MATERIALS. THE ACCURACY AND COMPLETENESS OF THE INFORMATION PROVIDED HEREIN AND THE OPINIONS STATED HEREIN ARE NOT GUARANTEED OR WARRANTED TO PRODUCE ANY PARTICULAR RESULTS, AND THE ADVICE AND STRATEGIES CONTAINED HEREIN MAY NOT BE SUITABLE FOR EVERY INDIVIDUAL. NEITHER THE PUBLISHER NOR AUTHOR SHALL BE LIABLE FOR ANY LOSS OF PROFIT OR ANY OTHER COMMERCIAL DAMAGES, INCLUDING BUT NOT LIMITED TO SPECIAL, INCIDENTAL, CONSEQUENTIAL, OR OTHER DAMAGES. FULFILLMENT OF EACH COUPON OFFER IS THE RESPONSIBILITY OF THE OFFEROR.

Trademarks: All brand names and product names used in this book are trade names, service marks, trademarks, or registered trademarks of their respective owners. IDG Books Worldwide is not associated with any product or vendor mentioned in this book.

is a registered trademark or trademark under exclusive license to IDG Books Worldwide, Inc. from International Data Group, Inc. in the United States and/or other countries.

IDG BOOKS WORLDWIDE

About the Authors

Marie Rama is coauthor of *Cooking For Dummies*. She has worked as a professional pastry chef and recipe developer for numerous food companies and associations, including The McIlhenny Company and The United Fresh Fruit and Vegetable Association. Marie served as Director of Romance, Weddings, and Entertaining for Korbel Champagne and as a spokesperson for Sunkist Growers. She is a regular guest-chef on hundreds of TV and radio shows in the U.S. and Canada, and she lives with her husband, Mark Reiter, and their two sons, Nick and Will, in Bronxville, New York.

John Mariani is the author of several of the most highly regarded books on food in America today. His first book, *The Dictionary of American Food & Drink* (Ticknor & Fields, 1983), was hailed as the "American Larousse Gastronomique" and was chosen "best reference book on food for 1983" by *Library Journal*. After a decade, during which the book was declared a "classic" of American food studies, Hearst Books issued a completely revised edition in 1994. His latest book, *The Dictionary of Italian Food & Drink,* the most comprehensive study of Italian food published in the U.S., will be published in spring 1998 by Broadway Books.

He is currently food and travel correspondent for *Esquire;* Food, Wine, Beer & Spirits Board Expert for the PRODIGY interactive service, for which he also produces the weekly *Mariani's Virtual Gourmet Newsletter;* dining columnist for *The Wine Spectator;* food columnist for *Diversion;* columnist for *Eating Well;* Food & Drink columnist for *Sports Afield;* and columnist for *Restaurant Hospitality.*

Mariani was born in New York City and received his B.A. from Iona College and his M.A. and Ph.D. from Columbia University. He lives in Tuckahoe, New York, with his wife, Galina, and two sons, Michael and Christopher.

About the Photographer

Lou Manna resides in New York City, where he runs his own studio on Fifth Avenue. Through his specialty in food photography, he has worked with numerous restaurants, renowned chefs, and food critics since 1975, including a long-standing collaboration with Craig Claiborne and Pierre Franey. He also contributed the color photography in *Desserts For Dummies* as well as 24 other books, most notably *The Four-Star Kitchen, A Plaza Wedding,* and *Cuisine Rapide.* Lou began his career as a photographer for *The New York Times* and since then has worked with other national publications, corporations, and leading agencies worldwide.

ABOUT IDG BOOKS WORLDWIDE

Welcome to the world of IDG Books Worldwide.

IDG Books Worldwide, Inc., is a subsidiary of International Data Group, the world's largest publisher of computer-related information and the leading global provider of information services on information technology. IDG was founded more than 30 years ago by Patrick J. McGovern and now employs more than 9,000 people worldwide. IDG publishes more than 290 computer publications in over 75 countries. More than 90 million people read one or more IDG publications each month.

Launched in 1990, IDG Books Worldwide is today the #1 publisher of best-selling computer books in the United States. We are proud to have received eight awards from the Computer Press Association in recognition of editorial excellence and three from Computer Currents' First Annual Readers' Choice Awards. Our best-selling ...For Dummies® series has more than 50 million copies in print with translations in 31 languages. IDG Books Worldwide, through a joint venture with IDG's Hi-Tech Beijing, became the first U.S. publisher to publish a computer book in the People's Republic of China. In record time, IDG Books Worldwide has become the first choice for millions of readers around the world who want to learn how to better manage their businesses.

Our mission is simple: Every one of our books is designed to bring extra value and skill-building instructions to the reader. Our books are written by experts who understand and care about our readers. The knowledge base of our editorial staff comes from years of experience in publishing, education, and journalism — experience we use to produce books to carry us into the new millennium. In short, we care about books, so we attract the best people. We devote special attention to details such as audience, interior design, use of icons, and illustrations. And because we use an efficient process of authoring, editing, and desktop publishing our books electronically, we can spend more time ensuring superior content and less time on the technicalities of making books.

You can count on our commitment to deliver high-quality books at competitive prices on topics you want to read about. At IDG Books Worldwide, we continue in the IDG tradition of delivering quality for more than 30 years. You'll find no better book on a subject than one from IDG Books Worldwide.

IDG BOOKS
WORLDWIDE

John Kilcullen
Chairman and CEO
IDG Books Worldwide, Inc.

Steven Berkowitz
President and Publisher
IDG Books Worldwide, Inc.

VIII
WINNER

*Eighth Annual
Computer Press
Awards ≥1992*

IX
WINNER

*Ninth Annual
Computer Press
Awards ≥1993*

X
WINNER

*Tenth Annual
Computer Press
Awards ≥1994*

XI
WINNER

*Eleventh Annual
Computer Press
Awards ≥1995*

IDG is the world's leading IT media, research and exposition company. Founded in 1964, IDG had 1997 revenues of $2.05 billion and has more than 9,000 employees worldwide. IDG offers the widest range of media options that reach IT buyers in 75 countries representing 95% of worldwide IT spending. IDG's diverse product and services portfolio spans six key areas including print publishing, online publishing, expositions and conferences, market research, education and training, and global marketing services. More than 90 million people read one or more of IDG's 290 magazines and newspapers, including IDG's leading global brands — Computerworld, PC World, Network World, Macworld and the Channel World family of publications. IDG Books Worldwide is one of the fastest-growing computer book publishers in the world, with more than 700 titles in 36 languages. The "...For Dummies®" series alone has more than 50 million copies in print. IDG offers online users the largest network of technology-specific Web sites around the world through IDG.net (http://www.idg.net), which comprises more than 225 targeted Web sites in 55 countries worldwide. International Data Corporation (IDC) is the world's largest provider of information technology data, analysis and consulting, with research centers in over 41 countries and more than 400 research analysts worldwide. IDG World Expo is a leading producer of more than 168 globally branded conferences and expositions in 35 countries including E3 (Electronic Entertainment Expo), Macworld Expo, ComNet, Windows World Expo, ICE (Internet Commerce Expo), Agenda, DEMO, and Spotlight. IDG's training subsidiary, ExecuTrain, is the world's largest computer training company, with more than 230 locations worldwide and 785 training courses. IDG Marketing Services helps industry-leading IT companies build international brand recognition by developing global integrated marketing programs via IDG's print, online and exposition products worldwide. Further information about the company can be found at www.idg.com.

1/24/99

Authors' Acknowledgments

There is a long list of people we would like to especially thank, who helped make this book possible.

To gather accurate information for the sidebars and icons in this book, we turned to many food experts and associations. We'd like to thank Susan Lamb Parenti and the National Cattlemen's Beef Association; Robin Kline and Ed Newman, consultants for the National Pork Producers Council; the American Lamb Council; and the National Institute of Fisheries. We are also grateful for the invaluable contributions of Donna Myers, editor of *The BackYard BarbeQuer* newsletter — after more than 25 years as spokesperson for the Barbecue Industry Association, Donna knows as much about grilling equipment, manufacturers, and techniques as anyone we know.

We'd also like to thank Jane Uetz Johnson, our technical advisor, for her careful fact checking and formatting of all our recipes. And thank you illustrators extraordinaire, Liz Kurtzman and Rich Tennant.

We thank Galina Mariani and Ann Persico for their very precise and delicious recipe testing assistance, especially with Chapters 16 and 18. We'd also like to thank the following manufacturers who generously donated our very reliable testing grills, grilling equipment, and accessories: Sunbeam, Char-Broil, Ducane, Jackes-Evans, and E-Z Fit Barbecue Parts and Accessories. We offer more information about these and other equipment manufacturers in Chapter 2.

We thank our photographer, Lou Manna, food stylist Diane Simone Vezza, and prop stylist Monica Baig for producing beautiful photos of more than 40 different recipes over three long days.

Marie would like to thank her husband, Mark, and her sons, Nick and Will, for ever-so-patiently taste-testing all 175 recipes developed for this book — some which didn't make it in.

We owe special, heartfelt thanks to our Project Editor at IDG, Tere Drenth, and her supporting editorial team of Tina Sims, copy editor; and Darren Meiss and Paul Kuzmic, editorial assistants. Throughout all these months, they kept us on track with their tireless devotion, editorial skills, and insightful questions. We also thank IDG's acquisitions editor, Sarah Kennedy, for her continuous, invaluable support and clear-sighted counsel.

We'd like to thank IMG literary agent, Mark Reiter, who is blessed with many talents — not the least of which is knowing a good idea when he hears it.

And one final note: Marie would like to thank her friend, Ira Bart, who one perfect summer day, waved a two-inch-thick steak in front of his personally-designed brick grill and announced, "Marie, you ought to write *Grilling For Dummies*." So, we did.

Publisher's Acknowledgments

We're proud of this book; please register your comments through our IDG Books Worldwide Online Registration Form located at http://my2cents.dummies.com.

Some of the people who helped bring this book to market include the following:

Acquisitions, Development, and Editorial

Project Editor: Tere Drenth

Acquisitions Editor: Sarah Kennedy, Executive Editor

Copy Editor: Tina Sims

Recipe and Text Reviewer: Jane Uetz Johnson

Technical Reviewer: Donna Myers

Editorial Manager: Elaine Brush

Editorial Coordinator: Maureen F. Kelly

Acquisitions Coordinator: Ann K. Miller

Editorial Assistants: Paul Kuzmic, Darren Meiss

Acquisitions Assistants: Jill Alexander, Nickole Harris

Administrative Assistant: Allison Solomon

Production

Project Coordinator: Regina Snyder

Layout and Graphics: Traci Ankrom, Cameron Booker, Lou Boudreau, Linda M. Boyer, J. Tyler Connor, Angela F. Hunckler, Tom Missler, Anna Rohrer, Brent Savage, Kathie Schutte, Janet Seib, M. Anne Sipahimalani, Deirdre Smith, Rashell Smith, Michael A. Sullivan

Special Art: Elizabeth Kurtzman, illustrations; Lou Manna, photography; Diane Vezza, food styling; and Monica Baig, prop styling

Proofreaders: Kelli Botta, Christine Berman, Betty Kish, Brian Massey, Nancy Price, Janet Withers

Indexer: Sharon Hilgenberg

Special Help

Tamara Castleman, Senior Copy Editor; Holly McGuire, Acquisitions Editor; Stacey Riebsomer, Copy Editor

---

General and Administrative

IDG Books Worldwide, Inc.: John Kilcullen, CEO; Steven Berkowitz, President and Publisher

IDG Books Technology Publishing Group: Richard Swadley, Senior Vice President and Publisher; Walter Bruce III, Vice President and Associate Publisher; Steven Sayre, Associate Publisher; Joseph Wikert, Associate Publisher; Mary Bednarek, Branded Product Development Director; Mary Corder, Editorial Director

IDG Books Consumer Publishing Group: Roland Elgey, Senior Vice President and Publisher; Kathleen A. Welton, Vice President and Publisher; Kevin Thornton, Acquisitions Manager; Kristin A. Cocks, Editorial Director

IDG Books Internet Publishing Group: Brenda McLaughlin, Senior Vice President and Group Publisher; Diane Graves Steele, Vice President and Associate Publisher; Sofia Marchant, Online Marketing Manager

IDG Books Production for Dummies Press: Michael R. Britton, Vice President of Production; Debbie Stailey, Associate Director of Production; Cindy L. Phipps, Manager of Project Coordination, Production Proofreading, and Indexing; Shelley Lea, Supervisor of Graphics and Design; Debbie J. Gates, Production Systems Specialist; Robert Springer, Supervisor of Proofreading; Laura Carpenter, Production Control Manager; Tony Augsburger, Supervisor of Reprints and Bluelines

Dummies Packaging and Book Design: Patty Page, Manager, Promotions Marketing

♦

The publisher would like to give special thanks to Patrick J. McGovern, without whom this book would not have been possible.

♦

Contents at a Glance

Cartoons at a Glance

By Rich Tennant

page 7

page 47

"What kind of fuel am I using? Right now, 2 hunks of hamburger, 1 chicken wing and 3 shrimp."

page 167

"This is your all-in-one grilling system. It comes with a rotisserie, a smoker, warming ovens, self contained detachable slaughter house..."

page 107

page 323

Fax: 978-546-7747 • E-mail: the5wave@tiac.net

Recipes at a Glance

Table of Contents

· ·

Foreword

Howdy folks!

As you all know, I love great food. And what's better than mixing great food with the great outdoors? *Grilling For Dummies* is the perfect guide for all you aspiring backyard gourmets — with this book in one hand, your spatula in the other, and your "Kiss the Cook" apron around your neck, you're ready for grilling greatness!

Many of you may be saying to yourselves "I sure as heck don't know how to grill, but I'm no dummy either." Well, grilling novices and more-experienced grillers alike will love this book because it's more than just a bunch of recipes. Readers will learn all about the tools of the trade, types of grills, and tips and techniques from the pros. Also, master grillers from around the globe throw in recipes for their open-flame favorites for you to duplicate on your backyard grill. You'll set stomachs to rumbling and mouths to watering as delicious aromas waft from your grill for the whole neighborhood to take in.

Don't know a briquette from a Rockette? Fearful of igniting half the neighborhood every time you fire up the grill or squirt some lighter fluid? Well, cast aside those fears — not only will this book keep the fire department away, it will help you rustle up some mighty good grillin' vittles, too.

Watching your fat intake (like me)? Not to worry — *Grilling For Dummies* provides ideas for lowfat cuisine over the flame. Need some recipes for your vegetarian friends? Check out the chapter on delicious grilled fruits and veggies. There's even an entire chapter on side dishes!

Want more? No ...*For Dummies* book would be complete without a Part of Tens section. Here, you'll find tips on how to throw a great outdoor party, and how to tailgate like a master.

Well, don't just sit there. Get grilling! A whole smorgasbord of gastronomic grilling goodies awaits!

Willard Scott

TV Personality

Introduction

• •

*I*f your grilling experience is limited to flipping a few burgers on a kettle grill or roasting a hot dog on a branch over an open fire when you were a kid at camp, you've just scratched the surface of what can be a very exciting (and somewhat intimidating) way to cook. After all, you're dealing with an open fire, red-hot coals, and a certain amount of danger, not to mention the potential embarrassment of burning the heck out of a $10 steak.

Grilling For Dummies takes you through the basics of grilling and then shows you the infinite possibilities of this terrific cooking technique. Even if you've done a certain amount of serious grilling out on the patio, this book can help you to refine your technique. It also introduces you to many foods you may never even have considered suitable for grilling, including vegetables and fruits.

And we try very hard to take the intimidation factor out of the process and replace it with a whole lot of fun.

About This Book

Grilling For Dummies is a book that will make an expert grill master out of you — or at least make the exercise painless. But it's not just a book of recipes or of tips on how to buy a grill. The recipes and tips are all in here, but the book includes a great deal more.

Grilling has its own jargon and requires its own accessories. So we explain grilling jargon and tell you what accessories you need — and what accessories you don't need. Grilling has been so popular in the past decade, that the market has responded by improving features of basic grills and by providing a wider variety of grill options. Although all these new features make the grilling marketplace a bit confusing — relax! — you have this book to help you!

In here, we show you the differences — and they are numerous and significant — among different grills and tell you what you can expect to pay for grills and grill accessories.

When you get to the recipe chapters, you find that we discuss the kinds of food that are great on the grill and how to select them. The recipes range from classic to contemporary — all perfect for the grill.

We give you some quick information in the Part of Tens, including the ten best barbecue places in America and tips on how to throw an outdoor party — which, in the end, is the best reason to grill.

We include illustrations that show you exactly what we're talking about, and the color photos of our recipes (located in the center of this book) are so mouth-watering that you'll want to go directly to the recipes and start grilling.

You need not read the book straight through. In fact, we've deliberately arranged it for those who already know a bit about grilling as well as for those who are just beginners. Depending on your admitted level of expertise, you may want to skip directly to the recipes (see Parts II, III, and IV), or you may want to start with Chapter 2 to find out more about the differences between gas grills and charcoal grills. Go right ahead: Read the book in any order you want. That's why this book looks and reads the way it does.

Foolish Assumptions

We are making certain assumptions about you, the reader, in this book. First of all, you obviously have a real interest in good cooking and grilling beyond the obvious burgers and hot dogs, so we gear this book for the reader who really wants to take a little time to get the best results.

Although we never take our assumptions for granted, we believe that you are well aware of the dangers of working with an open fire. But we still continue to stress the safety rules throughout the book. If you wish to skip around this book for information, that's great. But we urge you to read every safety tip that you come across.

We use a lot of common cooking terms here we assume that you're familiar with, including:

- ✔ Sear
- ✔ Braise
- ✔ Sauté
- ✔ Marinate

If you don't feel comfortable with basic cooking terminology, check out *Cooking For Dummies,* by Bryan Miller and Marie Rama (IDG Books Worldwide, Inc.).

We keep our recipes as simple as possible in terms of their instructions, but we firmly believe that these recipes take grilling several steps higher than some of you may have thought possible. Even those with only basic cooking skills shouldn't have the slightest trouble following any recipe in this book. But if you've never done much grilling before, go step-by-step through our simple, classic recipes for items like steaks and burgers. Then try some simple seafood recipes, like a swordfish steak. By the time you master those recipes, you'll be able to reproduce anything in this book.

How This Book Is Organized

As with all the books in the *...For Dummies* series, *Grilling For Dummies* is arranged for maximum ease of use. We break down subjects into simple-to-understand units. We begin with a section we call a *part,* which is further broken down into chapters, within which we cover specific subjects and topics, often with lists for handy reference.

Part I: Gearing Up for Grilling

In this part, we go over everything you need to know to decide among the various kinds of grills on the market, their relative virtues and problems, their costs, and what all those grilling terms mean when you're ready to buy. We also provide a checklist of accessories.

This part also shows you the differences among hardwoods, charcoal, briquettes, self-igniting coals, flavoring woods, and anything else that makes for a good fire. This part also explains how to make a good fire for your particular intentions, whether you're grilling fish, barbecued ribs, or kebabs. We discuss the strategies of safely starting a fire and maintaining it for maximum effect, and then we make some recommendations about the best fire starters on the market, from electric coils to metal chimneys.

Part II: Adding Spice (And Side Dishes) to Your Life

This is where we really start to cook. First, we help you stock your pantry with the kinds of foods and seasonings that make for great grilling. Anyone can slap down a sirloin on a grill, but this part suggests herbs, spices, rubs, and marinades that can add flavor and texture to your grilled foods. We also include recipes for some side dishes to serve with the food that's coming off the fire.

Part III: Golden (Grilled) Oldies

Ready, set, grill. In this part, we cover old-fashioned favorites like burgers (there's more to a great burger than buying a frozen patty at the supermarket, you know), hot dogs, kebabs, and rotisseried foods. In Chapter 10, we also explain the distinctions between regular grilling and barbecuing (ribs, in particular), which can, in fact, be easily accomplished at home with a little patience and a lot of time.

Part IV: Grilling Everything Under the Sun

This part takes you beyond the old-fashioned grilled foods and invites you to try a variety of steak, lamb, and chicken recipes. We give you tips about how to buy the best cut for your purposes.

And if you thought grilling involved only meat and poultry, this part shows you that the grill is one of the most versatile cooking methods imaginable for adding taste to seafood and vegetables. And if you've never considered making pizzas or other sandwiches directly over coals, we think that you'll be surprised by the possibilities.

Part V: The Part of Tens

We finish the book with some fun information that will make outdoor cooking more enjoyable. Here, you get tips on throwing a great party featuring fabulous food from your grill. And, you get our personal pick of the best barbecue restaurants around the U.S.A., where you may pick up a few pointers that even we missed.

Icons Used in This Book

We fill our book with icons that alert you to something you may not have thought of but that will help make outdoor cooking a lot more pleasurable. Here's what they all mean:

This icon gives you tips on the best meats, seafood, vegetables, seasonings, and equipment.

These tips give helpful information about successful grilling techniques for individual foods, from temperature control to ease of clean-up.

Sometimes you just need to hear something again. This icon serves as a reminder of some advice that we offer elsewhere in the book. These are also helpful hints to keep in mind after you put this book down!

All cooking involves a certain degree of danger, and safety should always be on the mind of anyone cooking outdoors over an open fire. This icon reminds you of ways to avoid personal injury or property damage.

We asked several of America's very finest chefs, all known for their grilling proficiency and talent, to come up with some absolutely dazzling recipes that you can easily replicate at home. This icon points them out for you.

Grilling itself is a pretty healthy way to cook, but this icon tells you how to further cut the fat from grilled foods.

In addition, we offer two ways to stretch the recipes in this book:

Vary It! When you're grilling, there's never just one way to prepare a recipe. So, we highlight ways that you can improvise and give you ideas for varying the preparation or the ingredients.

Go-With: These give you ideas for side dishes to pair with tasty grilled main dishes; marinades and sauces that work well with your chosen meat; and grilled fruits and breads that go with delicious recipes throughout the book.

A Few Guidelines Before You Begin

Every cook has his or her preferences, so it's best to know ours before you begin sampling our recipes. Here are some guidelines:

- ✔ All recipe cooking times are just estimates. The wind, temperature of the air and the food, and the intensity of the fire all affect, sometimes radically, the amount of time needed to grill food.

  By testing gas grill thermometers, we've found that their temperature readings can be off by a great deal. Charcoal grills nearly always burn hotter and cook faster than gas grills. Our best advice is to experiment with your own grill and adjust the cooking times of our recipes accordingly.

- ✔ Marinate all foods in the refrigerator in non-metal or non-reactive containers like glass or ceramic. Plastic, resealable bags are excellent for this purpose and take up less space than dishes. (Flip to Chapter 5 for more on marinating.)

- Never use leftover marinade as a finishing sauce unless you thoroughly boil the marinade to kill any possible bacteria picked up from the raw food.

- Although some cookbooks may say to bring your food to room temperature before cooking, with few exceptions, we don't recommend this tip for outdoor cooking. If the temperature is in the 80s or 90s, foods can spoil quickly.

- Salt can add tremendous flavor and even a little texture to grilled food. The optimum time to salt food is just before you place it on the grill. You can add more salt and sprinkle on the pepper (which should always be freshly ground) after you remove the food from the grill.

- Before preheating a gas grill or building a fire (see Chapter 3 for how to do that), brush the grill grid with a vegetable oil, such as peanut or corn oil. (Some grillers find it easier to use a nonstick cooking spray.) This step helps to keep the food from sticking unpleasantly to the grill grid. Never brush or spray the grid while the grill is heating or after the fire has started, because this can cause dangerous flare-ups.

- Always read all safety information and every warning icon (like this one) in this book. Following the safety advice is absolutely essential if you want to have a pleasant grilling experience.

Part I:
Gearing Up
for Grilling

In this part . . .

Grilling has its own jargon, equipment, and strategies — completely different from traditional cooking. This part introduces you to the grilling basics: from a quick tutorial on Grill-Speak to guidelines on shopping for a grill, from tips for cleaning up those nasty bits of food and grease to sound advice for building a perfect charcoal fire — with or without wood chips. We also share a list of grilling gadgets and accessories that range from must-haves to nice-to-haves — many of them make perfect gifts for that special someone who lives to flip burgers on the weekends (as we do!).

Chapter 1

Mastering Grill-Speak

● ●

In This Chapter

▶ Grilling directly and indirectly

▶ Understanding the finer points of barbecuing

▶ Getting to know smoking

● ●

*N*othing — not roasting, not frying, not sautéing, and certainly not poaching — gives such wonderful, smoky flavor to food as grilling does. And because it's done outdoors, grilling is the most social of cooking techniques. For as long as man has known how great foods can taste when cooked over an open fire, grilling outdoors has been a social event that invites people to participate.

By some strange twist of fate, men seem to take to grilling like ducks to water. (Perhaps women have just let men think that they're better at it!) But we find that no matter who's doing the grilling, everyone has fun. Grilling brings the kitchen outdoors and often gathers friends, neighbors, and family members around the grill to share stories, watch the fire, and trade recipes.

Grilling over a charcoal fire is perhaps the most interactive of all cooking techniques. It demands that you respond like an athlete to the changes of a live fire. This intense interaction is one of the aspects of grilling that makes it so much fun. You have to play with and master the elements of fire, smoke, and heat — and this book shows you how (as well as how to use a gas grill).

But first, in this chapter, we start off with some translation for you — from Grill-Speak into everyday language.

Two Key Terms: Direct Grilling and Indirect Grilling

In your introduction to the language of grilling, we start you off with the two basic methods of grilling — direct and indirect.

Direct — no-frills grilling

Direct grilling means that the food is placed on the grill directly over the full force of the heat source, whether it's charcoal, hardwood, or gas. (See Figure 1-1.) Just about every food, from meats to vegetables, can be grilled directly over fire. Some foods, however, are better cooked over indirect heat, a great grilling technique that's introduced in the following section. Foods that are often grilled directly over the heat include hamburgers, hot dogs, pork chops, lamb chops, boneless chicken breasts, beef tenderloins, and all types of fish and shellfish.

Grilling over direct, intense heat sears the food, coating its exterior with a tasty brown crust that's loaded with flavor. Steamed or boiled foods don't have this flavor advantage, nor do foods that are stir-fried or microwaved. The techniques of sautéing, deep-frying, roasting, and broiling create this crusty effect, but grilling rewards you with a seared crust *and* the extra benefit of smoky flavoring that can come from grilling with charcoal, wood chips, and hardwood chunks. And unlike sautéing and deep frying, grilling doesn't cook food in a layer of hot fat to produce this sear — you get all the benefits of a rich, brown crust with fewer calories.

Figure 1-1:
In direct grilling, the coals are centered in the grill or evenly spread throughout. In indirect grilling, the coals either surround a drip pan or are mounded to one side of the grill.

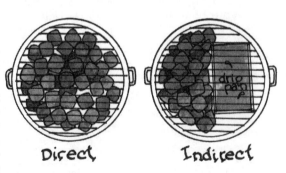

Direct   Indirect

Direct grilling, the primary focus of this book, is a fast cooking technique that doesn't require elaborate finishing sauces. Simple marinades (covered in Chapter 5), salsas (discussed in Chapter 6), and condiments (also in Chapter 6) are all you need to complement directly grilled meat.

The primary difficulty with direct grilling is that you must watch your food closely to prevent it from burning.

On a charcoal grill, the coals should be spread in a solid layer that extends about 1 to 2 inches beyond the edges of the food. In all our recipes, the grill grid — the metal latticework that you place the food on — is placed 4 to 6 inches from the heat. We find that most foods are best grilled over medium heat because you have more control and you end up with a nice brown crust without any nasty charring. However, fire temperatures vary according to what's being cooked. For example:

✔ You can sear $1^1/_2$-to 2-inch-thick steaks first over medium-high (or even high) heat and then finish cooking them over medium heat to end up with a crispy, brown crust and a rare to medium-rare center.

✔ Pork and chicken require moderate heat to give the interior a chance to cook completely. However, these same foods can be started on higher temperatures, which gives them a nice crust, and then moved to grill slowly over an indirect fire to finish cooking through.

Direct grilling can be done with or without using the grill's cover. The recipes in this book always tell you when to cover the food. Covering the grill instantly traps and raises the heat and tends to increase the smoky flavor, especially if you're using wood chunks or chips. However, covering food can increase the chance that you'll burn or overcook it, simply because you can't see the food. Sometimes, using the grill cover when direct grilling makes a lot of sense. We find that thick bone-in pork chops, for example, grill more evenly and better retain their succulence when grilled with the cover down.

When grilling directly in a covered grill, the vents — if you have them on your grill — are usually left open. Opening the vents allows more oxygen to enter the grill and increases the temperature of the coals. Closing the vents partially or totally has the opposite effect. If your fire is too hot and is browning food too quickly, either remove the cover or try closing the top grill vents.

Indirect — pushing food away from the fire

Indirect grilling grills foods slowly, off to one side of the heat source, usually over a drip pan (see Chapter 2) in a covered grill. If you want to use this technique, here's what you do:

- ✔ Place the food on the grill grid so that it's away from or to the side of the full force of the heat or fire. In a gas grill with two burners, you ignite only one burner and place the food over the unlit burner. If your gas grill has only one burner, place the food in an aluminum foil pan or on several layers of foil and grill over very low heat. Always preheat your gas grill with all burners on high and the lid down for about 15 minutes; then turn one of the burners off before cooking indirectly. In a charcoal grill, arrange the lit coals around the drip pan or bank them to one side of the pan.

- ✔ Whether you're using a gas or charcoal grill, place a drip pan directly under the food. Often you fill the pan with water or another liquid, such as broth or apple juice, to add moisture and keep the slow-cooking food from drying out.

- ✔ Close the grill lid to cover the grill, trap the heat and smoke, and mimic the desirable effects of slow, oven roasting.

- ✔ To collect pan juices (especially with large roasts), place the food in a roasting pan and then set the pan on the grill.

Be sure to clean out the ash catcher underneath a charcoal grill before starting the fire so that the bottom vents can properly draw air over the coals. When indirectly grilling on a charcoal grill, usually you can partially close both top and bottom vents to hold down the intensity of the fire.

Indirect grilling has a multitude of advantages:

- ✔ It slows down the cooking process. How many times have you used direct grilling to cook chicken and ended up with skin charred beyond recognition and meat that's practically raw in the center? Indirect grilling takes care of that problem. Food is cooked in a covered grill by heat that never directly touches it. Indirect grilling is comparable to oven roasting.

- ✔ Indirect cooking actually gives you two types of fires (or two levels of heat) in one grill. Think of it this way: You have a direct fire that can be used to sear food and an indirect fire to cook food slowly and thoroughly. For example, chicken, left whole or cut into pieces, can be first seared over the direct heat of the fire and then placed on the side over the drip pan without any direct heat. You then cover the grill to let the chicken finish cooking.

> ✔ Indirect grilling eliminates the possibility of dangerous flare-ups. Fat drips from the food into the drip pan, rather than onto the hot coals, lava rocks, or ceramic briquettes.

Indirectly grill any large cuts of meat or whole birds, poultry pieces, pork tenderloins, ribs, or large roasts for delicious results. The indirect cooking method is used in recipes for Just-Right Ribs (Chapter 10), Hickory Smoked Whole Turkey (Chapter 15), Whole Game Hens with Asian Flavors (Chapter 15), Sandra Lawrence's Mild Jerk Pork, Brined and Grilled Loin O' Pork, and Curry Pork Tenderloins (all in Chapter 13).

Another Term to Know: Barbecuing

Barbecuing is the technique of indirectly and slowly cooking large cuts of meat for a long period of time, over low heat and with lots of hot smoke. Compare this to direct grilling, which cooks small, tender pieces of food at higher temperatures for shorter grilling times. You might say that the two techniques are almost opposites.

Barbecuing generally takes tough cuts of meat and cooks or breaks down connective tissue into tender morsels that practically fall apart. Foods that are barbecued often include beef brisket, whole hogs, pork shoulder (which includes two pieces of meat — the Boston butt, which has the least amount of bone, and the picnic ham), and pork ribs. These foods are perfect for barbecuing because they actually *demand* to be cooked for long periods to break down their stubborn tissues and release flavor. Fish and vegetables can also be barbecued, not to break down the already tender tissue of these foods, but to add smoky flavor.

Barbecued food may or may not be seasoned, depending on the tastes of the cook. But many barbecuing chefs create elaborate rubs, basting sauces, and finishing sauces to enhance the flavor of barbecued foods.

A *barbecue pit* refers to a solidly built, upright grill apparatus with a deep hold for the fuel. The term also can mean an actual pit dug into the ground and filled with heated stones, over which the food is cooked, creating a steaming process. Most of the smoky flavor you get from using a barbecue pit comes not from fat dripping on the coals or coils, but from smoldering wood. (Flip to Chapter 3 for more on wood chips and chunks.)

A common kettle charcoal grill can come close to duplicating the effects of a barbecue pit. Simply build a small, indirect fire and use a combination of good quality charcoal briquettes and flavored wood chips or hardwood chunks. Give the flavored smoke a chance to have an effect — adding a handful of wood chips to a fire when grilling a piece of fish for a few minutes won't have much of an impact. But cooking the same piece of fish slowly and indirectly, adding a steady supply of presoaked wood chips as you go along, can produce excellent smoky flavor.

A few more techniques can help you turn your covered charcoal grill into a mini-barbecue pit.

✔ The grill must have a vented hood, and because the food is cooked indirectly, you'll need a drip pan under the food to catch the drippings. (See Chapter 2 for more on drip pans.) If the food requires a long cooking time, more than 30 to 40 minutes, fill the pan with water, apple juice, beer, or another flavored liquid to add moisture to prevent the food from drying out as it slowly grills.

Keep the top vents partially closed to trap the smoke and to decrease the supply of oxygen that fuels the fire. Position the lid so that the top vents are opposite the fire and directly above the food, to help draw the flavored smoke across the food. And don't lift the lid to peek — each time you do so, you release precious smoke and disrupt the cooking process.

✔ Keep a supply of preheated coals next to the grill in a metal bucket. Add a few every 40 minutes with long-handled tongs (see Chapter 2) to maintain the temperature of the fire. Lift the grill grid gently to add the hot coals, or use tongs to insert them into the space near the grid handles. Or add a few fresh briquettes to the edges of the fire every 20 to 30 minutes. When they're ashy, move them to the center of the fire.

✔ Use wood chips and chunks to infuse food with smoky flavor. Turn to Chapter 3 for more information.

More Vocabulary: Smoking

The technique of *smoking* food differs from barbecuing because it uses even lower heat to slow down the cooking process. Food cooks for hours, and becomes infused with hot, aromatic smoke. The cooking temperatures for smoking foods range from 180 to 250 degrees. You can choose from two methods — dry or wet — and both can be duplicated on your kettle grill. However, if you do use your kettle grill, you should place a temperature gauge on the grill to monitor and keep the heat within the proper temperature range. A 7-pound whole turkey or a 12- to 14-pound ham can take 9 hours or more to smoke. A 5- to 7-pound roast beef takes 5 to 6 hours to reach an internal temperature of 140 degrees. At many professional barbecue eateries and stores, beef and pork may be smoked for 12 hours or more at a very low heat.

Dry smoking requires indirect cooking in a closed charcoal grill. The food is placed on the grill, the lid is placed on top, and the air vents are adjusted enough to lower the flames but still keep enough oxygen inside to allow the fire to burn and create smoke. This smoke, in turn, flavors the food while the low heat cooks it. The degree of smoking is based on personal taste and the kind of food to be cooked. Alternatively, you can buy a dry smoker — a contraption that looks like a horizontal barrel and, depending on its size, can cook up to 50 pounds of food at one time. The dry smoker has two chambers: one for the food, and one that vents heat and smoke into the cooking chamber.

If you've tried smoking but find that the smoke flavor is too intense for your taste, cover food with foil about halfway through the cooking process.

Water smoking, also known as *wet smoking,* is an alternative to dry smoking. This technique involves placing a pan of water in the grill in order to maintain the moisture needed for more succulent, moister foods. Water smoking is an excellent method for delicate foods such as fish, shrimp, and lobster and does well with vegetables that would otherwise dry out quickly.

You can also buy a water smoker, shown in Figure 1-2. Water smokers are now being made by most grill manufacturers, but two companies — Brinkmann and Meco — specialize in such equipment. Water smokers come in three varieties:

- ✔ **Charcoal:** The most popular and least expensive water smoker; however, charcoal must be replenished every hour for long-term cooking. Charcoal water smokers also tend to have peaks and valleys of heat as the coals burn down.

- ✔ **Electric:** This is a very popular type of smoker that plugs right into an electric socket and offers consistent heat.

- ✔ **Gas:** This is the most expensive type of water smoker, but it's a cinch to use (and you don't have to be near an electric outlet to use it). They also provide consistent heat.

Water smoking is a very slow and easy method, but don't expect a real crusty exterior on your food — which, for many people, including us, is the whole point of good grilling.

Figure 1-2:
Water
smokers
are
generally
about 3
feet high.

water smoker

And the Rest of the Terms: A Griller's Glossary

To help you wade through the Grill-Speak that you may hear when shopping for accessories — or from your neighbor down the street — we compiled the following glossary of terms. Use these, and you'll be a grilling guru in no time!

- **Baste:** To brush a seasoned liquid over the surface of food to add moisture and flavor.

- **Brazier:** An inexpensive, open charcoal grill with a grill grid that is usually just a few inches from the coals. Best for quick grilling. Some braziers may have a partial hood or cover to better retain heat. Braziers sometimes also come with rotisserie attachments.

- **Ceramic briquettes:** These briquettes are made of radiant materials and are used in gas grills to transfer heat from the burners and spread it evenly under the grill grid. Briquettes made of ceramic don't burn up like charcoal briquettes do. *Lava rock* and *metal plates* are an alternative to ceramic briquettes.

- **Charcoal briquettes:** The most common fuel for a live fire, manufactured from ground charcoal, coal dust, and starch. They are compressed into a uniform, pillow shape and packaged for sale in 5- to 50-pound bags.

- **Charcoal chimney starter:** A metal, cylinder-shaped container that is filled with newspaper and charcoal and used to quickly ignite a charcoal fire. (See Chapter 2 for more on accessories.)

- **Charcoal grill:** A grill that uses charcoal as its principal fuel. A charcoal grill can be round, square, covered, uncovered, portable, or stationary. The most common type is a covered kettle grill.

- **Coal grate:** The rack that holds the charcoal in the firebox.

- **Drip pan:** A metal pan placed under the food to catch drippings when grilling indirectly.

- **Electric grill:** An indoor or outdoor grill whose heat comes from electric coils.

- **Fire starters:** Any number of gadgets or materials, such as the chimney starter, electric coil, wax or gel cubes, or compressed wood, used to ignite charcoal. (Flip to Chapter 3 for the lowdown on all these fire-starting gadgets.)

- **Firebox:** The underbelly or bottom of the grill that holds the fire or heat.

- **Flare-ups:** Flames caused by fat dripping onto hot coals or lava rock.

- **Gas grill:** A grill whose heating source is gas from a propane tank (or occasionally, a main gas line).

- **Grid:** The latticework of metal rods where you place your food on a grill is called a *grid,* or a *grill grid.* (Weber confuses things a little by calling this area the *grate,* which everyone else calls the metal piece on which the charcoal sits.) One grid is included with every grill.

- **Grill baskets:** Hinged, wire baskets that ease the grilling (and turning) of sliced vegetables, a delicate piece of fish, burgers, and other foods — Chapter 2 has more.

- **Hibachi:** A small, portable, uncovered grill, often made of cast-iron. Great for beach or tailgate grilling.

- **Kettle grill:** A relatively inexpensive, round charcoal grill with a heavy cover. It stands on three legs and is excellent for either direct or indirect grilling.

- **Lava rock:** This long-lasting natural rock results from volcanic lava, and is used as an alternative to ceramic briquettes. The irregularly-shaped lava rock heats evenly in gas or electric grills. Unlike charcoal briquettes, it can be used over and over.

- **Marinate:** To soak food in a seasoned liquid mixture in order to impart flavor to the food before it is cooked. The steeping liquid, often made with herbs, spices, oil, and an acidic ingredient like lemon juice or vinegar, is called a marinade.

- **Natural lump charcoal:** The carbon residue of wood that's been charred in a kiln — usually found in the form of chunks. This is one heating source for charcoal grills.

- **Roasting:** The process of cooking food in a pan in a closed-grill setup. By using indirect heat, you can roast an entire prime rib or turkey to perfection on a grill.

- **Rotisserie rod:** The spit or long metal skewer that suspends and rotates food over the grill's heat source.

- **Rub:** A concentrated, flavorful blend of dry or wet herbs, seasonings, and spices that is rubbed onto the surface of the food before grilling.

- **Sear:** To cook food directly above relatively high heat in order to seal in juices and impart flavor, a brown color, and a slightly crusty surface.

- ✔ **Smoker box:** Small, perforated steel or cast-iron container, placed directly on the lava rocks or ceramic bricks of a gas grill, that holds flavored wood chips and provides smoke.

- ✔ **Vent:** The holes in a grill cover or firebox that open and close like a shutter. An open vent increases the oxygen and heat of a fire, while a closed vent does the opposite. Some grills don't have vents.

- ✔ **Wood chips and wood chunks:** Natural hardwood materials added to the fire to impart smoky flavor to food as it grills.

Grilling Web sites to fire you up

If you can pull yourself away from your grill long enough, you may enjoy searching the World Wide Web for tips and recipes for outdoor cooking. Here are some sites to get you started.

- ✔ **Woodbridge Vintage Barrel Chips:** You can spend hours viewing the grilling-related material at this site, at www.woodbridgechips.com. Naturally, the site also promotes its wood chips, which are recycled from 100-percent-oak wine barrels.

- ✔ **World Wide Weber:** The mouth-watering recipes at this site, at www.weberbbq.com, will send you scurrying to your grill. (And, of course, if you don't have one, the Weber folks tell you all about their products here.) The Burning Questions section features frequently asked questions and expert grilling tips. Turn to the Portion Guide to find how much food you'll need for each menu item at your next cook-out.

- ✔ **The Mining Company:** Links to recipes, grilling books, cooking magazines such as *Gourmet* and *Bon Appétit,* and grilling tips make this site, at bbq.miningco.com,

a worthwhile visit. Click the link to Mastercook to search through thousands of recipes by topic. If you'd rather have someone else do the cooking, check out the list of some recommended barbecue restaurants around the country.

- ✔ **USDA Guide to Grilling and Smoking Food Safety:** This site, at www.usda.gov/agency/fsis/grilsmok.htm, doesn't offer the attractive graphics of some other sites, but you may find that the information from the U.S. Department of Agriculture is a good, basic grilling guide. The chart of approximate grilling times includes foods for people who prefer such exotic fare as ostrich and emu. The site contains facts on defrosting, marinating, grilling away from home, and serving food safely.

- ✔ **Good Housekeeping:** The Hot Off the Grill section of this magazine's site, at homearts.com/gh/food/08grilbl.htm, doesn't want to leave much to chance, so with each recipe, you have the option of selecting a wine to accompany the meal. You simply choose the style, price, and type of food you're serving, and you're given wine suggestions.

Chapter 2
Good Grill Hunting

*W*ithout a doubt, the most important grilling decision that you make is the type of grill you buy. How can you know what kind of grill (and accessories) will do the best job for you? This chapter helps answer that question.

Regardless of your needs or how you live and cook, you can find a grill that's just right for you. Today, you can buy big grills or small; basic grills or those with lots of bells and whistles; grills fueled by charcoal, gas, or electricity; or inexpensive grills that meet short-term needs or high-quality grills that are long-term investments, serving you well for many years. And after you choose a grill, you can find an amazing assortment of accessories at your local hardware or kitchen store.

Which Grill Is Right for You?

Your decision to buy a grill must depend, ultimately, on a few personal preferences.

A *gas grill,* powered by propane from a cylinder, stores easily; is economically priced (starting around $130), easy to set up, easy to turn on, and easy to work with; and uses low-cost fuel. Gas grills are also very easy to clean and maintain. (See Figure 2-1.)

Figure 2-1:
Gas grills
are easy
to clean.

Photo courtesy of Broilmaster.

A *charcoal grill* is one that's fueled by natural lump charcoal or charcoal briquettes and topped with a grill grid. (See Figure 2-2.) Many people also think that a *kettle grill* — a round, deep, metal kettle that is fueled by charcoal or briquettes and topped with a slatted grid (and sometimes has a gas igniter) — is synonymous with a charcoal grill, but that's not always the case. Charcoal grills come in all shapes and sizes, but they are all identical in their fuel source. They can range from inexpensive — $30 for small, portable models — to expensive — up to $450 for large kettles set into a rolling cart.

A *brazier,* sometimes called a *hibachi,* is really just a portable charcoal-style grill without any frills at all. It can be round, square, or rectangular, has a rudimentary metal grid on which food is placed, and is fueled by either charcoal or wood. Its portability is its greatest virtue (which makes it great for tailgating), but only if you're cooking for three or four people — the grill grid is usually quite small. You can usually find these for around $20. The term *brazier* also refers to a pot in which foods are cooked with a little liquid, but that's not what we're concerned with in this book.

Grills that don't have covers, such as hibachis and portable picnic grills, are mainly used for grilling small pieces of food quickly and directly over charcoal. Covered grills, on the other hand, give you the option of cover-cooking larger cuts of meat and poultry, such as beef roasts and whole turkeys, over a slow, indirect fire.

Figure 2-2:
Charcoal
grills offer
incomparable
flavor.

The kettle grill configuration is a trademark of Weber-Stephens Products Co.

An electric grill makes for clean grilling. You don't need to bother with charcoal, briquettes, wood, or ashes, and you don't have to refill propane cylinders. Although most don't provide the smoky charring and flavor that charcoal grills offer, they are a great answer for apartment dwellers. Find these at any home store or department stores, usually for $50 to $150.

Before you rush out to buy a particular grill based on the advice of a best friend (or even this book), head to a store that carries an assortment of grills from various manufacturers, and spend a few minutes playing with the floor models.

- Stand before the grill and lift up its hood. Does it seem sturdy and durable or cheap and flimsy?

- If it's a gas grill, do the knobs turn easily? Does it have two burners so that you can use the indirect cooking method?

- Does the grill offer expensive gadgets that you'll pay for but never use?

Buying a grill that suits your style and needs is a little like buying a car, except, unfortunately, you can't take it out for a test drive.

B-T-Whats?

BTUs (British thermal units) measure the heat intensity of a gas grill. For the average gas grill chef, 22,000 to 50,000 BTUs is plenty of heat. Don't be misled into believing that the higher the BTU, the better the grill will perform.

What's more important is that the grill burns fuel efficiently; otherwise, you're wasting gas and increasing your fuel costs. Ask your dealer about the fuel-burning efficiency of any grill before buying it.

The Great Grill Debate — Charcoal or Gas?

Because the two most popular grills are vastly different, buyers are faced with a difficult question: Buy charcoal or gas? Table 2-1 is a straight-up comparison of some features of the two basic types of grills — the simple charcoal grill, usually in the shape of a kettle, and the gas grill that uses a propane cylinder.

Table 2-1	Just Between Us Grills
Gas Grill	**Charcoal Grill**
Larger initial investment, from $150 up to $5,000 and more!	Less expensive, from $50 to $450
Heats up in 10 minutes	Coals need 20 minutes or more to heat up
Heats up to about 500 degrees — food takes longer to cook	Can go above 500 degrees — food must be watched closely
Steady supply of heat	Coals must be replenished
Easy to clean and maintain	A little messy to clean up
Adjustable flame controls	Not easy to adjust heat
Can grill all year 'round	Not fun to build a fire when outdoor temperatures drop
No fun 'n' games with fire	Get to light, tend, and watch the fire
Food tastes good	Food tastes great

Which grill produces better flavor?

Because taste is so subjective and personal, the debate will probably continue regarding whether charcoal or gas grilling produces superior flavor. Multitudes of taste tests have demonstrated that most people cannot tell the difference. However, we disagree and want to go on record as believing that a charcoal grill definitely gives a better flavor than a gas grill.

Location, location, location

Where you place your grill can affect its efficiency and your safety. Placement (of course) depends on how much room you have and how massive your grill is. But here are some general rules:

✔ Use the grill outdoors only! Never grill in your trailer, tent, house, garage, or any enclosed area.

✔ Place the grill away from anything — and we mean anything — that could possibly be construed as being flammable: piles of leaves or dry grass; structures of any kind; gasoline and any machines containing gasoline, especially automobiles; paint and aerosol cans; newspapers; awnings; children's toys; and trees.

✔ If you place the grill on a wooden deck, it's a good idea to use a deck protector under the grill. You can find one in most hardware stores.

✔ Don't place your grill in the path of strong winds, which may tend to stir up the embers and make them fly.

✔ Stay close to your kitchen for easy access to platters, utensils, and food.

✔ When grilling at night, place the grill near a light source.

Which grill lights easier?

Gas grills are a snap to light. You simply turn on the gas, push the igniter button, and adjust the control to high — in just 10 minutes you're ready to cook.

Despite the fact that many people would argue otherwise, charcoal grills are *not* difficult to light. The fact is, charcoal grills are extremely easy to light and take only about 30 minutes to reach a medium stage of heat. Using a chimney starter (see Chapter 3) can shave another 15 minutes off that time.

You can use several simple and foolproof ways to light a charcoal fire. Flip to Chapter 3 for all the details.

Which grill looks better?

This one's a tie. With people spending more and more money to spruce up their backyards, you have dozens of attractive grills to choose from, whether cooking with charcoal or gas. Grills come in high-tech, contemporary, gleaming stainless steel or wonderful bright-colored porcelain enamel.

Choose from bright red, cobalt blue, or even designer colors like teal. Even painted gas grills come in colors like hunter green or burgundy. Handsome carts or cabinets in stainless steel or wood finishes add to the sturdiness and beauty that will enhance your patio or deck.

Long Live Your Grill

Although the outer units of most grills carry a lifetime guarantee, keeping it oiled and clean and storing it correctly are just as essential to a long, happy grill life.

Oiling the grids

Keeping your grill grid lightly oiled helps improve your grilling in two ways:

- Prevents food ingredients from sticking while you're cooking
- Makes grid clean-up easier after each meal

Just use a little vegetable oil to do the job, wiped on with a soft cloth. Or you can use one of those aerosol vegetable oil sprays on a cold — but never a hot — grill.

Look before you light

Here are some hard-and-fast rules about gas grill safety you must follow:

- Always thoroughly check out the entire system of a gas grill after a winter's storage.

- Periodically check the tubes leading from the propane cylinder to the grill. Make sure that they are securely attached and free of stoppages like grease, insects, or cobwebs. (Since 1995, all grills are required to have three extra safety features to eliminate leaks.)

- Make sure that hoses are not cracked or don't have any holes.

- If you smell gas, do not attempt to light the grill.

- Keep all lighted cigarettes and matches away from the propane cylinder.

- Propane cylinders can, over several years, rust. If you notice any rusting (which may indicate a hole developing in the skin), get rid of it and buy a new one.

Grid size matters

Whether you choose a gas or charcoal grill, the size of the grill's cooking surface — the grid — is important. Be sure that the food grid is between 350 and 400 square inches so that you have the option of grilling several dishes at a time or of feeding a party crowd.

SHOPPING TIP

We would be less than honest, however, if we didn't mention that replacement grids are pretty cheap — about $15 to $20 at any good hardware store — and worthwhile replacing at the beginning of spring. That way, you don't have any old dirt, residue, or rust on the grill when you go to use it.

A clean grill is a good grill

Grills can last a lifetime if you take good care of them, as follows:

✔ After each use, use a wire brush to clean off the food particles remaining on the grid. Close the lid of the grill and, if you have a gas grill, turn up the heat for about 10 minutes to burn off any excess food remaining on the grid.

✔ Periodically clean the grids with a solution of warm, soapy water, using nylon or plastic woven pads to avoid damaging the grid. Use non-abrasive scouring powder on stubborn stains if you wish, but a small amount of grease left on the grids helps preserve the metal — it will burn off the next time you use the grill. Cast-iron grids should be seasoned after cleaning by applying a light coating of oil.

✔ You may clean the interior of the grill with the same soapy solution or with a can of aerosol grill cleaner. Scour with a scrub brush and then rinse with water and air dry. Never use anything but soapy water on the exterior of the grill because a cleaner may damage the paint or porcelain.

✔ Your grill won't work properly if the burners become clogged, so if you see an uneven flame, remove the burner and clean the ports with a wire. You can also force water through the removed burner until you are sure that it is coming through each hole. If the burners rust to the point of showing cracks or breaks, buy new ones.

✔ Lava rocks or ceramic briquettes get extremely greasy and contribute to flare-ups. Depending on how often you grill, you should turn the lava rock over periodically. Because they are quite inexpensive, replace the lava rock or briquettes at least once every 12 to 18 months (perhaps more often if you're a frequent griller) to ensure better grilled dishes.

Who 'ya gonna call?

Call the following grilling manufacturers for information on their grills and grilling accessories:

✔ Barbeques Galore: 800-Grill-Up

✔ Bradley Smoker Inc.: 800-665-4188

✔ The Brinkmann Corporation (largest manufacturer of smokers): 800-468-5252

✔ Broilmaster: 800-255-0403

✔ Char-Broil, Division of W.C. Bradley: 800-241-7548

✔ Ducane: 800-DUCANES

✔ Fiesta: 800-396-3838

✔ The Holland Company: 800-880-9766

✔ Masterbuilt: 706-327-5622

✔ Meco: 800-346-3256

✔ New Braunfels: 800-232-3398

✔ Sunbeam: 800-641-2100

✔ Thermador: 800-735-4328

✔ Viking Range Corporation: 888-845-4641

✔ Weber: For information on buying and shopping for grills, call 800-99-Weber; for information on grilling, call 800-Grill-Out (800-474-5568) from Memorial Day through Labor Day, 8 a.m. to 6 p.m. Central Time.

Storing your grill

Most people like to grill year-round, regardless of the weather. But, if you decide to pack your grill away for the coldest winter months, you certainly can. Be sure to thoroughly clean your grill before storing it and — for a gas grill — make sure that the gas lines are completely and tightly closed off and that the gas cylinder is removed.

If storing your grill indoors, always remove the propane cylinder and store it outside in a cool, shaded spot. Never, under any circumstances, store a propane cylinder inside your home or garage. It could be deadly.

Tools and Toys

In this section, we introduce you to time-saving, flavor-enhancing, safety-heightening accessories that no griller — beginner or guru — should be without. We also alert you to some advanced options that make you a pro in no time.

Getting to know grilling utensils

Step into a hardware store or kitchen gadget shop, and you'll see an amazing array of tongs, brushes, and spatulas in a variety of shapes and configurations. In this section, we list the utensils that we recommend, and in most cases, show you an illustration of the most common types. Keep in mind, however, that manufacturers and prices affect the exact sizes, shapes, and features.

Think of these accessories as investments and purchase the best ones that you can afford. Premium accessories are apt to have heavy-duty finishes and strong, comfortable handles.

Tongs

Outside on the patio, tongs are essential equipment. Tongs are a better choice than a long fork because you can flip food over without piercing the food (which can let out the juices) and they allow you to maneuver most foods better than a spatula does.

Buy with length in mind. Never use short, overly flexible ice tongs at the grill. A good pair of grilling tongs (see Figure 2-3) should be between 15 and 18 inches long and must have a wooden or insulated grip (hot metal burns!).

Fork and carving knife

A good knife is not nearly as important as a good *fork* when you're grilling. And a good fork is not nearly as important as a *long* fork — 16 inches or more — with a wooden handle and two tines. (See Figure 2-4.)

When moving around large pieces of meat — such as roasts — with a grill fork, try not to pierce the meat too deeply. By the same token, be careful not to spear the meat too delicately so that it falls off and causes flare-ups.

Given the fact that much of what comes off your grill (slabs of meat, ribs, or sausage) will need to be cut, invest in a good, heavy-handled, well-balanced carving knife (see Figure 2-4), curved butcher's knife, or chef's knife.

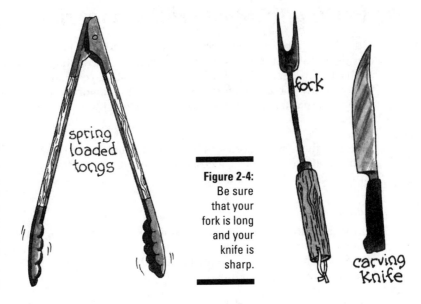

Figure 2-3:
Grilling
tongs
should be
long and
have a
good wide
opening.

Figure 2-4:
Be sure
that your
fork is long
and your
knife is
sharp.

Spatula

We never get tired of repeating ourselves on the issue of length: Use a spatula that is 15 to 18 inches long from the tip of the handle to the end of the blade. (See Figure 2-5.)

Also, be sure not to use the following:

- A Teflon or nonstick spatula for the kitchen used to flip pancakes, because it may burn or melt.

- An outdoor metal spatula with a metal handle. The handle will transfer heat to your hand.

- A long spatula used to spread icing on a cake. Such a tool is completely useless at a barbecue because it's too thin and flexible to hold a heavyweight piece of meat, poultry, or fish.

Grilling mitt

We cannot stress enough the importance of a good grilling mitt. A dishtowel or fireproof pot holder just doesn't give you the protection you need to grill safely. The mitts should be flexible and allow you to pick pots, pans, skewers, and other items off the grill with ease.

Figure 2-5:
A good grill
spatula
should be
sturdy, with
a fairly
wide blade.

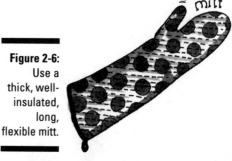

Figure 2-6:
Use a
thick, well-
insulated,
long,
flexible mitt.

A mitt also should be long enough to reach past your elbow — the longer
the better, at least 15 inches — and have a flame-retardant coating. (See
Figure 2-6.) Long-lasting, sturdy mitts start at about $7 and can run as high
as $20. If you can afford it, pay a bit extra to get a fully insulated, thick pair
with a thumb.

Basting brushes and mops

The most common *basting brush* (shown in Figure 2-7), is brush-shaped,
sometimes with an angled brush head, and is very useful for all kinds of
basting but is most often used for light basting sauces. The most important
virtue of such a brush is its length; look for ones at least 16 inches long so
that you can baste while the food is on the grill.

The bristles on a brush should be fairly pliable and extend at least 3 inches
from the end of the handle. You don't need to spend much on a good brush,
but don't spend too little either, or it will fall apart before long. Between $5
and $8 is a good range to look for.

A *basting mop*, sometimes called a *Texas-style barbecue brush,* is just that — a
little cotton mop for quickly slathering on thick sauce. (See Figure 2-7.) When
soaked with barbecue sauce, this brush is not likely to catch on fire, but be
attentive anyway.

Skewers

Skewers, shown in Figure 2-8, are wonderful grill accessories, allowing you to cook and easily turn foods like kebabs and satays. (Check out Chapter 9 for some outstanding kebab and satay recipes.) They should be between 15 and 18 inches long. Skewers that are 6 to 8 inches long, however, are perfect for cocktail party kebabs.

Bamboo skewers are popular and do a good job when you're grilling kebabs. Before using them, soak them in water for a half hour so that the ends don't catch fire.

Figure 2-7: Mops and brushes for your food — not your kitchen floor.

basting brushes

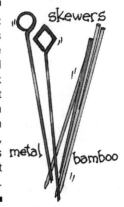

Figure 2-8: Skewers should be long and easy to pick up so that you can turn them on the grill, but always use a mitt to do so.

skewers

metal   bamboo

Thermometer and temperature gauge

One of the single biggest challenges faced by inexperienced — and even many experienced — grillers is turning out food that is moist, juicy, and cooked to perfection, both inside and out. A good food *thermometer* tells you the temperature inside the food being cooked and will solve this problem for you.

You can find two basic types of thermometers for use on a grill (see Figure 2-9):

- **Stainless steel insert thermometer:** This heat-resistant thermometer that you use for a roast in an oven works effectively on a grill, too. To use this thermometer, insert the stainless steel spike into the meat at the beginning of the cooking process and it registers the temperature on a glass-faced dial. This thermometer is intended only for foods that allow you to place the probe at least 2 to $2^1/_2$ inches into the grilled food. It is not intended for use on steaks, chops, chicken breasts, or other thin food.

✓ **Instant-read thermometer:** This type of thermometer does exactly what it says; that is, you can insert it into the meat at any moment and get — you guessed it — an instant reading! You must immediately remove the thermometer, however. Some models even display digital numbers; you don't have to buy this type, but if you do, be sure that the numbers are easy to read.

A *temperature gauge* tells you the temperature inside the grill itself. Just about all gas and electric grills now have built-in temperature gauges, but kettle and other charcoal-fueled grills usually do not. So you may find it worthwhile to buy a temperature gauge to set within the kettle, especially for closed-lid grilling and smoking. You can much more easily monitor cooking times this way.

Water bottle

Keep a water bottle, one equipped with a spray or spritzer top, close at hand to douse occasional flare-ups of flames and to lower the heat on a fire that has gotten too hot. (See Figure 2-10.) You can also spritz rotisserie grilled food with water (or other liquid) to retain moisture as the food rotates on the spit. You don't need anything fancy — a spray bottle of any kind will do — but make sure it shoots out a fine spray of water so that you don't extinguish the fire by spraying too much water on the wood or coals.

Cleaning brush

The only tool you need for cleaning your grill grid is a good, stiff wire brush (see Figure 2-11), which is sold at most hardware stores. A stiff brush does a better job than any scraper, but many cleaning brushes have a self-contained scraper on the top that allows you to scrape off the really tough grime that may build up over time.

Figure 2-9: Two types of thermometers work well at the grill — the instant-read and the stainless steel insert.

Figure 2-10: A water bottle is essential grilling equipment.

Oil your grill grid before grilling to alleviate the elbow grease needed to remove the cooking grease. But here's the easiest way to clean a grid: Attack the grid with a cleaning brush right after the meal, while the grill grid is still warm. It's more difficult to scrape away bits of food after the grill has cooled down.

A small, crumpled-up ball of aluminum foil makes a handy improvisational tool for scrubbing down the grill grid when you can't find your wire grill brush. A nylon or plastic scouring pad, sponge, and a pail of soapy water can also help with a thorough cleaning of the grill, inside and out. Never, ever use a wire brush or oven cleaner to clean the exterior of a grill because it can damage the finish.

Grill cover

A grill cover protects your grill from rain, wind, and heat and prolongs the life of your grill. Made from vinyl and cloth, grill covers come in all shapes and sizes to fit over the top of the grill. Just be sure to purchase one that fits your particular grill and always give the grill time to cool down completely before covering it.

Torch light

When twilight falls and the shadows creep across the grill, you can't see what you're cooking and certainly can't see the degree of doneness of the food. Torch lights come in very handy at that point. (See Figure 2-12.) *Torch lights* are poles atop which a lamp, fueled with oil or other fuel, is set. They can be stuck in the ground almost anywhere or set permanently in concrete. They come in all sizes and price ranges, and they always add a lovely flicker to a dinner after dark.

Work table

Even fancy grills with optional side tables don't provide enough space for your grilling chores. Set up a small table next to your grill for food, platters, and grilling tools.

More tools and toys for the serious griller

Beyond the utensils listed in the previous section, many more tools are really quite helpful as you move into grilling guruhood.

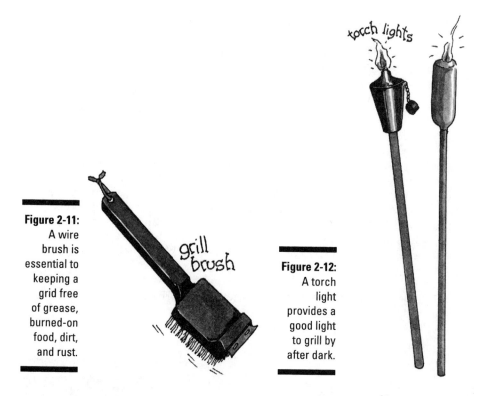

Figure 2-11:
A wire brush is essential to keeping a grid free of grease, burned-on food, dirt, and rust.

grill brush

Figure 2-12:
A torch light provides a good light to grill by after dark.

torch lights

Baskets

We are really big believers in hinged, wire, grilling baskets of every kind, and numerous shapes and sizes are available for every conceivable kind of ingredient. Baskets are a real aid for grilling delicate pieces of fish and shellfish, or for small pieces of food that aren't skewered and would otherwise fall through the grid. You can also use baskets to more easily turn onion rings and thinly sliced meat. We think that you can get away with a few basic baskets (see Figure 2-13).

✔ Into a boxlike basket, you can place just about any ingredient that is large enough not to fall through.

✔ A fish-shaped basket is ideal for a whole fish. (See Chapter 16.) Easy to turn, this basket keeps the flesh intact without adhering to the skin and produces a beautifully cooked fish.

✔ Other flat baskets aren't shaped like fish but are built to hold hamburgers, chicken, sausages, shrimp, and most fish fillets. (Steaks, lamb chops, and barbecued ribs are better when they're turned individually on the grill grid rather than locked into a basket.)

When purchasing a grilling basket, look for one with a handle that's long enough to extend well beyond the grilling surface. Because the baskets stand on the grill for several minutes at a time, the heat from the grill transfers to the basket handles, so always use a mitt when removing them. Baskets range in size and price. Most are made of steel and are designed not to be flexible. (You don't want to carry a flapping basket of fish or chicken from grill to table.) You can buy them at the hardware store for around $10.

Grill topper

A grill topper — sometimes called a perforated grid, fish grid, or delicate foods grid — is a porcelain grid with holes about half the size of a dime. (See Figure 2-14.) Place it on the grill grid (the one that comes with your grill, where you normally place the food) when you want to cook small foods (such as shrimp, scallops, delicate fish, mushrooms, and cut-up vegetables) that would otherwise fall into the fire. A grill topper makes it simple to turn delicate food. Lightly coating the food with oil makes the food even easier to turn.

Grill toppers come in several different sizes, so consider the size of your total cooking surface before selecting one, because you may want room to cook other foods on the regular grid at the same time. Prices range from $15 to $30.

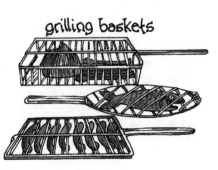

Figure 2-13:
Baskets are excellent for turning many pieces of food at one time.

Figure 2-14:
A grill topper helps you grill delicate food.

Vegetable holder

The *vegetable holders* that we've seen (see Figure 2-15) are little more than bent metal wires that hold baking potatoes and ears of corn upright on the grill. But these gadgets do allow vegetables to bake more slowly, without getting scorched. Basically, they allow you to be a bit less attentive than if you placed your vegetables right on the grid.

Rib rack

A *rib rack,* shown in Figure 2-15, is a lattice of metal rods that are arranged into a "U" shape, into which the ribs and other meats can be placed and kept slightly elevated above the heated grating. A rib rack allows you to cook more food on one grill.

When purchasing a rib rack, make sure that the metal rods are sturdy and the rack does not wobble on the grill.

Drip pan and charcoal divider

A drip pan, shown in Figure 2-16, is a shallow pan placed under the grid that catches the drippings from the meat that is cooking on the grill. You can buy inexpensive disposable aluminum foil pans at the supermarket or use a shallow metal rectangular baking pan (which is a bit messier to clean up afterwards). You can also make a drip pan out of heavy duty aluminum foil by folding up the edges of the foil to give it sufficient sturdiness.

Figure 2-15:
Vegetable holders and a rib rack are handy for grilling

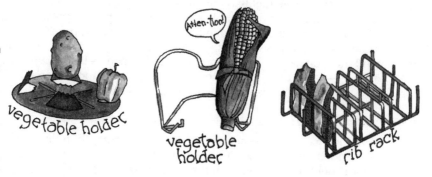

In a gas grill, set the pan directly on the lava rock or ceramic briquettes under the meat to be grilled. In a charcoal grill, place the pan on the charcoal grate with coals banked to one side or placed on either side of the pan and the meat directly over it.

When using a drip pan on a charcoal grill, use a *charcoal divider* (shown in Figure 2-17), a metal divider that holds the charcoal firmly in place so that it doesn't tumble into the drip pan (which is shallow). Although this gadget is not an absolute necessity, a charcoal divider — sometimes called a *rail* or *Char-basket fuel holder* — is a good investment.

Figure 2-16:
A drip pan catches dripping fat that can otherwise fall into the fire.

Figure 2-17:
A charcoal divider helps a drip pan do its work.

Smoker box

A *smoker box* (see Figure 2-18) is quite handy and very simple to use. It is nothing more than a lidded, heavy metal box with holes to allow the smoke to pour from burning wood chips (and, sometimes, a few aromatic herbs) that you've placed inside. A smoker box is a good, easy way to add smokiness to your foods.

If you use wood chips with a gas grill, a smoker box is a must, because it keeps the ashes from clogging the burner.

Side burner

One accessory we highly recommend for anyone who wants to do more than simple grilling is an attachable side burner. On pricier grills, they are standard, but you can buy one for your existing grill, too. These handy accessories (for gas grills only) allow you to do just about anything on the grill that you can do on a burner in your kitchen — from sautéing to sauce making — and are great just to have for reheating foods, too. They are even pretty simple to hook up. Side burner prices start at about $70.

Motorized rotisserie

Although we cover the subject of rotisseries in depth in Chapter 11, we want to mention here that they are a very useful accessory that the serious grill cook should consider. Some of the more expensive gas grills have them already built in, while others allow for rotisseries to be purchased as attachments.

The purpose of a rotisserie is to allow slow, even cooking that is especially good for doing roasts, whole chickens, and even ribs. Rotisseries are handy, too, because you don't have to tend them constantly; just baste the food occasionally with a marinade or sauce.

Ash can

Yes, the grill industry actually sells special cans in which you're supposed to put your spent charcoal ashes. An *ash can,* shown in Figure 2-19, may have come in especially handy in the nineteenth century when people used wood and coal for their hearths and fireplaces. These days, you use them to cart away ash residue after your fire is out. This is different from an *ash catcher,* which attaches under the body of a charcoal kettle grill.

Figure 2-18: A smoker box allows aromatic smoke from wood chips to pour out.

smoker box

Figure 2-19: An ash can helps you clean up your ashes.

ash can

Chapter 3

Playing with Fire

Chances are that if your food turns out perfect, your fire was perfect, too. This chapter shares the fine points of getting your fire — whether it's in a gas grill or charcoal grill — to burn the way it should for maximum results. In this chapter, we discuss the various kinds of fuel, fire-starting accessories, and fire-lighting tools for your grill.

Fuel Me Up, Scotty

For gas grills, choosing a fuel source is easy — that propane cylinder attached to the grill is your only option, unless your grill is built specifically to hook up to the main gas line from your house. Your most important decision will be when to replace the propane cylinder, which you can tell is low by three different methods:

✔ Buy a gauge that can measure the level. A gas cylinder usually doesn't come with a gauge already attached, but you can purchase one at any hardware store.

✔ Buy an *Accu-Level Tape* that you stick like cellophane tape to the side of the cylinder. When you pour boiling water over it, it shows you the level of propane left in the tank by changing color at the level where the propane has been used up. The tape costs about $3 and is available wherever propane tank supplies are sold.

✔ The simplest method is to weigh the cylinder. A full cylinder will weigh approximately 38 pounds, an empty one about 18 pounds. So if it weighs in at about 28 pounds, your supply is about half empty. Of course, if you're an optimist, it's half full.

Charcoal grill owners, however, have two options for their heating source: natural lump charcoal and charcoal briquettes.

Natural lump charcoal

Natural lump charcoal, shown in Figure 3-1, results when hardwoods such as maple, oak, and hickory are burned at super-high temperatures. The wood breaks down, dries out and, after hours of roasting, comes out ebony and almost weightless. The result is a clean-burning fuel, with a price — natural lump charcoal costs considerably more than the familiar briquettes. You may have to call around to find a reliable vendor, as well.

Natural lump charcoal is an excellent fuel source because it lights more quickly than charcoal briquettes and burns much hotter. However, if you've never cooked with natural lump charcoal, keep these tips in mind:

✔ A natural charcoal fire sparks and snaps, which may initially scare you, but there's no need for alarm, because these special effects are perfectly normal.

✔ Because natural lump charcoal burns very fast, your food cooks much faster than with briquettes. You may want to experiment with your cooking times.

✔ The temperature is always changing with natural lump charcoal. It starts out very hot, peaks quickly, and then drops rapidly.

✔ This intense initial heat results in quick searing, which imparts a bit more flavor to the food. For this reason, professional grillers and barbecue pitmasters prefer it to any other kind of fuel.

Figure 3-1: Natural lump charcoal burns hot and fast.

natural lump charcoal

Charcoal briquettes

Charcoal briquettes, shown in Figure 3-2, are made from powdered charcoal that has been compressed, bound with coal dust and starch, and formed into a uniform little brick. Briquettes don't burn as intensely as natural lump charcoal but can be much easier to control. They give a good, hot, enveloping, even heat and, because of their uniform size, give you consistent results — you're always working with a predictable fuel source!

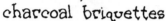
charcoal briquettes

Figure 3-2:
Charcoal
briquettes
are easy
to control.

SHOPPING TIP

To find the best briquettes, you have to do some sleuthing among the brands available in your markets: Try buying different brands a few times and keeping track of how they perform. You may notice that some burn more quickly than others, which means that they provide a less consistent heat and you'll need more of them. You may find store brands that are as efficient as some of the more familiar brands, like Kingsford. It won't take long to discover which ones you like best.

SHOPPING TIP

The briquettes should be uniform in size — not crumbly — or you lose a good portion in the bag before you even set them in your grill.

You can step up to still more convenience with *fire-starter briquettes,* shown in Figure 3-3, to which charcoal lighter fluid has already been added. You can place a few of these in with your regular briquettes for fast, easy lighting or cook with them exclusively. We don't recommend them as the sole source of heat for longer term grilling, because they tend to burn more quickly and require frequent replenishment. You should reseal the bag tightly after removing briquettes or the lighter fluid will evaporate, leaving you with plain-old briquettes!

The ultimate in convenience is *light-the-bag briquettes,* which contain just enough fuel for a single fire. There's no fuss or muss, because you simply place the bag in the grill and touch a match to the corner of the bag. Then, as with regular briquettes, wait until they've reached an ashy gray color to start cooking.

Figure 3-3:
The most
convenient
briquettes
in the
world.

fire starter
briquettes

Go easy on the fuel!

Many people use far too much natural lump charcoal or far too many briquettes in their grill. How much you need depends on the size of your grill and the amount of food to be cooked.

Use these general guidelines:

✔ Thirty briquettes will grill about a pound of meat. Count on an average of 2½ pounds of charcoal for grilling meat directly over the coals.

✔ A single layer of coals should extend 1 to 2 inches beyond the food being cooked. Pour the briquettes into the grill and spread them out to determine how many you need; then stack them in a pyramid in the center before lighting. When most of the coals begin to burn, spread them out in an even layer.

✔ If you grill more than 45 minutes, add 12 to 15 briquettes to the outer edges of the fire after about the first 35 minutes to maintain a proper temperature. Pushing the coals closer together as they burn down (using long-handled tongs) also intensifies the heat.

✔ If you're grilling indirectly, start with about 25 briquettes (give or take, depending on the size of your grill) on either side of the drip pan in an average (22½ inch) kettle grill. Add 8 briquettes to each side every 45 minutes.

The School of Hardwood Chunks

If you're lucky enough to have access to a natural supply of old hickory, oak, or fruit-tree wood, it will serve as an excellent supplemental fuel, or even just flavoring for outdoor cookery. The appeal of hardwoods as supplements to briquettes is that they make the fire burn more intensely, which is a virtue when you want high heat for searing and quick cooking. They also burn longer. Finally, and most important, they add an intensely smoky flavor that enhances the fairly subtle smokiness that comes from charcoal.

Commercial bags of hardwood chips, sold at hardware stores and grilling-supply stores, are easy to use. Chips simply require presoaking in water for 15 to 30 minutes to keep them from burning up too quickly. For charcoal grills, scatter the presoaked wood chips — a handful or two will do — over the charcoal briquettes after the coals turn ashy gray, or just before you're ready to cook. When the chips burn out, or when the smoke stops pouring from the cover vents, you can add another handful as a replacement. Don't overdo it though — the chips may smother the glowing coals.

Wood chips burn very quickly, so you want to use them when you're grilling food very slowly in a covered grill. One exception to this rule, however, is grilled fish: Its delicate flesh quickly absorbs the smoke from chips, so you don't need a lengthy cooking time to reap the benefits of the wood chips.

For a more intense, smoky flavor, you can build a fire entirely with wood chunks, which do not require presoaking; however, you'll probably have a hard time controlling the fire because the chunks burn so intensely. In addition, your wallet may suffer because the chunks are expensive.

You can also mix half a dozen or more wood chunks into a charcoal briquette fire. However, wood chunks take a few minutes longer to burn than charcoal does; to keep the chunks from scorching your food, ignite them a few minutes before the charcoal or ignite them with the charcoal and then spritz them lightly with water. Another solution is to start the coals and chunks together and, when the charcoal is ashy gray, move the chunks to the edges of the fire so that they surround and barely touch the coals. This way, the chunks produce just what you want — a steady supply of smoke without any flame.

You can also add light, smoky wood flavoring to food when cooking with a gas grill.

✔ Use wood chips only when grilling indirectly, with the lid closed. Wood chips and chunks can ignite into flames on the grill; read your manual for specific information on how to use them safely with your grill.

Increasingly, gas grills offer special, built-in smoking drawers or boxes to hold wood chips. On some gas grills, presoaked chips can be placed in a small foil pan and then set directly on the lava rock or ceramic briquettes.

✔ You can wrap presoaked chips in heavy-duty aluminum foil, poke holes in the foil to allow the smoke to escape, and place the packet directly on lava rocks. The heat of the grill will cause the wood to smolder and smoke. After the grill has cooled, simply remove the packets and discard. (Douse the chips with water if they are still smoldering.)

✔ You can also purchase a small steel or cast-iron container, called a *smoker box* (see Chapter 2), to hold the chips. You place it directly on the heat source.

Flavoring your food with hardwood

Here are some hardwood varieties that we think work particularly well on the grill:

✔ **Apple:** Very good with poultry.

✔ **Alder:** Nice delicate flavor with seafood.

✔ **Cherry:** Wonderful with game birds.

✔ **Hickory:** Essential for real pork barbecue.

✔ **Mesquite:** Has a strong flavor for big red meats like beef and venison.

✔ **Maple:** Fine wood to use for ham and pork.

✔ **Pecan:** Best for poultry and seafood.

One good source for ordering hardwoods is Barbecue Wood Flavors Company, 141 Lyons Road, Ennis, Texas (972-875-8391).

It Only Takes a Spark

Fire starting doesn't have to be a struggle if you own a charcoal grill — just choose a good firestarting strategy from the following list:

✔ **Lighter fluid:** This is the most popular method of starting a charcoal fire, and it is easy to use. Squirt $1/4$ to $1/3$ cup on the coals, wait a minute to let the fluid soak into the briquettes, and light the fire. (Check out the lighting options in the section entitled "Flaming Your Fire.") If you fear a chemical taste from the lighter fluid, don't worry! You won't place the food over the coals until 20 to 30 minutes after you start the fire, and by then, the fumes will have long since burned off.

If you think the fire is a bit sluggish and needs more lighter fluid, never squirt it into burning coals, because the fire can flare up or travel back up the stream of fluid to the can and cause a disaster. Rather, take a few new briquettes, place them in a clean can (such as a coffee can), and add enough lighter fluid to soak them. Then with long-handled tongs, carefully place the soaked briquettes among the other briquettes.

A word of caution: Never use gasoline or kerosene as a lighter fluid because either can cause an explosion.

✔ **Kindling:** Kindling is any material that is highly and quickly combustible and creates a fast flame that will burn long enough to ignite a fuel like charcoal or briquettes. We recommend wood or newspaper.

- **Wood:** Make sure that the wood you use for kindling is very, very dry and brittle. Any moisture or "greenness" will result in a slow start, a poor burn, and bitter smoke. Old twigs and cut-up branches are best, and you should snap them to expose the more flammable inner core of the wood.

- **Newspapers:** Newspapers make excellent kindling, but be aware that you may need several wads and that burnt newspaper can fly all over the place, which is both messy and dangerous. If you do use newspaper, roll it loosely into thin, branchlike cylinders, leaving plenty of air between the wrappings — air is oxygen, and oxygen is necessary for a good fire. Place the newspaper on the bottom of the grill and then place a single, uneven layer of charcoal on top. Light the newspaper (see lighting options in the section entitled "Flaming Your Fire") and allow the charcoal to begin to burn. After you notice that most of the charcoal looks ashy gray, add more charcoal, as needed.

✔ **Miscellaneous fire starters:** The grill industry has come up with a lot of useful items for fire starting: compressed sticks of wood compound or sawdust that's soaked or treated with a safe, combustible fuel; wax by itself; wax in wood; and various chemical mixtures. You merely place these around the edges of your briquettes or natural lump charcoal and light the fire starters. They will burn quickly and ignite the charcoal.

Using two temperatures for maximum results

So, when lighting a fire, do you have to choose between direct or indirect grilling? Well, sort of. Although you do need to determine which type of fire is better for the particular foods you're cooking, you can have both on the same grill. The fact is, different parts of the grill grid will vary in heat intensity, making it ideal for cooking a variety of foods at the same time. If you're using a direct fire, start foods like pork chops or chicken breasts in the center of the grid and then move them to the outside edges where the fire is less intense and they can finish cooking without burning or drying out the meat. Foods that need longer, slower cooking — such as chicken thighs and legs — can be placed directly over the coals initially to brown and crisp the skin and then moved over the drip pan of an indirect fire to finish cooking more slowly and thoroughly. (See Chapter 1 for more on direct and indirect fires.)

Flaming Your Fire

You may come across a bunch of gadgets for creating a flame with which to ignite a fire, and quite honestly, we believe that just about all of them beat a match. Here are the alternatives to burning your fingers with a stubby match.

Electric charcoal igniter

An *electric charcoal igniter* is a metal coil, usually made of stainless steel, that is placed underneath the charcoal briquettes and heated up to a red-hot, glowing point that transfers heat to the immediate area. (See Figure 3-4.) Left in place for a maximum of 8 minutes, the igniter starts coals glowing, and those coals rapidly ignite the coals that surround them. This method is a safe, easy way to start a grill, but be very careful when removing the coil, which can stay hot for several minutes. Unplug it first, remove it from the grill, and set it away from the grill on a nonflammable surface to cool. Such gadgets cost about $10.

Here's how to use the coil for best results.

1. **Plug the electric charcoal igniter into an electrical outlet and place the coil on the charcoal grate of the kettle grill.**

2. **Pile charcoal on top of the coil and wait about 8 to 10 minutes.**

   You'll see a little smoke rising from the kettle, and several of the coals atop the coil will be glowing brightly.

3. **Unplug the coil.**

4. Carefully remove the coil (if you leave it in much longer than 10 minutes, the coil itself may be damaged from the heat it has generated) and store it safely away to cool.

5. Using long-handled tongs, shuffle the coals around to make them level, and let them sit.

Within 20 to 30 minutes, you'll have perfect ashy gray charcoal ready for grilling.

Figure 3-4: Electric charcoal igniters are very easy to use and work by transferring heat from a red-hot metal coil to the coals above them.

Butane lighter

Butane lighters look like screwdrivers with a long nose that ignites a small flame at the flick of a switch. (See Figure 3-5.) You can use them to light paper, fire-starter briquettes, or gas grills, and they come in very handy. Good ones have a safety lock, a regulator for the flame, and even a little viewing window so that you can see how much butane is left. They are either disposable (cheaper) or refillable and cost about $10.

Figure 3-5: A giant lighter.

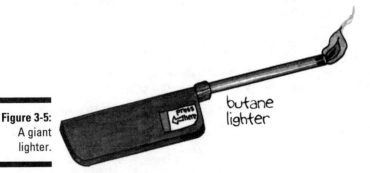

Giving it gas

One advantage of gas grills is that they are so easy to light. Today nearly all of them come with an automatic ignition.

Check the manual that came with your grill before trying to light it but, after that, follow these steps:

1. **Open the cover of the grill — and keep it open while lighting it!**

2. **Fully open the valve on the gas cylinder.**

3. **Turn the burner control(s) to high.**

4. **Immediately push in the ignition button to light the grill.**

5. **If the grill does not light instantly, push the ignition button again.**

6. **If the grill still doesn't light, turn off all burner controls and close the valve on the cylinder. Wait 5 minutes for any gas fumes to dissipate. Then repeat Steps 1 through 5.**

After the flame lights, set the controls to high for preheating (which should last about 10 to 15 minutes). Always be sure that the flame is burning before closing the cover.

Many contemporary gas grills have a built-in temperature gauge that tells you when they are hot enough to cook on. Some indicate actual temperatures — 350 degrees is medium and 500 degrees is hot — while others are marked "low," "medium," and "high," which corresponds to the directions in most of our grilling recipes.

Chimney starter

The other way to light a charcoal fire is with the amazing chimney, shown in Figure 3-6, which is really, really cool — and cheap. A *chimney starter* is nothing more than a wide-mouthed tin pipe that has a grate in the bottom and a handle. One usually costs around $10.

Figure 3-6: Igniting coals quickly with a chimney starter.

A chimney starter works as follows:

1. **Stuff a crumpled-up newspaper in the bottom of the chimney.**

2. **Add charcoal briquettes to the chimney.**

3. **Place the chimney on the lower grating of the grill and light the newspaper at the bottom. Be careful: Wear a mitt for this part of the operation.**

    By forcing intense heat up through the shaft, the burning newspaper ignites the charcoal, which starts to burn brightly within a few minutes.

4. **Release the burning charcoal from the chimney into the charcoal in the kettle, either by squeezing the handle or by picking up the chimney and dumping the contents into the grill.**

    That's it!

Bossing Your Flame Around

The general rule for knowing when your coals are ready for grilling is to make sure that 80 percent or more of the coals are ashy gray (at night, they glow red with no flame). If you have less than that, the coals are not ready, and if all of them are glowing red hot, the fire is probably too hot. A fire that's too hot will scorch your food and rob it of all its flavor.

Use the following simple technique to gauge the temperature of the coals. Place the palm of your hand just above the grid. If you can hold your hand in that position for two seconds (counting "one-thousand one, one-thousand two"), the coals are hot; a three-second hold tells you the coals are medium-hot; four seconds is medium; and five is low.

Here are a few steps you can take to adjust the temperature of your fire:

- ✔ If it is too hot, spread the coals out a bit more, which makes the fire less intense.

- ✔ Raise or lower the grid if the grill has an adjustable grid.

- ✔ Partially close (not entirely, of course) the vents in the grill, which allows less oxygen and damps down the fire.

- ✔ Use the indirect grilling method, with coals to either side of a drip pan and the food over the pan rather than directly over the coals.

- ✔ In the event of a severe flare-up, spritz the flames with water in a squirt bottle. Be careful, though — spraying with water tends to blow ash around and make a mess. To control a grease fire, we suggest baking soda. You may also want to keep a fire extinguisher, garden hose, or bucket of sand nearby.

Part II:
Adding Spice (And Side Dishes) to Your Life

In this part . . .

When you grill, much of the food's flavorful juices are lost into the fire — that's why we suggest enhancing the flavor of your food (before it sizzles on the grill grid), with marinades, rubs, flavored oils, and basting sauces. In this part, we give you ideas and recipes for marinating, seasoning, and basting grilled meat, poultry, fish, and vegetables. We also offer you shopping advice for stocking up your refrigerator and pantry with convenient store-bought products for spur of the moment cooking — the way most of us really cook today.

Chapter 4
A Griller's Pantry

Grilling in its simplest form requires nothing more than a hot fire and a piece of meat. But anyone who wants to take up grilling in all its diversity should stock his or her pantry with savory foods and condiments.

In this chapter, we share our recommended list of nonperishable items for your grilling pantry — bottled sauces, condiments, oils, vinegars, herbs, and spices — and end with a brief description of fresh vegetables and fruits that can serve as strong seasoning agents in marinades, rubs, and barbecue sauces.

Kitchen Helpers — Bottled and Canned Goods

In a perfect world, every barbecue sauce and marinade would be made from scratch with the freshest of ingredients. But in this time-pressed world, we rely heavily on good commercial products. Having even a few of the following items on hand in your pantry or refrigerator allows you to whip up an assortment of barbecue sauces, dressings, and marinades in a hurry.

- **Bottled barbecue sauce:** Every year you can find new sauces flavored with hickory, mesquite, Jamaican jerk seasonings, habañero peppers, peaches and pineapple, bourbon, rum, and every kind of imaginable hot chile pepper. Barbecue sauces are not meant for ribs or chicken only. Use them to baste salmon, shrimp kebabs, pork, or lamb chops.

  Before purchasing a product for the first time, read the ingredient label to get a general idea of its flavor. Try to avoid products in which the primary ingredient is sugar, salt, or fat — or that's all you'll taste. Purchase and taste-test a few different brands of sauces, condiments, and other bottled goods to determine which ones you like best.

  Remember, most barbecue sauces are loaded with sugar and should be applied only during the last 10 to 15 minutes of cooking to prevent the food from charring.

- **Bottled marinades, dressings, and other basting and finishing sauces:** These ingredients provide the grilling cook tremendous variety and convenience. Bottled vinaigrette can substitute as a last-minute marinade for poultry, vegetables, or pork. Check out the many new Asian and especially the Thai-style products including sauces for satay, kebabs, poultry, and ribs.

  Wish-Bone's new Oriental Salad Dressing — made with sherry, soy sauce, garlic, red pepper, Dijon-style mustard, and sesame seeds — makes a tasty marinade or basting sauce for beef, chicken, seafood, and vegetables.

- **Canned favorites:** Corn kernels, beans, chickpeas, and artichoke hearts are a few canned items to have on hand for making last-minute salads and salsas.

- **Capers:** These are pickled flower buds of the Middle Eastern caper bush (shown in Figure 4-1). The smallest capers are called *nonpareil*. They add a distinctive saltiness to dishes. Always rinse and drain before using in marinades, sauces, and dressings.

Figure 4-1:
Capers
range in
size from
tiny to those
as large as
a small
pearl.

- **Hoisin sauce:** A favorite of Chinese cuisine, hoisin sauce is made from soybeans, garlic, hot pepper, and spices. Depending on the brand, its texture can range from runny and thin to very thick. Use in marinades and basting sauces for grilled poultry, pork, or lamb. See Chapter 5 for a Hoisin Marinade that's delicious with pork, chicken, or lamb.

  We like Ka-Me Hoisin Sauce because it has wonderful flavor and a smooth consistency (without the addition of MSG — monosodium glutamate — or a thickening food starch).

- **Mayonnaise:** No kitchen pantry is complete without a jar of mayonnaise, but for the most part, think of mayonnaise as an incomplete dressing. We like to add a range of ingredients to mayonnaise, such as sun-dried tomatoes, basil, mustard, horseradish, rosemary, Tabasco sauce, or grated lemon peel, to create a whole assortment of dressings, sauces, and spreads.

  Substitute reduced-fat mayonnaise, if you wish, whenever the real thing is called for, or combine them equally to reduce calories and retain flavor.

- **Olives:** Olives add a luscious saltiness to many dishes. Sprinkle them into quick fresh tomato sauces for grilled fish (Chapter 16) or burgers (Chapter 8). Stir them into mayonnaise-based sauces or salsas (Chapter 6). Add them to pizzas, quesa-dillas, or grilled sandwiches (all in Chapter 18).

- **Peanut butter:** Use peanut butter to duplicate some of the sauces and dishes of Pacific Rim cuisine. (See Chapter 9 for Satay with Peanut Dipping sauce or Chapter 6 for Creamy Asian Peanut Sauce with Noodles.)

- **Soy sauce:** A vital ingredient in so many flavorful marinades, basting sauces, barbecue sauces, and dressings, soy sauce adds distinctive flavor, brown color, and saltiness.

  Light soy sauce is sodium-reduced and therefore less salty. You can substitute this anytime for soy sauce when less salt is preferred.

- **Tahini paste:** Made from sesame seeds, tahini is a staple ingredient in Middle Eastern cooking and is used in dips and sauces, or as a sandwich spread. See Chapter 17 for Baba Ghanoush, a grilled eggplant dish made with tahini paste.

- **Worcestershire sauce:** This sauce is a combination of vinegar, molasses, water, sugar, anchovies, and other savory ingredients.

  Vary It! Add Worcestershire sauce according to your taste to marinades, dressings, basting sauces, or hamburger patties; splash over finished grilled foods such as steaks, lamb chops, poultry, or roasted potatoes.

Condiment-ry, My Dear Watson

A condiment is any small side dish or accompaniment to food that adds flavor, texture, and contrasting color. Condiments can be vinegary (like ketchup), sweet (like preserved watermelon rind), hot and spicy (like salsa), sour (like dill pickles), or salty (like sun-dried tomatoes). The following list is a few of our favorites, available in any major supermarket.

- **Chutneys:** These sweet, tart, and spicy combinations of cooked fruits or vegetables make delectable accompaniments to grilled foods. Keep bottles of store-bought mango or tomato chutney on hand as a last-minute topping for grilled burgers, steaks, poultry, lamb, or pork. Or, look through Chapter 6 for a number of simple, homemade chutney recipes.

- **Horseradish:** A delicious condiment for grilled fish, horseradish also adds zing to dressings, dips, and sauces made with ketchup, sour cream, or mayonnaise.

- **Ketchup:** Ketchup is the ultimate ying-yang of condiments — a blend of tangy vinegar, sweeteners like sugar or corn syrup, and pureed tomatoes. Before being knocked off its throne by the now more popular salsa, ketchup was America's favorite condiment. Dress it up by adding chopped scallions, minced ginger, or horseradish. Or use ketchup as an ingredient in marinades, basting sauces, and salsas.

- **Mustards:** There are really two types of prepared mustards: those that are creamy smooth and those that contain coarse seeds. Either type may be flavored with herbs and spices, red or white wine, Champagne, honey, sugar, chiles, or peppercorns. Here are a few types of mustards:

  - **Dijon mustard:** This French classic, made with brown mustard seeds and flavored with white wine and other seasonings, is an extremely useful ingredient for the time-pressed grilling cook.

    Vary It! Combine it with melted butter and Worcestershire sauce as a quick sauce for steaks and burgers. Blend with honey as a basting sauce for turkey or ham steaks. Add to creamy-based salad dressings or to marinades and barbecue sauces.

  - **Classic yellow mustard:** With its mild taste and creamy texture, yellow mustard is the American choice — perfect for a grilled hot dog.

  - **Honey mustard:** This condiment combines these two compatible ingredients. Buy it bottled or make your own by combining equal amounts of honey and mustard (or mixing them according to taste).

Vary It! Use honey mustard as a basting sauce for sausage, ribs, ham steaks, chicken, turkey, duck, or lamb.

- **Whole-grain mustard:** Made with whole mustard seeds, whole-grain mustard has a pleasant crunchy texture and can be flavored with any number of ingredients, such as chiles, wine, mixed herbs, honey, or vinegar.

  Vary It! Whole-grain mustard is also a good addition to marinades for beef or pork.

✓ **Salsa:** Although salsas are usually tomato-based, the salsa product line is growing to include salsas with roasted corn, red pepper, black olives, and other ingredients. Store varieties range from mild to hot.

Vary It! Use salsa as a quick condiment for hot dogs, grilled burgers, steaks, chicken, or fish. Try it as a spread for quesadillas, fajitas, or other sandwich wraps. Add it to vegetable salads made with chopped tomatoes, corn, or canned beans. Use it to add flavor and heat to creamy macaroni salads.

✓ **Sun-dried tomatoes:** Sold either as oil-packed or dried, sun-dried tomatoes are somewhat chewy and intensely flavored. You can use them to flavor salads, dressings, and spreads. See Chapter 7 for Macaroni Salad with Sun-Dried Tomato Mayonnaise.

✓ **Tabasco sauce:** An all-purpose spicy seasoning and condiment made from hot Capsicum peppers, vinegar, and salt, Tabasco sauce adds heat and a pleasant sharpness to marinades, dressings, and finished grilled foods.

Oils and Vinegars, Demystified

Oils range in taste from the nearly neutral flavor of ever-so-subtle peanut oil, to bold and buttery olive oil, to nutty, almost bitter-tasting, dark sesame oil. Avoid exposing oils to light and air, because they cause the oils to deteriorate more rapidly — always store oils in a cool, dark place. Keep oil containers tightly sealed after opening and use within several months to one year. Throw out any oils that develop a musty or rancid smell.

✓ **Olive oil:** Use olive oil in dressings, marinades, and basting and finishing sauces. Olive oil is indispensable to the grilling chef — it infuses marinades, dressings, sauces, and salsas with its rich, fruity flavor. Try olive oil drizzled over grilled breads, grilled vegetables, roasted red peppers, and all kinds of grilled chicken or fish.

Don't be misled by olive oil labeled as *light.* This is a refined oil with little color and flavor but has the same number of calories — 120 — as a tablespoon of any other kind of oil.

- ✔ **Sesame oil:** Made from sesame seeds, sesame oil has a rich, distinctive flavor. Use it sparingly to accent marinades made with Asian ingredients like soy sauce, ginger, and garlic.

- ✔ **Nut oils:** Extracted from roasted walnuts, almonds, hazelnuts, and other nuts, these oils are very expensive and rich in flavor. Delicious in salad dressings and some salsas, especially when the recipe uses the nut as an ingredient. However, they are highly perishable and must be refrigerated.

Peanut, corn, safflower, soy, and other mild vegetable oils can be mixed with equal amounts of olive oil to enrich their flavors.

The shelf life of oil depends on its variety and how it's stored. Olive oil can be kept for up to a year if tightly capped and stored in a cool, dark place. But nut oils last only a few months, so purchase them in small quantities.

Flavored oils, seasoned with an assortment of ingredients such as lemon slices, whole peppercorns, dried herbs, garlic, and chiles, are now sold in fancy kitchenware stores and in the gourmet food section of many major supermarkets. They are terrific drizzled over grilled breads, grilled pizzas, grilled vegetables, or grilled steaks, fish, chicken, lamb, or vegetables.

Don't try to make your own flavored oils at home unless you're prepared to use them immediately. Homemade flavored oils can spoil in just a few hours.

Vinegars tenderize cuts of meat as they marinate, but they also add a pleasant tartness to sauces, dressings, and marinades. Vinegars are almost always paired with oils to balance their harshness. We are partial to balsamic vinegar, which is slightly sweet, less harsh, and more complex in flavor than other vinegars. If by accident you add too much vinegar to a dressing or marinade, you can tone down the acidic effect by adding a pinch of salt, more oil, or by whisking in a bit of sugar or other sweetener, such as honey, to taste. Here are some types of vinegar to keep in your pantry:

- ✔ **Balsamic vinegar:** Bold, rich, and slightly sweet, real balsamic vinegar is outrageously expensive and made only in the area near Modena, Italy. Most of the bottles sold in the supermarkets are imitations. But being a "fake" doesn't mean it's bad, it's just less aged. Balsamic vinegar is delicious in marinades, dressings, and finishing sauces. Try splashing it to taste on grilled lamb, chicken, or pork.

- ✔ **Apple cider vinegar:** Good for almost all recipes where vinegar is an ingredient, apple cider vinegar is especially good with marinades and dressings that contain a fruit or citrus juice or that have an element of sweetness.

- ✔ **White wine vinegar:** This type of vinegar can be fruity or very dry. It's delicious in relishes and chutneys to counterbalance sweet flavorings.

Solving the olive oil shopping conundrum

When shopping for a quality olive oil, look on the front of the bottle for a sign of its grade, or quality. The purest, most expensive olive oils are marked *extra-virgin* and have the richest aroma and strongest flavors. Other, less expensive grades of olive oil include *virgin olive oil* and *olive oil*. You may want to stock one bottle of the expensive kind and one of the less expensive grade. Save the more pricey extra-virgin oils to drizzle onto fresh salads, salsas, grilled breads, or grilled vegetables and fish. Use the virgin olive oil when a larger amount is required in recipes for marinades, or for barbecue sauces in which the oil's distinctive flavor is more likely to be masked by the other strongly-flavored ingredients.

✔ **Red wine vinegar:** Use this bold and pleasantly pungent vinegar in marinades for beef, pork, or poultry.

✔ **Rice vinegar:** Slightly milder than other vinegars, rice vinegar works well with sherry or sake in marinades.

Sweetening Up Sauces and Marinades

When preparing a sauce or a condiment, you may want it to be boldly sweet, or you may want just a hint of sweet taste. Much like salt, sweet ingredients, used in moderation, can help blend all the other flavors within a recipe.

✔ **Honey:** Honey can add anywhere from a slight to an overwhelming element of sweetness to marinades and basting sauces, and it mixes particularly well with Asian ingredients like soy sauce, ginger, hoisin sauce, garlic, and sesame oil.

Like other sweeteners, however, honey can cause grilled food to char and burn. To lessen the chances of burning, grill the food indirectly or scrape all the marinade off the food before placing it on the grill. For the best effect, apply any basting sauces containing honey only during the final minutes of grilling.

✔ **Molasses:** A common ingredient in barbecue sauces, molasses adds sweetness and color to marinades and barbecue and basting sauces.

✔ **Light and dark brown sugar:** Brown sugar is white sugar combined with molasses to give it color and moisture. The lighter the color, the less intense (or less molasses-like) the flavor.

✔ **Fruit jams and preserves:** Jams and preserves enhance grilled foods as ingredients in glazes and finishing sauces.

Vary It! Turn a pork chop or a rack of ribs into something sublime by coating it with a warm glaze of apricot jam, minced ginger, and lemon juice. A spit-roasted duck needs only a slather of black cherry or black currant jam to make it perfect. A broiled lamb chop pairs up nicely with a good-quality mint jelly and some freshly ground black pepper.

When to Wine

Like vinegars, all wines are tenderizing agents, but their chief function in a marinade or sauce is to add bold flavor. For marinades or sauces, you don't need to spend more than about $8 on a good bottle of red or white wine — and at that price, whatever wine remains in the bottle is good enough for serving with the meal.

✔ **Dry red and white wine:** These acid-based ingredients are tenderizing agents, but more importantly, they add a complexity of flavor to marinades and basting sauces. Add herbs and spices according to taste and always have an oil component in a red or white wine marinade to take off some of the acidic edge.

✔ **Marsala:** A *fortified* wine (which means that another alcohol, such as brandy, has been added to the wine to raise its alcohol content), Marsala is good in marinades for poultry and game birds, adding a tinge of sweetness.

✔ **Sake:** A Japanese beer made from fermented rice, sake is excellent in marinades. You can use it as a substitute for dry vermouth or pale dry sherry. After it's opened, it can be stored in the refrigerator for 3 to 4 weeks.

✔ **Sherry:** Sherry is a fortified wine, which essentially means that it is an aged blend of different wines and brandy. Depending on its sweetness, sherry is labeled dry, medium dry, or sweet. Sherry can be used in marinades and basting sauces to flavor poultry, pork, or beef.

Walking through a Griller's Herb Garden

For most grilled recipes, we prefer fresh herbs and spices — they have more flavor than dried herbs and spices. One exception to this rule applies to rubs, which are a mixture of dried, ground spices (and sometimes dried herbs) made into a compact, dense, and flavorful coating that easily adheres to the food's surface.

Most varieties of fresh herbs are available year-round in supermarkets and Middle Eastern and Asian specialty stores, and many can be grown in a pot on the windowsill or outdoors in mild climate.

Fresh herbs should be washed, dried thoroughly, and stored in damp paper towels in the crisper drawer of the refrigerator, where they will stay fresh for up to 5 days. To keep them longer, treat them like freshly cut flowers and place the herbs in a glass of water in the refrigerator. Dried herbs and spices should be stored in a cool place, away from direct sunlight and heat. The top of your stove is not a good place for a spice rack!

Avoid buying dried or preground herbs and spices in large quantities, even though they may be price discounted. Although there is no fixed rule about how long dried herbs and spices should be stored, dried herbs seem to lose their original potency after about a year. Ground spices have a longer shelf life. If you doubt the freshness of a dried herb or spice, just smell it. It should smell fresh and aromatic.

Vary It! The amount of herbs and spices that are blended in a sauce, marinade, rub, salsa, or dressing is usually a matter of personal taste. Experiment with different combinations, adding them to taste, usually at the end of cooking, when they will best retain their color and flavor. (Take a look at Figure 4-2 for tips on chopping herbs.) When substituting dried herbs for fresh herbs, use about ¹/₃ the amount of fresh herbs called for in the recipe.

Chopping Parsley & Other Fresh Herbs

Figure 4-2: The recommended way to chop fresh herbs.

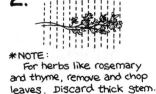

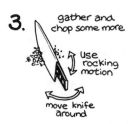

✔ **Allspice:** Spice berries from the evergreen pimento tree are combined with tastes of cinnamon, nutmeg, and cloves — hence the name. An important ingredient in Jamaican jerk seasonings and Caribbean sauces, allspice adds an almost sweet element. Use it in barbecue sauce, rubs, and marinades.

✔ **Basil:** Fresh basil has a slightly sweet, pungent flavor (some say it reminds them of licorice) that goes with garlic, mint, lemon peel or lemon juice, tomatoes, grilled fish, lamb, or poultry. Basil is the main ingredient in pesto sauce (Chapter 6) and is easy to grow outdoors in temperate climates. To maximize flavor, add basil at the end of cooking or sprinkle chopped, fresh basil leaves generously over grilled foods.

Dried basil has little flavor and is a poor substitute for fresh. Instead, freeze fresh, washed basil in a freezer bag, using it as needed when fresh basil isn't available.

✔ **Cayenne or red pepper:** This hot, powdered, red-colored mixture of several chile peppers is usually sold ground. Use it in small amounts in marinades, rubs, and sauces.

✔ **Chili powder:** This is a fiery mixture of dried chiles, cumin, oregano, garlic, coriander, and cloves — sold ground.

Vary It! Use chili powder as a multipurpose seasoning when you want to add heat as well as flavor. It's especially popular in Tex-Mex-style kebabs, marinades, and sauces. Chili powder mixes especially well in rubs for chicken or beef with cumin, oregano, ground chile peppers, cayenne or red pepper, and salt.

✔ **Fresh cilantro:** Also called *Chinese parsley* and fresh *coriander,* this herb is cherished by Chinese, Southeast Asian, Mexican, and Latin American cultures and cooks. Its parsley-look-alike leaves have a distinctive taste.

Vary It! Use cilantro in marinades for fish, chicken, or beef. Cilantro mixes well with ginger, citrus juices and peels, mint, hot chiles, and garlic. To make a delicious dipping sauce for chunks of French bread, skewered chicken, or fish, mix together extra-virgin olive oil, finely chopped cilantro leaves, salt, and freshly ground black pepper.

Salt talk

Most of the regular or fine-grained salt that finds its way to the supermarket and eventually to your table is rock salt mined from salt deposits. *Sea salt,* prized by chefs for its more complex taste, is made by evaporating sea water and contains minerals from the sea.

Many chefs and good home cooks prefer the seasoning effect of coarse-grained *kosher salt* — with its more oversized crystals, kosher salt clings to foods better than fine-grained salt.

- **Cinnamon:** A sweet and aromatic spice harvested from the bark of a tropical tree, cinnamon is commonly sold as whole dry sticks or ground. Cinnamon is a popular ingredient in Caribbean sauces and rubs where its sweetness contrasts with the heat of chiles and other spicy ingredients.

  Vary It! Add cinnamon to poultry rubs and barbecue sauces or sprinkle it on grilled fruits.

- **Cumin:** This aromatic, nutty-flavored spice is sold as whole dried seeds or in ground form. Cumin is essential to Middle Eastern and Southwestern cooking in the United States. Ground cumin is one of the main ingredients in curry powder and some chili powders. Cumin is terrific with grilled fish, lamb, pork, or beef, and in rubs, marinades, and barbecue sauces.

- **Curry powder:** This pungent spice blends more than a dozen different herbs and spices that often include cinnamon, cloves, cardamom, chiles, mace, nutmeg, turmeric, red and black pepper, and ground sesame seeds. Use curry when you want a Middle Eastern or Indian accent, or as the main ingredient in chicken, lamb, or pork rubs.

- **Five spice powder:** This aromatic seasoning powder, used throughout China and Vietnam, usually combines the following ground ingredients: star anise (a star-shaped spice filled with small seeds), Szechwan peppercorns, cinnamon, cloves, fennel seed, and sometimes ginger or cardamom (a mellow spice frequently used to make curries, spiced cakes, and garam masala — the most important spice blend of north Indian cooking). Five spice powder, available in Asian markets and many supermarket spice sections, may become one of your favorite grilling ingredients. Use it as a seasoning rub for chicken, pork, lamb, or fish or add it to marinades made with other Asian ingredients like soy sauce, sesame oil, or garlic.

- **Fresh ginger root:** Found in the produce section of the supermarket (and shown in Figure 4-3), fresh ginger root is peeled and then sliced, minced, or grated before it's added to marinades, dressings, and basting sauces. It mixes well with garlic, soy sauce, sesame oil, hot peppers, and other Asian seasonings. Fresh ginger also contains an enzyme that breaks down and softens animal gelatin and can be an effective tenderizing agent when used in meat marinades. Store fresh ginger in the refrigerator wrapped in a paper towel and then placed in a plastic bag punctured with a few holes to let in some air. It will stay fresh for up to 3 weeks.

- **Ground ginger:** Sold in the spice section, ground ginger blends well with spices common to Indian cuisine, such as cumin, curry, turmeric, and coriander, or with Caribbean cooking spices, like allspice, nutmeg, and cinnamon. You may substitute ground ginger for fresh ginger when you have no choice; however, ground ginger is much spicier than fresh.

ginger root

Figure 4-3:
Pieces of fresh ginger root can look a little like a small, gnarled hand.

Use it cautiously when substituting and taste after each addition. For a flavorful steak rub, mix together to taste powdered ginger, fresh minced garlic, black pepper, and salt. Cover and refrigerate meat for several hours before grilling.

✔ **Mint:** A fresh, sweet, pungent herb, mint is sold in fresh bunches or crumbled dry and is easily grown outdoors in mild climates. The two most common varieties are peppermint and spearmint.

Vary It! Mint is terrific with fresh vegetables, and in rice, fruit salsas, and fruit salads. (See Chapter 7 for a refreshing Yogurt Cucumber Salad with mint.) It combines especially well with basil or lemon peel in salads or dressings. Sprinkle chopped, fresh mint on grilled chicken, fish, pork, or lamb or add it to salsas or flavored butters.

✔ **Oregano:** Oregano has intense flavor and is best if fresh, but it can be purchased crumbled dry. Use it in marinades and dressings for grilled fish, lamb, beef, or chicken.

✔ **Paprika:** Lush red in color, paprika varieties range from faintly sweet and spicy to intensely hot and are usually sold ground. The Hungarian variety is considered the best. Excellent in rubs for poultry, pork, or beef, paprika also mixes well with cayenne.

✔ **Parsley:** Sold year-round, parsley is available in fresh bunches or crumbled dry. The most common fresh varieties are curly parsley and the stronger-flavored Italian flat-leaf. Parsley is an all-purpose herb that can be added liberally to marinades, dressings, sauces, or compound butters.

Vary It! *Gremolata,* a parsley and garlic topping classically served on *osso buco* — a hearty, Italian dish of braised veal shanks, white wine, tomatoes, garlic, anchovies, grated lemon peel, and other ingredients — makes a terrific lowfat garnish for grilled foods. Mix together 1 large clove peeled and finely minced garlic, the grated peel of one large lemon, $^1/_4$ cup chopped parsley, and salt and pepper to taste. Sprinkle over grilled fish, chicken, pork, or beef.

✔ **Peppercorns:** Like salt, pepper is a universally prized seasoning ingredient. It is used in recipes for foods that range in flavor from savory to sweet. Peppercorns of all types, whether black, green, or white, come from the *Piper nigrum* vine. Peppercorns can be combined to create peppery coatings for grilled meats or poultry. You also can buy bottles of mixed peppercorns in the spice section of major supermarkets.

Freshly crushed pepper is far more aromatic and potent than pre-crushed pepper in a can. Always use a pepper mill to crush black peppercorns into freshly ground pepper. You can use a couple of other ways to easily crush whole peppercorns before adding them to rubs, sauces or marinades. Gather them in the middle of a cutting board and press them with the bottom of a heavy skillet. Or wrap them in heavy-duty aluminum foil and pound the package with a meat mallet or a rolling pin until they are crushed to a desired size.

✔ **Rosemary:** Any serious grilling cook knows that rosemary is a very important herb. Fresh rosemary sprigs have just the right intensity of flavor for rubs and marinades.

Vary It! Rosemary is perfect for grilled pork, poultry, fish, lamb, potatoes, tomatoes, summer squash, and eggplant. Grill kebabs, fish steaks, or fish fillets on top of fresh, oiled rosemary sprigs. Or strip all the needles and use the stems as flavorful wooden skewers for small pieces of lamb, chicken, or fish. Dried rosemary is also an excellent rub ingredient. Mix it to taste with ground thyme, crushed peppercorns, dried oregano, garlic salt, or other seasonings and press onto chicken, steaks, lamb, or fish before grilling. Blend chopped, fresh rosemary leaves and lemon juice into butter for a rich herb butter.

✔ **Saffron:** Saffron — the world's most expensive spice — is pungent and aromatic; however, a little goes a long way to add flavor and a golden color to mayonnaise dressings or creamy sauces for grilled fish or chicken. (See Chapter 7 for Bow Ties with Peppers, Peas and Saffron Mayonnaise.)

Saffron is sold as a powder or as whole yellow, orange, or red threads. The threads, shown in Figure 4-4, are better quality. Soak the threads briefly in a little hot water before adding them (along with the soaking water) to the dish.

Figure 4-4: Saffron threads are dainty.

saffron

Spice is just a phone call away

Check out the supermarket spice section for an array of special spice mixes — from mixed peppercorn blends to jerk seasoning — made by McCormick, Paul Prudhomme, Zatarain's, and other companies. You can also mail-order rubs directly from Vanns (800-583-1693), Penzeys, Ltd (414-574-0277), or Mo Hotta Mo Betta (800-462-3220). Penzeys publishes a catalog that reads more like a cookbook, with pictures, tips, recipes, and descriptions of over 250 herbs, spices, and seasoning blends. The Mo Hotta Mo Betta catalog is a must-have for any fan of hot pepper sauces, salsas, rubs, barbecue sauces, and spicy condiments.

✔ **Thyme:** Fresh or dried, thyme is a terrific herb for accenting tomato and wine-based sauces and marinades for beef, pork, or poultry. Thyme mixes very well with basil, sage, rosemary, parsley, marjoram, and garlic. Sprinkle chopped, fresh thyme over grilled vegetables such as potatoes, eggplant, tomatoes, summer squash, mushrooms, or onions.

Adding Zest with Fruits and Veggies

A griller's pantry should include a range of fresh fruits and vegetables that can be used as seasoning ingredients to add spice, heat, pungency, and other intense flavors to foods. We recommend that you stock the following:

✔ **Chiles:** Sorting through chiles in the supermarket can be confusing. Chiles are sold fresh, dried crushed, flaked, and ground. The pungency of a chile can range from almost sweet to excruciatingly hot. Fresh chiles commonly found in Mexican dishes include *jalapeño* (hot), *habañero* (very hot), and *poblano* (mild) — see Figure 4-5. Remember that chiles infuse a dish with additional flavor, as well as with spiciness.

Handle all chiles, but especially fresh chiles, with care. To prepare a fresh chile, remove the seeds and ribs, the hottest parts, to reduce the intensity of the pepper by about 90 percent, and then finely chop the chiles into marinades and sauces. Wash your hands and avoid touching your eyes after handling, and you may want to wear rubber gloves!

Some of the more common dried chiles available in supermarkets today are the ancho, pasilla, and chipotle — a smoke-dried jalapeño with a wonderful, hot, smoky flavor. (Check out Chapter 16 for a Grilled Swordfish Steak with Chipotle Salsa recipe.)

Figure 4-5:
These
chiles
aren't
chilly!

Cayenne and paprika are chiles that have been ground to a fine powder and range in heat from very hot to mild. Ground chiles, mixed with cumin, garlic, and other spices, are often made into blends of chili powder.

Vary It! Sprinkle your favorite chili powder (or make your own blend) onto fish, chicken, or pork and coat the meat with a little oil before grilling for a delicious quick spice rub. (Chapter 5 has more on rubs.)

✔ **Citrus juice from lemons, limes, and oranges:** These juices are mildly acidic and add a fresh, bold flavor to marinades, dressings, and basting sauces. To some degree, citrus juice is a tenderizing agent in marinades.

Vary It! Garnish platters of grilled fish, chicken, or lamb with lime or lemon slices. Grill delicate fish fillets on slices of lemons, oranges, or limes. (Chapter 16 is filled with fish ideas.) Lemon juice is a delicious marinade ingredient for grilled lamb, veal, chicken, or pork. Orange juice adds natural sweetness to marinades and combines especially well with hoisin sauce and soy sauce — flip to Chapter 5 for a Hoisin Marinade for pork ribs, lamb, or chicken.

✔ **Citrus peel from lemons, limes, and oranges:** Grated citrus peel, also called *zest*, contains natural oils that can add intense flavor to grilled meat, fish, poultry, and vegetables. Grated citrus peel does not have the slightly harsh acidic quality of the juice; instead, like salt, it helps punctuate the natural flavor of a food.

Vary It! Add grated peel generously to dressings, marinades, basting sauces, and rubs. Add peels to white wine vinegar with fresh herbs to make citrus-flavored vinegars. Be sure to grate only the outer, colored portion of the peel because the *pith,* the white layer underneath the peel, imparts bitterness.

Throw whole peels directly into the coals to create flavorful smoke when grilling pork, fish, or lamb.

✔ **Garlic:** The potential of garlic for the grilling cook is unlimited — we cannot praise garlic too much. Raw garlic cloves are indispensable to all types of marinades. Minced or pressed garlic adds depth and dimension to basting and finishing sauces, dips, salsas, condiments, and side dishes. There is a reason why garlic is a recognizable ingredient in so many ethnic cuisines and dishes — it combines without objection with other strong ethnic seasoning like fresh ginger, soy sauce, chile peppers, hot spices, curries, onions, olive oil, and fresh herbs. When foil-wrapped and roasted, garlic loses some of its sharpness and mellows to an almost nutty taste. (See Chapter 17 for tips on roasting garlic.)

Vary It! When a marinade, dip, or salsa seems to taste flat and lacking in flavor, try adding a little minced garlic.

✔ **Red and yellow onions, scallions, and shallots:** In addition to being marvelous choices for grilling on their very own (see Chapter 17), all of these vegetables add flavor to marinades and sauces. You should always stock these items in your pantry.

- Red onions add color as well as an element of sweetness to salsas and condiments.

- Yellow onions, in good supply all year-round, are the workhorses of the griller's pantry. Dice and add them to marinades, salsas, chutneys, and relishes.

- Scallions, which have long green leaves and small white bulbs, are especially welcomed in Asian-style sauces and marinades. (Use both the green and white parts.)

- Shallots (see Figure 4-6), with their faint purple interior and papery bronze skin, are not some high-minded ingredient of the rich and famous. Shallots are readily available in all supermarkets and noteworthy because of their distinctive nutty flavor.

Figure 4-6:
The lonely
shallot.

Chapter 5

The Magic of Marinades, Oils, and Rubs

In This Chapter

▶ Marinating for taste and tenderness

▶ Coating foods with flavored oils

▶ Massaging with tasty rubs

You can't overestimate the importance of marinating food that's destined for the grill. Marinades change food in two very important ways — by softening or slightly tenderizing meat, and by adding flavor. A tender, succulent ribeye steak may need nothing but a dusting of salt and pepper before it's grilled, but a top blade or shoulder steak will greatly benefit from a little soaking to soften its tougher tissues. Tender cubes of sirloin can be cut and skewered with vegetables and fruits for kebabs, but marinating those cubes first in a seasoned liquid gives you an endless number of flavoring options. Indeed, adding flavor is the main benefit of marinating.

Oils and rubs are the little cousins of marinades — they add moisture and flavor but don't have acid ingredients such as lemon juice, vinegar, or wine, which also slightly soften food. Oils can be combined with chopped herbs, grated citrus peel, minced garlic, salt, pepper, and other seasonings to make a thick paste that you can apply to cuts of meat, fish, or poultry. Rubs can be any tasty blend of spices and seasonings.

You may say that marinades, oils, and rubs are to grilling what sauces are to French cooking: They layer on flavor to transform ordinary poultry, fish, meat, and vegetables into something divine and memorable. Except, unlike a fancy finishing sauce, marinades, oils, and rubs work their magic before the food is actually cooked.

The March of the Marinades

You're standing in your kitchen looking at a thick and juicy piece of steak that you hope to grill to a perfect medium-rare. And you're thinking that, in addition to a dusting of salt and pepper, you could add more pizzazz by plunging the meat into a spicy marinade. Good idea. But now comes the hard part: deciding what ingredients to use.

The typical marinade is a combination of an oil, an acid, herbs, and spices. The fat that lubricates and moisturizes the food is usually a vegetable oil. The acid component may be a vinegar, lemon juice, or other citric acid, yogurt, or wine. Although these acids don't actually tenderize the food, they can soften the surface tissues of tougher cuts.

Marinades come in endless flavors — spicy, sweet, savory, tangy, herby, oily, acidic, salty, and so forth. We give you plenty of marinades in this chapter and throughout the book, but there's no reason to use only our recipes. What you put into the marinade is a matter of personal taste — if you feel like experimenting on your own, use the marinade combinations that follow as guidelines, adjusting specific ingredient amounts to mix a potion that works for you.

When breaking away from a recipe to blend your own marinade, always consider the food that's being soaked:

✔ Is it lean — for example, chicken breast or white fish?

As a rule, the leaner the food, the better it does in marinades with a fairly high concentration of oil.

✔ Is it high in fat, like the well-marbled red meat of a ribeye steak?

Richer foods hold their own against more robust acidic ingredients like red wine vinegar or wine.

And think about how ingredients work best together:

✔ Soy sauce is compatible with the flavors of ginger, sesame oil, scallions, and garlic. Spicy Asian-flavored marinades for fish, pork, beef, or chicken often combine dark soy sauce, rice vinegar, garlic, sugar, chiles, fresh ginger, peanut oil, scallions, and coriander leaves.

✔ White or red wines mix well with olive oil, chopped garlic, onions, or shallots, and fresh herbs such as tarragon, thyme, and rosemary or bay leaf. Red wine marinades are good with beef, game, and dark-meat poultry. White wine marinades go well with pork, poultry, fish, and shellfish. (Turn to Chapter 11 for rotisserie chicken in a white wine, lemon-herb marinade, or to Chapter 12 for a red wine marinade in grilled tenderloin au poivre.)

✔ Fresh or dried chiles, chili powder, cayenne pepper, crushed red pepper, and Tabasco sauce can punch up the flavor in a marinade and leave your mouth with an appealing hot and spicy aftertaste.

✔ Honey, molasses, brown sugar, and granulated sugar add sweetness to your grill foods. Compose a tasty marinade for all kinds of poultry by ~~~~er corn oil, ketchup or molasses, dry sherry, Worcester-~~~~by sauce, crushed garlic, chopped onions, Tabasco sauce, ~~~~er (all to your tastes).

~~~~ry mild, while sesame oil is bold and best if used in ~~~~s in a marinade.

~~~~me, or orange peel is rich in aromatic citrus oil and can ~~~~erally in marinades.

~~~~nced, or pressed, seems to improve nearly every

~~~~rd added to a marinade of dry white wine, olive oil, ~~~~lemon peel, and chopped fresh herbs like parsley, ~~~~thyme is delicious for poultry or fish.

~~~~d that blends nicely with cumin, turmeric, curry, ~~~~nger, paprika, chopped onion, and garlic to coat and ~~~~mb, chicken, or fish. (See Chapter 9 for Chicken Tikka ~~~~works with pork or lamb.)

~~~~e recipes in this book are interchangeable. For ~~~~le for Caribbean Pork Chops (Chapter 13) also ~~~~y, or chicken. The Best-Ever Fajita marinade ~~~~od for other cuts of beef, with chicken, or with ~~~~. If you like its flavor, steal the marinade from ~~~~ith other foods.

~~~~ten in many other cookbooks, adding salt to a ~~~~pel food to release its natural juices, nor does it ~~~~r dry out. Water or liquid flows towards those ~~~~ense or concentrated, in a natural effort to ~~~~ls of the food sitting in the marinade take in ~~~~tle salt. So, if you wish, add the salt.

~~~~ut 1 to 2 cups of marinade for every 1¹/₂ to 2 ~~~~gh marinade to completely surround the ~~~~or delicate fish, vegetables, and certain cuts of ~~~~meat, benefit from several hours of marinating time, and many foods like to stand in the liquid overnight. Turn over the food (or the plastic bag) in the marinade a few times to moisten all the food surfaces.

Revolutionary Grill-Cleaning Tool

Cleans your BBQ grill with the power of *Steam*

Instructions

Select a container that's the proper size and shape — in which the food fits snugly and is immersed in the liquid. You can use a mixing bowl for your marinade, but make sure that it's glass, ceramic, or plastic, because acidic ingredients and alcohol can react with aluminum and iron, giving the meat and liquid a metallic flavor and gray color. (See Figure 5-1.) However, we think a large, resealable plastic bag works best. (Check out Figure 5-2.) Just mix the marinade right in the bag, toss in the food, seal the bag, and chill, turning occasionally. Foods marinated in a bag take up less room in your refrigerator.

Figure 5-1:
The good and the bad of marinade containers.

Figure 5-2:
Using a plastic bag is less hassle.

Place food in a plastic bag.

Pour marinade into the bag.

Press all of the air out of the bag.

Seal shut, making sure the food is surrounded by the marinade, folding over if necessary.

Hoisin Marinade and Basting Sauce

Hoisin sauce, which you can find in any major supermarket, is a convenient, versatile product that can add sparkle to many grilled foods — especially ribs, chicken, lamb, and shrimp. It's a mixture of sugar, vinegar, soybeans, chile peppers, and garlic. The sugar content is relatively high, so for best results, use the indirect grilling method (see Chapter 1) to prevent the food from charring.

Preparation time: 15 minutes

Yield: About 1 cup

$^1/_2$ cup fresh orange juice

$^1/_3$ cup hoisin sauce

2 tablespoons soy sauce

2 tablespoons peeled and minced fresh ginger

2 teaspoons honey

1 teaspoon sesame oil

Pepper to taste

$^1/_4$ cup finely chopped scallions (white and green parts)

In a small mixing bowl or measuring cup, whisk together the orange juice, hoisin sauce, soy sauce, ginger, honey, sesame oil, and pepper; stir in the scallions. Use as a marinade and basting sauce for about 2 pounds of pork, lamb, chicken, or shrimp. Marinate the meat or poultry for several hours or overnight; marinate shrimp for 30 minutes or less. Grill food indirectly or monitor carefully if grilling over a direct fire, to prevent charring. To use as a finishing sauce, bring any remaining marinade to a boil in a small saucepan and drizzle over grilled food.

Vary It! For a simple hoisin barbecue sauce, combine equal parts hoisin sauce, ketchup, and water. Use with chicken, ribs, or shrimp, basting the last 10 to 15 minutes of grilling.

Very often the same marinade that's used to soak the uncooked food can be reheated and poured over the grilled food to serve as a delicious finishing sauce. However, if any kind of raw fish, meat, or poultry was first soaked in the marinade, then it must be heated to boiling and allowed to simmer a minute or two to destroy any possible bacteria from the raw food.

Spicy Soy and Cilantro Marinade

This marinade is delicious with any cut of beef and also works with chicken, fish, or pork. Any leftover marinade can be boiled for a finishing sauce or tossed into cooked noodles with just enough additional peanut oil and soy sauce to coat. You can use any kind of hot chile pepper, such as jalapeño, serrano, or habañero, but beware — habañero is about as hot as peppers get! Using a red pepper rather than a green one adds a nice contrasting note of color to the finished dish.

(continued)

Preparation time: 15 minutes

Yield: About 1^1/$_3$ cups

^{1}/$_2$ cup dark soy sauce

^{1}/$_4$ cup plus 2 tablespoons rice vinegar

^{1}/$_4$ cup peanut oil

^{1}/$_4$ cup chopped cilantro leaves

4 cloves garlic, peeled and chopped

3 scallions, trimmed and chopped
(white and green parts)

1 tablespoon plus 1 teaspoon peeled,
grated fresh ginger

2 teaspoons sugar

1 to 2 chile peppers, seeded and finely
minced

Combine all the ingredients in a small mixing bowl or measuring cup and pour over
1^1/$_2$ to 2 pounds of meat, chicken, or fish. For best results, marinate fish for 30
minutes to 1 hour, and other foods for 6 hours or overnight, turning occasionally.

Gingery Grilled Vegetable Marinade

This vegetable marinade combines soy sauce, ginger, and sesame oil with the zing of
Tabasco sauce and is especially delicious with tomatoes, onions, summer squash
(zucchini or yellow squash), and mushrooms. However, it clashes with the bitterness
of eggplant, so choose vegetables with an element of sweetness, and you won't go
wrong. Plum or Roma tomatoes work especially well.

Preparation time: 25 minutes

Marinating time: 30 minutes to 1 hour

Yield: 6 servings

^{1}/$_2$ cup white wine vinegar

^{1}/$_3$ cup light soy sauce

6 tablespoons olive oil

2 tablespoons sesame oil

2 tablespoons peeled and minced fresh
ginger

1 tablespoon brown sugar, packed

2 large cloves garlic, peeled and minced

2 teaspoons Tabasco sauce

Salt and pepper to taste

6 to 7 cups sliced vegetables

1 In a medium mixing bowl or glass measuring cup, make the marinade by combining all the ingredients except the vegetables.

2 Place the sliced vegetables in a 1-gallon, resealable plastic bag or other large container; pour the marinade over the vegetables in the bag or container.

3 Press the air out of the bag and seal tightly, or cover the container. Refrigerate for 30 minutes to 1 hour, turning the bag over once or occasionally tossing the vegetables in the container.

4 Grill over a medium-hot fire. Grilling time will depend on the thickness of the vegetables — see Chapter 17 for more information on grilling vegtables.

Go-With: Arrange the attractive veggies on a large platter, surrounding grilled fish, meat, poultry, or pork, or toss them into hot, steamy pasta or a green salad. Leftovers can be diced up into a tasty relish for hot dogs, hamburgers, and grilled steaks.

Ignore the advice of cookbooks and recipes that instruct you to marinate meat, fish, or poultry at room temperature for 2 to 3 hours before grilling. You can safely marinate meat, fish, or poultry at room temperature for only about 30 minutes; after that, you risk the danger of contamination from airborne bacteria. Be on the safe side: Keep foods well chilled in the refrigerator. Grilling chilled meats takes a little longer, but you avoid the possibility of contaminating your food.

Flavored Oils — the Slick Solution

Sometimes all you need to boost the flavor of tender cuts of meat, boneless poultry, or delicate fish is a light brushing of oil, to which you have added chopped herbs, a little garlic, or a few spices. Refrigerate for 1 to 2 hours (or even less, if you don't have the time).

Use any of the following oils to generously brush $1^1/_2$ to 2 pounds of steak, chicken, fish, or pork. Brush both sides before grilling.

Be sure to discard all unused oil. In a short time, the fresh ingredients you add to the oil become a breeding ground for harmful bacteria, so toss it out as soon as you've finished coating the food.

- **Lemon-Rosemary Oil:** Because you must make this oil with fresh rosemary, you may decide to plant a rosemary pot in a sunny outdoor spot, or even indoors on a kitchen windowsill. Infuse the oil with rosemary and other seasonings by pureeing all ingredients in a blender. Whirl until smooth 6 tablespoons olive oil, $1/4$ cup minced rosemary leaves, 3 cloves peeled and crushed garlic, 2 teaspoons lemon juice, and 2 teaspoons grated lemon peel.

    Go-With: Brush this oil on about 2 pounds of sirloin steaks, or tender beef kebabs; on fish fillets or fish steaks; on boneless chicken breasts; or on sea scallop kebabs. Grill over a medium to medium-hot fire.

- **Ginger-Soy Oil:** Whisk together $1/4$ cup peanut or vegetable oil, 2 tablespoons soy sauce, 1 tablespoon sesame oil, 1 tablespoon peeled and grated ginger (or $1/2$ teaspoon ground ginger), 1 clove peeled and crushed garlic, and salt and pepper to taste.

    Go-With: This oil is delicious brushed on $1^1/2$ to 2 pounds of tender beef cuts, chicken or turkey parts, or fish.

- **Mustard-Worcestershire Oil:** Spoon $1/4$ cup Dijon-style mustard in a small mixing bowl. Add $1/2$ cup olive oil in a slow, steady stream, beating constantly with a fork or wire whisk to blend the mustard into the oil until the sauce is smooth and creamy. Whisk in 2 teaspoons Worcestershire sauce (or more or less to taste). Season to taste with salt and pepper.

    Go-With: Brush this sharp, mustard-flavored oil on pieces of chicken, fish, pork, or tender cuts of lamb or beef before grilling.

Rub-a-Dub-Dub

Rubs are usually a dry combination of herbs and spices, although sometimes a little oil is added to moisten the mixture. You simply massage rubs onto the surface of the food and end up with a wonderful crispness to the crust. Rubs are fast becoming the darlings of the grilling cook because, unlike marinades, they can be applied just before the food is grilled. However, if you have the time, let the food absorb the spice mixture in the refrigerator for several hours or overnight. Small tender pieces of fish or shellfish will benefit from about 30 minutes of standing time. A whole, spice-rubbed turkey should be plastic-wrapped to hold the rub tightly against its skin and then refrigerated overnight.

Rubs that are completely dry, without any oil or liquid ingredient, can be stored indefinitely in airtight containers in a cool, dry place. The amount of rub used to cover the surface of a piece of meat is entirely a matter of taste, but our rule calls for about 1 tablespoon for every pound of food.

To help the rub cling to the food's surface, apply it to food that is either completely dry or coated with a little oil. When seasoning poultry, spread the rub evenly over the surface and also under the skin as much as possible, being careful not to tear it.

Rub mixtures often call for crushing whole spices. You can best accomplish this task with a mortar and pestle; but if you don't have this kitchen tool, place the spices in a plastic bag and pound them with a rolling pin or a meat mallet until finely crushed.

Hot and Sweet Spice Rub

This rub gives an interesting sweet and spicy flavor to all kinds of meat.

Preparation time: 5 minutes

Yield: 2 tablespoons

2 teaspoons chili powder

1 teaspoon paprika

1 teaspoon brown sugar, firmly packed

$^1/_2$ teaspoon flour

$^1/_2$ teaspoon garlic salt

$^1/_4$ teaspoon ground cinnamon

$^1/_4$ teaspoon ground allspice

Pinch of pepper

Kosher or table salt (optional)

Combine all ingredients and use as a rub for 2 to 2$^1/_2$ pounds of beef, poultry, or pork. Coat the food lightly with oil before applying. Sprinkle grilled food lightly with additional kosher or table salt before serving (if desired).

Cajun-Style Steak Rub

This is an all-purpose rub for tender steak cuts that need no marinating. Try it on sirloin, T-bone, porterhouse, tenderloin, and ribeye. (See Chapter 12 for more on beef cuts.)

(continued)

Preparation time: 5 minutes

Yield: Enough for about 2 pounds of meat.

1 tablespoon olive oil

3 cloves garlic, peeled and minced (about 1 tablespoon)

1¹/₂ teaspoons chili powder

³/₄ teaspoon ground cumin

³/₄ teaspoon dried thyme leaves

³/₄ teaspoon dried oregano leaves

¹/₄ teaspoon cayenne pepper

¹/₄ teaspoon black pepper

¹/₄ teaspoon salt

Combine all ingredients in a small bowl. Using your fingers, generously rub the mixture on both sides of the steaks; cover with plastic wrap and let stand for 20 to 30 minutes as the grill preheats. Grill over medium heat until done as desired. Season with additional salt after grilling (if desired).

Pepper and Herb Rub

Here's a tasty all-purpose rub that's good with pork, poultry, or beef.

Preparation time: 10 minutes

Yield: About 3 tablespoons, or enough for about 2 to 2¹/₂ pounds of pork, chicken, or beef

1 tablespoon paprika

1 teaspoon garlic powder

1 teaspoon cayenne pepper

¹/₂ teaspoon onion powder (optional)

¹/₂ teaspoon ground white pepper (optional)

¹/₂ teaspoon dried thyme

¹/₂ teaspoon dried oregano leaves

¹/₂ to ³/₄ teaspoon salt

¹/₄ teaspoon black pepper

2 teaspoons grated lemon peel

1 Brush the food generously with vegetable or olive oil on all sides before rubbing with the herb mixture.

2 In a jar with a tight-fitting lid, combine all ingredients except the lemon peel. Add the grated lemon peel just before rubbing on chops, ribs, tenderloins, or kebabs. If you have the time, cover the rubbed food with plastic wrap and refrigerate for 30 minutes to 2 hours before grilling.

Peppery Parsley Rub for Tender Steaks

In this recipe, 1 tablespoon of crushed black peppercorns gives a subtle peppery flavor. To kick up the heat, use $1^1/_2$ to 2 tablespoons.

Preparation time: *15 minutes*

Grilling time: *14 minutes*

Yield: *4 servings*

6 tablespoons finely chopped Italian parsley

4 large cloves garlic, peeled and minced (about 4 teaspoons)

1 tablespoon (or more, if desired) whole black peppercorns, crushed

2 tablespoons olive oil

2 teaspoons dried basil

2 teaspoons grated lemon peel

4 tender beefsteaks, 6 to 8 ounces each, cut 1-inch thick and trimmed of fat

$^1/_4$ teaspoon salt, or to taste

1 In a small mixing bowl, combine the parsley, garlic, crushed peppercorns, olive oil, dried basil, and lemon peel.

2 Rub the mixture generously on both sides of the steaks. Wrap the steaks in plastic and refrigerate for 30 minutes or until ready to grill.

3 Prepare a medium fire in a charcoal or gas grill.

4 Remove the steaks from the refrigerator and sprinkle them with salt. Place on an oiled grid, directly over the heat. Grill, uncovered, for 14 minutes for medium-rare, or until desired doneness, turning every 4 to 5 minutes.

5 Carve the steak across the grain into thin slices. Season with additional salt (if desired).

Five-Spice Asian Rub

Five-spice powder is an aromatic mixture of equal parts cinnamon, cloves, fennel seed, star anise, and sometimes ginger or crushed Szechwan peppercorns. Commercial blends of five-spice powder are available in Asian markets and many supermarket spice sections. This recipe is sufficient rub for about a pound of steak. You can double or triple the ingredients to cover more food (if desired). It is also an excellent rub for pork and poultry.

Preparation time: *10 minutes*

Grilling time: *14 minutes*

Yield: *2 servings*

2 teaspoons five-spice powder	*$1/_4$ teaspoon salt*
2 cloves garlic, peeled and minced	*Pepper to taste*
2 teaspoons vegetable oil	*2 tender beef steaks, about 8 ounces each, cut 1-inch thick and trimmed of fat*

1 In a small mixing bowl, combine the five-spice powder, garlic, oil, and salt and pepper.

2 Using your fingers, generously rub the spice mixture on both sides of the steaks.

3 Place the steaks on a large, shallow plate. Cover and refrigerate from 30 minutes to 2 hours.

4 Prepare a medium fire in a charcoal or gas grill.

5 Place the steaks on an oiled grid, directly over the heat. Grill, uncovered, for 14 minutes for medium-rare, or to desired doneness, turning every 5 minutes.

6 Season the steaks with additional salt (if desired). Carve the steaks across the grain into thick slices and serve.

Chapter 6
The Secret's in the Sauce

In This Chapter

▶ Serving up savory sauces
▶ Concocting classic condiments
▶ Creating compound butters

*E*very grilling chef needs an arsenal of recipes for condiments, salsas, sauces, and compound butters — concoctions that elevate a humble steak, grilled chicken, pork chop, or hamburger into something more sublime. You can prepare many of these recipes ahead of time and store them in the refrigerator, thereby allowing you to focus your full attention on the grill. All of them complement the unique flavors of grilled foods while adding taste, color, and pizzazz.

Sauces

When you grill, the wonderful cooking juices that ordinarily end up in the pan (with top-of-stove or oven roasting techniques) are lost into the fire. To compensate for this sad fact, grilling gurus — like yourself — keep a file of quick and easy sauces that add a last-minute finish to that sizzling steak, chop, piece of chicken, or fish fillet. In this section, we give you a few of our favorite sauce recipes for all kinds of grilled foods.

Creamy Horseradish Sauce

This sauce combines sour cream, horseradish, fresh lemon juice, and ripe, chopped tomatoes.

Preparation time: *10 minutes*

Yield: *About ²/₃ cup*

¹/₂ cup sour cream

¹/₄ cup chopped ripe tomatoes

2 tablespoons bottled horseradish, drained

1 tablespoon mayonnaise

2 teaspoons fresh lemon juice

Pepper to taste

Combine all the ingredients in a small bowl; cover and chill until ready to serve.

Vary It! You can substitute 3 tablespoons peeled and chopped cucumber or scallions for the tomato. Or for a snappy raw vegetable dip, add 2 tablespoons ketchup or chili sauce, and Tabasco sauce to taste.

Go-With: This sauce is terrific with grilled sausage, fish steaks, shellfish, burgers, or poultry.

Tahini Dressing

Tahini, a paste made from sesame seeds, is an important ingredient in Middle Eastern cuisine. This recipe combines tahini with lemon juice and honey into a semi-sweet dressing. If you'd like more tart lemon taste, use only 2 teaspoons of honey rather than 1 tablespoon.

Preparation time: *10 minutes*

Yield: *About ¹/₂ cup*

¹/₄ cup tahini

1 tablespoon fresh lemon juice

1 tablespoon honey

1 teaspoon olive oil

3 to 4 tablespoons water

¹/₂ teaspoon grated lemon peel

Salt and pepper

In a blender container, combine the tahini, lemon juice, honey, oil, and as much water as necessary to make a smooth, thick dressing. Transfer to a small bowl; stir in the grated lemon peel and season with salt and pepper. Drizzle over grilled chicken, turkey, lamb, beef, or vegetables, or use as a dressing for sandwich wraps made with flour tortillas, grilled chicken, chopped tomatoes, and shredded lettuce. This dressing can be covered and stored in the refrigerator for up to 2 weeks.

Ginger Cream

If it's more convenient, make this sauce in advance, refrigerate, and gently reheat in the top of a double boiler. It's a delicious finishing sauce for grilled swordfish, salmon fillets, or shrimp.

Preparation time: *5 minutes*

Cooking time: *10 minutes*

Yield: *About 1¹/₄ cups*

¹/₂ cup dry white wine

¹/₂ cup chicken broth

2 tablespoons peeled and minced shallots

2 teaspoons peeled and grated fresh ginger, or ³/₄ teaspoon powdered ginger

¹/₃ cup seeded and finely chopped tomato

1 cup heavy cream

¹/₂ teaspoon grated lemon peel

Salt and pepper to taste

1 In a medium saucepan, combine the wine, chicken broth, shallots, and ginger. Bring to a boil over medium-high heat; boil, uncovered, for several minutes until reduced to about half its volume.

2 Add the tomato and cream; return to a gentle boil over medium heat and cook until thickened and reduced to about 1 ¹/₄ cups, stirring and occasionally scraping the bottom of the pan with a wooden spoon. Remove from heat and stir in the lemon peel; adjust seasoning with salt and pepper.

Vary It! For a mustard-flavored sauce, omit the ginger and add 1 to 2 teaspoons Dijon-style mustard. For a saffron-flavored sauce, omit the ginger and stir in 4 to 5 threads of saffron with the tomatoes and cream.

Mustard and Rosemary Grilled Chicken Sauce

This basting sauce works well with any grilled chicken — especially if the chicken's been brined. (See Chapter 15.) However, if you choose not to brine, be sure to sprinkle the chicken pieces with salt before grilling.

Preparation time: *10 minutes*

Yield: *About $^1/_2$ cup*

$^1/_4$ cup butter

2 medium cloves garlic, peeled and minced

$^1/_4$ cup Dijon-style mustard

3 tablespoons chopped fresh rosemary leaves, or 1 tablespoon crumbled dried rosemary

Pepper to taste

1 Warm the butter in a small saucepan over low heat and, before the butter is completely melted, add the garlic; cook for about 30 seconds, being careful not to let either the butter or the garlic brown. Remove from the heat immediately; stir in the mustard, rosemary, and pepper.

2 Divide the sauce in half, reserving about $^1/_4$ cup to serve with the grilled chicken. Brush the other half generously on the chicken during the last 4 to 5 minutes of grilling.

Watercress and Sour Cream Dressing

This creamy, light green sauce is whirled together in the blender in just a few seconds.

Preparation time: *10 minutes*

Yield: *About $^3/_4$ cup*

$^3/_4$ cup sour cream

$^1/_2$ cup rinsed and dried watercress leaves and small stems, packed

$^1/_2$ teaspoon Dijon-style mustard

Salt and pepper to taste

1 Place the sour cream, watercress, and mustard in a blender container and puree until smooth, stopping the blender as necessary to push the watercress down.

2 After pureeing, adjust the seasoning with salt and pepper. Spoon 2 to 3 tablespoons of the dressing over grilled or smoked fish.

Go-With: This dressing is delicious with salmon, trout, scallops, or shrimp.

In a perfect world, every kitchen would store an assortment of pesto sauces. Basil pesto, red pepper pesto, and pesto with pine nuts or walnuts all can be used as a sandwich spread, a dipping sauce, in dressings and marinades, or as a sauce for steamed pasta.

Pesto Sauce

Here is our favorite pesto recipe. For a lemony pesto that also works well with grilled shrimp and other fish, stir in the grated peel of half a lemon to the finished sauce. If you don't have the time to make your own pesto, buy a good-quality bottled or refrigerated pesto at any supermarket.

Preparation time: 15 minutes

Yield: About $1/2$ cup

2 cups, loosely packed fresh basil leaves, stems removed (about 2 ounces)	3 large cloves garlic, peeled and chopped
$1/2$ cup extra-virgin olive oil	Salt and pepper to taste
3 tablespoons pine nuts or walnuts	$1/4$ cup grated Parmesan cheese

1 Rinse and pat dry the trimmed basil leaves.

2 In the container of a food processor or blender combine basil leaves, oil, pine nuts or walnuts, garlic, and salt and pepper. Blend to a fine texture but not a smooth puree, stopping once to scrape down the sides of the container.

3 Add the Parmesan cheese and blend for just a few more seconds. Cover and chill until ready to use.

Creamy Asian Peanut Sauce with Noodles

This sauce recipe, flavored with peanut butter, is especially good drizzled over grilled pork chops. Use it to baste pork or chicken kebabs, or as a rich and elegant finishing sauce for grilled pork tenderloin. In this recipe, it's used as a sauce for a side dish of noodles (see the color photo section for an example).

Preparation time: *20 minutes*

Yield: *About 1 cup sauce, or a side dish serving of noodles for 4*

8 ounces uncooked, Chinese egg noodles, Japanese noodles, or linguine

2 tablespoons soy sauce

2 tablespoons dry sherry

2 tablespoons creamy peanut butter

1 tablespoon fresh ginger, peeled and grated

2 teaspoons sugar

2 teaspoons honey

2 cloves garlic, peeled and minced

$1/_4$ teaspoon crushed red pepper flakes

$1/_4$ cup peanut or vegetable oil

4 scallions, both white and green parts, chopped

Pepper to taste

1 Bring a large pot of lightly salted water to a boil; add the noodles and cook according to package directions. Before draining the noodles, reserve 2 tablespoons of the boiling water.

2 Meanwhile, prepare the sauce. In a small bowl or measuring cup, whisk together the soy sauce, sherry, peanut butter, ginger, sugar, honey, garlic, and red pepper flakes. Slowly add the oil in a steady stream, whisking as you pour, until the sauce is smooth and creamy. Stir in the scallions and black pepper. Set aside.

3 Drain the noodles thoroughly in a colander over the sink. Transfer them back to the pasta pot; add the sauce and, only if necessary, add 1 to 2 tablespoons of the reserved noodle liquid. Add only enough liquid to help bind the sauce to the noodles, but not so much that the sauce becomes thin and watery.

Go-With: Serve with pork tenderloin slices or grilled pork chops. (See Chapter 13.)

Vary It! If you want to use this sauce for grilled pork and have no reason to boil noodles, simply substitute 1 to 2 tablespoons hot tap water for the water from the pasta pot.

Roasted Garlic and Red Pepper Puree

Pureed vegetable sauces made from blends of tomatoes, cucumbers, greens like watercress or arugula and a binding ingredient like yogurt, sour cream, olive oil, or mayonnaise, are wonderful accompaniments to fresh grilled fish fillets. They are easy to assemble in the blender and often give the white, anemic looking fish a lovely ribbon of color.

Preparation time: *10 minutes*

Grilling time: *15 to 20 minutes*

Yield: *About 1 cup*

2 large sweet red peppers

4 large cloves garlic with skin

1 tablespoon butter

$^1/_4$ cup light cream or half-and-half

Salt and pepper to taste

1 Prepare a hot fire in a gas or charcoal grill.

2 Place the peppers and garlic cloves directly on an oiled grid.

3 Grill the garlic cloves for 8 to 10 minutes or until their papery skin is lightly browned and the flesh is soft, turning once. Remove from the grid. Cool slightly and press the cloves out of their skin. Set cloves aside.

4 Grill the peppers for a total of 15 to 20 minutes, turning every 5 to 10 minutes, until their skin is completely blackened all over. Immediately place the peppers in a brown paper bag and let stand for 10 minutes to steam off their skin.

5 When the peppers are cool enough to handle, use a paring knife to peel, core, and remove their seeds. (If the skin does not slip off easily, grill the pepper for a few minutes more.) Cut peppers into large pieces and place in a blender container with the roasted and peeled garlic cloves; puree until smooth. (For a terrific low-calorie sauce with plenty of flavor, stop at this point. Serve the sauce over grilled fish or chicken.)

6 In a small skillet, melt the butter over medium-low heat. Add the pureed pepper mixture and the half-and-half or light cream. Cook, stirring, 1 minute or just until warmed through. Remove from heat and season to taste with salt and pepper. Spoon over grilled fish fillets or fish steaks.

Condiments

Bottled ketchup, mustard, relish, and tomato salsa are the most popular condiments on any griller's table, and we think that using only those stand-bys is a mistake. This section takes you to a new level of grilling greatness, with recipes for homemade salsas, flavored mayonnaise dressings, savory pastes, and easy chutneys. Before you run screaming from the room, clutching the ketchup bottle to your chest, why not try a couple?

Guacamole

Here's our version of the Mexican classic, shown in the color photo pages of this book.

Preparation time: *15 minutes*

Yield: *1 cup*

2 ripe avocados, peeled and pitted (see Figure 6-1)

1 small onion, peeled and finely chopped

2 tablespoons chopped fresh cilantro or parsley

1 1/2 tablespoons fresh lemon or lime juice

1 clove garlic, peeled and squeezed through a garlic press, or minced

Salt to taste

Tabasco sauce (optional)

In a medium bowl, roughly mash the avocados with a fork to make a coarse puree. Add the onion, cilantro or parsley, lemon or lime juice, garlic, salt, and Tabasco sauce (if desired); mix well. Cover, chill, and serve within 1 hour.

Go-With: Guacamole is also delicious as a garnish or condiment for any kind of tender grilled steak (Chapter 12) and also goes well with Best-Ever Fajitas (Chapter 18).

Vary It! You can add all sorts of ingredients to the Guacamole to change its flavor in a heartbeat. Experiment by adding any of the following ingredients to taste:

- Bottled salsa
- Chopped black olives
- Scallions (rather than onions)
- Chopped sun-dried tomatoes or chopped fresh tomatoes
- Seeded, chopped chile peppers

How to Pit and Peel an Avocado

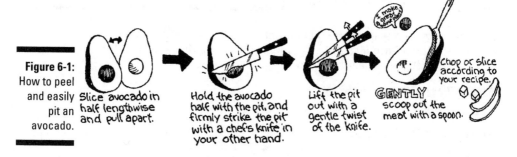

Figure 6-1: How to peel and easily pit an avocado.

Slice avocado in half lengthwise and pull apart.

Hold the avocado half with the pit, and firmly strike the pit with a chef's knife in your other hand.

Lift the pit out with a gentle twist of the knife.

I make a great guacamole!

GENTLY scoop out the meat with a spoon. Chop or slice according to your recipe.

Tapenade

This oh so rich, classic French paste makes a great condiment for grilled steaks or fish and is especially wonderful served as an appetizer on grilled slices of hard-crusted Italian or French bread.

Preparation time: *15 minutes*

Yield: *About $^2/_3$ cup*

1 cup pitted black olives

3 canned anchovy fillets, blotted dry with paper towels

2 cloves garlic, peeled and minced

2 teaspoons capers, rinsed and drained

$1^1/_2$ teaspoons fresh lemon juice

2 tablespoons olive oil

Pepper to taste

2 tablespoons finely chopped fresh basil, red onion, or tomato, for garnish

In a blender or food processor, combine the olives, anchovies, garlic, capers, lemon juice, oil, and pepper. Process into a coarse puree. (If using a blender, stop as necessary to scrape down the sides.) Transfer to a non-reactive container. Cover and refrigerate. Garnish with basil, red onion, or tomato before serving. Use within one week.

Barbecued Onions

Slow cooking onions in a little oil and butter and then adding a favorite barbecue sauce turns them into a slightly caramelized topping that's perfect for grilled burgers, hot dogs, sausage, or steaks.

Preparation time: *10 minutes*

Cooking time: *20 minutes*

Yield: *About 1¹/₃ cups*

4 large yellow onions

3 tablespoons butter

1 tablespoon vegetable oil

1 tablespoon light brown sugar, packed

¹/₂ cup bottled or homemade barbecue sauce

1 Peel the onions; cut each onion in half vertically through the core, lay the halves flat, and slice thinly into half rounds.

2 In a large heavy-bottomed skillet, heat the butter and oil over medium-low heat. Add the onion slices and brown sugar; stir well, coating the onions in the oil and sugar. Cook for 15 to 20 minutes or until the onions are very soft and browned, stirring often and occasionally scraping the bottom of the pan.

3 Stir in the barbecue sauce; continue cooking for 2 to 3 minutes more, stirring often until the onions are very tender and the sauce is warmed through.

Salsa

Salsa (SAHL-sah) is the Mexican word for sauce and can denote a combination of cold or hot ingredients. We use salsa in this book as a condiment or as a savory mixture of chopped, fresh, cold ingredients. Fresh salsas take little time to prepare and are colorful companions to grilled dishes.

Fresh Tomato Salsa

Fortunately for us, juicy, ripe tomatoes come to market just when the grilling season really kicks into gear. We give you a look at this condiment in the color photo section of this book.

Preparation time: *15 minutes*

Yield: *About 2 cups*

2 large ripe tomatoes, seeded and diced

1 small onion, peeled and diced

1 clove garlic, peeled and minced

3 tablespoons chopped fresh cilantro or parsley

$^1/_2$ to 1 jalapeño pepper, seeded and chopped

1 $^1/_2$ tablespoons olive oil

Juice of half a lime

Salt and pepper to taste

Tabasco sauce to taste

In a small mixing bowl, combine all the ingredients. Cover and let stand at room temperature for at least 15 minutes before serving.

Go-With: You must try this salsa with our Best-Ever Fajita recipe in Chapter 18, but it's also good with plain, grilled fish (Chapter 16) or chicken (Chapter 15).

Vary It! Substitute 2 tablespoons tequila for the lime juice.

Black Bean and Red Pepper Salsa

This salsa is such a pretty mix of colors. It's the best kind of recipe to make — easy and terrific.

Preparation time: *5 minutes*

Yield: *About 2 $^1/_2$ cups*

1 15-ounce can black beans, rinsed and well drained

$^1/_2$ cup diced red bell pepper

$^1/_3$ cup peeled and chopped red onion

$^1/_2$ to 1 small jalapeño pepper, seeded and finely diced

2 tablespoons chopped fresh cilantro or parsley

(continued)

Juice of 1 lime (about 1 ¹/₂ tablespoons)

2 tablespoons olive oil

1 large clove garlic, peeled and minced

Pinch of sugar

Salt and pepper to taste

In a medium, non-reactive mixing bowl, combine all the ingredients. Cover and chill. Serve with grilled fish, poultry, beef, or pork.

Mayonnaise

Mayonnaise, either commercially prepared or homemade, can be flavored with any number of ingredients and transformed into a simple finishing sauce for grilled fish. Try adding these ingredients to suit your taste:

- Grated lemon peel
- Dijon-style mustard
- Balsamic vinegar
- Chopped fresh herbs, such as tarragon or dill
- Grated fresh ginger
- Horseradish
- Plain yogurt
- Pureed roasted garlic

Sun-Dried Tomato and Basil Mayonnaise

This recipe has more uses than we can list — it's great in macaroni or grilled chicken salads, as a garnish for grilled chicken or fish, or as a spread for sandwiches stuffed with grilled vegetables.

Preparation time: *10 minutes*

Yield: *About ¹/₂ cup*

¹/₂ cup mayonnaise

2 tablespoons oil-packed sun-dried tomatoes, drained and coarsely chopped

1 tablespoon chopped fresh basil leaves

1 teaspoon fresh lemon juice

Pepper to taste

Combine all the ingredients in a blender or food processor. Puree until smooth, stopping as necessary to scrape down the sides of the container. Chill before serving.

Go-With: Serve with grilled fish or use as a dressing for grilled chicken, pork, or macaroni salads.

Chutney

Chutney is a condiment of Indian origin containing fruits or vegetables, vinegar, sugar, and spices.

Tomato Chutney

This recipe treats tomatoes like the fruits they are — sweetening them with brown sugar — to make a chutney that's great with grilled foods. If you wish, remove the tomato skins before making the chutney. To do this, plunge the whole tomatoes into boiling water for about 15 seconds or until the skins begin to split. Then chill in a bowl of ice water before slipping off the skins.

Preparation time: *15 minutes*

Yield: *About 2 cups*

2 tablespoons olive oil

1 onion, peeled and chopped

$^1/_2$ cup light brown sugar, packed

3 tablespoons apple cider vinegar

$^1/_2$ to 1 large jalapeño pepper, seeded and chopped

3 cups peeled, seeded, and chopped tomatoes

$^1/_2$ teaspoon fresh ginger, peeled and grated

1 In a medium sauté pan or skillet, heat the oil over medium heat; add the onion and cook for 7 minutes or until lightly browned and very soft, stirring occasionally.

2 Add the brown sugar, vinegar, and jalapeño pepper; cook for 4 to 5 minutes, stirring occasionally until the mixture is dark brown and syrupy.

3 Stir in the tomatoes, raise the heat to medium-high, and boil gently for 5 more minutes or until the liquid is reduced and the mixture has thickened. Remove from heat and stir in the ginger, adding more to taste (if desired). Serve warm, or cover and chill.

Go-With: This chutney goes well with grilled beef, poultry, or pork.

Summer Squash Chutney

Summer squash is combined with sweet orange juice, tart lemon juice, honey, and red onion for this chutney.

Preparation time: *15 minutes*

Cooking time: *20 minutes*

Yield: *About 2 1/2 cups*

1 tablespoon extra-virgin olive oil	1/2 cup fresh orange juice
1/2 cup peeled and chopped red onion	2 teaspoons fresh lemon juice
2 small yellow squash (about 1 pound total), diced	2 teaspoons honey
2 small zucchini (about 1 pound total), diced	1 teaspoon grated orange peel
2 teaspoons fresh ginger, peeled and grated	Salt and pepper to taste

1 In a heavy, medium saucepan, heat the olive oil over medium heat; add the red onion and cook for about 2 minutes, stirring often until the onion is soft and wilted. Add the squash, zucchini, and ginger; cook, stirring just to coat the vegetables in the oil.

2 Add the orange and lemon juices; raise the heat to high and bring the mixture to a boil. Reduce the heat to low, partially cover, and simmer for 20 to 25 minutes or until the vegetables are soft. (If the liquid has evaporated, cover completely during the last 5 minutes of cooking or add a little more orange juice to moisten.)

3 Remove from heat and stir in the honey and orange peel. Adjust seasoning with salt and pepper. Cover and chill for a few hours before serving.

Go-With: Serve with grilled chicken, pork, lamb, or beef.

Compound Butters

Compound butter is butter that's dressed up with a few herbs, spices, or other intense seasonings. A small pat on a sizzling steak can increase the pleasure of a beefy meal. Compound butters are great with all sorts of foods, including grilled meats, fish, poultry, and many vegetables, and are more appropriate than a heavy sauce in warm weather.

Compound Butter

Prepare according to Figure 6-2. Following this basic compound butter recipe is a list of tasty variations.

Preparation time: *15 minutes*

Yield: *4 servings*

1 stick of softened, unsalted butter   *Herbs and spices to taste*

1 Use a food processor, blender, or sharp chef's knife to grind up or finely mince the seasonings.

2 Using a rubber spatula, wooden spoon, or your hands and a small bowl, soften the butter until it's malleable but not too soft.

3 Work in the seasonings with a fork or with your hands.

4 Spoon the mixture onto a sheet of waxed paper and use the paper to shape the butter mixture into a cylinder or log that has a diameter of about 2 inches.

5 Wrap well and refrigerate or freeze until ready to use. The butter keeps frozen for 1 to 2 months. When ready to use, simply slice off into butter pats 1- to $1^1/_2$-inches thick.

6 Place a pat of butter on top of a thick steak, boneless grilled chicken breasts, or grilled fish; or toss grilled vegetables with butter to taste.

Steps for Making Compound Butters

Figure 6-2:
Compounding
your butter
options.

Put the butter in a bowl and let it get soft.... but DON'T MELT IT!

Use a fork to blend in your seasonings!

Turn butter out, onto a piece of waxed paper and roll into a uniform cylinder.

Refrigerate or freeze and cut off pats as you need them.

Vary It! In place of "herbs and spices to taste" in the Compound Butter recipe, substitute the following:

✔ **Lemon and Fresh Herb Butter:** Use 2 tablespoons finely chopped herbs (such as dill, basil, tarragon, thyme, marjoram, parsley, or sage), 1 teaspoon fresh lemon juice, 1 clove garlic, peeled and minced, and salt and pepper to taste. This butter works well with fish, pork, chicken, beef, and roasted vegetables.

✔ **Spicy Chili Butter:** Sprinkle in $1\frac{1}{2}$ teaspoons chili powder, $\frac{1}{4}$ teaspoon paprika, 8 drops Tabasco sauce, and salt and pepper to taste. This butter is delicious with grilled corn, chicken, or fish or as a spread for grilled breads.

✔ **Toasted Cashew and Brandy Butter:** Add $\frac{1}{4}$ cup toasted and chopped cashews, 1 tablespoon brandy or cognac, and salt and pepper to taste. Pair with grilled steaks or chicken.

✔ **Ginger and Scallion Butter:** Use 3 tablespoons finely chopped scallions, 2 teaspoons peeled and grated fresh ginger (or $\frac{3}{4}$ teaspoon ground ginger), a pinch of garlic salt, and salt and pepper to taste. Try this butter with fish, pork, and grilled vegetables.

✔ **Roasted Garlic Butter:** Take 1 whole head of garlic and remove some of the outer, papery leaves, leaving the cloves attached at the base. Slice across the top of the head, about $\frac{1}{4}$ inch, to expose the ends of the cloves. Drizzle about $\frac{1}{2}$ teaspoon olive oil over the top and wrap the head in aluminum foil. Then grill, covered, over medium heat, for 45 to 50 minutes or until the cloves are very soft, turning occasionally. (When cloves are fully cooked, they will be easy to press or squeeze out of their papery skins.) Remove from the foil and let the cloves cool for a few minutes. Squeeze about 20 cloves out of their skin. (Save and use any remaining cloves for adding to mashed potatoes or for spreading on grilled slices of Italian bread.) Mash the cloves coarsely before blending into butter with salt and pepper to taste. The garlic can also be foil-wrapped and roasted in a 350° oven for 45 minutes to 1 hour.

Chapter 7

Dishes on the Side

In This Chapter

▶ Rediscovering the classic sides and then some

▶ Introducing salads and sides your mom never made

▶ Perking up grilled dishes with easy side-dish casseroles

*Y*ou grill long enough and you'll have to face an important fact — you spend most of your energy tending the fire and grilling the food; the last thing you want to have to do is give yourself more pressure trying to assemble a bunch of complicated side dishes. So, in this side dish chapter, we promise not to torture you with any 25-step recipes that call for phyllo dough, puff pastry, or any other "I can't handle that" ingredient.

These recipes are simple side shows to the main event — the grilled food. That said, we put our own interesting accent on many of them. Our macaroni salad is a happy Mediterranean mixture of sun-dried tomatoes, black olives, basil, and lemon juice in a mayonnaise dressing. Our potato salad is made with sweet potatoes rather than white potatoes, and our coleslaw has orange sections, ginger, and spicy jalapeño peppers. So plunge into these recipes. We hope you're pleasantly surprised by the unusual flavors we've added to these old favorites. Most of them take 30 minutes or less to prepare.

Go-With: Serving suggestions follow each recipe. Use them only as guidelines. Compose your own favorite meal combinations by leafing through Parts III and IV to pair these sides with any of our main dishes.

Sides That Cool and Refresh

On hot summer days, nothing goes better with grilled food than cool salads — prepared ahead of time and waiting in the fridge.

Tomato and Red Onion Salad

This recipe combines some of our favorite fresh veggies available in the summer-time — ripe tomatoes, red onion, and fresh mint — into a salad that's easily tossed together.

Preparation time: 15 minutes

Yield: 4 servings

4 medium, ripe tomatoes, finely chopped (about 2 cups)

1 small red onion, peeled and finely chopped (about $1/2$ cup)

$1/4$ cup mixed, chopped fresh mint and parsley

2 tablespoons olive oil

1 tablespoon plus 1 teaspoon balsamic vinegar

Salt and pepper to taste

Combine all the ingredients in a medium bowl and serve. This salad is best made about 30 minutes to 1 hour before serving, but it can be prepared several hours in advance and refrigerated until serving time.

Go-With: Serve with grilled chicken, fish, beef, or pork.

Vary It! To turn this into a delicious cold rice salad, add 2 cups chilled cooked rice and, (if desired) 2 tablespoons pignoli nuts. Moisten with additional oil and balsamic vinegar and season with more salt and pepper to taste.

To draw out the most flavor in fresh tomatoes, keep them at room tempera-ture and away from heat and direct sunlight. Refrigerating tomatoes dimin-ishes their taste.

Yogurt Cucumber Salad

Made with yogurt, chopped cucumbers, and mint, this salad is guaranteed to refresh you on a hot summer day. Salads with yogurt dressings have a natural affinity for lamb and also for dishes with lots of spicy seasoning.

Preparation time: *20 minutes*

Yield: *4 servings*

1 large cucumber, peeled, seeded, and finely chopped; about 2 cups (see Figure 7-1)

1 small red onion, peeled and finely chopped (about ¹/₂ cup)

¹/₄ cup plain yogurt

¹/₄ cup mayonnaise

2 tablespoons chopped fresh mint

2 teaspoons white wine vinegar

¹/₂ teaspoon sugar

Pinch salt

Pepper to taste

In a medium mixing bowl, combine all the ingredients well; cover and refrigerate for at least 1 hour, or until serving time.

Go-With: Serve with grilled chicken (Chapter 15), fish (Chapter 16), or lamb (Chapter 14).

How to Seed a Cucumber

Figure 7-1: Getting rid of cucumber seeds.

 Remove the peel with a knife or peeler.

 Cut in half, lengthwise...

 and scoop out the seeds with a small spoon.

Minty Cucumber Salad

This cool cucumber salad, made without mayonnaise or yogurt, is a lighter variation of the preceding recipe. It's featured in the color photo section of this book.

Preparation time: *15 minutes*

Yield: *4 servings*

1 large cucumber, peeled, seeded, and finely chopped (about 2 cups)

1 medium red onion, peeled and finely chopped (about ²/₃ cup)

¹/₂ cup finely chopped fresh mint leaves

2 tablespoons olive oil

2 tablespoons white wine vinegar

1 tablespoon sugar

Salt and pepper to taste

1 In a medium mixing bowl, combine the cucumber, red onion, and mint leaves.

2 In a small mixing bowl, whisk together the oil, vinegar, and sugar. Pour the dressing over the cucumber mixture, tossing well. Season with salt and pepper. Chill before serving.

Go-With: This salad tastes especially good with grilled lamb (Chapter 14) or with beef (Chapter 12).

Orange-Ginger Coleslaw

Everybody has a favorite coleslaw recipe, and this is ours. (It's featured in the color photo section of this book.) We toss lots of sliced cabbage with fresh ginger, orange sections, carrot, and green pepper and then coat it all in a dressing that's both sweet and sour. This salad actually tastes best if allowed to sit in the refrigerator for a few hours (or even a day) before serving, to blend together the flavors.

Preparation time: *25 minutes*

Yield: *6 to 8 servings*

²/₃ cup mayonnaise

3 tablespoons fresh orange juice

1 tablespoon finely grated orange peel

2 tablespoons cider vinegar

2 teaspoons peeled and freshly grated ginger (optional)

1¹/₂ teaspoons sugar

1 large clove garlic, peeled and minced

¹/₂ teaspoon salt, or to taste

Pepper to taste

1 small head thinly sliced green cabbage (about 8 cups) (see Figure 7-2)

2 navel oranges, peeled, cut into bite-size pieces, and well drained

1 large carrot, scraped and coarsely grated

1 medium green pepper, finely diced

¹/₃ cup minced onion

1 To make the dressing, in a small bowl or measuring cup, combine the mayonnaise, orange juice, orange peel, vinegar, ginger (if desired), sugar, garlic, and salt and pepper.

2 In a large salad or serving bowl, combine the remaining ingredients; pour the dressing over the salad and toss well. Cover and refrigerate for 2 to 3 hours before serving.

Preparing Cabbage for Slaw

Figure 7-2: Cutting up cabbage.

Cut the cabbage in half, then in quarters.

Remove the core from each quarter.

Place a quarter on a flat surface, curved side down. Hold with one hand at the wedged top and cut thin slices on the bias with the knife in your other hand!

Go-With: This slaw is delicious with grilled burgers (Chapter 8), chicken (Chapter 15), pork (Chapter 13), or beef dishes (Chapter 12).

Vary It! Omit the ginger and add 1 to 2 seeded and chopped jalapeño peppers for a hot, peppery slaw.

Black Bean, Corn, and Rice Salad

Make this salad, please, we beg you! It's loaded with chopped fresh vegetables and so good for you. Plus, it's such a pretty mixture of colors — from the red peppers, yellow corn, black beans, and cilantro leaves, to the white rice — all mixed into one bowl (you can see an example in the color photo section of this book). Spoon it alongside the next hamburger you grill to charm your family, your dinner guests, or yourself.

(continued)

Preparation time: *25 minutes*

Yield: *4 servings*

1 15-ounce can black beans, rinsed and drained

1¹/₂ cups cooked, chilled white rice

1 cup frozen and cooked (or canned) corn kernels, drained

1 small sweet red pepper, cored and finely diced

1 small red onion, peeled and finely chopped

¹/₃ cup chopped fresh cilantro or parsley

¹/₃ cup olive oil

1¹/₂ tablespoons cider vinegar

2 cloves garlic, peeled and minced

1 small jalapeño pepper, seeded and chopped

¹/₂ teaspoon ground cumin

Salt and pepper to taste

1 Combine the beans, rice, corn, red pepper, onion, and cilantro or parsley in a large bowl; toss well.

2 Combine the olive oil, vinegar, garlic, jalapeño pepper, and cumin. Add to the rice mixture; toss well. Adjust seasoning with salt and pepper. Cover and chill before serving.

Go-With: Serve with any grilled fish dish (Chapter 16), chicken recipe (Chapter 15), pork dish (Chapter 13), or with Just-Right Pork Ribs (Chapter 10).

Tabbouleh

Tabbouleh — a salad that's usually made with bulghur wheat, tomatoes, parsley, mint, onions, lemon juice, and olive oil — is especially good with lamb and chicken dishes. You can find bulghur in most major supermarkets and health food stores. To make tabbouleh, soak the bulghur in boiling water until soft and plump. (Read the package for soaking directions; they vary.) If you'd rather open a box than make your own, we recommend the Near East Food Products brand, which is available in any quality supermarket — the company makes a complete line of convenient, whole-grain side dishes that include tabbouleh, couscous, and rice pilaf.

Preparation time: *30 minutes, which includes soaking the bulghur wheat*

Yield: *4 servings*

1 cup bulghur wheat

1 large, ripe tomato, diced (about 1 cup)

$^1/_2$ cup peeled, seeded, and finely chopped cucumber

$^1/_3$ cup chopped scallions

$^1/_3$ cup finely chopped fresh mint, or 1 tablespoon plus 1 teaspoon dried mint

$^1/_4$ cup chopped parsley

$^1/_4$ cup extra-virgin olive oil

3 tablespoons fresh lemon juice

Salt and pepper to taste

1 Put the bulghur wheat in a large bowl; cover with at least $^1/_2$ inch boiling water and let stand for 30 minutes or more, until the wheat is swollen and tender. (Read the package directions, because the soaking time can vary from 30 minutes to 2 hours.)

2 Drain the bulghur in a colander over the sink, pressing out as much liquid as possible. Transfer the bulghur to a salad or mixing bowl. Add the tomato, cucumber, scallions, mint, parsley, olive oil, lemon juice, and salt and pepper. Blend well. Cover and chill before serving.

Vary It! You can add chopped black olives or capers or chopped carrots, and a clove of pressed garlic or you can substitute red onion for the scallions.

Go-With: Serve with Lemony Fresh Lamb Kebabs or Chicken Tikka (Chapter 9), any of the rib recipes (Chapter 10), a grilled steak (Chapter 12), or a simple hamburger (Chapter 8).

Sweet Potato-Apple Salad with Maple Dressing

When you make salad with sweet potatoes, you get all the qualities that a white potato brings to the dish — like those delicious, chunky, fill-you-up potato wedges. But by using sweet potatoes, you also get a natural, sugary taste that gives the salad a charming dessert-like quality. In this recipe, we mix sweet potatoes with lots of crunchy foods — chopped celery, apples, pecans, and onion — and toss it all in a maple-mayonnaise-sour cream dressing.

Preparation time: 25 minutes

Yield: 4 to 6 servings

(continued)

2 pounds sweet potatoes (about 3 large potatoes), peeled and cut into $^1/_2$- to $^3/_4$-inch cubes

1 cup chopped celery

1 large sweet apple, such as Red Delicious or Yellow Delicious, cored and diced

$^3/_4$ cup chopped pecans

$^1/_3$ cup peeled and chopped onion

$^1/_2$ cup mayonnaise

$^1/_4$ cup sour cream

2 tablespoons cider vinegar

2 tablespoons maple syrup

$^1/_2$ teaspoon salt, or to taste

Pepper to taste

1 Put the potatoes in a medium saucepan of boiling, salted water. Cover and boil gently for 5 to 6 minutes until just tender and still firm enough to hold their shape. Turn into a colander and rinse under cold running water. Drain well.

2 Transfer the potatoes to a large salad bowl; add the celery, apple, pecans, and onion.

3 In a medium bowl or measuring cup, make the dressing by mixing together the mayonnaise, sour cream, vinegar, and maple syrup. Gently toss the dressing into the sweet potato-apple mixture. Season with salt and pepper. Cover and chill before serving.

Go-With: Serve with grilled pork (Chapter 13), lamb (Chapter 14), chicken (Chapter 15), or beef (Chapter 12).

Macaroni Salad with Sun-Dried Tomato Mayonnaise

This macaroni salad is not your usual blend of cold pasta coated with mayonnaise. Instead, we jazz it up with two salty-savory ingredients — sun-dried tomatoes and black olives — and add chopped fresh basil and lemon juice to give it a Mediterranean taste.

Preparation time: 20 minutes

Yield: 4 to 6 servings

$^1/_2$ pound elbow macaroni

$^3/_4$ cup mayonnaise

3 tablespoons oil-packed sun-dried tomatoes, drained and finely chopped

2 tablespoons chopped fresh basil leaves

2 teaspoons fresh lemon juice

$^1/_3$ cup peeled and diced onion

1 cup chopped celery

$^1/_4$ cup chopped pitted ripe olives

Salt and black pepper to taste

1 Cook the macaroni in a large pot of boiling, salted water for 7 to 8 minutes, until tender but still firm. Turn into a colander and rinse under cold water. Drain well.

2 In a large serving bowl, mix together the mayonnaise, sun-dried tomatoes, basil, lemon juice, and onion. Add the cooked macaroni and toss to coat. Gently fold in the celery and olives. Adjust seasoning with salt and pepper. Cover and refrigerate for at least 1 hour before serving.

Go-With: This salad is delicious with grilled chicken (Chapter 15), beef (Chapter 12), or fish (Chapter 16).

Bow Ties with Peppers, Peas, and Saffron Mayonnaise

One of the steps in this bow tie pasta salad softens tiny saffron threads in a little hot water in order to release their precious, flavorful oils. (See Chapter 5 for more information on saffron.) The threads are then combined with mayonnaise and sour cream to make a yellow, saffron-infused dressing. If you love saffron, use about $^1/_4$ teaspoon of the threads. If you want only a hint of the spice or are trying saffron for the first time, then start with between $^1/_8$ and $^1/_4$ teaspoon. Chilling the salad in the refrigerator for an hour before serving develops the flavors more fully. (Check out an example of this dish in the color photo section.)

Preparation time: 25 minutes

Yield: 4 servings

$^1/_2$ pound farfalle (bow-tie-shaped pasta, see Figure 7-3)

1 medium clove garlic, peeled

$^1/_4$ teaspoon coarse kosher salt, or $^1/_2$ teaspoon salt

6 tablespoons mayonnaise

2 tablespoons sour cream

Pinch cayenne pepper, or to taste

Scant $^1/_4$ teaspoon saffron threads softened in 1 tablespoon hot water

1 medium red pepper, cored, seeded, and diced

1 cup frozen peas, thawed

$^1/_3$ cup finely chopped scallions

Salt and black pepper to taste

(continued)

1 Bring a large pot of salted water to a boil; add the farfalle. Stir to keep the pasta from sticking together. Bring to a boil again and cook for about 12 minutes or according to package directions, until just tender.

2 As the pasta cooks, use the flat side of a chef's knife to crush the garlic on a wooden cutting board; sprinkle the garlic with the kosher salt and mince together with the knife into a paste. (Or pound the garlic with the salt in a mortar.) Transfer the paste to a small bowl; add the mayonnaise, sour cream, cayenne pepper, and the softened saffron, including the liquid.

3 Drain the cooked pasta in a colander in the sink, rinse under cold running water, and drain again.

4 Put the pasta in a salad bowl; add the red pepper, peas, scallions, and saffron-mayonnaise mixture. Stir well to coat all the ingredients evenly. Adjust seasoning with salt and pepper. Cover and refrigerate for at least 30 minutes before serving.

Go-With: This salad is terrific with a grilled sirloin steak (Chapter 12), Rock Cornish Game Hens with Molasses Rum Marinade (Chapter 15), or Grilled Lamb Chops with Orange and Rosemary (Chapter 14).

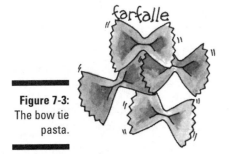

Figure 7-3:
The bow tie
pasta.

Warm and Cozy Sides

When grilling on chilly early-spring or late-fall days (or for you die-hard grillers who shovel through snow to get to the grill), we include some warmer side-dish recipes that go beautifully with the meat and vegetable dishes in Parts III and IV. Make these on your stovetop or in your oven and let them cook while you head out to the grill.

Couscous with Apples, Onions, and Raisins

Precooked couscous cooks in about 5 minutes and is a pleasant alternative to rice or noodles. Made from the same semolina wheat as pasta, couscous can be dressed up with a variety of seasonings and vegetables. It's exceptionally tasty when cooked in a beef or chicken stock, such as in this recipe. We give this dish a slightly sweetened slant by adding apple, pecans, raisins, and cinnamon. It makes a lovely bed of grain on which to serve the Apple and Tarragon Pork Kebabs in Chapter 9.

Preparation time: *15 minutes*

Cooking time: *5 minutes*

Yield: *5 to 6 servings*

1 tablespoon butter

1 tablespoon olive oil

1 large onion, peeled and finely chopped (about 1 cup)

1 large firm apple (such as Granny Smith or Golden Delicious), peeled, cored, and diced

$^1/_2$ teaspoon cinnamon

1 10-ounce package precooked couscous (about 1$^1/_2$ cups)

2$^1/_2$ cups fresh or canned chicken broth, heated to boiling

$^1/_3$ cup dark raisins

$^1/_4$ cup chopped fresh coriander or parsley

$^1/_3$ cup chopped walnuts or pecans (optional)

Salt and pepper to taste

1 Heat the butter and oil in a medium saucepan over medium-high heat. Add the onion and cook, stirring occasionally, until the onion wilts, for 3 to 4 minutes. Stir in the apple and cinnamon and cook for 1 more minute.

2 Add the couscous, boiling chicken broth, and raisins; stir to combine. Cover tightly, remove from heat, and let stand for 5 minutes. Just before serving, stir in the coriander or parsley and the walnuts or pecans (if desired). Season with salt and pepper.

Go-With: This couscous dish is especially good with grilled pork (Chapter 13), grilled lamb (Chapter 14), or beef kebabs (Chapter 9).

Three-Bean Bake

This baked bean casserole — shown in the color photo section — is so rich and luscious that you'll want to serve it with a hunk of crusty bread to sop up the delicious dark molasses and vinegar sauce. You can assemble it a day or two in advance and bake to perfection about 1 hour before serving time.

Preparation time: *20 minutes*

Cooking time: *1 hour*

Yield: *4 to 6 servings*

¹/₄ pound bacon	*1 10-ounce package frozen lima beans*
1 large onion, peeled and chopped	*1 16-ounce jar or can baked beans*
¹/₂ cup molasses	*1 16-ounce can red kidney beans, drained*
¹/₂ cup chili sauce	*Pepper to taste*
¹/₂ cup ketchup	
2 tablespoons cider vinegar	

1 In a medium skillet or fry pan, sauté the bacon over medium heat until lightly browned, turning occasionally; drain on paper towels, reserving bacon drippings in the skillet. When the bacon is cool enough to handle, tear into small pieces and set aside.

2 Add the onion to the drippings in the skillet and cook over medium heat until transparent, for 3 to 4 minutes, stirring often. Stir in the molasses, chili sauce, ketchup, and vinegar; bring to a boil, reduce heat, and simmer for about 5 minutes, stirring occasionally.

3 Place the beans in a large ovenproof casserole fitted with a lid; add the molasses-chili sauce mixture. Stir well to combine. Sprinkle the bacon pieces over the top. Cover the casserole and bake in a 375°oven for 30 minutes or until bubbly; remove the cover and bake for 15 minutes more.

Go-With: Great dishes to serve with this casserole include Grilled Chicken Quarters with Barbecue Sauce (Chapter 15), Texas Beef Barbecue (Chapter 12), any of the rib recipes in Chapter 10, Grilled Pork Chops with Rosemary Oil or Apricot Glazed Pork Chops (both in Chapter 13), Western Beef Kebabs with Red Peppers and Onions (Chapter 9), or Grilled Turkey Tenderloins with Honey-Mustard Glaze (Chapter 15).

Middle Eastern Rice

This top-of-the-stove rice casserole is a mix of pleasing flavors — turmeric, cinnamon, pine nuts, and parsley. Flip to the color photo section of this book for a vivid example.

Preparation time: 20 minutes

Cooking time: 25 minutes

Yield: 4 to 5 servings

1 tablespoon butter

1¹/₂ tablespoons olive oil, divided

3 tablespoons peeled and chopped onion

1 large clove garlic, peeled and minced

1 cup long-grain white rice

1 teaspoon turmeric

1³/₄ cup chicken broth (heated just to boiling)

¹/₄ cup dark or golden raisins (optional)

1 lemon slice, seeds removed, about ¹/₄-inch thick

¹/₄ teaspoon salt

¹/₄ cup pine nuts

1 large plum tomato or Roma tomato, chopped

3 tablespoons chopped fresh parsley

¹/₄ teaspoon cinnamon

1 In a sauté pan with a heavy bottom or in a casserole designed for stovetop cooking, melt the butter with 1 tablespoon of the oil over medium-low heat. Add the onion and garlic and cook until the vegetables start to soften, about 3 minutes, stirring occasionally.

2 Add the rice and the turmeric to the pan; cook for about 3 minutes over medium heat, stirring occasionally with a wooden spoon. Add the hot broth, raisins (if desired), lemon slice, and salt. Bring to a boil over high heat, stir with a fork, and then reduce the heat to low. Cover and simmer for about 20 minutes or until the rice is cooked and the liquid is evaporated.

3 While the rice cooks, heat a small skillet or fry pan over medium heat; add the pine nuts and toast for 2 to 3 minutes, shaking the skillet and tossing the nuts with a fork to prevent them from browning too fast. Remove them immediately from the skillet when lightly toasted.

4 When the rice is cooked, stir in the toasted pine nuts, tomato, parsley, cinnamon, and the remaining ¹/₂ tablespoon olive oil. (Omit the oil if desired.)

Go-With: Middle Eastern Rice makes an excellent side dish for just about any grilled lamb main course (Chapter 14). You can also serve with grilled chicken (Chapter 15) or beef (Chapter 12).

Part III:
Golden (Grilled) Oldies

The 5th Wave   By Rich Tennant

"This is your all-in-one grilling system. It comes with a rotisserie, a smoker, warming ovens, self-contained detachable slaughter house..."

In this part . . .

*I*n this part, you start grilling from the ground up by first tackling the basics: hamburgers, hot dogs, and sausages. Then, you'll want to master assorted kebabs, real barbecued ribs, and rotisserie cooking (which you'll be pleased to discover is the easiest and most carefree way to grill).

Chapter 8

Burgers and Sausages and Hot Dogs — Oh My!

*B*elieve it or not, you can serve a great burger, hot dog, or sausage with as much finesse as you might serve duck or lobster. For, even though these may seem like the easiest, slap-'em-on-the-grill kind of dishes, they can be made well or poorly. In this chapter, however, we give you the basics of turning out the kind of burgers, hot dogs, and sausages that make your guests think that you've gone to great lengths or know some long-hidden secrets!

Everyone Loves a Burger

Ground meat patties have been a staple of world cookery for thousands of years. They may come in different sizes and shapes, but the ground meat patty is always a way of taking less-than-prime meat, tenderizing it, and then cooking it quickly for instant gratification. But it took some genius — a person still unknown to gastronomic history — to come up with the idea of tossing a patty on a soft bun and then heaping ketchup and other condiments on it to make a complete meal in itself. Well, a burger is *almost* a complete meal — as long as you have french fries on the side and top it with lettuce and tomato.

A hamburger that has been carefully shaped and plumped to a proper thickness, grilled to a perfect medium-rare, with a slightly charred exterior, set on top of a toasted bun, and served with homemade condiments is a grand, glorious, and very simple food.

Choose chuck

A grilled burger is probably the easiest and most commonly grilled food in America, but most of us are often disappointed with the results for two reasons: Either the burger patty is too thick to begin with and cooks to a frazzle on the edges, while remaining too pink or even raw in the middle, or the patty meat is too lean.

Although your choice of burger meat is a matter of personal preference, we believe that the juiciest hamburgers are made with ground beef that is about 80 to 85 percent meat and 15 to 20 percent fat. This is about the ratio that you find in chuck — the best all-around cut for a perfect, juicy hamburger.

Handle the patties with care

Try to mold the meat into a uniform, fairly flat patty, no thicker than $3/4$ inch. A thicker patty, mounded high in the center, is less likely to cook evenly — though we have to admit that big, fat burgers don't taste half bad. And be sure not to press the patty with the flat side of a spatula as it grills, even though you may be tempted to do so. Pressing squeezes out the flavorful juices and can also cause dangerous flare-ups. (See Figure 8-1.)

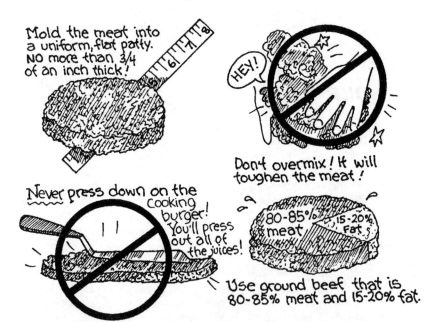

Figure 8-1: Making the perfect hamburger.

Basic Burger

Ah, there's nothing like a beautifully grilled burger. This isn't your run-of-the-mill, gotta-grab-a-quick-bite burger. This is the kind of burger that you'll think about long after it's gone. For a look at the finished product, turn to the color photo section of this book.

Preparation time: *15 minutes*

Grilling time: *10 to 15 minutes*

Yield: *4 servings*

$1^1/_2$ *pounds ground chuck*	$^1/_4$ *teaspoon pepper*
$^1/_4$ *teaspoon salt, or to taste*	*4 hamburger buns*

1 Prepare a medium fire in a charcoal or gas grill.

2 While the grill or coals are heating, combine the ground chuck, salt, and pepper in a medium mixing bowl, mixing lightly but thoroughly, using your hands. Shape the mixture into four patties, each $^3/_4$-inch thick in the center and at the edges. (Even thickness ensures even cooking and prevents the edges from drying out before the center is cooked.)

3 Place the patties on an oiled grill grid. Grill directly over the heat for 5 to 7 minutes per side for medium, less for rare to medium-rare, and 7 to 9 minutes per side for well done, turning once. (According to the U.S. Department of Agriculture, all ground meat should be cooked to at least medium doneness — 160° — or until the center of the patty is no longer pink.) Make a small incision in the center of each patty to determine doneness.

4 Toast the buns by placing them, split side down, on the edges of the grill grid for about 1 minute or until lightly browned.

5 Remove the burgers from the grill and serve on toasted hamburger buns.

Brush the grill grid with vegetable oil or nonstick cooking spray to prevent food from sticking to the grid. To avoid dangerous flare-ups, brush the grid *before* preheating the grill or igniting the charcoal.

Keep in mind that all grilling temperatures are only estimates. Variables — such as the intensity of your grill's heat, weather conditions, and the thickness of the meat — all affect the exact time it takes to cook your burger. To avoid overcooking, test the interior color of your burger. Do this by making a small incision with a thin knife in the center of the patty 1 or 2 minutes before you're done grilling.

Several grilling cookbooks recommend bringing ground meat to room temperature before placing it on the grill. We disagree. Instead, keep ground meat in the refrigerator until just before grilling. This minimizes exposure to airborne bacteria. And always place cooked burgers on a clean plate. Never return them to the plate used to carry them to the grill because it may be contaminated with bacteria from the uncooked meat.

Vary It! Use these hamburger variations (see Figure 8-2) to spark your own burger creations. Each of these seasoning combinations works for $1\frac{1}{2}$ pounds of raw ground meat.

- **Italian Burger:** Add the following ingredients to the ground meat mixture: 1 egg yolk, $\frac{1}{4}$ cup grated onion, 1 large clove garlic minced, 2 tablespoons chopped fresh basil or 2 teaspoons dried crushed basil, $\frac{1}{2}$ teaspoon dried oregano, and salt and pepper to taste. Place grated Parmesan cheese on top of each burger (if desired) about 2 minutes before the burger is done and grill, covered, until the cheese melts.

- **Mexican Burger:** Add the following ingredients to the ground meat mixture: $\frac{1}{4}$ cup finely chopped onion, $\frac{1}{2}$ to 1 teaspoon seeded and chopped jalapeño pepper, $\frac{3}{4}$ teaspoon ground cumin, and salt and pepper to taste. Serve on toasted buns or in warmed tortillas with a prepared tomato salsa or taco sauce, and slices of ripe avocado.

- **Middle Eastern Burger:** Add the following ingredients to the ground meat mixture: 2 tablespoons finely chopped onion, 2 tablespoons finely chopped raisins, $\frac{1}{2}$ teaspoon cinnamon, $\frac{1}{2}$ teaspoon paprika, and salt and pepper to taste. Serve in warmed pita pockets with Tabbouleh. (Flip to Chapter 7 for the recipe.)

- **Asian Spiced Burger:** Add the following ingredients to the ground meat mixture: $\frac{1}{4}$ cup finely chopped scallions; 3 tablespoons teriyaki sauce; 1 large clove garlic, minced; and salt and pepper to taste.

- **Veggie-Stuffed Burger:** Add the following ingredients to the ground meat mixture: $\frac{1}{3}$ cup finely grated carrot; 2 tablespoons finely chopped onion; 6 tablespoons fine dry bread crumbs; 1 beaten egg; 2 cloves garlic, minced; 1 teaspoon dried crushed marjoram or basil; and salt and pepper to taste. Serve on toasted sesame seed buns with slices of ripe tomato and alfalfa sprouts.

Go-With: The perfect grilled side dish for hamburgers is — hands down — corn on the cob. Check out Chapter 17 for all sorts of interesting ways to grill vegetables, and see Chapter 7 for other side dish ideas.

Vary It! How can you turn an ordinary burger into something divine? Search your pantry or refrigerator for the following ingredients and add them to the raw meat: Tabasco sauce, Worcestershire sauce, ketchup, pickle juice, dry sherry, wheat germ, onion soup mix, cayenne pepper, ground ginger, coriander, cumin, garlic salt, chopped canned or fresh mushrooms, chopped parsley, tarragon, thyme, sage, other fresh herbs, ground walnuts or pecans, Dijon-style mustard, horseradish, lemon juice, and grated lemon peel.

Figure 8-2: Use your imagination to create these burger variations!

Turkey Burger

Turkey burgers are a great alternative to beef burgers, and they're a tasty dish. Seasonings — like those used in this recipe — make a *big* difference in flavor.

Preparation time: *20 minutes*

Grilling time: *12 minutes*

Yield: *4 servings*

(continued)

1¹/₄ pounds ground turkey

1 small red pepper, cored, seeded, and finely chopped

2 scallions, thinly sliced

2 tablespoons parsley, finely chopped

2 tablespoons chopped fresh cilantro

1 large clove garlic, peeled and minced

¹/₂ teaspoon dried thyme

¹/₂ teaspoon ground cumin

1 teaspoon Tabasco sauce

Salt and pepper to taste

4 hamburger buns, toasted on the grill

Mayonnaise or Dijon-style mustard (optional)

1 Prepare a medium-hot fire in a charcoal or gas grill.

2 In a medium mixing bowl, combine the ground turkey, red pepper, scallions, parsley, cilantro, garlic, thyme, cumin, Tabasco sauce, and salt and pepper; mix well. Gently shape the turkey mixture into 4 burger patties, each about ³/₄-inch thick.

3 Place the patties on a well-oiled grill grid. Grill for 10 to 12 minutes or until done, turning once. Burgers are done when the juices run clear and the center of the patty is cooked to brown with no sign of pink; cut to test.

4 Serve immediately on buns that have been toasted until lightly browned on the edge of the grill. Top burgers with the mayonnaise and mustard (if desired).

Lamb Burger

Ground lamb patties can be seasoned simply with a sprinkling of salt and pepper for a child's finicky palate. But why not use favorite spice combinations from world-class cuisines to alter the taste of ground lamb?

Preparation time: *20 minutes*

Grilling time: *12 minutes*

Yield: *4 servings*

1¹/₄ pounds lean ground lamb

1 tablespoon grated red or yellow onion

2 tablespoons dark raisins, chopped (optional)

2 tablespoons chopped fresh parsley or cilantro

³/₄ teaspoon ground cumin

¹/₄ teaspoon cinnamon

¹/₄ teaspoon paprika

¹/₄ teaspoon salt, or to taste

Pepper to taste

4 pita breads, each about 5 inches in diameter

Chutney (optional)

Chopped tomatoes and cucumbers (optional)

1 Prepare a medium-hot fire in a charcoal or gas grill.

2 In a large mixing bowl, combine the ground lamb, onion, raisins (if desired), parsley or cilantro, cumin, cinnamon, paprika, and salt and pepper. Mix well. Shape the meat into 4 oblong patties, each 3 to 4 inches long and $^3/_4$-to 1-inch thick. Wrap the pitas in heavy-duty aluminum foil.

3 Place the lamb patties on a lightly oiled grill grid. Cook the patties for 6 to 8 minutes per side for medium, or to desired doneness. (Cut into the center of each patty to check meat color. The USDA recommends cooking all ground meat to medium or until the center is no longer pink.) About 3 minutes before the patties finish cooking, place foil-wrapped pitas at the edge of the grid; heat until warmed through, turning once.

4 To serve, place each patty in a bread pocket; allow each diner to top with chutney, chopped tomatoes, or cucumbers (if desired) or other condiments of choice.

Go-With: Serve with the Middle Eastern Rice recipe found in Chapter 7.

That tops the burger

Some burger fans insist on eating their burgers without any extras; not even a pickle hides under their burger bun. But the rest of us pride ourselves on piling on the toppings. In addition to down-home, old-fashioned ketchup, here are some of our favorite toppings:

✔ **A slice of cheese:** Try Cheddar, Swiss, Muenster, Gruyère, or fontina — any cheese that melts into a thin, velvety layer. Place the slice on the meat a minute or two before the burger is ready and cook, covered.

✔ **Tomato slices:** You can brush tomato slices with your favorite bottled vinaigrette and heat them on the grill for about 2 minutes per side or until they're very lightly browned.

✔ **Raw or grilled onion slices:** Yellow onions are great, but so are milder red onions.

✔ **A dollop of fruit chutney:** Try adding a generous dollop of tomato, peach, or mango chutney. (Flip to Chapter 6 for more information on chutney.) It's a nice counterpoint to grilled meat.

✔ **Avocado:** Slice or mash ripe avocado into a spread with a little lemon juice and Tabasco sauce.

✔ **Pesto sauce:** Buy it or make your own. (Refer to Chapter 6 for a recipe.) For a smoky flavor, spread pesto sauce on the buns before toasting them on the grill.

- ✔ **Crisp strips of bacon:** You can add bacon with or without the lettuce and tomato.

- ✔ **Sautéed or grilled mushrooms:** Portobello mushrooms, with their meatlike texture and woodsy taste are terrific sliced, brushed with oil, and grilled. Turn to Chapter 17 for a complete recipe.

- ✔ **Pickles:** Choose from dill or sweet pickle slices.

- ✔ **Salsa:** Try making your own (see Chapter 6) or use any of the better bottled brands, such as Newman's Own Salsa.

Vary It! To make some simple sauces to adorn burgers when guests come for a patio dinner (or to treat yourself), jump to Chapter 6, where you find recipes for all sorts of spreads and sauces.

Simple Sausages and Fancy Franks

Sausage-making is a food art practiced around the world. Sold fresh (or uncooked), cooked, smoked, and cured, sausages are made with a variety of meats and seasonings and shaped into links that vary in thickness and length.

With few exceptions, sausages are made with a fair amount of fat, but some lower-fat varieties are starting to pop up in grocery stores.

Here are just a few of the endless varieties of sausage available for grilling:

- ✔ **Bockwurst:** May be cooked but is usually sold fresh. Bockwurst is usually seasoned mildly with parsley and chives.

- ✔ **Bratwurst:** A German pork or veal sausage, generally sold fresh, but also available precooked and smoked. Moderately spicy and seasoned with ginger, nutmeg, coriander, and caraway.

- ✔ **Chorizo:** A Mexican fresh pork sausage or a Spanish smoked pork sausage. Both varieties tend to be hot and spicy and flavored with garlic, chili powder, and other hot spices.

- ✔ **Frankfurter:** A precooked, smoked sausage, mildly seasoned, and better known as a *hot dog* or *frank*. Hot dogs or franks can be made from beef, pork, turkey, chicken, or veal and are usually packed into a casing. Its size ranges from the tiny, delicate *cocktail frank* to the impressive *footlong*. Kosher franks are all-beef and often heavily flavored with garlic. Franks labeled "all-beef" must be made (according to U.S. law), without fillers such as cereals or soybean products.

- ✔ **Italian:** Fresh pork sausage, sold hot (with hot peppers, fennel, and garlic) or sweet (minus the hot peppers).

- **Knackwurst (also known as knockwurst):** Fully cooked and smoked sausage made of beef, pork, and/or veal. Flavored with lots of garlic, this sausage is mild, not spicy.

- **Polish kielbasa:** Fully cooked and smoked sausage that's usually made of pork but sometimes also made of veal and beef. Flavorings include onion and garlic, so it can be quite spicy.

- **Salami and cervelat:** Both of these are uncooked sausages that are safe to eat without further cooking because they have been preserved by curing. Salami, which includes the popular pepperoni, is air-dried (which makes it firm-textured), is usually heavily seasoned with spices and garlic, and is great for slicing thinly over a pizza destined for the grill. Cervelat sausages, such as mortadella, are preserved by curing, drying, and smoking.

Although many sausages are cured and/or cooked, they cannot be held indefinitely in warm weather. It is always best to preserve their flavor and quality by placing them in the coldest part of your refrigerator — 36 to 40 degrees is the ideal temperature range. Freezing sausages is not a good idea, because the sausages lose flavor, but if you do freeze them, place them in vaporproof plastic bags and thaw them overnight in the refrigerator. The flavor really starts to decline after about 2 months of freezing, so don't leave them in the freezer any longer than that.

Knowing how long to cook 'em

There's no trick to grilling franks and sausages; the cooking time is all you need to know.

- Uncooked sausage needs to be precooked before grilling to release some of the natural fat, which can cause dangerous flare-ups on the grill.

  To do this, prick each sausage several times and then simmer in water (flavored, if you wish, with wine, beer, or apple juice) for 5 to 10 minutes or until they're fully cooked with no trace of pink in the center. Grill over medium heat until browned and crisp on all sides, turning often.

- Cooked sausages need only a few minutes of grilling to acquire that lovely, smoky taste and the bubbly skin that makes them irresistible on a summer afternoon.

- Remember to keep turning sausages — whether they are precooked or fresh — because they can burn very quickly. The best method is to use a square or rectangular grill basket (see Chapter 2) that holds a dozen or more sausages so that they can all be turned at once.

- Grill frankfurters for about 8 minutes or until browned on all sides, turning frequently.

Hot dog history

No one knows for sure when the first frankfurter appeared in America, but the best bet is that it was first served under that name in St. Louis in the 1880s by a German immigrant named Antoine Feuchtwanger, whose principal contribution was the soft roll.

The fame of the frank really took off in 1901 after Harry Magely, director of catering at New York City's Polo Grounds (where the New York Giants used to play), exhorted customers to "Get your red hots!" and served the frankfurters on a *heated* roll with various condiments.

The term "hot dog" was coined by Hearst Newspaper sports cartoonist Tad Dorgan, who often caricatured German figures as dachshunds and, as of 1906, as talking sausages.

So widespread was the name "hot dog" that, to calm patrons' fears, Nathan's Famous Hot Dog Stand in Coney Island, Brooklyn, New York, put up a sign explaining that its sausages did not contain any dog meat.

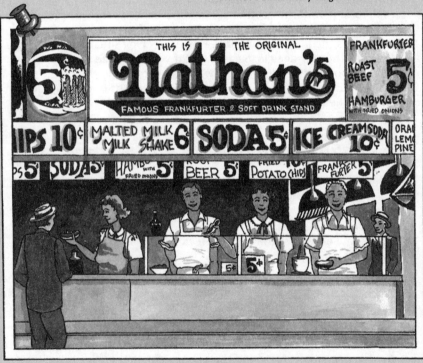

Grilled Kielbasa with Creamy Mustard Sauce

Make these kielbasa when you need dinner on the table in just a few minutes or when you're tailgating in the stadium parking lot of your favorite team. (Look at Chapter 20 for more tailgating tips.)

Preparation time: 30 minutes

Grilling time: 10 minutes

Yield: 4 servings

¹/₄ cup sour cream	*Pepper to taste*
3 tablespoons Dijon-style mustard	*Tabasco sauce (optional)*
2 tablespoons prepared horseradish, drained	*1 to 1¹/₄ pounds fully cooked sausage (such as kielbasa or knackwurst)*

1 Prepare a medium fire in a charcoal or gas grill.

2 Meanwhile, prepare the Creamy Mustard Sauce by combining the sour cream, mustard, horseradish, pepper, and Tabasco sauce (if desired) in a small bowl. Cover and refrigerate.

3 Slice the sausages, if necessary, into 4 pieces of equal length. Cover and arrange the sausages on a lightly oiled grill grid. Grill, turning 2 or 3 times, until well browned on all sides and warmed through, about 10 minutes.

4 Divide the sausages among 4 individual plates and top each link with a generous dollop of Creamy Mustard Sauce.

Go-With: Try serving the kielbasa sandwich-style, between wedges of crusty Italian bread. Orange-Ginger Coleslaw (Chapter 7) makes a good side dish.

Grilled Italian Links with Caraway Sauerkraut

In this recipe, the sausages are parboiled (gently boiled) in beer before grilling. You can also cook them in equal parts apple juice and water, or in a fruity white wine, such as Riesling.

(continued)

Preparation time: *20 minutes*

Grilling time: *12 minutes*

Yield: *4 servings*

8 sweet Italian sausages, cut into 3- to 4-inch links (about 1¹/₂ pounds total)

1 cup beer

¹/₂ cup water

2 14-ounce cans sauerkraut, drained

3 tablespoons cider vinegar

1 teaspoon caraway seeds

Dijon-style mustard (optional)

1 Prepare a medium-hot fire in a gas or charcoal grill.

2 Meanwhile, prick each sausage 2 times. Place the sausages in a skillet or sauté pan large enough to hold them in one layer. Add the beer and water; cover and bring to a boil over high heat. Reduce the heat to medium-low and simmer the sausages for about 5 minutes. Remove the sausages, reserving the liquid in the skillet.

3 Add the sauerkraut, vinegar, and caraway seeds to the liquid in the skillet; stir to mix well. Simmer, uncovered, for about 5 minutes or until nearly all the liquid has evaporated. (The sauerkraut should be moist.) Remove the skillet from heat and set aside. Cover the skillet to keep warm.

4 Place the sausages directly over the heat on an oiled grill grid. Grill for 5 to 6 minutes per side or until nicely browned, turning once. Sausage meat is cooked when it's no longer pink in the center. Cut each sausage in the center to determine doneness.

5 Serve with the Caraway Sauerkraut and Dijon-style mustard (if desired).

Loading up on toppings

Good as they are unadorned, frankfurters and sausages are even better with a topping or two. Mustard and ketchup are the world's favorite toppings, but for a little more pizzazz, the next time you fire up the grill and slap down franks for a crowd, offer an assortment of hot dog toppings — some home-made and others straight out of a can or bottle.

Let your guests pick and choose from among plates of coleslaw, baked beans, canned and warmed chili, relishes, pickles, grated Cheddar cheese, flavored mustards and chutneys, guacamole, roasted red and green peppers, grilled and raw onion slices, sauerkraut, spicy salsas, and barbecue sauces. See Chapter 7 for more side dish ideas.

Chapter 9

Swordplay: Grilling Kebabs and Satay

Kebabs (and their Middle Eastern cousin, satay) are some of the simplest and most popular foods to grill — you simply thread morsels of pork, beef, chicken, or other foods onto a skewer before grilling over an open fire. And they're a popular grilled dish for all of the following reasons:

✔ Kebabs require limited preparation time.

✔ The thin strips of beef, fish, or poultry quickly absorb the flavors of a marinade or spice rub.

✔ You can use cheaper cuts of meat such as top round, chicken thighs, and lamb shoulder.

✔ Small cubes, strips, and chunks of food skewered on a stick grill in no time.

✔ You can grill a meal that's almost complete on just one skewer.

✔ The plate presentation can be quite dramatic when assorted colorful foods are strung along the same skewer.

✔ Kebabs are fun to eat and make especially good party appetizers.

Ladies and Gentlemen — Choose Your Skewers!

Kebabs can't exist without skewers, so before you can grill kebabs, you need to choose your skewers. Skewers come in many forms and sizes, from 6- to 9-inch-long bamboo (or wooden) skewers used in Southeast Asia to long, swordlike metal skewers that flamed dramatically at restaurants in the 1970s. Some are even quite decorative.

When buying skewers for your own use, you can choose between metal and wood, which both have advantages and disadvantages:

✔ Metal skewers tend to be long — ranging from 10 to 18 inches long — so that you can pack them with food.

✔ Metal skewers are either flat, which makes sliding the food off easier, or square, which keeps slippery food on more firmly.

✔ Some metal skewers have a sliding block at one end to allow you to push the food down and off the blade.

✔ Metal skewers are an investment — you have to pay for them now, but you can use them for years to come!

✔ Decorative metal skewers can look quite dramatic on a platter.

✔ Bamboo or wooden skewers, which are usually sold and packaged by the dozens or hundreds, are significantly cheaper than metal ones.

✔ Because of the material they're made of, wooden skewers must be soaked in water for at least 30 minutes before using, lest they burn in the fire. Wrapping the tips in aluminum foil also works.

✔ Check out Chapter 2 for more information and illustrations on the different types of skewers available.

Even after you soak the wooden skewers in water, the ends of the skewers tend to burn anyway. Be careful when you transfer them to a plate.

Grilling Up Kebabs

Here are some pointers for skewer or kebab cooking:

✔ Pack the pieces of meat tightly on the skewer if you want the meat cooked rare or medium-rare. If you want it medium to well, pack the cubes or strips more loosely, with a little space between each piece, allowing more heat to circulate.

✔ Cut the cubes of food into pieces that are uniform in size to ensure even cooking. A 1-inch beef cube grills to medium in about 10 minutes over a medium fire.

✔ Any firm-fleshed fish can easily be cut into kebabs about 1-inch thick. You want all the pieces of food on the skewer to be done in the same amount of time. Turn and brush fish kebabs frequently with a basting sauce, marinade, or herb butter to keep them from drying out. One-inch pieces of fish take 6 to 8 minutes to cook through.

✔ You can turn hot dogs or sausages into simple kebabs by threading them end-to-end on a skewer, as shown in Figure 9-1.

✔ When serving an entire meal of grilled meat and vegetable kebabs, you may want to grill each separately. True, it looks prettier and is more convenient to grill the entire meal on one skewer, but packing these foods alternately onto the same skewer gives you less control and may result in food that is unevenly cooked.

✔ Be sure that round-shaped vegetables, like mushrooms, or slices of zucchini and yellow squash lie flat, with their widest surface exposed to the heat of the grill. Pierce them from edge to edge, rather than through their centers. (See Figure 9-2.)

✔ Foods such as cherry tomatoes or shrimp have a tendency to spin around as the skewer is turned. Try piercing these items with two parallel skewers, rather than one, to hold them in place, as shown in Figure 9-2. Or use square rather than round metal skewers.

Figure 9-1:
Threading
hot dogs
end to end
on a
skewer.

Skewering end to end
for easy turning.

Figure 9-2:
Various ways to skewer vegetables.

Use 2 skewers to prevent spinning.

Skewer round vegetables flat side down!

✔ A splash of balsamic vinegar, other flavored vinegar, or fresh lemon juice is the perfect fat-free flavoring accent for grilled pork or lamb kebabs.

✔ For pretty appetizers, cut your ingredients into small cubes or chunks of 1 inch or less and thread foods onto 6-inch skewers.

Use caution when turning your kebabs and always wear an insulated mitt (described in Chapter 2). The skewer handles get hot enough to sear the tips of your fingers.

Artichoke, Mushroom, and Cherry Tomato Kebabs

The vegetables in this kebab recipe — cherry tomatoes, bottled artichoke hearts, and mushrooms — grill very quickly and make pretty appetizer kebabs when threaded on short skewers. See the color photo section for a peek at this colorful dish.

Preparation time: 15 minutes

Marinating time: 30 minutes to 1 hour

Grilling time: 8 minutes

Yield: 6 appetizer servings

1 6-ounce jar marinated artichoke hearts

12 medium mushrooms

6 cherry tomatoes

3 tablespoons extra-virgin olive oil

Juice of 1 lemon

Grated peel of 1 lemon

1 clove garlic, peeled and minced

Kosher or table salt to taste

Pepper to taste

1 Drain the artichoke hearts, reserving the marinade. Brush the mushrooms clean with a damp paper towel; slice off and discard their stems. Remove the stems of the cherry tomatoes. Place all vegetables in a medium mixing bowl or a resealable plastic bag.

2 In a small mixing bowl, combine the remaining ingredients with the reserved artichoke marinade; pour over the vegetables. Cover the bowl or seal the bag, and marinate for 30 minutes to 1 hour.

3 Prepare a medium-hot fire in a charcoal or gas grill.

4 Thread 2 mushrooms and 2 artichoke hearts, alternately, on 6 skewers, leaving room to add a cherry tomato at the top of each skewer. Skewer whole mushrooms lengthwise through the caps so that they lie flat on the grill and can brown evenly on both sides. (If using wooden skewers, soak the skewers in water for at least 30 minutes in cold water to prevent them from burning.) Brush the vegetables generously with the marinade.

5 Place the skewers on a lightly oiled grill grid and grill for about 4 minutes per side, turning once. Brush with the remaining marinade and thread a cherry tomato through the top of each skewer. Grill for 1 to 2 minutes more or until the tomatoes are tender but still intact, turning once. Serve with hamburgers, steak, grilled fish, or lamb.

Vary It! Add extra-large or jumbo shrimp or 1-inch cubes of green pepper to the marinade with the vegetables. Grill as described but use longer skewers. For a complete meal, remove grilled vegetables from kebabs and toss with steaming pasta, extra-virgin olive oil, chopped fresh parsley, and grated Parmesan cheese. If you don't have time to make the marinade, use a favorite bottled vinaigrette or Italian dressing instead.

Kebabing for Beef

Most agree that the best beef kebabs are made from tender cuts like sirloin, top loin, and tenderloin. However, less expensive beef cuts, such as top round, chuck, or flank steak, also work if you marinate the meat before grilling. Nothing is worse than a charred, dried-out kebab, so timing is critical with beef kebabs. You can honor individual preferences for doneness by cooking kebabs for different lengths of time to get them well-done, medium, or rare.

Preparing a complete meal with the main and side dishes all cooked on one grill can be tricky when the cooking times and temperatures differ. On a gas grill, you can adjust the burners, raising or lowering the heat, much as you do on your kitchen range. You don't have this luxury with a charcoal grill, but you can use the edges of the grid for warming and moderate cooking, and the center for foods that need intense heat. Another option is to use your kitchen broiler to grill side dishes. Broiling doesn't produce those wonderful smoky flavors of the grill, but it can help you get the whole meal on the table at once.

Western Beef Kebabs with Red Peppers and Onions

In this recipe, you save the marinade that soaks the raw food and boil it to make a delicious finishing sauce for the grilled food. This particular marinade combines many ingredients common to American Southwestern cooking — lime juice, grated lime peel, garlic, jalapeño peppers, and ground cumin. A touch of butter is added, just as the sauce is reheated, to blend together the various flavors.

Preparation time: *25 minutes*

Marinating time: *6 hours or overnight*

Grilling time: *10 to 12 minutes*

Yield: *4 servings*

$1^1/_2$ to 2 pounds sirloin, or other tender beef such as top loin or round tip steak

2 medium red peppers

1 medium onion

$^1/_2$ cup apple juice, divided

6 tablespoons lime juice (about 3 large limes)

$1^1/_2$ teaspoons grated lime peel

6 tablespoons vegetable oil

3 cloves garlic, peeled and coarsely chopped

1 to 2 large jalapeño peppers, seeded and chopped

³/₄ teaspoon cumin

1¹/₂ teaspoons chili powder

¹/₂ teaspoon paprika

Salt and pepper to taste

2 tablespoons butter

1 Working on a cutting board, trim all visible fat from the beef; cut the meat into cubes of about 1¹/₂ inches. Place the cubes in a large, resealable plastic bag or other non-reactive container.

2 Core and seed the red peppers and slice them into strips about 1¹/₂ inches wide; slice each strip crosswise into 1- to 2-inch pieces. Cut the onion in half lengthwise and remove the skin. Cut each half into thirds; break them apart into slices. Place the peppers and onions in the bag or container with the beef cubes.

3 Combine 6 tablespoons of the apple juice with the lime juice, grated lime peel, oil, garlic, jalapeño peppers, cumin, chili powder, and paprika, in a blender container; whirl the mixture for a few seconds into a coarse puree. Pour the resulting marinade over the beef and vegetables; seal the bag or cover the container, and refrigerate for at least 6 hours or overnight, turning occasionally.

4 Prepare a medium-hot fire in a charcoal or gas grill. (Sprinkle coals with a handful of presoaked hickory or mesquite wood chips, if desired.)

5 Remove the beef from the marinade. Reserve any remaining marinade and place in a small saucepan. Thread 3 to 4 beef cubes, alternating with pieces of pepper and onion, on skewers. (Soak wooden skewers in water for at least 30 minutes to prevent them from burning.) Sprinkle kebabs with salt and pepper.

6 Place the skewers on a well-oiled grill grid; grill the kebabs for about 10 minutes for medium-rare, or about 12 minutes for medium, turning every 5 to 6 minutes.

7 As the kebabs grill, bring the marinade in the saucepan to a boil over high heat on top of the stove; reduce heat and simmer for 1 minute. Whisk in 2 tablespoons butter and 2 tablespoons of the remaining apple juice. Spoon sauce over the grilled kebabs just before serving.

Go-With: Serve with buttered rice or any of the side dishes in Chapter 7, with Grilled Potato Planks, or with Grilled Corn on the Cob (both in Chapter 17).

For best results, follow the marinating times suggested in recipes. But when you're in a hurry, marinate for as much time as you have. The flavor may not be as intense, but the dish should still taste fine.

Everybody likes their meat cooked to different degrees of doneness: One person's rare is another's medium-well. Always check the meat for doneness a few minutes before the end of the estimated cooking time by making a small cut with a sharp knife into the center of a few of the kebab cubes.

Teriyaki Steak Kebabs

Grilling succulent oranges (and other citrus fruits) releases the intensely rich and flavorful oils locked in the peel of the fruit. In this recipe, shown in the color photo pages of this book, oranges are threaded onto skewers with teriyaki-marinated red onions, peppers, and beef.

Preparation time: *25 minutes*

Marinating time: *6 hours or overnight*

Grilling time: *12 to 14 minutes*

Yield: *4 servings*

¹/₂ cup teriyaki sauce

3 tablespoons vegetable oil

2 tablespoons brown sugar, packed

2 cloves garlic, peeled and minced

1 tablespoon peeled and freshly grated ginger

¹/₂ teaspoon black pepper

1¹/₂ to 2 pounds well-trimmed beef top round steak, cut into 1¹/₂-inch cubes

2 medium seedless oranges, quartered

2 medium red onions, each cut into 6 pieces

2 large green bell peppers, seeded and cut into 2-inch chunks

1 In a large bowl or large, resealable plastic bag, combine the first six ingredients. Add the beef and toss (or shake the bag) to mix. Cover the bowl or seal the bag, pressing out any air; refrigerate the meat for 6 hours or overnight, turning it several times. Drain off and reserve the remaining marinade.

2 Prepare a medium fire in a charcoal or gas grill.

3 As the grill preheats, alternate pieces of beef, orange, onion, and green pepper on skewers, beginning and ending with the beef. (If using wooden skewers, soak them in water first for 30 minutes to prevent them from burning.) Brush the meat and vegetables with the reserved marinade.

4 Place the kebabs on a well-oiled grill grid. Brush the kebabs once with the remaining marinade during the first 5 minutes of grilling. Grill 12 minutes for medium-rare, and 14 minutes for medium, turning about every 5 minutes to prevent charring.

Porky Pig on a Stick

Pork kebabs can be cut from almost any part of the pig, including leg, loin, or shoulder, but the best meat for kebabs comes from the tenderloin and boneless loin. The meat should be cut into 1-inch-thick cubes and then marinated before cooking over direct heat. Grill for 10 to12 minutes total, turning and basting the kebabs frequently to keep them from drying out.

Apple and Tarragon Pork Kebabs

The flavor of pork works well with virtually any kind of vegetable and a range of succulent, sweet fruits. In this recipe, apples and apple juice team up with white wine and tarragon to flavor grilled pork kebabs.

Preparation time: 25 minutes

Marinating time: 4 to 24 hours

Grilling time: 12 to 14 minutes

Yield: 4 servings

$^1/_4$ cup apple juice

$^1/_4$ cup dry white wine

1 tablespoon soy sauce

2 cloves garlic, peeled and crushed

2 tablespoons chopped fresh tarragon, or 2 teaspoons dried tarragon

1 tablespoon Dijon-style mustard

Salt and pepper to taste

$1^1/_4$ to $1^1/_2$ pounds lean boneless pork loin, cut into 1-inch cubes

2 Granny Smith or Golden Delicious apples, peeled, cored, and cut into $1^1/_2$ -inch cubes

(continued)

1 Combine all ingredients except the pork and apples in a shallow, non-reactive dish or large, resealable plastic bag.

2 Add the pork, turning to coat in the marinade. Cover the dish or seal the bag, pressing out any air; refrigerate for at least 4 hours, but not more than 24 hours, turning occasionally.

3 Prepare a medium-hot fire in a charcoal or gas grill.

4 Remove the pork cubes from the marinade, reserving any remaining marinade.

5 Arrange the pork and apple cubes on the skewers. (If using wooden skewers, soak them in water for at least 30 minutes to prevent them from burning.)

6 Place the skewers on a lightly oiled grill grid. Grill the kebabs 6 to 7 minutes, turning and basting them frequently with the reserved marinade. Continue to grill for about 6 to 7 minutes, turning frequently, without basting, until the pork is well browned on all sides and cooked through.

Go-With: Serve over a bed of Couscous with Apples and Raisins (Chapter 7) or with any of the fruit chutneys in Chapter 6.

 Be sure to grill the kebabs for at least 5 to 7 minutes after the last application of the basting marinade — this destroys any bacteria from the raw pork, which may contaminate the marinade.

Lamb Kebabs — the Real Deal

Kebabs originated in the Middle East, where lamb is virtually a staple. The most authentic (and some say, the most tasty) kebabs that you can grill up are made with fresh lamb.

Lemony Fresh Lamb Kebabs

These lambs kebabs come to life with the flavors of fresh lemon juice, grated lemon peel, crushed garlic, and fresh rosemary. Lamb kebab cubes grill quickly, in only about 10 minutes. Be sure to hover over the kebabs, checking often for doneness, because they easily overcook and lose their juicy tenderness. They make terrific party appetizers.

Preparation time: 20 minutes

Marinating time: 6 hours or overnight

Grilling time: 10 minutes

Yield: 4 servings

6 tablespoons olive oil

Grated peel of 1 large lemon (about 2 teaspoons)

Juice of 1 large lemon (about 3 tablespoons)

1 tablespoon finely chopped fresh rosemary, or 1 teaspoon dried, crushed rosemary

2 large cloves garlic, peeled and minced

$^{1}/_{2}$ teaspoon salt, or to taste

Pepper to taste

2 pounds lamb (from the leg), cut into 1- to 1$^{1}/_{4}$-inch cubes

8 to 10 long sprigs fresh rosemary (optional)

Oil for brushing rosemary sprigs

Lemon wedges for garnish

1 In a medium mixing bowl or large, resealable plastic bag, combine the olive oil, lemon peel, lemon juice, rosemary, garlic, and salt and pepper; add the lamb cubes, tossing to coat in the marinade. Cover the bowl or seal the bag, pressing out any air. Refrigerate for 6 hours or overnight.

2 Prepare a medium fire in a charcoal or gas grill.

3 Remove the lamb from the marinade, reserving any remaining marinade. Thread the lamb on skewers. (Be sure to presoak wooden skewers in water for 30 minutes to prevent them from burning.) Brush the lamb with the reserved marinade.

4 If using rosemary sprigs, brush them generously with oil. Place the sprigs on a lightly oiled grill grid. Set the lamb kebabs on the rosemary sprigs (or directly on the oiled grid, if you're not using the rosemary). Grill the kebabs for about 5 minutes; brush them with more marinade and turn. Grill for about 5 minutes more for medium-rare. Cut to test: The lamb should be pink to rosy in the center of each kebab when done. Transfer immediately to a serving platter, garnished with lemon wedges.

Lamb and Eggplant Kebabs with Tarragon Marinade

As much as lamb is complemented by the sharp tartness of lemon, as in the preceding recipe, it also partners well with sweet ingredients like chutneys, jam glazes, honey, and fruit juices. In this recipe (shown in the color photo section of this book), honey, apple juice, and tarragon are combined to infuse lamb and vegetables with a tinge of sweetness. This marinade is especially tasty with eggplant and summer squash, and we encourage you to use it on any number of other vegetable kebabs.

Preparation time: *30 minutes*

Marinating time: *8 hours or overnight*

Grilling time: *10 minutes*

Yield: *4 to 6 servings*

1 cup apple juice	*1 clove garlic, peeled and halved*
$1/3$ cup cider vinegar	*$3/4$ teaspoon salt, or to taste*
$1/3$ cup olive oil	*$1/4$ teaspoon pepper*
$1/3$ cup chopped scallions (green and white parts)	*$1^1/2$ to 2 pounds lean boneless lamb, cut into $1^1/4$-inch cubes*
3 tablespoons honey	*$1/4$ cup olive oil (for vegetable marinade)*
2 tablespoons A-1 steak sauce (or your favorite brand)	*1 small eggplant (about 1 pound), cut into 1-inch pieces*
$1^1/2$ tablespoons chopped fresh tarragon, or $1^1/2$ teaspoons dried tarragon	*2 small yellow squash, cut into $1/2$-inch rounds*

1 In a medium saucepan, combine the apple juice, vinegar, $1/3$ cup olive oil, scallions, honey, steak sauce, tarragon, garlic, and salt and pepper; simmer the mixture for 10 minutes over low heat, uncovered. Cool to room temperature.

2 Place the lamb in a large, resealable plastic bag or mixing bowl; pour $1^1/4$ cups of the marinade over the lamb, reserving the remaining $1/4$ cup marinade. Cover the remaining marinade and refrigerate until ready to marinate the vegetables. Seal the bag, pressing out any air, or cover the bowl and refrigerate for 8 hours or overnight, turning the meat occasionally.

3 About 1 hour before you are ready to grill, combine the reserved marinade with the $1/4$ cup olive oil. Place the vegetables in a large, resealable plastic bag or a bowl; pour the marinade-oil mixture over the vegetables, tossing to coat. Seal the bag or cover the bowl, and refrigerate for about 30 minutes to 1 hour, turning occasionally.

4 Prepare a medium fire in a charcoal or gas grill.

5 Remove the lamb and vegetables from their marinades, reserving the lamb marinade. Thread lamb, eggplant, and squash pieces alternately onto long skewers. Thread pieces of squash and eggplant so that they lie flat on the grill. (If using wooden skewers, presoak them in water for at least 30 minutes to prevent them from burning.) Brush kebabs generously with the reserved lamb marinade and (if desired) sprinkle with additional salt and pepper.

6 Place the skewers on a well-oiled grill grid. Grill for 5 to 7 minutes; brush with marinade, and turn. Grill for about 5 to 7 minutes more for medium-rare or until the lamb is browned on the outside but pink and juicy inside and the vegetables are lightly browned and crisp-tender. Cut into a kebab to test for doneness.

 Threading pieces of food tightly together on skewers increases the overall cooking time. Leave a little space between each piece of food to allow the heat to surround and cook the food evenly and more quickly.

Chicken Kebabs for the Soul

Tender, plump, boneless chicken breasts are easily cut up into thin strips, chunks, or cubes for threading on skewers. Chicken's mild flavor makes it suitable for any number of sweet or spicy marinades, barbecue sauces, or rubs.

Use soy sauce, ginger, and crushed red pepper together in a marinade; or garlic, lemon, olive oil, and fresh rosemary. Or you can simply squeeze a little lemon or lime juice over the chicken chunks or strips and then sprinkle them with a commercial jerk seasoning before grilling.

Chicken Tikka

In this Indian recipe, you marinate cubes of chicken in yogurt along with spices common to Indian curries — turmeric, cumin, and cayenne pepper. The turmeric gives these kebabs a yellow glow, as you can see in the color photo section of this book.

(continued)

Preparation time: 25 minutes

Marinating time: 6 hours or overnight

Grilling time: 10 to 12 minutes

Yield: 4 servings

2 pounds boneless, skinless chicken breasts

$^1/_2$ cup plain yogurt

1 medium onion, peeled and quartered

3 large cloves garlic, peeled and crushed

2 tablespoons fresh lemon juice

1 tablespoon peeled and grated fresh ginger

2 teaspoons vegetable oil

1 teaspoon salt, or to taste

$^1/_2$ teaspoon ground cumin

$^3/_4$ teaspoon cinnamon

$^1/_2$ teaspoon turmeric

$^1/_4$ teaspoon cayenne pepper

Black pepper to taste

15 to 20 cherry tomatoes

1 Rinse the chicken breasts under cold running water and pat dry with paper towels; trim any loose fat and cut into $1^1/_4$-inch cubes. Place the chicken in a large, resealable plastic bag or a medium mixing bowl.

2 In a blender container, combine the remaining ingredients, except the cherry tomatoes; puree the mixture until smooth. Pour the marinade over the chicken in the bag or bowl; toss to coat well. Seal the bag, pressing out any air, or cover the bowl, and refrigerate for at least 6 hours or overnight.

3 Prepare a medium-hot fire in a charcoal or gas grill.

4 As the grill preheats, remove the chicken from the marinade and thread on skewers, 3 to 4 pieces to a skewer. (If using wooden skewers, presoak them in water for 30 minutes to prevent them from burning.)

5 Place the skewers on a well-oiled grill grid; grill the kebabs for 5 to 6 minutes per side or until done and nicely browned, turning once. Using a barbecue mitt to protect your hands from the heat, place a cherry tomato on the top of each skewer after grilling for 5 minutes.

Go-With: Serve on a bed of white rice and boiled peas and complete the meal with one of the cucumber salads in Chapter 7 or with Summer Squash or Tomato Chutney (Chapter 6).

Vary It! The yogurt-flavored marinade can also be used with about 2 pounds of skewered beef or lamb cubes or with extra-large shrimp.

Gone Fishin' (For Kebabs)

What seafood is best for kebabs? Any firm-fleshed fish or shellfish that you can easily cut into chunks about 1-inch thick. That includes large sea scallops, monkfish, halibut, tuna, salmon, swordfish, and, of course, large to jumbo-sized shrimp. You want all the pieces of food on the skewer to be able to grill in the same length of time.

You may find it necessary to parboil tougher vegetables and fruits before skewering them with tender, quick-cooking fish.

Mixed Grill Seafood Kebabs with Fresh Lemon Sauce

These mixed seafood kebabs are doused twice with the lively flavor of fresh lemons — one time in the marinade and again in the finishing sauce.

Preparation time: *25 minutes*

Grilling time: *6 to 8 minutes*

Yield: *4 servings*

Fresh Lemon Sauce

Grated peel of 1 lemon

3 tablespoons fresh lemon juice (about 1 large lemon)

1 tablespoon minced fresh parsley, or 1 teaspoon dried parsley

1 tablespoon minced fresh herbs, such as oregano, thyme, rosemary, basil, or dill, or 1 teaspoon dried herbs

2 teaspoons Dijon-style mustard

Salt and white pepper to taste

$^1/_2$ cup virgin olive oil

In a jar with a tight-fitting lid, combine all the ingredients except the olive oil; seal the jar and shake until the ingredients are well blended. Add the olive oil, about $^1/_4$ cup at a time, tightly sealing the jar and shaking after each addition.

Mixed Grill Seafood Kebabs

$^3/_4$ pound firm fish, such as halibut, shark, swordfish, monkfish, salmon, or tuna, cut into 1- to 1$^1/_4$ -inch cubes

$^3/_4$ pound shellfish, such as peeled, deveined extra-large shrimp, whole sea scallops, or lobster tail meat cut into large chunks

(continued)

1 large red pepper, seeded and cut into 2-inch pieces

8 fresh herb sprigs, such as thyme, rosemary, oregano, or dill

1 medium red onion, peeled and cut into 2-inch pieces

Oil for brushing herbs

1 Prepare a medium-hot fire in a charcoal or gas grill.

2 Arrange the seafood, red pepper, and red onion on 8 metal or wooden skewers, alternating different pieces of fish with the vegetables. (If using wooden skewers, presoak them in water for at least 30 minutes to prevent them from burning.)

3 Pour half (about ⅓ cup) of the Fresh Lemon Sauce into a small bowl; baste the skewered fish and vegetables with the sauce. Reserve the remaining sauce to drizzle over grilled kebabs.

4 Just before grilling the kebabs, brush the herb sprigs with oil and place directly on a well-oiled grill grid.

5 Place the kebabs on the herbs, one to a sprig. Grill, basting and turning the kebabs every 2 to 3 minutes, for a total of 6 to 9 minutes or until the fish is opaque. (Do not baste during the last 3 minutes of cooking.) Cut the shellfish with a thin-bladed knife; the shellfish should be firm and opaque but still moist throughout.

6 Remove the kebabs from the grill and place on a large serving platter; drizzle with the reserved lemon sauce. Serve over steaming white rice (if desired).

You can always turn up the heat on your gas or charcoal grill by using the grill cover. For example, if the fish and vegetable kebabs don't seem to be cooking fast enough, cover with the grill hood during the final 2 to 3 minutes. If your grill doesn't have a cover, use a large overturned pot or an aluminum drip pan.

Grilled Shrimp with Scallions in a Soy Marinade

These skewered extra-large or jumbo shrimp (16 to 20 per pound), shown in the color photo section of this book, are brushed with a sweet-sour glaze. To add a little contrasting color and crunch, wrap a long green scallion around and through each skewered shrimp. Or cut the scallions into 2-inch pieces and alternate them on the skewers with the shrimp.

Remember that tender-fleshed shrimp, like other seafood, quickly absorb smoky flavors from wood chunks and chips. Build your charcoal fire by using a few hard-wood chunks — pecan, apple, and mesquite are all good with fish — or toss a handful of presoaked chips onto the fire or into a smoker box before grilling.

Preparation time: *20 minutes*

Marinating time: *30 minutes to 1 hour*

Grilling time: *6 minutes*

Yield: *4 servings*

26 to 28 extra-large shrimp, shelled and deveined (about 1¹/₂ pounds)

6 tablespoons soy sauce

3 tablespoons sesame oil

3 tablespoons vegetable oil

3 tablespoons balsamic vinegar

2 tablespoons honey

3 cloves garlic, peeled and minced

1 tablespoon peeled and coarsely chopped fresh ginger root

1 to 2 teaspoons seeded, minced fresh hot chile pepper, such as jalapeño or habañero

8 scallions, trimmed (optional)

1 Rinse and drain the shrimp under cold running water.

2 In a medium mixing bowl or a large, resealable plastic bag, make the marinade by combining the remaining ingredients, except the scallions; add the shrimp to the marinade, tossing them to coat well. Cover the bowl or seal the bag, pressing out any air; refrigerate for about 30 minutes to 1 hour.

3 Prepare a medium-hot fire in a charcoal or gas grill.

4 Arrange the shrimp, 3 to 4 to a skewer, on 8 skewers. (Be sure to presoak wooden skewers in water at least 30 minutes to prevent them from burning.) Pierce a scallion through its white bulb with the tip of a skewer (if desired), and then thread the long green part through and around the shrimp to hold in place. Repeat with remaining scallions and skewers. Brush the scallions and shrimp generously with the mari-nade, dabbing on bits and pieces of the chopped ginger and chiles.

5 Grill the kebabs on a lightly oiled grill grid about 3 minutes per side or until the shrimp are opaque and pink, brushing with the marinade once before turning.

Allowing fish to marinate longer than an hour, particularly when the mixture contains an acid like lemon juice or vinegar, can cause the fish flesh to begin to toughen. One way to strengthen the flavors of the marinade without risking this undesirable firming up is to chill the marinade in the refrigerator a few hours *before* adding the fish. When the fish is finally added, the marinade flavors are at their peak.

Please Satay for Dinner

If you travel throughout Malaysia, Singapore, and Indonesia, you can see vendors grilling all kinds of satay (pronounced sah-TAY) along the roadside on small portable hibachis. *Satay* is sort of a kebab, except that the meat (beef, lamb, or pork) or poultry is cut into thin strips instead of cubes or chunks. After grilling, the strips are served with a thick and scrumptious peanut sauce.

Whether made with pork, beef, lamb, or chicken, satay-like dishes make a great party appetizer or, when a big platter of them is brought to the table, a hefty main dish, accompanied by spicy side dishes.

Satay with Peanut Dipping Sauce

We use chicken as the meat of choice for this satay recipe, but you can easily substitute other meats such as pork or beef with very good results. Take a look at this dish in the color photo section of this book.

Preparation time: 25 minutes

Marinating time: 4 hours or overnight

Grilling time: 8 minutes

Yield: 4 main servings, or 8 to 10 appetizer servings

2 whole boneless, skinless chicken breasts (about 2¹/₂ pounds)	*2 tablespoons fresh coriander, chopped with stems*
¹/₃ cup olive oil	*2 small scallions, trimmed and chopped*
¹/₄ cup lime juice	*1 teaspoon Tabasco sauce*
2 tablespoons grated lime peel	*1 large clove garlic, peeled and minced*

1 Lay one chicken breast on a cutting board or other flat surface between 2 pieces of waxed paper. Using a meat mallet (a rolling pin or the bottom of a heavy skillet also works), pound the breast to flatten slightly; cut across the grain into 1-inch-thick strips. Repeat this step with the second breast. Place the strips in a large, resealable plastic bag or mixing bowl.

2 In a small mixing bowl or glass measuring cup, make the marinade by combining the remaining ingredients; pour the marinade over the chicken strips. Seal the bag, pressing out any air, or cover the bowl; marinate in the refrigerator for at least 4 hours or overnight.

3 Prepare a medium-hot fire in a charcoal or gas grill.

4 Remove the chicken from the marinade and thread on bamboo or metal skewers. (Presoak wooden skewers in water for 30 minutes to prevent them from burning.)

5 Place the skewers on a well-oiled grill grid. Grill for about 4 minutes on each side or until done. Serve with Peanut Dipping Sauce (recipe follows).

Peanut Dipping Sauce

An inspired, spicy peanut sauce, sweetened with just the right amount of creamy coconut milk, is the traditional dipping sauce for skewered pieces of pork, chicken or beef satay.

Preparation time: *15 minutes*

Yield: *About 1¹/₄ cups sauce*

1 tablespoon corn oil	*2 tablespoons soy sauce*
1 clove garlic, peeled and minced	*1 tablespoon lime juice*
1 teaspoon peeled and minced fresh ginger	*1 tablespoon rice vinegar*
²/₃ cup canned coconut milk	*1 teaspoon Tabasco sauce, or to taste*
¹/₃ cup crunchy peanut butter	*2 tablespoons chopped fresh coriander leaves*

1 In a medium skillet or sauté pan, heat the oil over medium heat; add the garlic and ginger and cook for 1 to 2 minutes, stirring, until the garlic is softened. (Be careful not to let the garlic brown.)

2 Add the coconut milk, peanut butter, soy sauce, lime juice, rice vinegar, and Tabasco sauce to the pan. Stir well to combine. Bring the mixture to a boil, reduce heat, and simmer for 1 to 2 minutes. Transfer the sauce to a small bowl and sprinkle it with coriander. Serve with grilled chicken strips as a dipping sauce.

Chapter 10

All about Ribs

In This Chapter

▶ Shopping for various cuts of ribs

▶ Discovering regional distinctions in rib preferences

▶ Grilling ribs to perfection

▶ Creating rib rubs and sauces

*I*n this chapter, we take a bit of a breather from grilling, which is loosely defined as cooking relatively tender foods quickly and directly over intense heat. Although barbecuing is the complete opposite — the cooking of relatively tough foods, long and slow, with lots of smoke — sometimes these cooking methods overlap. A person with good grilling skills can barbecue without building a smoke pit in the backyard; the old, reliable charcoal kettle grill will do just fine. In this chapter, we give you the techniques that enable you to barbecue ribs like a Kansas City pitmaster.

If ever a single food item seems perfectly matched to a covered charcoal grill, it's ribs. Barbecued ribs are very much a passion for the grilling chef, and succulent, tender, finger lickin' ribs are not all that difficult to achieve. We find that most die-hard barbecuers call for pork and not beef ribs. The last recipe in this chapter is a beef rib recipe that really takes us back to the grilling method. It cooks very tender, thinly cut Korean-style beef ribs directly over the heat of the grill in about 10 minutes.

Solving Pork Rib Riddles

Pork rib cuts can be a source of confusion. Three types of pork ribs are available at your grocery store, so you should get to know the distinctive characteristics of each type of rib before tossing them on the grill.

✔ **Back ribs:** Also called *baby back ribs,* back ribs are cut from the blade and center section of the loin chops, close to the spine, and include the finger meat between the ribs. This cut is very meaty, tender, and small enough to almost qualify as dainty finger food. Plan on a pound of ribs per person. A slab (or rack) of back ribs weighs about 1$\frac{1}{2}$ to 2 pounds and will take about 1$\frac{1}{2}$ to 2 hours to cook indirectly on the grill.

✔ **Spareribs:** The most popular pork rib choice, spareribs come from the underside or belly of the pig, next to the bacon. Although they're the least meaty portion of the pig, they're packed with tremendous flavor. A full slab (or rack) of spareribs can weigh from 3 to 5 pounds — plan on a pound of ribs per serving. Set the heat medium to medium-low and cook from 1¹/₂ to 2 hours. Use a covered grill, turn the ribs once, and brush them with sauce during the last 15 minutes of cooking (if desired).

✔ **Country-style ribs:** These ribs are cut from the shoulder or the blade end of the loin and have the most amount of meat in proportion to bone. They come from the top of the backbone instead of the rib cage. Because they're loaded with meat, you may want to braise them in a small amount of water on top of the stove until very tender, then grill them. One pound serves 3 to 4 people.

Robin Kline, spokesperson for the National Pork Producers Council, likes her baby backs and spareribs to have a little "bite." She recommends grilling them over low, indirect heat (with the coals banked to one side) for a long time — about 1¹/₂ to 2 hours. Country-style ribs, which have more meat, says Kline, are best not grilled but braised or slow-cooked in the oven or on top of the stove in a covered container with a little water to make them very moist and tender. If desired, after braising for 45 minutes to 1 hour, place them on the grill over direct heat to finish cooking and to give them a nice brown exterior.

The Great Pork Rib Controversy

Depending on whom you ask, you'll find a conglomeration of assorted techniques, methods, and preferences for cooking pork ribs. Some like the meat falling off the bone and smothered in barbecue sauce. Others like their ribs a little bit chewy and crispy, with just a hint of sauce and a lot of hickory wood flavoring. We talked with cooks who strongly believe in *degreasing* — to rid pork ribs of excess fat by first roasting them in the oven or parboiling them on the stove before finishing on the grill. And other cooks recommend foil-wrapping the ribs before cooking them over direct heat in a covered grill. The foil is removed when the ribs are tender, and then the basting sauce is applied just a few minutes before they are fully grilled.

These methods produce a pork rib with meat that is very moist and tender. And generally, either of these methods cooks the ribs in less time than it takes to grill them. But by not cooking pork ribs on the grill from beginning to end, we think that you lose much of that rich, slow-cooked barbecue flavor that only grilling indirectly and slowly over hot coals can produce. Pork ribs need long, slow, indirect grilling, and in the following recipe, we help you perfect this technique.

Regional ribs

Not everyone in the U.S. agrees on the best way to cook ribs. Here are some regional differences:

- People in the South overwhelmingly prefer pork to any other meat for ribs.

- You can find tomatoey barbecue in parts of western North Carolina, where the folks call it *Lexington-style* barbecue, after Lexington, North Carolina. Very often, barbecue in this part of the world is chopped pork taken from the bone or pork shoulder, but ribs are very popular too.

- Eastern North Carolinians prefer vinegar-based rib sauces with chile pepper flakes and spices like cinnamon, nutmeg, oregano, and paprika.

- Kansas City, Missouri, rib sauces are famous for their thick, ketchupy consistency.

- In Louisiana, Cajun spices — cayenne pepper, black pepper, garlic powder, Tabasco sauce, and thyme — often reign in rib rubs and sauces.

- In the Pacific Rim states — California, Washington, Oregon, and Hawaii — rib sauces can have a distinct sweetness, usually from fruits like pineapple.

- Ironically, a Midwestern state — Ohio — hosts the annual National Rib Cook-Off in Cincinnati, serving up 350,000 pounds of ribs during one weekend.

- Memphis, Tennessee hosts the International Barbecue Cooking Contest; the rules state that "any nonpoisonous substances" may be used in the sauces and require vinegar to be one of those substances.

Some spots on the grill will be hotter than others. Move rib slabs to hotter or cooler spots to speed up or slow down cooking.

Today, rib rubs often replace sweet, tomato-based barbecue sauces that have for so long been a traditional part of Southern U.S. barbecue. Dry spice rubs add flavor without completely masking the natural taste of the pork, which overly rich sauces can do if applied throughout the cooking process.

Rubs, which can be mixed from any number of spices or herbs probably already on hand in your kitchen, are usually free of the unwanted calories in oils and other fats that are often loaded into rich barbecue or finishing sauces. Flip to Chapter 5 for more recipes and information on how to apply and use rubs.

Ribbing the right way

The following is a summary list of important points to consider before heading out to barbecue pork ribs.

1. Build an indirect fire by piling the coals on one side of the grill. (This is our preferred method because it gives you plenty of room to place the large rib slabs away from the heat of the fire.) You also can stack the charcoal in a circular ring around the edges of the grill. (Turn to Chapter 1 for complete instructions.) You can cook the ribs indirectly in a gas grill, but a charcoal fire gives them more flavor.

2. Cook the ribs slowly for $1\frac{1}{2}$ to 2 hours, over medium heat (325° to 350°) and over a drip pan half filled with water. Long, slow cooking makes for moist and tender ribs with a crisp crust. If in the first 30 minutes the ribs are browning too quickly, shut the grill vents.

3. Determining when pork ribs are done is a little tricky, but after $1\frac{1}{2}$ to 2 hours, you can be virtually certain that the ribs are fully cooked. However, the meat's color is not an indication of doneness. Smoke from the coals or from burning wood chips can turn the interior of the meat pink and leave you with the impression that it's not cooked. If you can move the rib bones back and forth without a lot of resistance after $1\frac{1}{2}$ to 2 hours, the meat is cooked.

4. Add any basting sauce that has a component of tomato or other sweet ingredient to the ribs during the last 20 minutes of cooking. Adding the sauce late in the process keeps the sauce from burning.

5. You can toss in a large handful of presoaked wood chips each time you add fresh coals to the fire. Or build the fire by using a combination of charcoal and hardwood oak or hickory chunks to achieve extra smoky flavor.

Just-Right Pork Ribs

To make our pork ribs, we combine three recipes — a spice rub, a basting sauce, and a barbecue sauce. Apply the Gingery Spice Rub — a mixture of ginger, brown sugar, lemon peel, and salt and pepper — to the slab of raw ribs and allow it to stand for about 30 minutes (or about as long as it takes to build an indirect fire in a charcoal grill). After you place them on the grill, brush the ribs about every 20 minutes with the Apple-Beef Basting Sauce to keep them fully moist. Finally, 15 to 20 minutes before they are removed, you brush again, but this time with a rich and delicious Country-Style Barbecue Sauce that gives them a glossy finish and also doubles as a dipping sauce (see the color photo section for a beautiful example).

Step 1: Mixin' the Gingery Spice Rub and Rubbin' the Ribs

You can prepare the Gingery Spice Rub up to a week ahead of time, using all the ingredients except the grated fresh lemon peel. Add the grated peel just before smearing the rub onto the ribs, to retain the fragrant oil in the peel. If you have any leftover rub, store it in an air-tight container and use within a few days on other pork cuts, grilled fish, or chicken.

Preparation time: *5 minutes*

Yield: *Enough rub for 3 to 4 pounds of pork ribs*

1 tablespoon brown sugar	*1 to 2 teaspoons pepper, according to taste*
2 teaspoons ground ginger	
2 teaspoons salt	*1 teaspoon grated lemon peel (optional)*

1 Combine all the ingredients in a small, clean jar or container with a tight-fitting lid. Seal the jar and shake until well mixed.

2 Set the ribs on a flat cookie sheet. Trim any loose or large pieces of fat from the ribs. Cut the slabs into pieces 8 to 10 inches wide. This makes it easier to turn the ribs as they grill.

3 Sprinkle the ribs with the rub, pressing the seasoning firmly into the meat on both sides. Cover loosely and set in the refrigerator for about 30 minutes or as long as it takes to prepare the fire.

Vary It! For a spicy dry rib rub, add cayenne pepper, seeded and chopped jalapeño pepper, or Tabasco sauce to taste. For a jerk-flavored rub, add cayenne pepper, allspice, and cinnamon to taste.

Step 2: Fixin' the Apple-Beef Basting Sauce

Thick, sugar-loaded barbecue sauces mopped (with a special brush — see Chapter 2) onto the ribs too early can burn and char the surfaces of the meat. To keep pork ribs moist as they slow-cook for a long time on the grill, use a simple, low-sugar (or sugar-free) basting sauce made from any number of ingredients. Some grill chefs like a peppery solution of crushed red pepper and water. Others mix a smoky-flavored whiskey like bourbon or Scotch with a little water to taste. In this Apple-Beef Basting Sauce recipe, we use a simple combination of apple juice and beef broth. Although the apple juice does contain a little natural sugar, it's not enough to char the meat. (You can also use this sauce to keep pork loins and other large cuts of meat moist as they grill.)

Preparation time: *5 minutes*

Yield: *1 cup*

$1/2$ cup apple juice	*$1/2$ cup beef or chicken broth*

(continued)

In a small glass measuring cup or mixing bowl, combine the apple juice and beef or chicken broth. Use as a basting sauce to brush on 4 to 5 pounds of pork ribs, about every 20 to 25 minutes as they grill.

Step 3: Saucin' and Grillin' Time

As the ribs grill, you have time to prepare the Country-Style Barbecue Sauce. Or, if you prefer, you can make and refrigerate the sauce up to 3 days prior to grilling. Be sure to reheat it, though, in a small pan on top of the stove before basting the ribs.

Preparation time: 35 minutes

Grilling time: $1^1/_2$ to 2 hours

Yield: 4 to 6 servings

1 3- to 4-pound rack of pork spareribs, seasoned with Gingery Spice Rub (see previous recipe)

Country-Style Barbecue Sauce

2 tablespoons vegetable oil

1 small onion, peeled and finely chopped (about $^1/_2$ cup)

2 cloves garlic, peeled and minced (about 2 teaspoons)

$^3/_4$ cup water

$^2/_3$ cup ketchup

6 tablespoons cider vinegar

$^1/_2$ cup dark brown sugar, packed

1 tablespoon Worcestershire sauce

1 tablespoon molasses

1 teaspoon ground cumin

Salt and pepper to taste

1 Prepare a fire in a covered grill with 45 to 50 charcoal briquettes. Using long-handled tongs, bank the briquettes when they are hot to one side of the fire grate. On the other side of the fire grate, place a large drip pan half filled with water next to the banked coals. (See Figure 10-1.) The pan should be large enough to completely sit under the ribs. A grill or oven thermometer should read about 350° over the drip pan in the *covered* grill when the fire is ready. Try to maintain this moderate temperature as the ribs continue to cook.

2 Brush the grill grid with oil and set in place. Place the ribs on the grid, fat side up. (Or place the ribs in a rib rack.) Cover and cook over indirect heat for $1^1/_2$ to 2 hours, turning and basting the ribs every 20 minutes with the Apple Basting Sauce.

Be sure to adjust the grill vents to maintain an even, moderate heat. If the heat is too hot and the ribs are browning too quickly, close the top vents to lower the temperature of the fire. Add hot briquettes to the fire every 30 to 40 minutes, or as necessary to maintain a steady, moderate heat.

grid
(4-6" over
the coals)

H2O

drip pan

Figure 10-1:
Preparing an
indirect fire.

3 Meanwhile, prepare the Country-Style Barbecue Sauce. Heat the oil in a medium saucepan over medium heat. Add the onion and garlic and cook, stirring, until the onion wilts, for 3 to 4 minutes.

4 Add the remaining ingredients. Raise the heat to high and bring to a boil. Reduce the heat and simmer for 20 to 25 minutes or until thickened, stirring often.

5 About 15 minutes before removing the ribs from the grill, apply the barbecue sauce, turning and basting the ribs 2 to 3 times.

6 The ribs are done when you can easily cut through the end rib with a sharp kitchen knife and you can move the bones back and forth without much resistance. Remove the ribs from the grill and cut into serving-size portions. Bring the remaining sauce to a rapid boil in the saucepan and serve with the ribs.

For foods that take longer than 40 minutes to grill, you need to replenish the fuel in your charcoal fire in one of two ways:

✔ Add 10 to 12 fresh briquettes to the burning coals every 30 minutes.

✔ Keep a metal pail filled with burning briquettes next to the grill and add a half-dozen (or more, depending on the size of the fire) every 40 minutes.

Go for the gold

Assuming that you're going to be proficient at barbecuing ribs after using our tips, you may want to try out your expertise at one of the dozens of barbecue contests held around the U.S. each year. Check with your local county or state fair to see if one is held in your area. Here are some of the best "open competitions" and phone numbers and addresses for more information.

✓ May: Annual Memphis in May World Championship Barbecue Cooking Contest, Memphis, Tennessee; 901-525-4611.

✓ May: Louisiana State Barbecue Championship, Shreveport, Louisiana; write to 239 Hanging Moss Trail, Shreveport, Louisiana 71106.

✓ June: The Great Lenexa Barbecue Battle, Lenexa, Kentucky; 913-541-8591.

✓ July: Midwest Regional Barbecue Championship, Gladstone, Missouri; 816-436-4523.

✓ September: Blue Springs Blazeoff, Blue Springs, Missouri; 816-228-0137.

✓ September: Ribfest, Chicago, Illinois; write to Ribfest, 435 North Michigan Avenue, Chicago, Ilinois 60611.

✓ September: Super Bowl of Brisket, Abilene, Texas; write to Box 3452, Abilene, Texas 79604.

✓ September: World Championship Barbecue Cook-Off, Pecos, Texas; write to Pecos Chamber of Commerce, Box 27, Pecos, Texas 79772.

✓ October: International Barbecue Society Tournament of Champions, Grand Prairie, Texas; write to Doug Beich, Traders Village, 2602 Mayfield Road, Grand Prairie, Texas 75051.

Donna Myers's Baby Back Ribs with Sweet-Hickory Barbecue Sauce

As a spokesperson for the Barbecue Industry Association for the last 25 years, Donna Myers probably knows more barbecuing and grilling secrets than most seasoned pitmasters. In this recipe, Donna protects baby back ribs from the intense heat of the grill by wrapping them in aluminum foil until nearly cooked. In the final 30 minutes, the ribs are then grilled over indirect heat where they develop a nice brown crust without any charring or overbrowning. Donna's rib barbecue sauce is savory-sweet with a hint of liquid hickory smoke seasoning, which you should be able to find at most grocery stores. It's one of our very favorite sauces in the book and delicious with any kind of poultry, beef ribs, steaks, or even burgers.

Preparation time: *20 minutes*

Grilling time: *1¹/₂ hours*

Yield: *3 to 4 main dish servings or 6 to 8 appetizer servings*

2 full racks baby back pork ribs (about 3¹/₂ pounds)

4 tablespoons water

2 teaspoons liquid hickory smoke seasoning

1¹/₂ cups Sweet-Hickory Barbecue Sauce (see following recipe)

1 In a covered grill, prepare a medium charcoal fire or preheat a gas grill to medium.

2 Cut each rack of ribs in half to make 4 equal-sized pieces, with about 6 to 7 ribs to a piece. Lay 2 pieces of the ribs side-by-side on a long sheet of heavy-duty aluminum foil. Wrap tightly, using a drugstore wrap, but leave one end of the foil packet open. (Figure 10-2 illustrates how to use a drugstore wrap.) Repeat with the 2 remaining rib pieces and a second long sheet of foil.

Drugstore Wrap

Figure 10-2: Doing the drugstore wrap.

Place the food in the center of a rectangle of foil. Leave enough foil to fold the sides and ends.

Bring the sides together at the top and fold down + over several times.

Fold the short ends up + over several times and crimp to seal the package.

ready to grill!

3 Combine the water and liquid smoke seasoning; spoon half of the liquid smoke-water mixture into each foil packet; seal the ends tightly to prevent leakage.

4 Place both packets flat on the preheated grill grid; cover and cook for a total of 60 minutes, turning the packets over about every 20 minutes. Remove the packets from the grill to a large baking pan and let rest.

5 If you're using a gas grill, raise the heat on one burner to create a medium-hot indirect fire. If using a charcoal grill, add more coals to the fire to raise the temperature of the fire to medium-hot, and then bank them to one side. (See Chapter 1 for information about building an indirect fire.)

6 Remove the foil wrapping; place the ribs on a lightly oiled grid, opposite the fire or heat. Cover the grill and cook for about 30 minutes or until the ribs are done, turning and basting both sides with the Sweet-Hickory Barbecue Sauce about every 10 minutes. Heat the remaining sauce just to boiling in a small saucepan and serve with the ribs.

Go-With: Good with Garlic-Grilled Portobello Mushrooms or Grilled Tomatoes with Basil and Bread Crumb Stuffing (both in Chapter 17).

Sweet-Hickory Barbecue Sauce

Preparation time: *About 15 minutes*

Yield: *About 2 cups*

$^1/_3$ *cup soy sauce*	$^1/_4$ *cup ketchup*
$^1/_2$ *cup water*	$^1/_4$ *cup corn syrup*
4 scallions, cut into 1-inch pieces	$^1/_4$ *cup honey*
6 large cloves garlic, peeled and crushed	*1 teaspoon liquid hickory smoke seasoning*
$^1/_4$ *cup chili sauce*	

In a small bowl, whisk together all the sauce ingredients; cover and refrigerate several hours or overnight to meld flavors. The sauce can be stored in the refrigerator for about a week.

Know Your Beef Ribs

Much like pork ribs, beef ribs come in different styles and from different sections of the animal. The most tender beef ribs for grilling come from the rib portion of the steer and are sold as either back ribs (also known as beef spareribs) or beef rib short ribs. The National Cattlemen's Beef Association recommends slow grilling over indirect heat to infuse beef back ribs with lots of smoky flavor. If you purchase short ribs from the chuck portion of the steer and grill them without any precooking, you may be disappointed. Chuck short ribs are too tough for grilling and are really best when they're first braised in the oven or on top of the stove and then finished off on the barbecue grill to give them the smoky flavor you want.

Beef short ribs are also known as Korean ribs because they are often marinated in a sauce that includes soy sauce, ginger, scallions, sake, and other ingredients common to Asian cuisine. These ribs are cut from the spare rib rack so that each rib piece has 3 crosswise-cut rib bones (see Figure 10-3). Ask your butcher to cut the ribs into 3-inch lengths, about $^3/_8$- to $^1/_2$-inch thick, for best results on the grill. They are juicy and meaty, and best of all, unlike other cuts of beef and pork ribs, they grill quickly in only about 12 minutes. The following recipe is ideal as a party appetizer if you cut each rib into 3 small pieces after grilling.

Korean Beef Short Ribs

Korean short ribs are traditionally grilled quickly over medium heat, with frequent applications of a sesame-soy marinade. The result is a rib with a pink, medium-rare interior color and a rich, bronzed exterior. But if you prefer your ribs more tender and with the meat falling off the bone, cook them indirectly for a longer period of time.

Preparation time: *25 minutes*

Marinating time: *4 hours to overnight*

Grilling time: *10 to 12 minutes*

Yield: *4 to 6 main dish servings or 10 appetizer servings*

4 green onions, trimmed and finely chopped

¹/₂ cup soy sauce

¹/₄ cup sake, dry sherry, or dry vermouth

¹/₄ cup water

¹/₄ cup sesame oil

3 tablespoons dark brown sugar, packed

2 tablespoons sesame seeds, lightly toasted in a dry skillet (toasting instructions follow this recipe)

1 tablespoon peeled and grated fresh ginger, or 1 teaspoon ground ginger

3 cloves garlic, peeled and minced

¹/₄ teaspoon cayenne pepper

¹/₂ teaspoon crushed red pepper flakes

3 to 4 pounds beef short ribs (also called flanken short ribs), trimmed of excess fat and cut crosswise about ¹/₂-inch thick (see Figure 10-3)

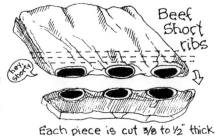

Figure 10-3:
Cutting beef short ribs.

Each piece is cut 3/8 to ½" thick and contains 3 cross-cut rib bones.

1 Combine all ingredients in a large, resealable plastic bag or a large non-reactive container. Seal the bag or cover the dish, and refrigerate for 4 hours or overnight, turning occasionally.

2 Prepare a medium fire in a charcoal or gas grill.

(continued)

3 Remove the ribs from the marinade, reserving the marinade. Place the ribs on a well-oiled grill grid.

4 Grill for 5 to 6 minutes; baste both sides of the ribs with the reserved marinade. Cover and continue cooking for 5 to 6 minutes on the other side. The ribs should be a rich golden brown on both sides, with a pink interior.

Toast sesame seeds in a dry skillet, in a single layer, over medium-low heat until lightly browned. Remove the seeds immediately from the skillet to keep them from overbrowning or burning.

Go-With: Serve with Stuffed Summer Squash or Grilled New Potato Salad with Fresh Mint (both in Chapter 17).

Chapter 11
One Good Turn Deserves Another

In This Chapter

▶ Discovering the benefits of rotating your food

▶ Getting the best results from a rotisserie

▶ Using a thermometer to ensure doneness

▶ Using rotisserie drippings for sauce

▶ Experimenting with recipes for the rotisserie

The very first grills were some primal form of rotisserie — just a stick that someone turned every once in a while over a fire. Today, electric rotisseries are available as grill accessories and make this once time-consuming chore a leisure-time activity. In this chapter, you find out about the benefits of rotisserie cooking and how best to use a rotisserie in a covered gas grill. We discuss cooking times — which differ a great deal from tossing food directly on a grill — and give you the low-down on sauces that you can make by reclaiming juices from the rotisserie drip pan.

As the Food Turns

Although we spend most of this book exalting the pleasures of cooking directly *on* a grill grid, we now state unequivocally that rotisserie cooking a few inches *above* the grid not only offers a few benefits but also imparts wonderful taste and textures to those foods.

A rotisserie that turns at a constant, never-varying speed allows the same degree of heat to cook every inch of the food, thereby guaranteeing that a roast or bird will be succulent throughout. The food holds its moisture better than in an oven because the surface of the food sears quickly and therefore seals in natural juices.

Rotisserie cooking is also healthier in some ways because you need to add very little extra fat, or none at all, before the food is placed on the *spit* — the rod of the rotisserie that holds the food above the fire — for cooking. The meat self-bastes.

Marinate and baste with any combination of liquids, herbs, and spices, but keep sugared ingredients to a minimum in your marinades. Don't baste with a sauce that has a high sugar content until the last 15 to 20 minutes of cooking to prevent the sauce from charring.

Use a spray bottle to mist and add moisture to rotisserie meats or poultry as they spit-roast. Fill the bottle with any combination of flavored liquids, such as soy sauce, sherry, apple juice, or beef broth, and your favorite herbs and spices. Mist about every 20 minutes.

Rotisserie cookery is best for "round" food, that is, large roasts, whole poultry, and whole fish. The more delicate the flesh, the better results rotisserie grilling provides. Of course, rotisserie cookery is not ideal for every food. We wouldn't stick a skewer through a whole steak or lamb chop or beef fillet, and many of our kebab recipes are best placed directly on the grill so that they pick up flavor from the burning coals. But if you like moist, juicy roasts and if you have the time to spend, rotisserie cookery is a wonderful process — and, thanks to electric rotisserie units, almost foolproof.

Rotisserie Rules

Rotisserie cooking has its own set of simple rules:

- ✔ As with grilling, many factors, such as wind, air temperature, humidity, and the size and thickness of the food, affect the performance and actual cooking times of your rotisserie. Recipes can only give approximate cooking times. Always check the manufacturer's manual for cooking times and guidelines.

- ✔ Keep the pieces of food, such as cut-up chicken, of more or less equal size in order to ensure consistency in the cooking time. For larger food, such as a roast, make sure that the food is balanced on the skewer before placing it over the grill.

- ✔ Poultry wings and legs, which may flop around on the rotisserie, should be trussed or tied securely (though not too tightly) to the body with heavy cotton kitchen twine. Too much weight or an imbalanced weight can cause the machine motor to malfunction and burn out. Weights are often provided on electric rotisseries to help achieve this balance.

✔ Always use a drip pan under your rotisserie grilled foods because otherwise a good deal of fat will drip onto the coals — fat that you can use to make a sauce later. If you do not plan to baste or make a sauce, fill the pan half full with water, which adds moisture. Never allow the liquid in the drip pan to evaporate.

✔ The drip pan should be large enough to accommodate the length and width of the food being cooked but not so large that it blocks the heat of the grill.

✔ If the food browns too quickly, reduce the temperature setting on your rotisserie. The food may take a little longer to cook, but you'll avoid scorching it.

✔ It's always a good idea to wear a heavy mitt when raising the rotisserie hood.

Checking for Doneness

If ever there was a good reason to go out and buy a meat thermometer (see Chapter 2), a rotisserie is it. You can easily pluck a steak or grill basket off the fire and cut into the food to see if it's cooked the way you like it, but you really can't do that with ease or safety if the rotisserie is turning. Even if you turn the rotisserie off and cut into the meat, you'll still create a pocketlike gash in the meat that will thereafter get more heat than the rest of the surface and interior when you turn the rotisserie back on. Not good.

So, for rotisserie cooking, the meat thermometer should be inserted in the deepest part of the food. If you think that the thermometer may fall out when the food turns, secure the thermometer with a string.

To avoid overcooking the food, check the temperature about 15 to 20 minutes before the final *estimated* cooking time. The temperature will rise more rapidly at the end of cooking time than at the beginning. Unlike oven-roasted food, food that is rotisserie cooked does not increase in temperature and does not continue to cook after it's taken off the rotisserie. However, all roasts should rest for 5 to 10 minutes after cooking to allow the juices to settle and to make carving easier.

Rotisserie cooking takes a bit longer than placing the food directly on the grill but really no longer than if you cook it in a kitchen oven.

For the best results, check your manufacturer's instruction manual for tips, recipes, temperature settings, and cooking times that are specific to your rotisserie and to the foods you're cooking.

Meat, Fish, and Poultry Make the Rotisserie Go Round

Here are a few general tips for rotisserie cooking different cuts of beef, poultry, pork, lamb, and fish. For more specific jargon and shopping tips, refer to the specific meat chapter in Part IV of this book.

Beef roasts

The rotisserie seems made for beef roasts because it keeps them juicy inside and nicely crisp on the outside. Beef roasts that are perfect for rotisserie cooking include the boneless beef top sirloin roast, round tip roasts (also called the sirloin tip), boneless ribeye roasts, and the eye of round roast. Beef roasts practically baste themselves in their own juices as they turn on the spit. Coat the exterior lightly with olive oil and sprinkle with salt, pepper, and other seasonings, such as garlic powder. Rub the surface with dried herbs and spices to give the exterior a nice brown crust when it's finally cooked.

Cooking times and temperatures will vary according to the heat intensity of your rotisserie, but a good rule is that the less tender the cut, the more slowly the roast should be cooked. For lean round tip and eye round roasts, set the temperature on medium or medium-low for long, slow cooking. Top sirloin and ribeye roasts, which are more tender and contain more fat, can be cooked over higher temperatures — from medium to medium-high. However, for best results, check your grill manual for recommended temperature settings and grilling times. The internal temperature should reach 135 to 140 degrees before the roast is removed from the spit. In most cases, a 3- to 4-pound roast yields 6 to 8 servings.

Vary It! Rotisserie cooks often use large beef, pork, or poultry roasts and are left with delicious, next-day leftovers — just another added benefit! Shred or thinly slice leftover meat for hearty sandwiches or add the meat to homemade soups and tossed green or pasta salads. You also may want to mix the leftovers with shredded lettuce and roll the mixture up in soft tacos.

Pork

Pork is a favorite for rotisserie cooking. The interior of the meat stays naturally moist while the outside surface develops a nice brown crust. Cook until the internal temperature of the roast reaches 155 degrees. Ribs and boneless pork loins (see recipes for Rotisserie Pork Spareribs and Rotisserie Boneless Pork Loin with Herbes de Provence in this chapter) are favorite cuts, but rolled shoulders and boned fresh hams are also delicious. Ribs that are rotisserie cooked do not have that soft, "fall off the bone" texture that you get from indirect grilling. Instead, they have a firmer, chewier meat, which some people find more desirable.

Keep the seasoning simple so that the rotisserie taste of the meat comes through. Try brushing the surface of the roast or ribs with a commercially produced flavored oil — such as roasted garlic or herb oil — and then sprinkle with salt and freshly ground black pepper to taste.

Lamb

A leg of lamb, with its bone intact, is one of the more difficult meat cuts to balance on a spit. For best results, ask your butcher to remove the bone and butterfly the leg. Boned and rolled shoulder roasts and racks of lamb can also be spit roasted.

Marinate any of these cuts (if desired) or simply season with olive oil, garlic, salt, and pepper. Fasten to the spit and cook on medium-high to high heat, or according to the instructions in your grilling manual, until the temperature reaches 135 degrees for rare or 140 or 145 degrees for medium.

Turkey

Turkeys are best if they are first butterflied by your butcher. Whole turkeys have very large bones that tend to prevent even cooking on a spit. The final result can be thigh meat that's undercooked and breast meat that's overcooked and dry. Season the butterflied turkey inside and out and tie it back together for rotisserie cooking. You can even add a thin layer of cranberry stuffing or dressing to the inside before you tie the bird. Cook on high and remove the turkey from the spit when the internal temperature reaches 175 degrees. Boneless turkey breasts, two at a time, are also great choices to rotisserie cook.

Saucing things up

One of the best benefits of rotisserie cooking is being able to make a sauce from the drippings that fall into the aluminum pan that you placed under the food. By using these drippings to baste the food, you not only keep the food moist but you create more drippings for use in a sauce, just as if you had cooked the food in your kitchen oven.

Other poultry

You can cook a pair of chickens or even four Cornish game hens or squab together on one spit. (See Chapter 15 for more information on Cornish game hens and squab.) Most spit rods can hold about 12 pounds of meat at one time. The length of the rod and barbecue determine the actual number. Be sure to tie the legs and wings of each bird securely to their bodies before cooking to prevent them from flopping around as the spit turns. Except for turkey, all poultry should be cooked to an internal temperature of 180 degrees. You also can stuff poultry before rotisserie cooking, but the cooking times will be longer.

Fish

Fish should really be rotisserie cooked in a swinging basket that rocks back and forth over the heat. Fish flesh is so fragile that it can easily fall apart if tied to the spit and rotated over the fire. Rotisserie baskets are becoming increasingly popular; they are available at major department stores that carry a full line of grill equipment, restaurant supply stores, and through the toll-free numbers of many grill manufacturers. Fish fillets are better than whole fish for rotisserie cooking. Whole fish tend to release and splatter their oils all over the inside of the grill, causing it to smell pretty fishy for a long time. Brush cod, salmon, or flatfish fillets with a little oil and then dip them lightly into fresh, seasoned bread crumbs to give them a little protective coating. Place them in the basket and cook over medium heat for about 8 to 12 minutes or until the flesh is opaque.

Let the Rotisserie Games Begin!

Rotisserie cooking interjects yet another dimension of fun and games into the grilling story. As a rotisserie chef, you get to attach food onto a metal rod or spit and watch with fascination as it spins around or rotates over the heat of the grill. Except for seasoning and securing the food to the spit, you need to do little else to guarantee success. Just baste a few times and avoid overcooking. In this section, we give you rotisserie recipes for chicken, ribs, duck, and pork, just to get you started. After you're hooked (or should we say skewered), you'll to want to experiment with recipes of your own.

Rotisserie-Grilled Chicken

If you've never used a rotisserie attachment, start with this chicken recipe — it's shown in the color photo section of this book. The bird produced is juicy, tender, and packed with flavor. You may even decide to forever abandon the technique of roasting poultry in the oven!

Preparation time: 30 minutes

Marinating time: 3 hours

Rotisserie time: 1¹/₄ hours

Yield: 4 servings

1 3¹/₂- to 4-pound chicken

Marinade

1 cup dry white wine

¹/₂ cup olive oil

3 cloves garlic, peeled and coarsely chopped

2 teaspoons minced lemon peel (about 1 lemon)

Juice of 1 lemon (about 3 tablespoons)

3 fresh rosemary or thyme sprigs, about 3 to 4 inches long

1 teaspoon salt, or to taste

Pepper to taste

Spice Rub

1 teaspoon ground thyme

¹/₂ teaspoon paprika

¹/₂ teaspoon salt, or to taste

¹/₂ teaspoon grated lemon peel

¹/₄ teaspoon ground ginger

Pepper to taste

1 Remove all excess fat and giblets from the chicken cavity. (Wrap and freeze the giblets for adding to soups or stocks, if desired.) Rinse the chicken in cold water; pat dry with paper towels. Truss the bird to keep its wings and legs from drooping as the spit turns. (See Figure 11-1.)

2 In a medium mixing bowl or a large, resealable plastic bag, make the marinade by combining the white wine, olive oil, garlic, 2 teaspoons lemon peel, lemon juice, rosemary or thyme sprigs, 1 teaspoon salt, and pepper. Add the chicken to the marinade. Cover the bowl with plastic wrap, or press the air out of the bag and seal it shut. The chicken should fit snugly in the bowl or bag, with the marinade covering it as much as possible. Refrigerate for about 3 hours.

3 Preheat a covered grill with a rotisserie attachment to high (or to the temperature recommended by your grill manufacturer for cooking chicken on a rotisserie).

4 While the grill is preheating, in a small bowl, make a spice rub by mixing together the ground thyme, paprika, ¹/₂ teaspoon salt, ¹/₂ teaspoon lemon peel, ginger, and pepper. Remove the chicken from the marinade; pour the marinade into a drip pan that is only slightly larger than the chicken. Rub the spice mixture all over the chicken, sprinkling some into the cavity as well.

5 Following the rotisserie instructions of your grill manufacturer, arrange the bird on the spit, securing it with the pronged rotisserie forks. (See Figure 11-2.) Set the drip pan with the marinade on the grill grid, directly under the chicken. As the bird cooks, the pan collects juices that flavor the basting sauce.

(continued)

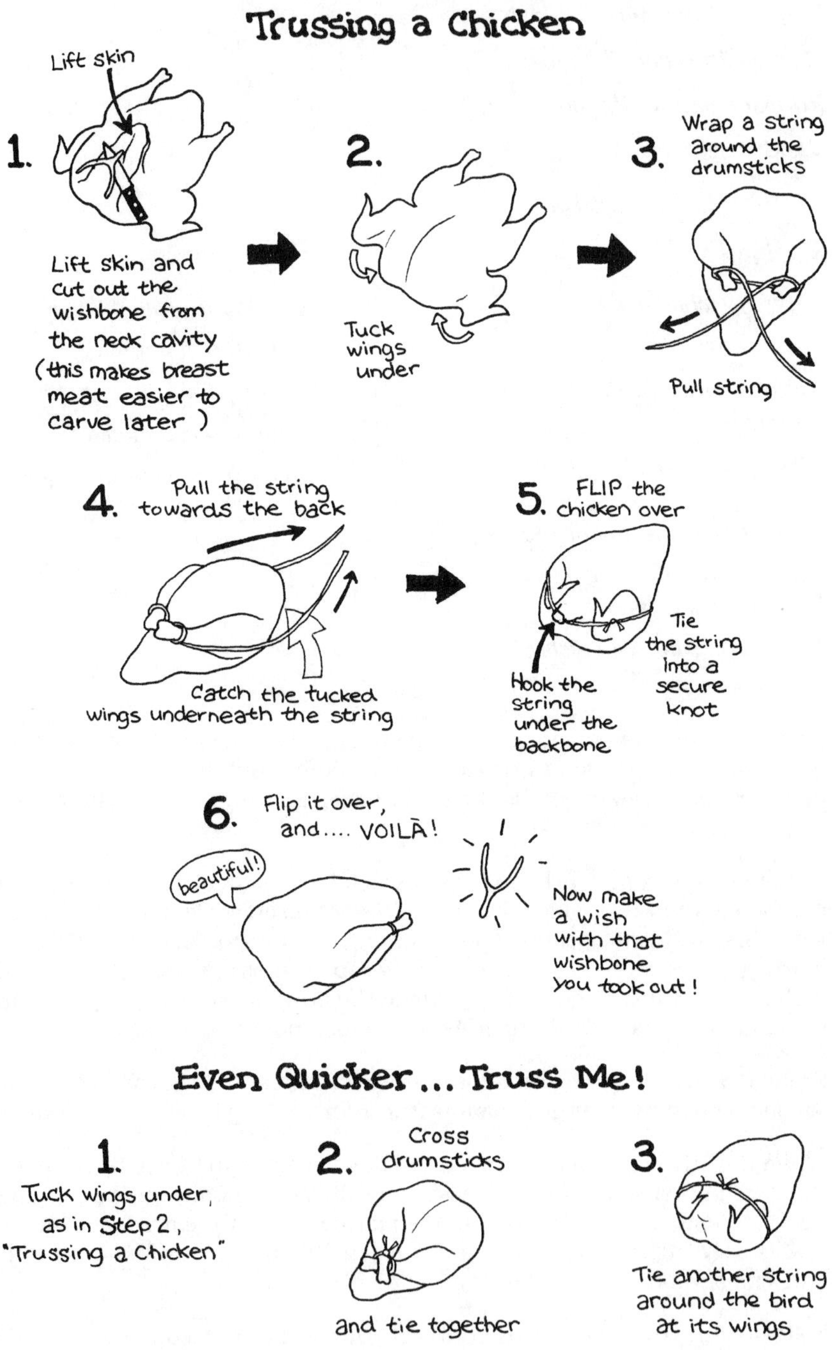

Trussing a Chicken

1. Lift skin

Lift skin and cut out the wishbone from the neck cavity (this makes breast meat easier to carve later)

2. Tuck wings under

3. Wrap a string around the drumsticks

Pull string

4. Pull the string towards the back

Catch the tucked wings underneath the string

5. FLIP the chicken over

Hook the string under the backbone

Tie the string into a secure knot

6. Flip it over, and.... VOILÀ!

beautiful!

Now make a wish with that wishbone you took out!

Figure 11-1:
Two ways to truss a chicken. The easier, quicker way is just fine for rotisserie cooking.

Even Quicker... Truss Me!

1. Tuck wings under, as in Step 2, "Trussing a Chicken"

2. Cross drumsticks and tie together

3. Tie another string around the bird at its wings

Figure 11-2:
The right way to secure and balance a chicken on a rotisserie spit.

How to Fasten Meat or Poultry to the Rotisserie Spit

Tie wings and legs (on poultry) to prevent the bird from flopping.

Thread one of the prongs onto the spit and run the spit from the neck through the tail.

prong · spit

Push the prongs into the bird and fasten by turning and tightening the screws.

screw

6 Cook, with the spit turning, in a covered grill for about 1¹/₄ hours or until done, basting 3 times, or about every 20 minutes, with the juices in the drip pan. (For a crispy skin, omit basting during the last 20 minutes.) When the chicken is done, an instant-read thermometer inserted into the chicken between its thigh and breast will register between 180° and 185°.

7 Remove the chicken from the spit onto a serving plate; cover loosely with aluminum foil and let stand for 10 to 15 minutes before carving. Serve with pan juices or Lemon-Herb Gravy (if desired). (See the following recipe.)

Go-With: Suggested side dishes include mashed potatoes, Middle Eastern Rice, or Bow Ties with Peppers, Peas, and Saffron Mayonnaise (Chapter 7).

Lemon-Herb Gravy

You can make a delicious gravy from the rotisserie chicken pan juices. Strain the juices in the drip pan through a strainer or sieve over a glass measuring cup. Discard the solids left in the strainer. Pour off and discard all but 2¹/₂ tablespoons of the fat. (The fat is the darker liquid that rises to the surface of the measuring cup.) Save all the other juices in the measuring cup. At this point, you can spoon some of these juices over the carved chicken. Or you can use these same juices to make this Lemon-Herb Gravy. It's especially wonderful with mashed potatoes. See the color photo section for an example.

Preparation time: 15 minutes

Yield: ³/₄ cup

(continued)

2¹/₂ tablespoons fat from rotisserie chicken pan juices

2¹/₂ tablespoons flour

³/₄ cup pan juices (fat removed)

¹/₂ cup chicken broth or water

Pepper

Pour the fat into a small saucepan over medium heat. Using a fork or wire whisk, blend the flour into the fat to make a *roux,* or thickening paste. Gradually whisk in the reserved pan juices and the chicken broth or water. Keep whisking over medium heat until the gravy comes to a boil; boil 1 minute. Adjust the seasoning with pepper to taste.

When spit roasting poultry, run the spit through the breast, parallel to the backbone and out through the body cavity, centering the rod as much as possible. The spit prongs should be attached through the breast and tail areas to firmly secure the bird. Be sure that the bird is properly balanced on the rod; test the balance by turning the shaft in the palms of both hands. (See Figure 11-3.) If during the course of cooking, the spit prongs become detached from the bird, simply shut off the motor and, using a protective mitt, push the prongs back into the bird and retighten the fastening screws.

Balance Your Bird "🪶"

wheee

Figure 11-3: Do the balance test.

The bird should rest as much as possible in the center of the spit. Test the balance by turning the shaft in the palms of both hands. If it flops around on the spit, reposition and try it again!

Rotisserie Pork Spareribs

Pork spareribs are an excellent choice for rotisserie cooking. Spit cooking naturally bastes the ribs and keeps them from burning, while the fat melts into the drip pan, becoming part of a delicious basting sauce. Apply sweet barbecue sauces only during the last 15 minutes of cooking time to prevent charring. The delicious drip pan juices in the following recipe may be stored frozen in a covered container for adding to gravies or stews.

Preparation time: 20 minutes

Marinating time: 3 hours or overnight

Rotisserie time: 45 minutes

Yield: 4 servings

1 3- to 4-pound rack of pork spareribs

1 tablespoon lemon juice

1 tablespoon brown sugar

2 teaspoons salt

1 teaspoon pepper

2 teaspoons ground ginger

$^1/_2$ teaspoon garlic powder

1 cup apple juice or cider, or more if necessary

1 cup beef broth, or more if necessary

1 cup bottled or homemade barbecue sauce for basting ribs

1 Sprinkle the ribs on both sides with the lemon juice. In a small bowl, combine the brown sugar, salt, pepper, ginger, and garlic powder. Rub the seasonings all over both sides of the ribs. (Cover with plastic wrap and refrigerate for several hours or overnight for best flavor.)

2 Preheat a covered grill with a rotisserie attachment to medium-hot. (Grill temperatures and heat settings on gas grills vary from one manufacturer to the next. Check your grill manual for the recommended heat setting and estimated times for rotisserie cooking pork ribs.)

3 Slide one of the metal spit prongs onto the spit rod. Starting midway up and at one end of the rack, stick the spit rod between the first and second rib. (See Figure 11-4.) Skip 2 or 3 ribs and skewer again until the entire rack of ribs is "accordion-pleated." Fasten the second spit prong into place on the rod; slide both prongs into the ribs to help secure the ribs to the rod. The rack should be balanced on the spit to ensure even cooking and to keep the rotisserie motor from straining as it turns. (Refer to Figure 11-3.)

Accordion-Pleated Rack of Ribs

Figure 11-4:
Here's how to accordion-pleat spare ribs onto a rotisserie spit rod.

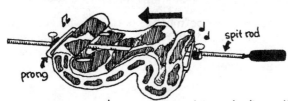

Thread the rib rack accordion style onto the spit rod holding securely in place with skewer prongs.

(continued)

4 Center on the grill a disposable aluminum drip pan that is just large enough to fit under the ribs. (If the pan is too large, it may obstruct the heat of the grill.) Pour the apple juice and beef broth into the pan. Put the spit in place and baste the ribs with the apple-broth mixture. Cover and cook for 45 minutes to 1 hour, basting every 15 minutes with the drip pan juices, until the ribs are tender when pierced with a thin, sharp knife. (Actual cooking time depends on the heat of the rotisserie.) Be sure to keep the drip pan filled with at least an inch of the apple-broth mixture (or water if you run out) at all times to prevent the ribs from charring.

5 Brush the ribs with your favorite barbecue sauce (or use Country-Style Barbecue Sauce in Chapter 10). Cover and rotisserie cook for another 15 minutes or until the meat is fully cooked but still moist. (Unlike ribs cooked indirectly in a covered grill, rotisserie ribs will not result in meat that "wiggles" or falls off the bone. The rotisserie cooked meat will be firmer in texture.)

Go-With: Serve with Orange-Ginger Coleslaw; Black Bean, Corn, and Rice Salad; Three-Bean Bake (all in Chapter 7); or Grilled Tomatoes with Basil and Bread Crumb Stuffing (Chapter 17).

 If you want to keep the ribs or other rotisserie foods warm while taking 15 to 20 minutes to assemble the side dishes for the rest of the meal, leave the food on the spit in the rotisserie with the cover down and with the heat off.

Rotisserie Boneless Pork Loin with Herbes de Provence

When it comes to rotisserie cooking, few people are more qualified to give advice than Ed Newman. A chef and restaurateur for more than 30 years, Ed currently runs Solutions, Inc., a Florida-based food consulting company.

In this recipe, Ed calls for seasoning the boneless pork loin with herbes de Provence — a blend of dried herbs commonly used in French cooking. Several herb and spice companies, like McCormick, sell this blend, or you can make your own because you probably already have these dried herbs in your kitchen pantry.

Smoked Salmon Fillet (Chapter 16), Grilled Tomatoes with Cumin Butter (Chapter 17)

(clockwise from upper left)
Basic Burger (Chapter 8) with Orange-Ginger Coleslaw (Chapter 7), Three-Bean Bake (also in Chapter 7), Grilled Chicken Quarters with Barbecue Sauce (Chapter 15), Grilled Corn on the Cob (Chapter 17)

(clockwise from upper left) Sun-Dried Tomato and Mozzarella Cheese Pizza (Chapter 18), Best-Ever Fajitas (also in Chapter 18) with Fresh Tomato Salsa and Guacamole (Chapter 6), Open-Faced Grilled Eggplant and Goat Cheese Sandwich (Chapter 18)

Just Right Ribs with Country-Style
Barbecue Sauce (Chapter 10); Black
Bean, Corn, and Rice Salad (Chapter 7)

Rotisserie Grilled Chicken (Chapter 11), and Grand Marnier Grilled Sweet Potatoes (Chapter 17), Lemon-Herb Gravy (Chapter 11)

(clockwise from upper left)
Satay with Peanut Dipping Sauce; Teriyaki
Steak Kebabs; Chicken Tikka; Lamb and
Eggplant Kebabs with Tarragon Marinade;
Artichoke, Mushroom, and Cherry Tomato
Kebabs; Grilled Shrimp with Scallions in a
Soy Marinade (all in Chapter 9)

(clockwise from upper left)
Apricot Glazed Pork Chops (Chapter 13);
Bow Ties with Peppers, Peas, and Saffron
Mayonnaise (Chapter 7); Soy Pork
Tenderloin with Asian-Flavored Vegetables
(Chapter 13) and Creamy Asian Peanut Sauce
with Noodles (Chapter 6)

(clockwise from upper left)
Grilled Steak Salad (Chapter 12), Minty Cucumber
Salad (Chapter 7), Butterflied Leg of Lamb with
Honey-Mustard Dressing (Chapter 14) with Middle
Eastern Rice (Chapter 7), Roasted Sweet Pepper
Salsa, Stuffed Summer Squash (both in Chapter 17)

(clockwise from upper left)
Flatfish Fillets Grilled on Lemon Slices with Mediterranean Skillet Sauce, Asian-Style Salmon Fillets with Vegetables, Whole Grilled Trout with Thyme and Almond Butter Sauce
(all in Chapter 16)

Foil-Wrapped Baked Apples,
Grilled Bananas with Caramel Sauce,
Grilled Pound Cake and Fruit with
Brandy Sauce (all in Chapter 17)

Preparation time: *15 minutes*

Marinating time: *8 hours or overnight*

Rotisserie time: *30 to 35 minutes*

Yield: *4 servings*

2 pounds center-cut boneless pork loin

$^1/_4$ cup olive oil

2 tablespoons dried herbes de Provence (or a combination of 3 or 4 of the following dried herbs: oregano, thyme, basil, chervil, marjoram, rosemary, summer savory, or sage)

2 tablespoons cracked black peppercorns

1 tablespoon garlic powder

1 tablespoon Dijon-style mustard

$^1/_4$ teaspoon salt

1 Place the loin in a shallow baking dish. In a small mixing bowl, combine all the remaining ingredients; rub the mixture over the pork. Cover with plastic wrap and refrigerate for at least 8 hours, or overnight.

2 Preheat a covered grill with a rotisserie attachment to hot. (Grill temperatures and heat settings on gas grills vary. Check your grill manual for the recommended heat setting and estimated cooking time for rotisserie cooking pork.)

3 Remove the pork from the dish. Center and secure to the spit rod. Put the spit into place over the grill. Place a disposable aluminum pan under the pork on top of the grill grid. The pan should be half filled with water to catch juices and provide moisture to the roast as it turns. It should be only slightly larger than the pork. (Using a pan that's too large cuts off the grill's heat.)

4 Cook for a total of 30 to 35 minutes. After about 25 minutes, check the internal temperature with an instant-read thermometer inserted into the thickest part of the roast. When the pork is done, the internal temperature will register 155°, and the carved slices will be very moist with a light pink blush.

5 Let rest for 5 to 10 minutes on the rod. Remove the spit rod and carve the roast across the grain into thin slices.

Go-With: Suggested side dishes and condiments include Grilled Potato Planks (Chapter 17) and Tomato Chutney (Chapter 6).

Part IV:
Grilling Everything Under the Sun

The 5th Wave   By Rich Tennant

"What kind of fuel am I using? Right now, 2 hunks of hamburger, 1 chicken wing, and 3 shrimp."

In this part . . .

1f you haven't guessed, we're crazy about grilling! We firmly believe that just about everything that you can cook on a stove or in the oven tastes better when cooked outdoors. In this part, we give you recipes for meats, poultry, and seafood. Each chapter begins with quick hints and tips — like temperature settings and the best cuts of meat — before you set out to sizzle that juicy steak or luscious piece of salmon. And if you think that fresh vegetables and fruits taste best when eaten raw, steamed, or boiled, we hope to alter that opinion with an entire chapter on fruits and veggies. Finally, in this part, we expand your grilling repertoire with recipes and tips for sandwiches and pizzas — fast, friendly food choices for your outdoor summer parties.

Chapter 12

Beef Is What Grills Were Made For

Beef — thick, juicy, and full of flavor — is the quintessential grilled food. Whether you like your beef rare or well done, rubbed and marinated or plain, in the form of filet mignon or a T-bone, this chapter has tips and tricks for all your beef grilling needs.

This chapter isn't the only place you can find beef recipes in this book. For tips on grilling the perfect hamburger, turn to Chapter 8. For grilling a variety of beef kebabs, flip to Chapter 9. In Chapter 10, you can find a delicious recipe for Korean-style beef ribs. You can also find a large assortment of rubs, flavored oils, and compound butters — perfect for a variety of beef cuts — in Chapter 6.

Hearty — and Pretty Healthy

Concerns over the high fat and cholesterol in beef, in our opinion, have been overemphasized by zealots who neglect to mention beef's healthful properties. True, a 16-ounce steak with baked potato and sour cream, onion rings, and a piece of cheesecake for dessert is not what you'd call a low-cal dinner, but it's not the beef that accounts for most of those calories.

Beef is an excellent source of protein, iron, zinc, niacin, phosphorus, and B vitamins. And both fat and cholesterol — in moderation — are essential to a human diet. A "portion," in today's definition, is a piece the size of a deck of cards.

Because beef, like other animal products, can carry all sorts of bacteria, follow these precautions:

✔ If the meat has been frozen, do not thaw it at room temperature. Bacteria can build up during the thawing process, and thawing in the refrigerator overnight makes for a better texture in the meat.

✔ Always store meat of any kind in the refrigerator or freezer after purchase.

✔ Cook all ground beef hamburgers to 160 degrees (or medium), with no trace of pink remaining in the center of the patty, and you will kill off bacteria that can cause food-borne illnesses.

You can cook other beef cuts to slightly lower internal temperatures.

✔ Never place the cooked or grilled meat on the same platter that held the raw meat.

The relative quality of beef depends on its grade and on the cut you choose.

Making the grade

Since 1927, the U.S. Department of Agriculture has graded beef through a voluntary program on behalf of the meat packers. For consumers, *grade* is a gauge for determining eating quality.

The more *marbling* (flecks of fat within the meat) — which, by the way, should be evenly distributed — the more flavorful the steaks. In addition to marbling, meat graders look for characteristics such as age or maturity, color, and meat texture.

Although the USDA has eight beef grade categories, here are the three most often found at your supermarket. The grade of a particular piece of meat is usually clearly displayed on the package label.

✔ **Prime:** Young beef with the most marbling is given this prime (highest quality) grade. Most prime is sold to better-quality restaurants and to specialty butcher shops and grocery stores, especially in major cities. Because only about 2 percent of meat today is graded as prime, it's almost impossible to find in grocery stores.

✔ **Choice:** Choice is a juicy, tender grade of meat, though not quite as tasty as prime. Currently about 44 percent of graded beef is choice — it's the most widely available grade of beef.

✔ **Select:** Select has the least amount of marbling of the three grades and, although it may be less expensive than prime or choice, it's usually not as juicy, flavorful, or tender, either. About 27 percent of graded meat is classified as select.

Checking for doneness

Doneness is a matter of taste, but remember that even the finest prime beef has little taste or texture left if you cook it beyond medium. The National Cattlemen's Beef Association defines the approximate degree of doneness in beef as the following:

- Very rare: 130 degrees
- Rare: 140 degrees
- Medium-rare: 145 degrees
- Medium: 160 degrees
- Well-done: 170 degrees
- Very well-done: 180 degrees

These temperature guidelines are helpful when you're using a meat thermometer to take the guesswork out of cooking large roasts, but for steaks and smaller cuts, doneness is defined by the meat's interior color. Rare meat is bright red and juicy. Medium meat has a light pink center with light brown edges. Well-done meat is brown-gray throughout.

The intensity of the heat of gas and charcoal grills varies. Keep in mind that the cooking times throughout this chapter are only estimates. Check the interior of the meat by making a small cut with a sharp knife a few minutes before the estimated time of doneness, to avoid overcooking your steak. Unfortunately, after a steak is overcooked, you can't reverse the results.

Let the steak rest, loosely covered with foil, for a few minutes after taking it off the grill. The juices will stabilize, and it will cook a bit more.

Also, about 27 percent of all meat is ungraded and sometimes referred to as *no roll.*

Prime, choice, and select grades of meat are suitable for grilling, but prime or choice is more tender, juicy, and savory than select. So, if you have a choice, choose prime or choice grades for grilling.

The cut of your beef

Names of meat cuts can be confusing because there are regional and colloquial differences in the way butchers describe a particular cut. For instance, Midwesterners may refer to a luscious short loin without the fillet and bone as a New York strip, while people in New York call the exact same cut a Kansas City strip. Elsewhere it might be called a shell steak. London broil, often sold as a particular cut of beef, started out as a recipe made with flank steak. Today the term London broil is often used to identify beef top round, beef chuck shoulder steak, or flank steak.

When shopping for cuts most suitable for grilling, here's what you'll find at your supermarket (see Figure 12-1):

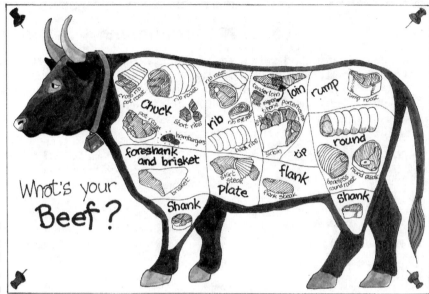

Figure 12-1:
The cut of
your beef.

✔ **Top loin (strip) steak:** The classic beef steak — also known as Kansas City strip, New York strip, and club. The top loin or strip steak is considered by many steak lovers to be the single finest cut because of its rich marbling, perfect texture (which is neither too firm nor too mushy), and its real beefy flavor. Strip steaks are usually sold boneless, although the bone provides an added succulence to the finished product.

✔ **Tenderloin:** A rather long, boneless piece of meat with three sections. The middle is called the center section, the larger thicker end is called the butt, and the tapered end is the tip. The whole tenderloin weighs about 4 to 6 pounds, but can be cut and bought as a smaller roast, as individual steaks, or as tenderloin tips that are good for kebabs.

✔ **Filet mignon:** A term for steaks cut from the small end of the tenderloin — the most tender beef cut available. These steaks cook quickly and are best if cut between 1 and 2 inches thick. A 1-inch-thick filet, grilled directly over medium heat, takes about 13 to 15 minutes for medium-rare to medium.

✔ **T-bone and porterhouse steaks:** Cut from the short loin section of the animal, these two are basically the same. Each of these steaks has two muscles — the tenderloin and the top loin (also called the *strip*). The distinctive T-bone (a bone down the middle of the steak that's shaped like the letter "T") helps identify each of these steaks. The difference between them is the size of their tenderloin muscles: The porterhouse has a tenderloin muscle about the width of a silver dollar or bigger, while the T-bone's tenderloin muscle is smaller than a silver dollar. The porterhouse is also called a *sweetheart steak,* because it's really two steaks in one and big enough for two servings.

✔ **Ribeye:** Boneless cut from the rib section. Ask for ribeye steaks from the *small end,* which is farthest from the chuck and closest to the more tender loin. The small end also has less fat, which is better for grilling. Cut them about 1-inch thick and grill over medium heat for about 11 to 14 minutes, uncovered. If sold with the bone, these steaks are called *rib steaks,* and cook in less time, about 9 to 12 minutes over medium heat for 1-inch thick.

✔ **Sirloin:** Situated next to the round and actually cut from the loin or hip portion of the animal, most sirloin steaks are sold boneless. They are fairly economical, tender, and versatile — they make great cubes for kebabs or strips for stir-frying. A 1-inch-thick sirloin, grilled over medium heat, takes about 15 to 17 minutes to grill to medium.

✔ **Flank:** Although considered less tender than the other cuts in this list, the flank steak has wonderful flavor when grilled and needs only a little marinating to soften. Cook only to medium-rare, carving across the grain into thin slices. Turn to Chapter 18 for Best-Ever Fajitas, made with flank steak.

Preparing and Grilling Your Steaks

Is the thickness of a good steak merely a matter of personal preference? Not to us. The best thickness for grilling any type of steak is 1 inch, although the most commonly sold steak in the supermarket is only $3/4$ inch. A steak that's 1-inch thick allows you more control than a thinner steak. A $3/4$-inch steak's degree of doneness can change in a heartbeat from medium-rare to medium on a medium-hot grill. So ask your butcher to cut your steaks 1-inch thick. You don't need to score the fat on a steak, but you may want to trim the fat, leaving it $1/8$- to $1/4$-inch thick. A little fat makes the steak moist and juicy. Too much fat causes dangerous flare-ups.

We recommend a medium heat to grill a 1-inch-thick steak. Medium heat (a four-second, hand-held count over the hot coals) gives you a nice brown crust without any serious charring. If you use charcoal, be sure to build an adequate fire — one that extends about 2 inches beyond the edges of the meat — so that you don't run out of fuel during the last few minutes of grilling.

Always thoroughly wash and dry your utensils and cutting surfaces after handling any form of beef (and chicken, too!). Also make sure that you wash your hands just as thoroughly.

Love them tender

Some beef is tender — some, not (see Figure 12-2). Although we like our tender steaks relatively plain — without gussying them up with other flavors — we have some tips on handling those tougher cuts.

Tender beef steaks, such as sirloin, porterhouse, T-bone, ribeye, and tenderloin, don't require marinating to break down or soften the exterior surface of their tissues. These cuts can be simply rubbed with combinations of seasonings that flavor the exterior of the meat as it grills. Use the rub and flavored oil recipes in Chapter 5, create your own rub from your spice rack, or check out your supermarket spice section for the commercial rubs suitable for beef.

Although you don't need to marinate ribeye, top loin, porterhouse, T-bone, tenderloin, and sirloin to improve their tenderness, these steaks may benefit from a little dunking — from 15 minutes to 2 hours — to absorb additional flavors.

Overmarinating tender beef cuts in liquid with an acid ingredient, such as lemon juice or wine, can turn the surface tissues slightly mushy.

Less-tender and less-expensive cuts — flank, skirt, top round, eye round, and chuck steaks — need a longer marinating time. Marinate less-tender cuts in the refrigerator for at least 6 hours, or even overnight. Marinating adds flavor and helps to soften their tougher muscle tissues. When marinated and then grilled to medium-rare, these cuts can be quite juicy and delicious.

Within the categories of round and chuck, some cuts are tougher than others. Top blade and chuck eye (very tender cuts though they come from the chuck) don't need to be marinated longer than 6 hours. However, other chuck and top round steaks benefit from long marinating — 6 hours or overnight.

Figure 12-2:
Some beef cuts are tougher than others.

Grilling 'em up!

Usually, you don't need to *sear* a steak — that is, cook the steak for a few minutes over very high heat until well browned on both sides — as the initial step in the cooking process. However, bigger pieces of meat, like a thick roast or a 2-inch-thick steak may benefit from searing first, followed by cooking slowly over lower heat. For these bigger cuts, sear them, but not enough to blacken the exterior.

We are squarely in the camp of those who insist that allowing grilled meat to stand a few minutes before carving makes for a better steak. The juices inside will stabilize and redistribute throughout the meat.

Grilled Steak 101

Compared to the more expensive ribeye or porterhouse, a sirloin steak gives you lots of flavor for the money, and more versatility, too, because it's also perfect for cutting into kebab cubes. (See Chapter 9 for steak kebab recipes.)

This recipe features the flavor of a simply grilled sirloin and relies on only a little garlic, olive oil, and salt and pepper as seasoning. However, if you care to embellish a little, turn to Chapters 5 and 6 for an assortment of flavored oils, seasoned rubs, sauces, and compound butter recipes.

Preparation time: *5 minutes*

Grilling time: *15 minutes*

Yield: *4 servings*

2 tablespoons olive oil

1 clove garlic, crushed

2 boneless sirloin beef steaks, cut 1-inch thick (about 2 pounds total)

Salt and pepper to taste

1 Prepare a medium fire in a charcoal or gas grill.

2 In a small bowl, combine the olive oil and garlic. Generously rub or brush the flavored oil on both sides of the steaks. Sprinkle the steaks lightly with salt and pepper.

3 Place the steaks on a well-oiled grill grid, directly over medium heat. Grill, uncovered, 14 to 16 minutes for medium-rare to medium doneness, turning every 5 minutes.

4 Remove the steaks from the grill; cover loosely with foil and let the steaks rest for a few minutes before thinly slicing across the grain. Season with salt and additional pepper (if desired) before serving.

(continued)

Go-With: Serve with any of the side dishes in Chapter 7; with the Tapenade, Pesto Sauce, Tomato Chutney, or Guacamole all in Chapter 6; or with any of the compound butters in Chapter 6.

Vary It! You can substitute porterhouse steaks, cut 1-inch thick, totaling about 2 pounds, for the sirloin steaks.

Chuck Steaks Marinated in Red Wine

If you're looking for a way to turn inexpensive chuck shoulder steaks into a very tasty grilled dinner, try this recipe. For other steak marinades recipes, which are also good with tougher steaks, flip to Chapter 5.

Preparation time: 15 minutes

Marinating time: 8 hours or overnight

Grilling time: 15 minutes

Yield: 4 servings

2 boneless beef chuck shoulder steaks, cut about 1-inch thick (about 1¹/₂ to 2 pounds)

1 cup dry red wine

¹/₂ cup chopped onions

3 tablespoons olive oil

2 tablespoons peeled and grated fresh ginger

1 tablesooon red wine vinegar

2 large cloves garlic, peeled and minced

¹/₂ to 1 large jalapeño pepper, seeded and minced (optional)

¹/₄ teaspoon salt, or to taste

Pepper to taste

1 Place the steaks in a large, resealable plastic bag or a shallow non-reactive dish.

2 In a small mixing bowl, make the marinade by whisking together the remaining ingredients.

3 Pour the marinade over the steaks in the bag or dish, turning to coat. Close the bag securely, pressing out any air, or cover the dish, and refrigerate for 8 hours or overnight, turning occasionally.

4 Prepare a medium fire in a charcoal or gas grill.

5 Remove the steaks from the marinade, discarding the marinade. If desired, sprinkle with additional salt and pepper to taste. Place the steaks on an oiled grill grid, directly over the heat.

6 Grill, uncovered, 14 to 16 minutes for medium-rare to medium, or until desired doneness, turning every 7 to 8 minutes. (Check for doneness by making a small cut into the center of the meat with a sharp knife. For best results, less-tender steaks should be cooked from medium-rare to medium.) Carve into thin slices across the grain.

Go-With: Serve with any of the side dishes in Chapter 7, or with the Garlic-Grilled Portobellos in Chapter 17.

Vary It! Flank and top round also work well with this red-wine marinade. A flank steak about 1¹/₂ to 2 pounds will cook to medium-rare or medium in 17 to 21 minutes, depending on thickness. One beef top round steak (1-inch thick) takes 16 to 18 minutes for medium-rare to medium doneness.

Texas Beef Barbecue

This marinade uses beer, lots of chili powder, cumin, and red pepper flakes to give an inexpensive piece of top round an authentic hometown barbecue flavor — without actually barbecuing.

Preparation time: 10 minutes

Marinating time: 3 hours or overnight

Grilling time: 14 minutes for medium-rare

Yield: 4 servings

1 cup bottled chili sauce	*1 teaspoon ground cumin*
¹/₂ cup beer	*¹/₂ teaspoon dried red pepper flakes*
¹/₃ cup vegetable oil	*1 boneless beef top round steak, cut 1-inch thick (about 1-¹/₂ to 2 pounds)*
¹/₄ cup finely chopped green onion (white and green parts)	*Salt to taste (optional)*
3 tablespoons chili powder	

1 In a medium bowl, make the marinade by combining all the ingredients except the steak.

2 Place the steak in a glass baking dish or a large, resealable plastic bag. Pour the marinade over the steak, turning to coat. Cover the dish or seal the bag, pressing out as much air as possible. Refrigerate 3 hours or overnight.

3 Prepare a medium fire in a charcoal or gas grill.

(continued)

4 Remove the steak from the marinade, shaking off any excess. Discard the marinade. If desired, sprinkle the steak with salt. Place the steak on a well-oiled grill grid and grill 12 to 14 minutes for medium-rare or about 15 minutes for medium, turning every 5 to 6 minutes.

5 Transfer the steak to a cutting board and let rest for 5 minutes, loosely covered with foil. Thinly slice across the grain.

Vary It! You can substitute 1¹/₂ to 2 pounds of flank steak for the chuck steak in this recipe.

Go-With: This steak is absolutely heavenly with the Three-Bean Bake casserole in Chapter 7 or with the Barbecued Onions in Chapter 6.

 Cook any type of beefsteak according to your personal preference, but remember that overcooking tightens and toughens muscle. The more a steak is cooked, the less juicy it becomes. Cooking to medium-rare or medium gives you the most tender steaks.

 If you intend to use a marinade as a basting or dipping sauce, pour off and reserve a small portion *before* adding the raw, uncooked meat. Otherwise, any marinade that has previously come in contact with raw meat, fish, or poultry must be brought to a full rolling boil and then simmered a few more minutes before it can be used as a finishing sauce.

Grilled Steak Salad

In this recipe, grilled sirloin or top round strips are tossed with salad greens, bell pepper, red onion rings, and dressing (see the color photo pages for a peek at this colorful dish). Serve with a crusty loaf of French or Italian bread to complete the meal.

Preparation time: 25 minutes

Marinating time: 3 hours or overnight

Grilling time: 12 to 14 minutes for medium-rare

Yield: 4 servings

¹/₂ cup reduced-sodium soy sauce

¹/₄ cup rice wine vinegar

3 tablespoons water

2 tablespoons Asian-style sesame oil

2 cloves garlic, peeled and minced

1 tablespoon peeled and minced fresh ginger

1 teaspoon hot chili oil

1 pound boneless sirloin or top round steak, 1-inch thick

8 cups torn salad greens, such as spinach, watercress, romaine lettuce, or Boston lettuce

1 large red bell pepper, seeded and cut into thin strips

¹/₂ red onion, thinly sliced and rings separated

3 tablespoons minced fresh cilantro (optional)

1 In a small bowl or jar, make the dressing (which is also the marinade) by combining the first 7 ingredients. Mix or shake well.

2 Place the steak in a shallow glass dish or a large, resealable plastic bag; add ¹/₂ cup of the dressing. Turn the meat to coat. Cover the dish or seal the bag, and refrigerate 3 hours or overnight, turning occasionally. Refrigerate the remaining dressing.

3 Prepare a medium fire in a charcoal or gas grill.

4 Drain the meat; reserve the marinade. Place the steak on a lightly oiled grill grid. Grill 12 to 14 minutes for medium-rare, or to desired doneness, turning once and brushing once with the reserved marinade. When the steak is cooked to desired doneness, discard any remaining marinade. Allow the steak to stand 5 minutes, loosely covered with foil on a carving board. Slice thinly across the grain.

5 In a large bowl, mix the salad greens, red pepper, and onion; transfer to a serving platter. Top with the sliced steak. Pour the reserved, refrigerated dressing over the salad, sprinkle with cilantro (if desired), and serve.

Vary It! You can substitute 2 boneless beef top loin steaks (cut 1-inch thick and about 1 pound total) for the sirloin or top round steak.

Giving Grilled Beef Roast a Chance

Grilled beef roast is a wondrous thing. It takes on a lovely smokiness that you can't get when you cook it in an oven, and if turned carefully on a spit, it reproduces the most primal of all cooking processes. Although you won't have the wonderful aroma wafting through the house or enjoy the promise of Yorkshire pudding made with the pan drippings, you may never want to cook roast beef in your oven again after you try it on the grill.

The following is a short list of beef roasts that we recommend for grilling:

- **Tenderloin:** This most elegant piece of meat is so perfectly suited to grilling that our mouths water just thinking about it. A tenderloin is also one of the most expensive meats in the supermarket, so you want to grill it perfectly. The first rule when grilling a tenderloin is to remove it from the grill 5 to 10 degrees shy of the final, desired internal temperature. The internal temperature of a roast will increase 5 to 10 degrees after it has been removed from the grill and allowed to rest for 15 minutes under a tent of foil. For rare meat, remove the roast when the temperature is between 130 and 135 degrees; for medium-rare, remove between 135 and 140 degrees; for medium, remove when the internal temperature is between 145 and 150 degrees.

  The second cardinal rule when roasting a tenderloin is to be sure that the roast is evenly thick from end to end to ensure even cooking. A tenderloin has a thin and a thick end, and often the butcher tucks and ties the thin end underneath the roast to make it uniformly thick. However, to ensure even cooking, it's better to have the thin tail end cut off rather than tied. (Check out the recipe for Grilled Tenderloin Au Poivre with Herb Butter Sauce, later in this chapter.)

- **Ribeye roast:** This is a very tender, boneless roast that readily absorbs the strong, smoky flavors of a live charcoal fire. With the bone, this cut is called a *prime* ribeye roast. Cook it indirectly in a covered grill, over medium-low heat, for 15 to 20 minutes per pound.

- **Beef round tip roast:** Sometimes called sirloin tip, this economical cut comes boneless. It is packed with flavor and really is quite tender if cooked to medium-rare (about 135 degrees). Cook indirectly in a covered grill, over medium-low heat, for about 20 minutes per pound. This roast may also be rotisserie-grilled.

- **Tri-tip roast:** One of California's best kept secrets for years, the tri-tip roast can now be purchased in supermarkets and meat markets coast to coast. This relatively small, thin roast with its distinctive triangular shape weighs a maximum of 2 pounds. It cooks very quickly and over direct medium heat in approximately 30 minutes. For tri-tip steaks, cut the raw steak across the grain into 1-inch-thick steaks, beginning at the long, flat end of the roast. A 2-pound raw roast slices into 4 to 5 steaks, with some meat remaining for kebabs or stir-frying.

- **Boneless chuck roast:** Perhaps the most economical of meats, the boneless chuck roast comes from the shoulder and weighs about 3 to 4 pounds. Because it's not a very tender cut, marinate the roast for a long time, about 8 to 24 hours, before grilling. Grill it indirectly, covered, over medium-low coals, for about 25 minutes per pound for rare to medium-rare. Then slice it thinly across the grain.

✔ **Brisket:** A brisket needs several hours of long, slow, indirect cooking or water-smoking to tenderize its tough muscle tissue. After it's barbecued, the meat is usually sliced across the grain and is smothered in a thick, rich, tomato-based barbecue sauce.

Accompany any of these roasts with baking potatoes (like Idaho potatoes). Put them on the grid about 1 hour before the roast is done. (See Chapter 17 for more information on grilling potatoes.)

Grilled Tenderloin Au Poivre with Herb Butter Sauce

Beef lovers, you may never again roast a tenderloin in your oven. The smoke and heat of a covered charcoal grill cook this tender piece of meat beyond compare.

Poivre is French for *pepper,* and a red wine marinade and cracked peppercorns infuse this beef tenderloin with flavor and just the right touch of stimulating spice. (Turn to Chapter 15 for information on how to crack peppercorns.) For you pepper fans, about a tablespoon of pepper produces a roast that is quite peppery — use $1/2$ tablespoon or less if you want only a hint of heat. Grilling the tenderloin directly over medium coals and giving it a quarter turn every 5 minutes cooks it evenly and quickly, without any unpleasant charring. For best results, be sure to use at least a 2-pound tenderloin.

Preparation time: *15 minutes*

Marinating time: *2 hours*

Grilling time: *20 minutes*

Yield: *4 to 6 servings*

$1/2$ *cup dry red wine*

3 tablespoons olive oil

1 tablespoon coarse-grained mustard

2 large cloves garlic, peeled and minced

1 large shallot, peeled and minced, or 2 tablespoons minced onion

1 teaspoon dried oregano or thyme leaves, crumbled

$1/4$ *teaspoon salt*

$1/2$ *to 1 tablespoon whole black peppercorns, cracked (optional)*

1 beef tenderloin, 2 to 2$1/2$ pounds, trimmed

Herb Butter Sauce (optional) (see following recipe)

1 In a small bowl or large glass measuring cup, make the marinade by combining the first 7 ingredients. Place the meat in a large, resealable plastic bag or a shallow nonreactive dish. Pour the marinade over the meat, turning to coat. Cover the dish or seal the bag (pressing out all the air). Refrigerate for 2 to 3 hours, turning occasionally to coat the meat in the marinade.

(continued)

2 Remove the meat from the dish or bag; discard the marinade. Spread the cracked pepper evenly and onto all sides of the meat, pressing it into the surface with the palm of your hand. Cover loosely with foil or plastic wrap and allow the meat to warm slightly before grilling. The meat will grill evenly when brought to room temperature, which takes about 35 minutes, depending on the air temperature.

3 Prepare a medium fire in a charcoal grill, using wood chunks (if desired).

4 Place the tenderloin in the center of a well-oiled grid, directly over the heat. Cover and grill for 5 minutes; give the roast a quarter turn and grill for another 5 minutes. Proceed, grilling covered and turning every 5 minutes, until the roast reaches an internal temperature of between 135° and 140° for medium-rare. Check the temperature with an instant-read thermometer after 15 minutes and then each time you turn the roast.

5 Remove the roast to a carving board (preferably one that collects the juices); cover loosely with foil and allow to stand for 10 to 15 minutes. Carve into ¹/₂-inch-thick slices. Serve with Herb Butter Sauce (if desired).

Herb Butter Sauce

In a small pan, melt ¹/₄ cup butter; stir in 1 tablespoon Worcestershire sauce and 2 tablespoons chopped fresh parsley. Pour over tenderloin slices.

Go-With: Suggested side dishes include Garlic-Grilled Portobellos or Grilled Potato Planks (both in Chapter 17), or any of the side dishes in Chapter 7.

Vary It! If you are lucky to have any leftovers, use them to make tenderloin sandwiches the next day, spreading the slices of bread with chutney or mustard.

The internal temperature of a roast rises most rapidly at the end of the estimated cooking time. So check the temperature often toward the end of grilling to avoid overcooking the meat.

For a hunk of tenderloin that's even more flavorful, mix in a few pieces of hardwood hickory chunks with your charcoal. Keep in mind, however, that wood chunks burn hotter than charcoal. Light the chunks before lighting the charcoal to give them more time to burn to a medium stage. If the chunks are still too hot and the charcoal is ready, spritz the chunks with a little water or move them to the outer edges of the coals, where they will add smoke to the food without flaming and without burning the meat.

Chapter 13

Pork — The King of Barbecue

*T*oday's pork is among the most savory and healthful of meats and is a classic grilled favorite. In this chapter, we tell you just why some of the myths about pork should be forgotten and why pork can be a very healthful meat. We also help you choose the best cuts of pork for the grill. Finally, we make sure that you don't mistreat that beautiful piece of pork and cook it into a dried-out, gray wad — which in the past, too many people thought was the *correct* way to cook it! By the time you finish this chapter, you may be convinced that pork is actually one of the most delicious and delicate meats you can put over a fire.

The Skinny on Pork

Many people avoid eating pork because they think it's a fatty meat, and if they're talking hot dogs and sausages (covered in Chapter 8) or spareribs (in Chapter 10), they're right. But pork taken from the loin and leg is not particularly fatty. And for those concerned about cholesterol, here's some good news: According to the National Pork Council, a 3-ounce serving of pork actually contains less cholesterol than beef or lamb. Table 13-1 gives a comparison:

Hog wild!

Wild pigs, called *peccaries* or *javelinas,* came to North America across the Bering Straits during the Stone Age, but domesticated pigs only arrived when Spanish explorer Hernando de Soto brought 13 of them to Tampa, Florida, in 1539. From this small herd, all the domesticated pigs in the United States have been bred.

Table 13-1	How Pork Stacks Up to Other Meats			
Meat (1 ounce, uncooked)	Calories	Protein (g)	Total Fat (g)	Saturated Fat (g)
Beef T-bone steak	77	5.0	6.2	2.5
Ground beef	75	5.0	5.9	2.4
Lamb chop	106	4.1	9.8	4.3
Pork spareribs	81	4.9	6.7	2.7
Pork shoulder	40	5.6	1.8	0.6

Hit me with your best cut (of pork)

The main thing to look for in a cut of pork is a firm, finely-grained meat. Check to see that the lean part of the meat has a healthy pink color and that the fat is firm and white, not yellow. By the way, the iridescence that you sometimes see on the surface of pork is perfectly natural — it's a reflection of light off the cut ends of muscle fibers — and in no way affects the flavor of the pork.

You can find a dizzying array of cuts produced by the meat industry, though few — usually the choicest parts — show up at the butcher shop or supermarket. (See Figure 13-1.) You'll most likely find the following:

✔ **Leg and loin of pork:** The most tender and succulent cuts of pork, both of these cuts are available either with or without the bone. The leg and the loin are delicious prepared in any number of ways — from chops (covered in the section "Chop, chop who's there?") to kebabs (included in Chapter 9) — on the outdoor grill.

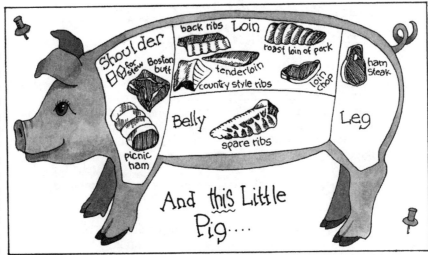

Figure 13-1:
Although
pork has
numerous
parts and
cuts, only
the best
pieces
come to
your local
supermarket
or butcher.

From the loin you also get the best, meatiest ribs, covered in Chapter 10.

The meat from the rear leg, which can weigh 15 pounds, basically consists of two delicious parts: the butt and the shank. It's often cut by the butcher into several boneless roasts called a fresh ham or a boneless fresh ham roast.

✔ **Shoulder:** The shoulder has two principal cuts:

- **Boston butt:** This cut weighs up to 6 pounds and is fatty but juicy — delicious for steaks or cooked whole. It's also the best meat you can use for making sausages. (See Chapter 8.)

- **Picnic ham:** This cut farther down — towards the leg — and is less tender than the Boston butt. The picnic ham is inexpensive and best cut into steaks or used as chunks for stews.

All three massive pork roasts — the Boston butt, the picnic ham, and fresh ham (meat from the rear leg) — can be turned into delicious barbecued dishes. However, the Boston butt, with its high proportion of fat, is prized most by pitmasters because it remains juicy and succulent during the long, slow barbecueing process. To make the barbecue classic called Pulled Pork Sandwich, the Boston butt is cooked for hours and then pulled apart or torn into thin strips, tossed with barbecue sauce, and served on white bread or hamburger buns.

Here's the rub: Treating pork with herbs and spices

Grilled foods don't produce the drippings that you get when you cook indoors. When you sauté, pan-fry, roast, or bake foods, the pan drippings (the browned bits left in the cooking pan) provide you with the start of an exquisite sauce to add flavor to your foods. But when you grill, the raw sauce materials drip, splatter, and waste away into the hot coals. That's why the marinades and rubs in this chapter become important ways to impart flavor to grilled foods.

A number of international spice and seasoning combinations work well with pork:

- ✔ French Provençal rubs: Combine dried, crushed herbs like rosemary, thyme, bay leaves, salt, and black pepper.

- ✔ Asian spice rubs: Combine anise seeds, cinnamon, ground cloves, ground ginger, and red pepper flakes.

- ✔ West Indian and Jamaican rubs: These have a lot of *heat,* or spice, usually in the form of cayenne, paprika, and hot peppers blended with the sweet complementary tastes of allspice, cinnamon, ginger, and dark brown sugar.

- ✔ For a Greek-style roast, make a marinade of olive oil, fresh lemon juice, oregano, garlic, salt, and pepper.

Cooking with rubs is beneficial because:

- ✔ Rubs can be added at the last minute. Although it's best to give a rub at least 30 minutes to penetrate and flavor the food, if you don't have the luxury of time, you can still get good results — unlike marinades, which sometimes need hours to penetrate the meat.

- ✔ Rubs usually contain little or no oil and therefore little fat. Flare-ups on the grill are eliminated.

- ✔ Rubs stick to the surface of foods better than marinades. They form a tasty crusty exterior that complements the food's interior flavors.

Peppery Dried Herb Rub for Pork

One of the charms of rub recipes is that they are flexible — they can be altered to satisfy your individual taste. For example, you can increase the spiciness in this rub by adding ground white pepper or additional cayenne pepper. For a touch of sweetness, you can add a little dark brown sugar. If you don't like thyme, delete it altogether and substitute another herb, like dried marjoram. Or use freshly grated orange peel instead of lemon peel.

Preparation time: *10 minutes*

Yield: *About 3 tablespoons, or enough for about 1^1/$_2$ to 2 pounds pork*

1 tablespoon paprika	*^{1}/$_2$ teaspoon ground thyme*
2 teaspoons grated lemon peel (about l lemon)	*^{1}/$_2$ teaspoon dried oregano leaves*
	^{3}/$_4$ teaspoon salt, or to taste
1 teaspoon garlic powder	*^{1}/$_4$ teaspoon freshly ground black pepper*
1 teaspoon cayenne pepper	*Vegetable or olive oil*

1 In a jar with a tight-fitting lid, shake together all the ingredients except the vegetable or olive oil.

2 Brush the pork generously with vegetable or olive oil on all sides before rubbing with the spice mixture. Use your fingers to apply the rub to 1^1/$_2$ to 2 pounds of chops, whole roasts, or ribs. (Double the recipe to cover larger amounts of meat.)

3 Cover the meat with plastic wrap or place it in a resealable bag and refrigerate 30 minutes or more before grilling.

If you love spicy foods, run to the store to buy yourself a bottle of Jamaican jerk seasoning. Why make it yourself when several superior products are now available in major supermarkets? Jerk is especially good on pork but also works with chicken and fish. Rub it into chops and tenderloins before grilling.

And This Little Pork was Done Just Right

Grilling pork can be tricky business, and it takes some practice to get it just right. Our grandmothers used to cook pork to an internal temperature of 185 degrees, believing that to cook it less would subject us to trichinosis. But we now know that trichinae are killed at 135 degrees. So, cooking pork to 155 or 160 degrees is considered plenty safe and yields a much juicier piece of meat. One way to determine this, of course, is by using a meat thermometer (discussed in Chapter 2).

Furthermore, today's pork is bred leaner than the pork of our grandparents' day, with far less fat. Overcooking pork to 185 degrees results in a tough, dry chop or roast. So hover over pork chops as they grill. Turn them over or move them to cooler spots on the grill if they are cooking too fast. Cover the grill to increase the heat if the meat is cooking too slowly or if the coals are losing heat too quickly. (It is not necessary to sear a chop or other piece of pork.)

Depending on the thickness of the pork cut and the amount of fat, muscle, bone, and grain of the meat, the cooking time for pork can vary considerably. Final cooking time depends on the thickness of the meat, the heat of the fire, and the distance the grill grid is placed from the heat.

- ✔ As you near the end of the estimated cooking time, cut into the meat near the bone to determine doneness before pulling the meat off the grill.

- ✔ A nice thick pork chop is cooked when its juices run clear and the meat is no longer pink near the bone.

- ✔ Brush glazes or sauces that contain any sweet ingredients like sugar or honey during the last few minutes of grilling to keep the meat from burning.

If you insist on grilling your pork until it's well done — we hope just because you like it that way! — you may still see some red areas in the meat, especially near the outer edges. Not to worry: In braising, this color comes from naturally occurring nitrites and nitrates (not additives); in grilling, the presence of exhaust gases from your grill may cause this red color. It's all perfectly natural.

Chop, chop, who's there?

Even those who are not particularly keen on roast pork or ribs are often delighted by the prospect of a nice, thick, juicy pork chop with trimmings like applesauce and sauerkraut. And grilling is one of the tastiest ways to cook pork chops, which are especially delicious marinated, rubbed, or glazed, or simply seasoned with a dusting of salt and pepper.

Pork chops for the grill should be cut about 1-inch thick for best results, so that they develop a nice exterior crust without drying out. In any recipe that calls for a pork chop, you can use a chop with or without a bone — but we find a lot more flavor in a chop with its bone intact.

Lemony Tarragon Pork Chops

Citrus juices are natural meat tenderizers, and lemon, orange, and lime are especially wonderful with pork. Tart, tantalizing lemon juice is the principal flavor in this recipe. You can use the Lemony Tarragon Marinade to marinate pork chops, pork roasts, or kebabs as well.

Even a few hours of marinating can make a difference in the flavor of a pork chop. The length of time needed to marinate pork can vary from 15 minutes (extremely tender pieces) to 24 hours (for tougher pieces of meat). Be sure to marinate in the fridge.

Preparation time: *15 minutes*

Marinating time: *12 to 24 hours*

Grilling time: *10 to 12 minutes*

Yield: *4 servings*

$^2/_3$ *cup olive oil*	*1 clove garlic, peeled and crushed*
$^1/_2$ *cup fresh lemon juice*	$^1/_4$ *teaspoon salt, or to taste*
2 tablespoons chopped fresh tarragon or sage, or 2 teaspoons dried	$^1/_4$ *white pepper, or more to taste*
	Black pepper to taste
2 teaspoons grated lemon peel (about 1 lemon)	*4 pork loin chops, each about 1-inch thick (about 2 pounds total)*

1 To make the marinade, combine all the ingredients except the pork chops in a large, shallow, non-corrosive baking dish or a large, resealable plastic bag. Stir until well blended.

2 Trim all but $^1/_4$ inch of fat from the edges of the chops. Add the trimmed chops to the marinade. Cover the dish or seal the bag and refrigerate for 12 to 24 hours, turning occasionally.

3 Prepare a medium fire in a covered charcoal or gas grill.

4 Remove chops from marinade and discard marinade. Place chops on a lightly oiled grill grid.

5 Cover and grill the chops with the vents open for about 10 minutes or until done, turning once. Cut near the bone to determine doneness. Chops are done when the meat is browned on the outside, with a slight pink blush in the center, and no longer pink near the bone.

(continued)

Go-With: If desired, serve with Black Bean and Red Pepper Salsa (Chapter 6).

Vary It! Punch up the flavor of these chops by adding Dijon-style mustard, red pepper flakes, Tabasco sauce, or other fresh herbs like basil, parsley, or rosemary.

 It's best to use a resealable, plastic bag to marinate food. You can discard the bag after the food is marinated, saving you a dish to wash. But more important, the bag allows more of the food to come into direct contact with the marinade. A dish, bowl, or pan has to be exactly the right shape and size for the marinade to cover the food. A bag, however, can be pressed to conform to the exact shape of the food. Be sure to press all the air out of the bag, and twist it tightly closed, to prevent leaking.

 Whenever you're grilling a relatively thin piece of meat — such as a chop — with the grill cover down, you lose some control over the grilling process because you can't see whether the food is cooking too fast or not fast enough. Remove the lid of the grill to check on how each chop is cooking before the chop is ready to be turned and make adjustments, if necessary, by moving, the chops to cooler or hotter spots.

Grilled Pork Chops with Rosemary Oil

In this grilled chop recipe, the marinade is actually a flavored oil, deliciously seasoned with a little honey, balsamic vinegar, red wine vinegar, grated orange peel, and rosemary. Grilling any kind of chop on fresh herb sprigs, as we suggest here, adds another dimension of flavor — but be sure that the sprigs are lightly oiled before placing them on the grill.

Preparation time: 15 minutes

Marinating time: 12 hours or overnight

Grilling time: 10 minutes

Yield: 4 servings

6 tablespoons olive oil

2 tablespoons honey

2 tablespoons red wine vinegar

2 tablespoons balsamic vinegar

1 tablespoon minced fresh rosemary, or 1 teaspoon dried rosemary

1 tablespoon grated orange peel (from 1 large navel orange)

2 cloves garlic, peeled and minced

¹/₄ teaspoon salt, or to taste

Pepper to taste

4 pork loin chops, cut 1-inch thick (about 2 pounds total)

4 3- to 4-inch long sprigs fresh rosemary, brushed with oil (optional)

1 Combine the olive oil, honey, vinegars, rosemary, orange peel, garlic, and salt and pepper in a large, shallow baking dish or resealable plastic bag. Trim all but ¹/₄ inch of fat from the edges of each chop. Place the chops in the dish or bag, turning the chops to coat all sides. Refrigerate for 12 to 24 hours. (The longer you marinate, the better the flavor.)

2 Prepare a medium fire in a covered charcoal or gas grill.

3 Remove the chops from the marinade, shaking off a bit of the excess; discard the remaining marinade.

4 Place the chops on the oiled grill grid, directly above the heat. Place a rosemary sprig on the top of each chop (if desired). Cover the grill and cook for 5 minutes. Turn chops so that the rosemary sits under them. Grill the chops, covered, for another 5 minutes or until the meat is browned on the outside with a slight blush of pink in the center and no sign of pink near the bone. Cut to determine doneness. Season with salt and additional pepper before serving (if desired).

Should you cover the modest pork?

So far, even the grilling experts haven't been able to decide whether or not you should cover the grill when cooking pork chops. Our advice: Do what makes you happy. We tested pork chops both with and without the grill cover, and each technique has its rewards and shortcomings.

✔ If you grill the chops without a cover, you risk ending up with unevenly cooked meat, especially near the bone where it takes longer to cook. If you choose to cover the grill, we recommend using moderate or medium heat and cooking 1-inch chops for about 5 minutes a side. But check them before this estimated time and remove them sooner, if necessary.

✔ Although covering eliminates the problem of unevenly cooked meat, it also cranks up the grill's heat and can overcook or even burn the chops, especially if they are marinated with any sweet ingredients. If you grill without the cover, then increase the heat to medium-hot and grill for 5 to 6 minutes a side. Covering requires more intense monitoring but also produces a more smoky flavor — an absolute advantage if you are using wood chips or chunks.

Whether you cover or not, move the chops around on the grill, to cooler or hotter spots, to keep them from burning and ensure even cooking.

In the end, you are trying to produce a fully-cooked, moist, and juicy chop, with a slight *give* in the center so that when you push gently with your finger or the tip of a spatula, the meat springs back. It's an art — the best results comes with practice.

Caribbean Pork Chops

In this recipe, pineapple juice gives the meat and bones of these chops a taste and crispness that is reminiscent of slow-cooked pork ribs. Use this marinade for other cuts of pork, adding some cayenne pepper to spice it up, if you wish.

Preparation time: *15 minutes*

Marinating time: *12 to 24 hours*

Grilling time: *10 minutes*

Yield: *4 servings*

1 cup unsweetened pineapple juice

¹/₄ cup honey

¹/₄ cup cider vinegar

1 tablespoon peeled and coarsely chopped fresh ginger

2 cloves garlic, peeled

1 jalapeño pepper, seeded and coarsely chopped

¹/₄ teaspoon ground allspice

4 loin pork chops, cut 1-inch thick (about 2 pounds total)

Salt and black pepper to taste

1 In a blender container, whirl all the ingredients, except the pork chops and the salt and pepper, for about 4 seconds, to make a coarse marinade.

2 Trim all but ¹/₄ inch of fat from each chop. Place the chops in a resealable plastic bag or a shallow baking dish; pour the marinade over the chops and refrigerate them for 12 to 24 hours.

3 Prepare a medium-hot fire in a charcoal or gas grill.

4 Remove the chops from the marinade, shaking off most of the excess; discarding the marinade. Season the chops lightly with salt and pepper. Place the chops on a well-oiled grill grid and cook them, uncovered, for 5 to 6 minutes per side, turning once. Cut to determine doneness. The chops are done when the meat has a light pink blush and there's no sign of pink near the bone.

Vary It! Just about any fruit-flavored sweet chutney, marmalade, or jam (such as plum, apple, pineapple, or orange) works as a quick glaze for pork chops. You can reduce its thickness and sweetness by mixing with a little water or lemon or lime juice.

Apricot-Glazed Pork Chops

In this recipe (shown in the color photo section of this book), apricot jam is mixed with cider vinegar, soy sauce, fresh ginger, and cayenne pepper for a sweet and spicy glaze.

Thick sweet glazes, laced with honey, brown sugar, jams, molasses, and other sweeteners, all work well with chops and ribs. But remember, the sugar content means that the glaze must be applied only during the last 5 minutes of cooking; otherwise, the glaze may burn and you may taste char instead of chop.

Preparation time: *15 minutes*

Grilling time: *10 minutes*

Yield: *4 servings*

1 cup apricot jam	*$1/4$ teaspoon cayenne pepper, or to taste*
3 tablespoons cider vinegar	*4 loin pork chops, cut 1-inch thick (about 2 pounds total)*
1 tablespoon plus 1 teaspoon soy sauce	
2 teaspoons grated fresh ginger	*Oil for brushing chops*
2 cloves garlic, peeled and minced	*Salt and pepper to taste*

1 Prepare a medium-hot fire in a charcoal or gas grill.

2 Meanwhile, in a small saucepan, combine the jam and the vinegar. Cook, stirring over low heat, until the jam melts. Stir in the soy sauce, ginger, garlic, and cayenne pepper. Remove from the heat and set the glaze aside.

3 Trim all but $1/4$ inch of fat from each pork chop. Brush the chops lightly with oil; sprinkle with salt and pepper.

4 Place the chops on a well-oiled grill grid. Grill the chops for 3 minutes on each side. Brush both sides generously with the glaze and grill for another 4 to 5 minutes or until done, turning once. Cut to determine doneness. The chops are cooked when the meat has a light pink blush and there's no sign of pink near the bone. Simmer the remaining glaze for 2 to 3 minutes and then drizzle over the grilled chops before serving (if desired).

Brine 'n dine

Brine is a solution of water and salt that deeply marinates food. It's an easy way to add flavor and moisture to large pieces of meat. (The most famous brined dish — corned beef — is first soaked in a brine before it's rinsed and finally boiled with cabbage and other vegetables.)

Brined and Grilled Loin O' Pork

In this recipe, a boneless pork loin roast is placed in a briney solution of water, sugar, salt, and seasonings for 2 days before it's cooked indirectly in a covered grill. The result is a deliciously tender and perfectly moist piece of pork. This is a great company dish and one of our favorite recipes.

Preparation time: 25 minutes

Marinating time: 2 to 3 days

Grilling time: 50 to 70 minutes

Yield: 8 servings

8 cups water

$^1/_2$ cup sugar

$^1/_3$ cup kosher salt

3 tablespoons fennel seed

2 bay leaves

2 tablespoons grated orange peel (about 2 large oranges)

3 whole cloves

2 teaspoons black peppercorns

4-pound boneless pork loin roast tied by a butcher

Applesauce (optional)

1 To make the brine, combine all the ingredients, except the pork loin roast and applesauce, in a medium saucepan. Cover, bring to a boil over high heat. Remove from heat and let cool.

2 Place the pork loin in a 2-gallon, heavy-duty plastic bag and then put the bag in a 9-x-13-inch baking pan (or other large rectangular pan). Pour the cooled brine over the roast and seal the bag tightly, pressing out any air. Turn the bag to coat the roast with the brine and refrigerate for 2 days, turning the bag over occasionally.

3 Prepare an indirect, medium-hot fire in a covered grill (use 55 to 60 briquettes for a charcoal fire), with a drip pan that's half-filled with water. Use presoaked wood chips or chunks (if desired). Be sure to add fresh briquettes to the fire about every 30 minutes, to maintain the temperature. (For more instructions on building an indirect fire, see Chapter 1.)

4 Remove the loin from the brine; discard brine; allow loin to stand at room temperature until the grill is ready. Place loin on the oiled grill grid directly above the drip pan and opposite from the heat.

5 Cover the grill and cook over indirect heat, turning once, for about 15 minutes per pound or until a meat thermometer inserted into the thickest part of the roast reads 155° (about 50 to 70 minutes). The exact grilling time depends on the intensity of the grill's heat and the thickness of the roast. Be sure to adjust the grill vents if necessary, to maintain a medium-hot temperature.

6 Remove the roast from the grill, cover it with foil, and let it rest for about 15 minutes. (The internal temperature will rise to 160°.)

7 Cut the roast across the grain into thin, $^1/_2$-inch slices and serve with applesauce (if desired) or any of the following side dishes.

Go-With: Serve with Couscous with Apples, Onions, and Raisins (Chapter 7); Bow Ties with Peppers, Peas, and Saffron Mayonnaise (Chapter 7); or Summer Squash Chutney (Chapter 6).

Vary It! Kosher salt is additive-free and all natural, and its individual grains are much coarser than those of table salt. Favored by many chefs as the salt of choice, it is especially delicious sprinkled over grilled meats and vegetables. For example, try it sprinkled over grilled new potatoes and crushed garlic.

Sandra Lawrence's Mild Jerk Pork

Sandra Lawrence, a long-time resident of Harlem, New York, learned to cook professionally from her grandmother and mother, resort and restaurant entrepreneurs. Sandra has a love for cooking that keeps her in the kitchen designing new recipes for cookbooks. Her recipe for Mild Jerk Pork is a refreshing use of some of the best commercial barbecue and grilling products available in any supermarket.

Preparation time: 25 minutes

Marinating time: 24 hours

Grilling time: $2^1/_2$ hours

Yield: 10 to 12 servings

4- to 5-pound boneless pork loin, tied by the butcher

3 cloves garlic, peeled and sliced into thin slivers

$^1/_4$ cup Jamaican jerk seasoning (Penzeys is a good brand)

2 tablespoons dried oregano leaves

2 tablespoon dried ground thyme

$^1/_4$ cup Allegro Hot and Spicy Marinade

1 15-ounce can pork gravy

$^1/_4$ cup Pickapeppa Sauce

$^1/_2$ teaspoon sugar

(continued)

1 Using a small paring knife, make shallow incisions all along the loin, just large enough for each cut to hold a sliver of garlic. Insert a garlic sliver into each cut. Rub the loin with the jerk seasoning, covering the entire surface. Sprinkle the oregano and thyme over the loin, spreading them evenly over its surface.

2 Place the loin in a large, resealable plastic bag. Place the bag in a shallow baking dish. (The dish is a safety net, in case the bag leaks.) Pour the Allegro marinade into the bag; press out all the air in the bag and seal it. Turn the bag to coat the meat with the marinade. Refrigerate for 24 hours, turning occasionally.

3 Prepare a medium, indirect fire in a charcoal or gas grill. (For a charcoal fire, use about 50 briquettes.) Place a drip-pan, half filled with water, on the side opposite the heat. (Flip to Chapter 1 for complete directions on building an indirect fire.)

4 Remove the pork from the plastic bag, discarding the marinade. Oil the grill grid and place the pork on the grid, directly over the drip pan. Cover and grill, with the top and bottom vents open, for a total of 2¹/₂ hours. (Be sure to add more charcoal to the fire, if using a charcoal grill, about every 30 minutes or as necessary to maintain a steady, moderate heat.) You don't need to turn or baste the roast.

5 Place the pork on a carving board, cover it with the foil, and let it rest for 20 minutes.

6 Meanwhile, prepare the gravy. In a medium saucepan, combine the pork gravy, Pickapeppa Sauce, and sugar. Cook over medium heat, stirring occasionally until the sugar is dissolved and the sauce is warmed through.

7 Thinly slice the pork and arrange the slices on a platter; pour half of the gravy over the slices. Pour the remaining gravy into a gravy boat or small bowl and serve on the side with the pork slices.

Tenderloin is the night

A pork tenderloin is a boneless, extremely tender piece of meat from the loin of the pig. It weighs only about 1 pound and is often sold in the supermarket meat case wrapped two to a package. Tenderloins can be rubbed or marinated with any number of seasonings and then cooked indirectly or directly. However, the indirect cooking method (see Chapter 3) assures that the meat will be moist, tender, browned, and cooked through (not charred!) in 20 to 30 minutes.

A whole pork tenderloin is completely cooked when the interior of the meat reaches a temperature of 160 degrees. However, remove the tenderloin from the grill when the thermometer inserted into the thickest part of the roast reaches 155 degrees. Let the tenderloin stand, loosely covered with foil, for 10 minutes before slicing. While the meat rests, the internal temperature will continue to rise, and the juices will settle into the meat, making it easier to carve. Be sure to pour any of the flavorful juices that run out of the roast after it's carved over the slices.

Curry Pork Tenderloins

Coating the surface of the meat with a mixture of herbs and spices is by far the simplest way to season a pork tenderloin. Slice the grilled meat about $1/2$-inch thick and arrange the slices on a large platter.

Preparation time: 20 minutes

Marinating time: 30 minutes to 2 hours

Grilling time: 20 to 30 minutes

Yield: 6 to 8 servings

2 pork tenderloins, about $3/4$ to 1 pound each

1 tablespoon olive oil

1 teaspoon light brown sugar, packed

1 teaspoon curry powder

$1/2$ teaspoon ground cumin

$1/2$ teaspoon ground ginger

$1/2$ teaspoon garlic salt

Pinch cayenne pepper, or to taste

Black pepper to taste

1 Place the tenderloins in a large shallow baking dish. If necessary, use kitchen twine to fold and tie the thin end of each tenderloin under the meat. (This step gives the meat uniform thickness and allows even cooking.)

2 Rub each loin with olive oil. Blend the brown sugar, curry powder, cumin, ginger, garlic salt, cayenne pepper, and black pepper in a small bowl; rub the spice mixture evenly over each pork tenderloin. Cover with plastic wrap and refrigerate for 30 minutes to 2 hours.

3 Build an indirect, medium-hot fire in a covered charcoal or gas grill. (Use about 50 briquettes if the fire is charcoal.) It's not necessary to place a drip pan under the pork. (See Chapter 1 for complete instructions on indirect grilling.)

(continued)

4 Place the tenderloins on the oiled grid, opposite the heat. Cover and grill for 10 minutes. Turn, cover, and grill for 10 to 15 minutes more (maybe longer for a gas grill — see note after this recipe) or until a meat thermometer inserted into the thickest part of the roast (not the folded part) registers 155°.

5 Let the roast stand for about 10 minutes, covered with foil, before slicing across the grain. The sliced meat should have a hint of pink.

Vary It! You can tone down or crank up the spice in this tenderloin recipe by adjusting the amount of cayenne and black pepper to suit your taste. Any leftovers can be served the next day as delicious grilled pork sandwiches. Lay the meat between dark bread slices and garnish with a fruit chutney or pickled watermelon rind.

Go-With: Serve with Grilled Nectarines (Chapter 17), Creamy Asian Peanut Sauce with Noodles (Chapter 7), Tomato Chutney or Summer Squash Chutney (both in Chapter 6), or any of the grilled vegetables in Chapter 17.

 When you turn the tenderloins over midway into grilling, also switch their positions by placing the tenderloin farthest from the coals closest to the heat.

 The heat of a gas grill is usually not as intense as that of a charcoal fire, so for most recipes in this book, we cover those differences by giving you approximate cooking times. However, pork tenderloins may take as much as 15 minutes longer to cook indirectly on gas grills than on charcoal kettle grills. Here's what we advise if you're cooking pork tenderloins on a gas grill:

1. **Preheat the grill with both burners on high.**

2. **After the grill is hot, turn one burner off and the other to medium-hot.**

3. **Cook the tenderloins, indirectly, for 25 to 40 minutes or until done, turning once or twice.**

   If after 40 minutes the tenderloins are not cooked, reduce the heat to medium, move them directly over the heat, and continue to cook until done.

Soy Pork Tenderloin with Asian-Flavored Vegetables

In this recipe, you heat the soy marinade and serve it as a finishing sauce for the grilled tenderloin slices and a colorful side dish of steamed carrots, red pepper, zucchini, and broccoli. You can see an example of this dish in the color photo section of this book.

Preparation time: *20 minutes*

Marinating time: *6 hours or overnight*

Grilling time: *20 to 30 minutes*

Yield: *6 to 8 servings*

Tenderloins

2 pork tenderloins, about $^3/_4$ to 1 pound each

6 tablespoons reduced-sodium soy sauce

1 small onion, peeled and finely chopped

$^1/_4$ cup light brown sugar, packed

2 tablespoons vegetable oil

2 tablespoons sesame oil

3 tablespoons water

2 cloves garlic, peeled and minced

2 teaspoons ground ginger

$^1/_2$ teaspoon black pepper

$^1/_8$ teaspoon cayenne pepper

1 If necessary, use kitchen twine to fold and tie the thin end of each tenderloin under the meat to give it uniform thickness and allow it to cook evenly.

2 Blend the remaining ingredients in a large, plastic resealable bag or other non-metallic dish; add the tenderloins to the bag or dish. Seal the bag, pressing out as much air as possible, or cover the dish with plastic wrap. Refrigerate for at least 6 hours, or overnight, turning occasionally.

3 Prepare a medium-hot, indirect fire in a charcoal or covered gas grill. Use about 50 briquettes if the fire is made with charcoal. It is not necessary to set a drip pan in place. (Turn to Chapter 1 for complete instructions on building an indirect fire.)

4 Remove the tenderloins from the marinade; pour the remaining marinade into a medium saucepan and reserve for making the Asian-flavored vegetables. Place the tenderloins on a lightly oiled grid, on the side opposite the coals or heat. Cover and grill for 10 to 15 minutes; turn, cover and grill for 10 to 15 minutes more or until a meat thermometer inserted into the thickest part of the roast (but not the folded part) registers 155°. The pork is done when you see a hint of pink in the center.

Asian-Flavored Vegetables

3 large carrots, trimmed and scraped

1 small red bell pepper

1 small zucchini or yellow squash, ends trimmed

2 cups broccoli florets

1 tablespoon vegetable oil

$1/4$ cup cold water

1 teaspoon cornstarch

1 While the grill preheats, quarter the carrots and then cut into 2-inch-long pieces. Core and seed the pepper; cut into 2-inch chunks. Cut the zucchini in half lengthwise and then into $1/2$-inch semicircle pieces. Place all cut vegetables in a bowl with the broccoli florets and set aside.

2 While the tenderloins are grilling, bring 1 inch of water and the vegetable oil to a boil in a medium saucepan. Add the carrots, cover, and boil for about 3 minutes. Add the broccoli, and boil, covered, about 3 minutes. Add the red pepper and zucchini and boil, covered, for about 2 minutes more or until all the vegetables are crisp-tender. Drain immediately, cover, and set aside.

3 In a small bowl, combine the $1/4$ cup cold water with the cornstarch, stirring to blend well. Bring the reserved marinade to a boil in a medium saucepan over medium-high heat. Add the cornstarch-water mixture and cook for 1 to 2 minutes, stirring constantly, until the sauce is slightly thickened and smooth.

4 Add the boiled vegetables to the saucepan; stir gently to coat in the sauce. Remove from heat as soon as the vegetables are warmed through. Cover to keep warm.

5 Remove the grilled tenderloins to a carving board and let stand 10 minutes, covered with foil. Slice thinly across the grain. Pour any juices that run out from the roast onto the carved slices. Arrange the tenderloin slices surrounded by the vegetables on a large platter. Spoon any remaining sauce over all and serve immediately.

Chapter 14

Put a Little Lamb in Your Life

*O*ften overlooked as an entrée for grilling, lamb is one of the most succulent meats you can prepare inside *or* outside the house. In this chapter, you find out which lamb cuts are the best to grill and discover that cooking lamb on the grill is a slightly different process than that used for beef. We feature recipes that represent the best of American barbecue style lamb — and one Middle Eastern lamb recipe, too.

Looking for Lamb in All the Right Places

Lamb comes in cutlets, loins, legs, rumps, racks, and several other cuts. It makes terrific ground meat dishes, sensational kebabs, and superb barbecue. After it's trimmed, lamb tastes splendid when prepared with herbs like rosemary and garlic, a gloss of olive oil, or a marinade of red wine or Eastern spices like cumin, coriander, and cardamom.

Figure 14-1 shows the principal cuts of lamb you can find in the American market.

✔ **Breast:** Good for braising, but the riblets make good barbecue, and the meat is excellent ground up for burgers.

✔ **Leg:** This cut may be the whole leg, center leg steaks, the boneless leg, the French-style leg, the shank half, or the butterflied leg, all of which come off well on the grill. Plus, cubes from the leg make great kebabs (see Chapter 9).

✔ **Loin:** Includes the thick loin chops, loin roast, boneless loin roast, and medallions, all of which are best prepared on either the broiler or the grill.

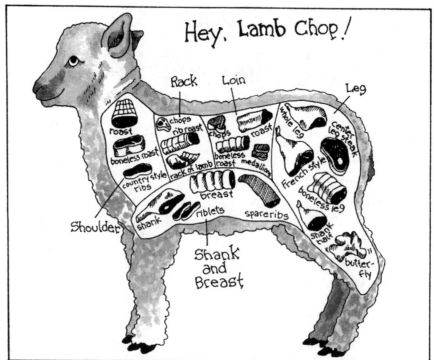

Figure 14-1:
Cuts of
lamb.

- **Rack:** The rack includes various smaller chops, such as rib chops and rack of lamb — which is delicious grilled.
- **Shank:** Best for braising and stewing.
- **Shoulder:** Includes everything from shoulder chops to boneless shoulder roasts.

When buying lamb, look for meat that is bright red in color, which indicates freshness.

Good lamb is raised in the rest of the world, as well — especially in England, Ireland, France, Italy, Greece, and Australia. New Zealand has nearly monopolized the export market with its lamb shipments, which are always frozen. Of good but not outstanding quality, New Zealand lamb is considerably cheaper than that from other countries.

Giving Your Lamb Some Spice

Lamb chops, steaks, and kebabs can be basted or glazed with endless, imaginative sauces and marinades. (You can find out more about lamb kebabs in Chapter 9.) Here are some easy, classic recommendations from the American Lamb Council. Happily, you can assemble most of them from common kitchen and pantry ingredients. Each basting recipe is enough for four ³/₄-inch-thick leg steaks or chops. Brush the lamb on both sides before grilling over medium-hot heat for 5 to 7 minutes per side or until cooked as desired. For more flavor, marinate the chops for a few hours before grilling.

- **Cracked Pepper:** Combine 2 tablespoons red wine, 1 tablespoon cracked pepper, and 2 tablespoons olive oil.

- **Curry:** Combine ¹/₄ cup plain lowfat yogurt, 1 clove peeled and pressed garlic, and 1 teaspoon curry powder.

- **Honey-Mustard Glaze:** Combine 2 tablespoons each honey and prepared mustard.

- **Lemon Pepper:** Combine 2 tablespoons olive oil, 1 tablespoon finely minced onion, 1 tablespoon red wine vinegar, and 1¹/₂ teaspoons lemon pepper.

- **Polynesian:** Combine 3 tablespoons apricot-pineapple jam, ¹/₂ teaspoon dry mustard, 1 tablespoon fresh lemon juice, and ¹/₄ teaspoon garlic salt.

- **Southwest:** Combine 2 tablespoons olive oil, 1 clove peeled and pressed garlic, ¹/₄ teaspoon cumin, 1 tablespoon fresh lime juice, and ¹/₂ teaspoon dried leaf oregano.

- **Teriyaki:** Combine 2 tablespoons soy sauce, 1 tablespoon honey, 1 clove peeled and pressed garlic, 1 tablespoon dry sherry, 1 teaspoon sesame oil, and 1 teaspoon grated fresh ginger.

Dear Ann Lambders

Lamb, by its very nature, has a good degree of fat — certainly more than beef — so you have to watch carefully for flare-ups. Follow this advice when grilling lamb:

- Trim unnecessary fat to about ¹/₄ inch of the bone or flesh.

- Cook lamb chops over a medium-hot fire for best results.

- Use a meat thermometer to determine the doneness of lamb roasts.

- Grill to between 145 and 150 degrees for medium-rare.

- Grill to between 150 and 155 degrees for medium, depending on your desired degree of doneness.

- Before carving, let a lamb roast stand for 10 to 15 minutes after removing it from the heat. This helps the meat settle down after all that fire. The juices will be more evenly distributed, and the meat will continue to cook slightly from internal heat.

Licking Your (Lamb) Chops

Lamb chops are delicious when cooked on the grill, whether they are the big thick loin chops or the smaller riblets, which take no more than a minute or two on each side to cook. (You can eat the riblets with your fingers.) A lamb chop needs little seasoning and is delicious when rubbed with a little olive oil, salt, and black pepper before grilling.

Avoid buying those skinny chops that you see wrapped in plastic in the supermarket refrigerator cases. Rib and loin lamb chops for the grill should be cut at least 1-inch thick; your goal is to keep the center of the chop pink and rosy, and the outside crisp and browned. A thinner chop gives you less control because it turns in a flash from medium to well-done.

Even grilling trimmed lamb can cause flare-ups. Keep a water bottle handy to douse any flames, and move the chops around to cooler spots from time to time. Covering the grill also extinguishes flare-ups.

Grilled Chops with Orange and Rosemary

In this recipe, we use a touch of garlic and two very compatible seasonings — orange and rosemary — that partner perfectly with these grilled lamb chops.

Preparation time: *15 minutes*

Marinating time: *1 to 4 hours*

Grilling time: *12 minutes*

Yield: *4 servings*

4 loin lamb chops, cut 1-inch thick

2 tablespoons olive oil

1 large shallot, peeled and minced

2 cloves garlic, peeled and finely minced

1 tablespoon grated orange peel (about 1 large navel orange)

Salt and pepper to taste

4 sprigs fresh rosemary, each about 4 inches long

Olive oil for brushing rosemary sprigs

1 teaspoon balsamic vinegar or to taste

1 If necessary, trim all but about ¼ inch of fat from the edge of each chop.

2 Using a small bowl and a wooden spoon, or a mortar and pestle, lightly mash together the 2 tablespoons olive oil, shallot, garlic, orange peel, and salt and pepper. Brush all surfaces of the chops with the mixture. Place the chops in a shallow baking dish or in a large, resealable plastic bag. Cover the dish or close the bag, and refrigerate the chops for 1 to 4 hours, turning occasionally.

3 Prepare a medium-hot fire in a charcoal or gas grill.

4 Remove the chops from the flavored oil, reserving any extra. Brush the rosemary sprigs generously with olive oil and set them on a lightly oiled grid. Place 1 chop on each sprig. Grill the chops for 5 to 6 minutes per side for medium-rare, or until desired doneness, brushing each chop with the remaining marinade once before turning.

5 Place the chops on a serving platter; sprinkle about ¼ teaspoon balsamic vinegar over each chop and (if desired) additional salt and pepper.

 All of our cooking times are just good estimates. Actual cooking times depend on the temperature of the air, the intensity of your grill's heat, the thickness of the cut, and other factors. Make a small incision in the lamb chops with a thin, sharp knife a few minutes before you think they're done to avoid overcooking.

The Lowdown on Lamb Shoulders

Arm and blade lamb chops from the shoulder are not the most tender cuts of meat. They contain a fair amount of connective tissue that, when grilled quickly, remains somewhat unattractive and sinewy. Therefore, we recommend that only ardent lamb lovers grill shoulder chops.

 Ask your butcher to cut shoulder steaks a bit thinner than the rib and loin chops. Thinner cuts allow the marinade to more fully penetrate and soften the sinewy meat.

Lamb Shoulder Chops with Yogurt and Curry Marinade

If you do choose to grill shoulder chops, you'll find them loaded with flavor and a much better buy than loin or rib chops. Marinate the chops for several hours or overnight, using this Middle Eastern yogurt and spice mixture, to help soften some of the connective tissue.

Preparation time: *20 minutes*

Marinating time: *6 hours or overnight*

Grilling time: *12 to 14 minutes*

Yield: *4 servings*

(continued)

4 shoulder lamb chops, cut ³/₄-inch thick

2 teaspoons peeled and grated fresh ginger

1 large clove garlic, peeled and minced

1 teaspoon ground cumin

³/₄ teaspoon ground turmeric

¹/₄ teaspoon cayenne pepper

¹/₄ teaspoon salt, or to taste

¹/₂ cup plain lowfat yogurt

1 medium onion, peeled and quartered

2 tablespoons finely chopped cilantro leaves (optional)

1 If necessary, trim all but ¹/₄ inch of the fat from the edges of the chops; place chops in a shallow baking dish.

2 In a small bowl, combine the ginger, garlic, cumin, turmeric, cayenne pepper, and salt. Spread the spice mixture over both sides of the chops. In a blender, whirl the yogurt and onion for a few seconds into a coarse puree; pour the yogurt mixture over the chops in the baking dish, turning to coat. Cover the dish and marinate for 6 hours, or overnight.

3 Prepare a medium-hot fire in a charcoal or gas grill.

4 Remove the chops from the marinade, shaking off the excess; discard any remaining marinade. Grill the chops on a lightly oiled grid, 6 to 7 minutes per side for medium-rare, or until desired doneness, turning once.

5 Place the chops on a serving platter; sprinkle with additional salt and pepper and chopped cilantro leaves (if desired).

Go-With: Serve with a Tomato Chutney or Summer Squash Chutney (Chapter 6) or Yogurt Cucumber Salad (Chapter 7).

Vary It! This yogurt marinade is also delicious with lamb kebabs, leg steaks, and whole roasts, such as a butterflied leg of lamb. To cover these larger roasts, you need to double the recipe.

A Leg Up on Lamb

Lamb leg steaks can also be delicious on the grill, as in the following recipe.

Western Lamb Steaks

Ask your butcher to custom-cut lamb steaks from the leg of the lamb for this recipe. Each leg steak will probably weigh just under 1 pound, so two steaks are enough to serve four diners. This marinade, or basting sauce, also works with shoulder lamb chops or a butterflied leg. If you are really desperate for time, a bottle of your favorite barbecue sauce, especially one with hickory-smoked flavoring, also makes a very good sauce for lamb steaks.

Preparation time: *20 minutes*

Marinating time: *4 hours or overnight*

Grilling time: *10 to 14 minutes*

Yield: *4 servings*

2 lamb steaks, center cut from the leg, about ³/₄- to 1-inch thick

¹/₂ cup chili sauce

2 tablespoons cider vinegar

2 tablespoons water

1 small onion, peeled, halved, and thinly sliced

1 large clove garlic, peeled and minced

1 tablespoon Worcestershire sauce

1 teaspoon chili powder

¹/₂ teaspoon ground cumin

Generous dashes Tabasco sauce

Salt and pepper to taste

1 If necessary, trim all but about ¹/₄ inch of fat from the edges of the steaks; place steaks in a shallow baking dish or large, resealable plastic bag.

2 In a mixing bowl or glass measuring cup, combine the remaining ingredients, except the salt and pepper; pour the marinade over the lamb steaks, turning the steaks to coat them. Cover the dish or seal the bag, pressing out any air, and refrigerate 4 hours or overnight.

3 Prepare a medium-hot fire in a charcoal or gas grill.

4 Remove the steaks from the marinade, reserving marinade. Sprinkle the steaks with salt and pepper. Place the steaks on a lightly oiled grid. Grill 5 to 7 minutes per side for medium-rare, or until desired doneness, brushing once with marinade before turning.

Go-With: Try Western Lamb Steaks with the Middle Eastern Rice recipe in Chapter 7.

We recommend that you keep all meats, fish, and poultry refrigerated until you're ready to grill. However, you'll get a better initial sear, particularly with fatty meats like lamb, if the meat is near room temperature or very nearly so. Our advice is to remove the lamb from the refrigerator as you prepare the fire. By the time the grill is preheated, the meat will be close to room temperature without sustaining any effects from airborne bacteria. Don't let meat, fish, or poultry stand at room temperature longer than 30 minutes.

Racking Up Lamb for the Grill

A rack of lamb may contain as many as eight ribs, but is more often cut by the butcher into individual portions of three or four chops per person.

Some cooks prefer to have their racks *French cut* so that the top of the rib bones are stripped entirely of their meat and fat. However, we recommend leaving the rib bone meat alone and intact, shown in Figure 14-2. Lamb ribs are a lot like pork ribs — tender, juicy, full of flavor, and great on the grill.

Figure 14-2: Preparing a rack of lamb for the grill.

Although some people consider rack of lamb to be a rather dainty dish, we think it's really finger-licking food. You'll want to sink your teeth into the tiny morsels of meat around the back and rib bones and, eschewing fork and knife, pick up the small chops with your fingers.

Trim (or have your butcher trim) most of the fat from the back of the ribs, leaving only a paper-thin layer. Slice 2 to 3 inches between each rib down towards the meatier "eye" end. Slash also about 1 inch through the back-bone to separate each chop slightly at the bottom of the rack, as shown in Figure 14-2. The rack should remain in one piece, but these slashes allow you to apply basting sauces and seasonings with better results.

Rack of Lamb with Hoisin Marinade

Because orange juice and honey are the principal ingredients in this recipe, the rack of lamb is grilled indirectly to prevent the meat from cooking too fast and charring. Indirect cooking is an excellent method of cooking racks and roasts — even if sweet ingredients are not present in the recipe. The final result is a moist and juicy piece of meat that needs little attending. In this recipe, the rack is left on the grill for at least 20 minutes before turning. This marinade is terrific with any cut of lamb, from chops to leg, and also works with pork and poultry.

Preparation time: 20 minutes

Marinating time: 12 to 24 hours

Grilling time: 45 minutes

Yield: 2 servings

1 8-rib rack of lamb, about 2¹/₂ pounds	1 tablespoon plus 1 teaspoon honey
²/₃ cup fresh orange juice	2 large cloves garlic, peeled and minced
3 tablespoons hoisin sauce	2 teaspoons peeled and grated fresh ginger
3 tablespoons soy sauce	
2 tablespoons olive oil	Salt and pepper to taste

1 Using a sharp knife, cut the rack in half, so that each half has 4 ribs. Make a 1-inch cut between each chop at the backbone end to make carving easier. Make a 2-inch cut between each rib down towards the meaty "eye" end. Trim the fat, leaving a paper-thin layer on the back of each rack (refer to Figure 14-2). (A good butcher can do all of this, if you prefer.)

2 In a small mixing bowl, make the hoisin marinade by combining all the remaining ingredients, except the salt and pepper.

(continued)

3 Place the lamb racks in a large, resealable plastic bag or a shallow baking dish; pour the marinade over the lamb. Try to work pieces of the ginger and garlic into the slashed areas. Seal the bag (press out all the air in the bag to surround the rack with the marinade) or cover the dish, and refrigerate 12 to 24 hours, turning occasionally.

4 Remove the lamb from the refrigerator and let it stand for about 30 minutes before grilling. Meanwhile, prepare a hot, indirect fire in a charcoal or gas grill, with a drip plan (half filled with water) in place. (For complete directions on how to build an indirect fire, turn to Chapter 1.)

5 Remove the rack of lamb from the marinade. Shake off the excess marinade and re-serve any remaining marinade. Season the lamb on both sides with salt and pepper.

6 Place the lamb on the grid, fat side down, over the drip pan on the side without heat. Cover and grill for 45 to 55 minutes, turning every 20 minutes, or until an instant-read thermometer registers 140° to 150° for rare to medium-rare or 150° to 155° for medium. Add hot briquettes to a charcoal fire after 30 to 40 minutes, or when necessary, to maintain heat. If desired, during the last few minutes of grilling, move the lamb to the side of the grid directly above the heat for 3 to 5 minutes per side, to brown the meat more thoroughly.

7 Remove the lamb from the grid and place on a carving platter. Cover the meat loosely with foil and let rest for about 5 minutes. Meanwhile, transfer the reserved marinade to a small saucepan. Boil for 1 to 2 minutes, stirring frequently. Carve the lamb into individual chops; spoon the sauce over the chops and serve.

Go-With: Rice, noodles, or whole potatoes roasted in a covered grill (see Chapter 7) make excellent accompaniments to this lamb dish.

The heat of a charcoal grill is much more intense than the heat of a gas grill, resulting in shorter cooking times, especially when you are using an indirect fire. Whatever your grill style, be sure to use a meat thermometer and to start checking the internal temperature about 15 to 20 minutes before the end of the estimated cooking time to get a good indication of how fast (or slow) the food is cooking. And remember, the internal temperature increases more rapidly during the final minutes of cooking, so check the meat thermometer often during the final minutes.

Grill Roasting a Leg

You can roast a 5- to 7-pound leg of lamb in a covered grill, with or without a rotisserie unit, with delicious results.

Prepare the leg for the grill by first trimming any large pieces of fat. A thin, transparent layer of tissue, called the *fell,* lies between fat and the meat. Don't remove this — it keeps the meat moist as it grills. With the tip of a sharp knife, make a half dozen or more incisions, or very small pockets, all over the leg. Insert slivers of peeled garlic, as shown in Figure 14-3, into each slit and then rub the leg with olive oil. Sprinkle the leg with pepper, grated lemon peel, and 1 tablespoon of a fresh herb such as rosemary, marjoram, or thyme. Grill, covered, over a medium, indirect fire (see Chapter 1 for more specific directions on building an indirect fire in a gas or charcoal grill), with a drip pan under the meat that is half-filled with water, broth, or apple juice. (If using charcoal, ignite 50 to 60 briquettes and bank them to one side of the grill after they are ashy gray. Replenish the fire with additional charcoal every 30 to 40 minutes.) Grill until an instant-read or oven thermometer registers 140 to 150 degrees for rare to medium-rare or 150 to 155 degrees for medium. If using a regular meat thermometer, insert it into the thickest part of the roast, without touching any bone, before grilling. Approximate grilling time is 15 to 20 minutes per pound, but start checking for doneness 30 minutes before the estimated final cooking time. Let the roast rest for about 10 to 15 minutes, loosely covered with foil, before carving into thin slices. Be sure to serve any remaining cutting-board juices with the meat.

A roasted or grilled leg of lamb offers meat of varying degrees of doneness. The meat at the thin shank end, which is close to the bone, will be brown and probably well-done. The meat at the thicker end is ideally quite pink and medium-rare.

The internal temperature of a roast will rise about 5 degrees after it's removed from the grill or oven, causing it to cook a little more. Remove the roast when the thermometer registers about 5 degrees less than the desired final temperature.

Inserting Garlic into a Leg of Lamb

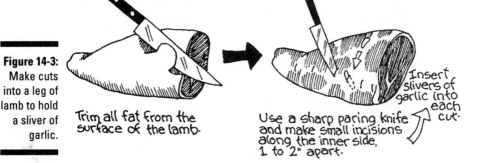

Figure 14-3: Make cuts into a leg of lamb to hold a sliver of garlic.

Trim all fat from the surface of the lamb.

Use a sharp paring knife and make small incisions along the inner side, 1 to 2" apart.

Insert slivers of garlic into each cut.

Giving Your Lamb Butterflies

After you try butterflied and grilled leg of lamb, you'll probably agree that it's one of the best meals you can serve to a crowd of backyard guests. To *butterfly* a leg, you bone it, slit the leg lengthwise, and spread it flat. The boned meat more readily accepts the flavors of its marinade, the grilling time is quick and even, the carving is a cinch, and the taste is delicious. Have your butcher butterfly the leg and trim the fat, or do it yourself by following the instructions in Figure 14-4.

Marinades for butterflied lamb can be as simple as salad dressing. (We know a few excellent home cooks who proudly announce that the best marinade for butterflied leg of lamb is a bottle of Wish-Bone Italian Dressing.) Or you may want to use something a bit fancier, perhaps a multi-ingredient curry marinade. Lamb, with its nearly gamey taste, readily accepts the flavors of yogurt, curry spices, red or white wine, lemon, hot peppers, black pepper, chili powders, balsamic vinegar, assorted herbs, and garlic — the best and simplest lamb seasoning. Follow your own likes and dislikes into your kitchen lab to assemble a marinade for a butterflied leg of lamb. Ask yourself: "Do I want a hint of orange, lemon, or rosemary? Do I want a slightly sweet taste or something more spicy? Do I like the pungency of balsamic or cider vinegar, or the complexity of a fruity red wine?" And then go for it.

Figure 14-4:
When a leg of lamb is butterflied, the bone is removed and the meat lies flat, resembling a butterfly.

How to Butterfly a Leg of Lamb

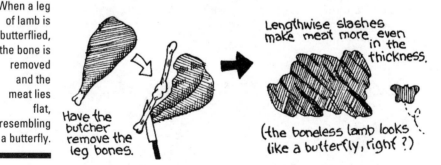

Have the butcher remove the leg bones.

Lengthwise slashes make meat more even in the thickness.

(the boneless lamb looks like a butterfly, right?)

Butterflied Leg of Lamb with Honey-Mustard Dressing

The small, boneless leg of lamb used in this recipe is available in most major super-markets and is perfect for a family of 4 to 6. The leg is often wrapped in a twine bag or netting. Remove the netting and lay the meat flat in the dressing. Be sure to let it marinate for at least 24 hours to completely absorb the vinegar, honey, and mustard flavors.

If you want to feed a crowd of 10 or more, the ingredient amounts can be doubled for a bone-in 6- to 8-pound leg that weighs about 5 pounds butterflied. Or you can use the same marinade with wonderful success on about 2 pounds of lamb for kebabs. A final note: If you really love garlic, use the full 2 cloves; for less garlic flavor, use 1 large clove. Check out the color photo section for a look at this dish.

Preparation time: *20 minutes*

Marinating time: *24 hours*

Grilling time: *25 to 30 minutes*

Yield: *4 to 6 servings*

A half or small butterflied leg of lamb (about $2^1/_4$ to $2^1/_2$ pounds without the bone)

1 to 2 cloves garlic, peeled and thinly sliced

6 tablespoons extra-virgin olive oil

$^1/_4$ cup balsamic vinegar

2 tablespoons honey

2 tablespoons Dijon-style mustard

Salt and pepper to taste

Chopped parsley for garnish

1 Trim all fat from the surface of the lamb. Using a sharp paring knife, make small incisions or cuts along the inner side (the side that held the bone), about 1 to 2 inches apart. Insert a sliver of garlic into each small incision.

2 Place the lamb in a large, shallow baking dish or resealable plastic bag.

3 In a small bowl, whisk together the oil, vinegar, honey, and mustard; pour the dressing over the lamb and turn to coat both sides. Cover the dish or seal the bag, pressing out any air, and refrigerate for 24 hours, turning occasionally.

4 Drain the lamb, reserving the dressing. Sprinkle the lamb with salt and pepper on both sides.

5 Prepare a medium fire in a charcoal or gas grill.

(continued)

6 Place the lamb on a lightly oiled grid. Grill, turning the meat about every 8 to 10 minutes, for a total of 25 to 30 minutes or until the internal temperature in the thickest part of the meat registers 135° to 140° for rare, 145° to 150° for medium-rare, or 150° to 155° for medium. Baste the lamb twice with the reserved marinade during the first 15 to 18 minutes of grilling.

7 Remove the lamb, place on a carving board, and let it rest, covered loosely with foil, 10 minutes before cutting against the grain into thin slices. Serve the meat with the carving board juices and sprinkle with chopped parsley.

Go-With: Suggested side dishes include Grilled Potato Planks, Garlic-Grilled Porto-bellos, or Grilled Tomatoes with Basil and Bread Crumb Stuffing (all in Chapter 17); Tomato Chutney or Summer Squash Chutney (Chapter 6) and any of the salads in Chapter 7. Make sandwiches with any leftovers, spreading the bread with honey mustard or a little fruit chutney.

If you're carving the meat and think that it needs a little more cooking, simply place it back on the grid for a few minutes.

Move the meat away from the hot spots of the fire if you see that it is charring or cooking too quickly.

Chapter 15

Birds of a Feather

In This Chapter

▶ Choosing cuts of chicken for the grill

▶ Finding the secrets of grilling chicken

▶ Brining chicken

▶ Grilled turkey — it's not just for Thanksgiving anymore!

▶ Discovering wild game birds, Rock Cornish hens, and little chickens for the grill

Chicken and other types of fowl offer more than great taste when prepared on the grill. They can also provide a healthy, nutritious meal.

Almost the whole world loves chicken, and for good reason: It can be used in so many recipes, it is a fairly inexpensive meat, and as far as we know, there are no religious taboos against it.

The mild flavor of chicken appeals to just about everyone but a strict vegan, and the meat of chicken adapts extremely well to marinades, rubs, and seasonings. When choosing chicken, keep in mind that legs and thighs are dark meat and they take a tad longer to cook on the grill. The white-meat breasts cook quickly and, if not watched carefully, can dry out.

If you are getting a little tired of using only chicken in your grilling repertoire, this chapter is for you. We share delicious turkey recipes — including one for a whole turkey! — and then give you tips for grilling up game birds, Rock Cornish game hens, and even poussins.

Free, free on the range

Free-range chickens are not penned and have the freedom to roam a yard eating both the natural foods that chickens scratch for and the feed provided by the grower. This is a much more expensive process than penning tens of thousands of chickens into a factory space and feeding them in a regimented fashion. But free-range chickens make for a tastier bird. However, they are not always the most tender bird, because they do roam around actively.

Handle Chicken with Care

Although American poultry production is carefully monitored and the facilities comply with all government sanitary and safety guidelines, salmonella and other bacteria that can cause sickness in human beings may still be found in chicken. Fortunately, these bacteria are killed off if the chicken is cooked until the internal temperature reaches 160 degrees for boneless, skinless breasts; 170 degrees for bone-in breasts and leg quarters; and 180 degrees for whole birds.

Here are a few guidelines for safe handling and preparation of chicken in your kitchen:

- Always keep poultry refrigerated, even when in a marinade, until it's ready for cooking.

- Always thaw frozen poultry in the refrigerator, never at room temperature. You can usually thaw a chicken this way overnight.

- If any part of the bird has an odd or "off" odor, discard the entire chicken.

- Before cooking the chicken, wash it, inside and out, with cold water and then pat it dry with paper towels. Discard the paper towels.

- Thoroughly wash your hands, the utensils, and the work surface when you're done.

Grilling chicken breasts

Chicken breasts offer plenty of interesting grilling options. They can be grilled with or without their skin and bones; seasoned with any number of alluring rubs, sauces, and marinades; and sliced into thin strips or thick cubes for sizzling kebabs. (See Chapter 9 for kebab recipes.)

Breast meat is juicier and more flavorful if the breast is grilled with the skin intact. However, the skin contains a lot of fat that can cause dangerous flare-ups. You may want to opt for skinless breasts or pull the skin off before grilling. We start this section with two easy skinless breast recipes that grill in about 10 quick minutes (another advantage of cooking without the skin and bone — it's so fast).

You can grill chicken breasts with the skin intact to add flavor and moisture to the meat, and then reduce calories by removing the skin before serving.

Jerk-Seasoned Chicken Breasts

The smoky heat of the grill, combined with spices common to Jamaican jerk seasoning — cinnamon, allspice, cayenne pepper, thyme, and jalapeño pepper — give these chicken breasts their splendid taste.

Preparation time: *15 minutes*

Marinating time: *6 hours or overnight*

Grilling time: *10 minutes*

Yield: *4 to 6 servings*

8 boneless, skinless chicken breast halves (about 2 to 3 pounds)	*1 small jalapeño pepper, seeded and finely chopped*
¹/₄ cup vegetable oil	*1 teaspoon brown sugar, packed*
¹/₄ cup orange juice	*¹/₂ teaspoon kosher salt, or to taste*
3 scallions, finely chopped (green and white parts)	*¹/₂ teaspoon ground allspice*
4 medium cloves garlic, peeled and finely chopped	*¹/₂ teaspoon dried leaf thyme*
2 tablespoons lime juice	*¹/₂ teaspoon cinnamon*
2 tablespoons soy sauce	*¹/₄ teaspoon cayenne pepper*
	¹/₄ teaspoon nutmeg

1 Trim the breasts of any loose fat; rinse them under cold running water and pat dry with paper towels.

2 In a medium bowl, combine the remaining ingredients, beating with a fork or whisk to incorporate the spices into the oil and orange juice.

3 Place the breasts in a large, resealable plastic bag or shallow dish; pour the marinade over the breasts. Seal the bag, pressing out any air, or cover the dish; refrigerate 6 hours or overnight, turning occasionally to coat the breasts in the marinade.

(continued)

4 Preheat a medium-hot fire in a charcoal or gas grill.

5 Remove the chicken breasts from the marinade; discard the marinade. Place the chicken breasts on an oiled grill grid. Grill for 10 to 12 minutes or until done, turning every 4 to 5 minutes. To test for doneness, cut into the breasts; the meat should be white and moist, with no sign of pink.

Vary It! To grill chicken breasts with skin and bone, place the breast pieces, skin side down over a medium-hot fire. Grill, uncovered, for 6 to 7 minutes or until the skin is browned. Turn the breasts over and grill for another 6 to 7 minutes or until lightly browned. Cover the grill and continue cooking for 10 to 15 minutes or until done, turning once. The chicken is cooked when an instant-read thermometer registers 170° in the thickest part, or when the meat shows no sign of pink near the bone.

Lemon Chicken Breasts

The lovely marinade of fresh lemon, olive oil, and herbs in this recipe keeps these skinless chicken breasts moist and plump on the grill.

Preparation time: 15 minutes

Marinating time: 2 to 6 hours

Grilling time: 10 minutes

Yield: 4 to 6 servings

8 boneless, skinless chicken breast halves (about 2 to 3 pounds)	*2 large cloves garlic, peeled and minced*
$^1/_2$ cup extra-virgin olive oil	*2 tablespoons chopped fresh oregano, or 2 teaspoons dried oregano*
$^1/_2$ cup fresh lemon juice	*1 teaspoon salt, or to taste*
Grated peel of 1 lemon (2 to 3 teaspoons)	*$^1/_2$ teaspoon pepper*

1 Trim the breasts of any loose fat; rinse them under cold running water and pat dry with paper towels.

2 Place the breasts in a large, resealable plastic bag or a shallow, non-reactive baking dish. In a small mixing bowl or large glass measuring cup, combine the olive oil, lemon juice, lemon peel, garlic, oregano, and salt and pepper; pour the marinade over the breasts in the bag or dish. Cover the dish or seal the bag, pressing out any air; refrigerate for 2 to 6 hours, turning the breasts occasionally to coat in the marinade.

3 Prepare a medium-hot fire in a charcoal or gas grill.

4 Remove the chicken breasts from the marinade; discard the marinade. Place the breasts on a well-oiled grid for 10 to 12 minutes or until done, turning every 4 to 5 minutes. To test for doneness, cut into the breasts; meat should be white and moist with no sign of pink.

Vary It! If you want dinner in a hurry and don't have time to assemble a marinade from scratch, substitute your favorite bottled vinaigrette or Italian salad dressing. Marinate 4 to 6 boneless, skinless breast halves for 20 to 30 minutes in about 1 cup of dressing, being sure to shake off the excess marinade before grilling, to avoid flare-ups. If you wish, about 2 minutes before the breasts are done, top each with a thin slice of Swiss, provolone, or Monterey Jack cheese. Cover and grill until the cheese is melted and the breasts are cooked through.

 Covering the grill automatically raises the grill's temperature. To maintain a medium heat, adjust the heat setting on a gas grill or close the vents on a charcoal grill. Closing the cover vents lowers the heat, while opening them adds more oxygen to the fire and increases the heat.

 When marinating any food, remember to use a non-reactive container — one made of plastic, glass, ceramic, or other nonmetallic material. Certain metals, such as aluminum, react with acidic ingredients like lemon juice or vinegar, causing the food and marinade to discolor.

Just wingin' it

Once discarded by many people as not worth eating, the chicken wing has become one of the most popular parts of the bird, thanks, in large part, to a cook in Buffalo, New York.

Back on the night of October 30, 1964, at the Anchor Bar in that city, owner Teressa Bellissimo's sons and their friends came in just before midnight with a roaring appetite. Mrs. Bellissimo had received an oversupply of chicken wings that day, so she popped them in the deep fryer and mixed together a little margarine and hot sauce as well as a blue cheese dressing. The boys gobbled it up, others in the bar loved the idea, and the Buffalo Chicken Wing was born.

Spicy Chili Chicken Wings

In this recipe, the delicate meat of a chicken wing is nestled around flavorful bone and wrapped in succulent skin. Serve these finger-lickin' grilled wings as part of a light dinner or make up a big batch when you need inexpensive party appetizers for a hungry crowd.

Preparation time: *20 minutes*

Marinating time: *2 to 4 hours*

Grilling time: *10 to 15 minutes*

Yield: *4 main dish servings or 8 to 10 appetizer servings*

3 to 3¹/₂ pounds chicken wings (about 15 to 18 wings)

3 tablespoons olive oil

3 tablespoons fresh lime juice

4 large cloves garlic, peeled and minced

2 teaspoons ground cumin

2 teaspoons ground coriander

2 teaspoons paprika

1 teaspoon peeled and grated ginger

1 teaspoon salt, or to taste

¹/₂ teaspoon hot chili powder or cayenne pepper

¹/₂ teaspoon cinnamon

1 Rinse the chicken wings under cold running water and pat dry with paper towels. Cut off the wing tips at the joints and discard the tips. (Or wrap and freeze the tips to use later to add flavor to canned or homemade soups and stocks.)

2 Combine all the remaining ingredients in a large, resealable plastic bag or mixing bowl, blending them well.

3 Add the chicken wings; toss well to coat the wings in the oil-spice mixture. Seal the bag, pressing out any air, or cover the bowl; refrigerate for 2 to 4 hours.

4 Prepare a medium-hot fire in a charcoal or gas grill.

5 Place the wings on a well-oiled grid. Grill, uncovered, for 10 to 15 minutes or until done, turning with tongs every 2 to 3 minutes to prevent burning and to ensure even cooking. To test for doneness, cut into the thickest part of the wing; the meat should be white, with no trace of pink, and the juices should run clear.

Orange-Garlic Chicken Wings

This dish has a slightly Asian flavor that comes from the soy sauce, the orange, and the garlic. It's as simple as any dish you can possibly make on the grill.

Preparation time: 20 minutes

Marinating time: 6 hours or overnight

Grilling time: 10 to 15 minutes

Yield: 4 main dish servings or 8 to 10 appetizer servings

3 pounds chicken wings (about 15 wings)

¹/₄ cup peanut or corn oil

¹/₄ cup sesame oil

2¹/₂ tablespoons grated orange peel

2 tablespoons soy sauce

1¹/₂ tablespoons peeled and minced garlic

2 scallions, green and white parts, finely chopped

2 teaspoons peeled and grated ginger

1 tablespoon plus 2 teaspoons Szechwan peppercorns (see Figure 15-1), roasted and crushed (see "Szechwan peppercorns" sidebar)

1 to 2 tablespoons kosher salt, or according to taste

1 Rinse the chicken wings under cold running water and pat dry with paper towels. Cut off the wing tips at the joint, discarding tips. (Or wrap and freeze the tips to use later to add flavor to canned or homemade soups and stocks.) Place the wings in a large, resealable plastic bag or a shallow baking dish.

2 In a medium mixing bowl or glass measuring cup, combine the peanut and sesame oils, orange peel, soy sauce, garlic, scallions, ginger, and 2 teaspoons of the peppercorns. Pour the marinade over the chicken wings in the bag, or dish, turning to coat all sides. Seal the bag, pressing out any air, or cover the dish, and refrigerate for 6 hours, or overnight, tossing occasionally to coat the wings in the marinade.

3 Prepare a medium-hot fire in a charcoal or gas grill.

4 Remove the wings from the marinade; discard the marinade. Place the chicken wings on a lightly oiled grid. Grill, uncovered, for 10 to 15 minutes or until done, turning every 4 to 5 minutes to ensure even cooking and prevent the wings from charring. To test for doneness, cut into the thickest part of the wing; the meat should be white, with no trace of pink, and the juices should run clear.

5 Place the grilled wings on a large platter. Combine the remaining 1 tablespoon Szechwan peppercorns and the kosher salt; sprinkle the mixture over the wings to taste.

Szechwan peppercorns

Though they resemble black peppercorns, Szechwan peppercorns (also known as Chinese pepper) are not part of the black and white peppercorn family at all. This mildly hot, aromatic spice is actually a berry with a tiny seed, from a tree that is native to the Szechwan province of China. To release their flavorful oils, heat the berries in a dry, heavy-bottomed skillet just until they give off an aromatic scent.

Discard any that blacken. Then crush by using a mortar and pestle or place them on a cutting board and press with the bottom of a heavy skillet. (See figure below.)

Szechwan peppercorns are available in spice sections of Asian markets or other specialty food stores and are often used in marinades and sauces with other Chinese seasonings.

How to Crush Szechwan Peppercorns

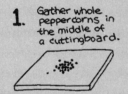

1. Gather whole peppercorns in the middle of a cuttingboard.

2. Use the heel of your hand to press the bottom edge of a pan.

3. Repeat Steps 1 & 2 until peppercorns are crushed to desired size.

Figure 15-1: These are not really peppercorns, but berries with mild spiciness.

We're Hot!

szechwan peppercorns

Chicken quarters — drawn and grilled

Choosing chicken quarters simplifies the grilling process because you have fewer pieces to watch and turn. And some grilling chefs believe that quartered pieces retain their moisture and succulence better than individual pieces of chicken. As a bonus, chicken quarters look so inviting on the plate and are especially good as a special occasion or company dish.

Grilled Chicken Quarters with Barbecue Sauce

This recipe calls for two easy steps — preparing the barbecue sauce and grilling the chicken quarters. We think that you'll like the way sweet, sour, and spicy flavors come together in this barbecue sauce (you can see an example in the color photo section of this book). If you want to crank up the heat, add more Tabasco.

Preparation time: 25 minutes

Grilling time: 25 to 30 minutes

Yield: 4 servings

Barbecue Sauce

1 cup ketchup

$^1/_2$ medium onion, peeled and finely chopped

3 tablespoons fresh lemon juice

3 tablespoons Worcestershire sauce

1 tablespoon olive oil

1 tablespoon molasses

$1^1/_2$ teaspoons cider vinegar

1 teaspoon Dijon-style mustard

1 clove garlic, peeled and minced

$^3/_4$ teaspoon salt, or to taste

$^3/_4$ teaspoon Tabasco sauce

$^1/_4$ teaspoon dried thyme leaves

Combine all the ingredients in a medium saucepan; bring to a boil, lower the heat, and simmer for 10 minutes, stirring occasionally. The sauce can be kept, covered, in the refrigerator up to a week.

Grilled Chicken Quarters

1 whole chicken (about 3 to $3^1/_2$ pounds), quartered

2 tablespoons olive oil

Salt and pepper to taste

1 Prepare a medium-hot fire in a charcoal or gas grill.

2 As the fire preheats, rinse the chicken under cold running water and pat dry with paper towels. Rub the chicken quarters with the oil, covering all surfaces; sprinkle all over with salt and pepper.

(continued)

3 Place the chicken parts, skin side down, on a well-oiled grid, directly over the heat, and grill for 15 minutes, turning every 4 to 5 minutes.

4 Baste the quarters thoroughly on both sides with the barbecue sauce. Continue grilling for another 7 to 10 minutes or until the chicken is done, turning every 3 to 4 minutes. Cut into the quarters to test for doneness; when cooked, the juices run clear, and the meat near the bone is no longer pink.

Keep that chicken moving!

Chicken, especially with its skin on, can be *seared* — browned very quickly — and can then turn charcoal-black just as quickly, without the inside cooked at all. This is something you want to avoid. The key to grilling chicken over direct heat is to keep turning the pieces and to move them to hotter or cooler spots on the grid when some pieces seem to be cooking faster than others. Follow these steps when using direct heat to grill chicken pieces with bone and skin:

1. Thicker, dark-meat pieces, which include the thighs and legs, take longer to cook than white-meat pieces. Place these pieces on the grill first, on the hottest part of your grid.

2. Add the other parts of the bird — the breast and wings — after about 10 minutes, or when the legs and thighs have browned on both sides.

3. Throughout the process, continually turn the pieces from side to side, or to hotter or cooler areas of the grid as necessary, making sure that none of them are cooking too fast or turning black.

4. When grilling chicken directly over the heat, don't leave it unattended. You have to be there, and you have to monitor it. The result of your attention will be a crispy, smoky chicken that's juicy inside and full of the flavor of the grill.

5. If you use an instant-read thermometer to check for doneness, the boneless, skinless breast meat should register 160 degrees, and bone-in breast and thigh meat should reach 170 degrees. To check for doneness without a thermometer, make a small cut into the thickest part of the chicken. The juices should run clear, and the meat should show no trace of pink.

6. Move any fully cooked pieces to the edges of the grid to keep them warm until the remaining pieces finish cooking.

Grilled Lime Chicken with Onion Compote

In this recipe, chicken quarters are first soaked in a luscious lime marinade, then grilled, and finally smothered with onions that are slightly caramelized from long, slow, top-of-the-stove cooking. The result is divine.

Preparation time: *45 minutes*

Marinating time: *6 hours or overnight*

Grilling time: *20 to 25 minutes*

Yield: *4 servings*

1 3- to 3^1/$_2$-pound chicken, quartered

^{1}/$_4$ cup olive oil

^{3}/$_4$ cup lime juice

Grated peel of 1^1/$_2$ limes

2 cloves garlic, peeled and minced

^{1}/$_2$ teaspoon coarsely cracked black pepper

Salt to taste

^{1}/$_4$ cup corn oil

3 Spanish onions, or 4 medium yellow onions, peeled, halved, and sliced about ^{1}/$_4$-inch thick

^{1}/$_2$ teaspoon dried thyme leaves

2 bay leaves, crushed

Pepper to taste

1 Rinse the chicken under cold running water and pat dry with paper towels; place the chicken in a large, resealable plastic bag or a shallow baking dish.

2 In a small mixing bowl or large glass measuring cup, combine the olive oil, lime juice, lime peel, garlic, cracked black pepper, and salt. Pour the marinade over the chicken in the bag or dish. Seal the bag, pressing out any air, or cover the dish; refrigerate for 6 hours, or overnight, turning occasionally to coat the chicken in the marinade.

3 Prepare a medium-hot fire in a covered charcoal or gas grill.

4 As the grill preheats, make the onion compote. In a medium skillet, heat the corn oil over medium heat; add the onions and sauté for 15 minutes, turning frequently. Stir in the thyme, bay leaves, and salt and pepper; continue cooking for 10 minutes or longer, until the onions are well browned, turning frequently. When done, remove from heat and set aside.

(continued)

5 Remove the chicken from the marinade, shaking off some of the excess; reserve the remaining marinade. Season the chicken lightly with salt and pepper and place on a well-oiled grid, skin side down. Cover and cook for 20 to 25 minutes or until the juices run clear and the meat near the bone is no longer pink, turning every 4 minutes.

6 Add the reserved marinade to the onions in the skillet and simmer over medium heat for 5 minutes. When the chicken is done, remove it from the grill onto a serving platter; spoon the onion compote over the chicken and serve immediately.

Lemon-Cilantro Chicken with Garlic-Ginger Mayonnaise

The fragrant marinade in this recipe is made with cilantro, fresh ginger, garlic, soy sauce, curry powder, and hot chili powder — ingredients all common to Pacific Rim cuisine. The mayonnaise garnish, laced with ginger, garlic, and lemon juice, gives it an American twist.

Preparation time: *30 minutes*

Marinating time: *6 hours or overnight*

Grilling time: *20 to 25 minutes*

Yield: *4 servings*

1 3- to 3¹/₂-pound chicken, quartered and scored (score by slashing through the skin and into the meat on both sides of each piece, using a sharp knife)

2 tablespoons soy sauce

1 tablespoon corn or vegetable oil

1 tablespoon peeled and grated fresh ginger

Grated peel of 1 lemon

2 scallions, trimmed and finely chopped

6 sprigs cilantro leaves and stems, chopped

2 cloves garlic, peeled and minced

³/₄ teaspoon curry powder

¹/₂ teaspoon hot chili powder

Salt and pepper to taste

1 Rinse the chicken under cold running water and pat dry with paper towels.

2 Place the chicken in a large, resealable plastic bag or a shallow baking dish.

3 In a small mixing bowl or glass measuring cup, combine the remaining ingredients; pour the marinade over the chicken in the bag or dish. Seal the bag, pressing out any air, or cover the dish; refrigerate for 6 hours or overnight, turning the chicken occasionally to coat in the marinade.

4 Prepare a medium-hot fire in a charcoal or gas grill.

5 Remove the chicken from the marinade, shaking off a bit of the excess. Season the chicken with salt and pepper; place, skin side down, on an oiled grid. Cover and grill for 20 to 25 minutes, turning every 4 minutes, until the juices run clear and the meat is no longer pink near the bone. Serve with Garlic-Ginger Mayonnaise (see the following recipe) and Grilled Asparagus (Chapter 17).

Garlic-Ginger Mayonnaise

Yield: *About ²/₃ cup*

²/₃ cup mayonnaise	1 tablespoon fresh lemon juice
1¹/₂ teaspoons peeled and grated fresh ginger	Salt and pepper to taste
2 cloves garlic, peeled and minced	

In a small mixing bowl, combine all the ingredients. Cover and refrigerate until ready to use with Lemon-Cilantro Chicken. You can make this mayonnaise ahead and store it, covered, in the refrigerator for up to 1 week.

Vary It! Garlic-Ginger Mayonnaise is also delicious with grilled fish (Chapter 16).

It's thigh time to grill some legs

The legs and thighs of chicken are dark meat with rich flavor. They are delicious grilled and lend themselves to being eaten with your fingers — always one of our prime considerations when grilling for a party!

Moroccan Chicken Legs and Thighs

The marinade in this recipe contains a good amount of honey, so to avoid scorching the skin, we use both direct and indirect grilling methods. (See Chapter 3 for instructions on how to grill indirectly.) For the first 5 minutes, the chicken pieces are placed directly over the fire to brown and crisp the skin. Be sure to hover over them at this point, flipping the pieces every 2 to 3 minutes. They should be nicely browned but not blackened. When the pieces are moved over to the side of the grid without any heat, you can relax and go grab a cold soda and a handful of chips.

Preparation time: 20 minutes

Marinating time: 6 hours or overnight

Grilling time: 35 to 40 minutes

Yield: 4 servings

4 chicken legs and thighs (about 2¹/₂ to 3 pounds total)

¹/₄ cup olive oil

¹/₄ cup honey

¹/₄ cup mixed, chopped fresh mint and parsley

¹/₄ cup plus 2 tablespoons fresh lemon juice

2 teaspoons grated lemon peel

2 large cloves garlic, peeled and minced

2 teaspoons peeled and grated fresh ginger

1 teaspoon ground cumin

¹/₄ teaspoon crushed red pepper flakes

¹/₈ teaspoon cayenne pepper

Salt and black pepper to taste

1 Rinse the chicken pieces under cold running water and pat dry with paper towels. Unless you purchased the chicken as separate pieces, divide the legs from the thighs by cutting through the thigh-leg joint with a sharp knife. Place the pieces in a large, resealable plastic bag or a large, shallow baking dish.

2 In a small mixing bowl or glass measuring cup, combine the olive oil, honey, mint and parsley, lemon juice, lemon peel, garlic, ginger, cumin, red pepper, cayenne pepper, and salt and black pepper. Pour the marinade over the chicken, turning to coat all sides. Cover and refrigerate for 6 hours or overnight, turning occasionally.

3 Prepare an indirect, medium-hot fire in a covered charcoal or gas grill. (Turn to Chapter 1 for instructions about building an indirect fire.) Place a drip pan under the side of the grill without heat.

4 Remove the chicken from the marinade, reserving the marinade. Place the chicken pieces, skin side down, on a lightly oiled grid, directly over the heat. Grill until well browned on both sides, turning every 2 to 3 minutes. (At this point, you need to hover over the grilling pieces to prevent the skin from burning.) Move the pieces over to the side of the grill without heat; baste with the reserved marinade. Cover the grill and cook for 15 minutes. Turn and baste again with any remaining marinade; cover and cook for 15 to 20 minutes more or until done. To test for doneness, cut into the chicken; the juices should run clear, and the meat near the bone should show no sign of pink. Place the chicken on a serving platter and serve with Tomato and Red Onion Salad. (See Chapter 7.)

Brining a whole chicken

Brining is an age-old process of soaking food in a solution of salt, water (and sometimes, sugar) to preserve it. However, brining can also be used to increase the amount of liquid inside food cells and make food juicy, tender, and full of flavor. Think of brining as a long, deep marinade, but without an acidic ingredient (such as lemon or vinegar). You can enhance the flavor of a salty brine with citrus peel, fresh ginger, cloves, garlic, hot peppers, peppercorns, and most herbs.

All poultry (and other meats, too) should be brined in a non-reactive container made of glass, plastic, or ceramic material — never aluminum. Salt reacts chemically with aluminum to discolor the brine and give the soaking food an undesirable flavor. You can place a weight, such as a heavy plate, on the food to completely submerge it in the brine. Refrigerate the brining food until it's fully seasoned, stirring the mixture occasionally.

After removing the chicken from the brine, rinse it thoroughly in cold water and pat dry with paper towels. You can leave the bird nearly unseasoned (adding only black pepper) or use the seasonings that we recommend in the recipe for Dry Poultry Rub for Brined Chicken. Be sure not to add extra salt until after grilling; the brine already has plenty of salt.

Brined and Grilled Chicken

After one attempt, you will see how easy and irresistible it is to brine chicken for the grill. Serve a pretty fruit or vegetable chutney, with contrasting sugar and vinegar flavors, alongside the finished dish. (Buy a bottle of chutney if you don't have the time to make your own. Or try the delicious, quick-cooking chutney recipes in Chapter 6.)

Preparation time: *15 minutes*

Marinating time: *1¹/₂ to 2 hours*

Grilling time: *20 to 25 minutes*

Yield: *4 servings*

1 quart water

¹/₂ cup kosher salt

¹/₂ cup sugar

1 bay leaf, or 1 teaspoon dried sage, thyme, or other herb

¹/₂ teaspoon black peppercorns

1 whole frying chicken (3 to 4 pounds), cut into pieces

Pepper (optional)

(continued)

1 In a large non-reactive container or a large, resealable plastic bag, combine the water, kosher salt, sugar, bay leaf or other herb, and black peppercorns. Stir the solution for 2 to 3 minutes, until the sugar and salt are nearly dissolved. Add the chicken pieces and submerge into the brine by using a heavy weight, or close the plastic bag, pressing out as much air as possible. Refrigerate for 1½ to 2 hours.

2 Remove the chicken from the brine, rinse well, and dry thoroughly with paper towels. Season with a little pepper (if desired) or use the following poultry rub.

3 Prepare a medium fire in a covered charcoal or gas grill.

4 Place the chicken pieces, skin side down, on a well-oiled grid. Cover the grill and adjust the temperature or hood vents to maintain medium heat (about 350°). Grill the chicken, covered, for a total of 20 to 24 minutes, turning every 3 to 5 minutes, or as necessary, to keep the pieces from browning too quickly. To test for doneness, cut into the chicken; the juices should run clear, and the meat near the bone should show no sign of pink.

Dry Poultry Rub for Brined Chicken

After brining pieces of chicken to make them moist and tender, you can rub them with this tasty seasoning blend before grilling. (Or turn to Chapters 5 and 6 for additional seasonings and sauces.)

Preparation time: *5 minutes*

Yield: *Enough for 4 pounds of chicken*

2 teaspoons olive oil	*1 teaspoon paprika*
2 cloves garlic, peeled and minced	*1 teaspoon grated lemon peel*
2 teaspoons ground sage	*½ teaspoon pepper, or to taste*

1 Rub the chicken with the olive oil, covering all surfaces.

2 In a small mixing bowl, combine all the remaining ingredients. Rub chicken pieces generously, applying the spice mixture under the skin and into the cavity, as well as on all surfaces.

3 Grill pieces as directed in the preceding recipe.

Dark meat takes longer to cook than white meat and therefore should be placed on the grill about 5 minutes before the breasts. Or you can start the pieces all at once and move the breasts after they are fully cooked to the cooler edges to keep them warm until the legs and thighs finish cooking.

Being Thankful for the Many Uses of Turkey

Turkey is low in fat, but unlike chicken, it needs a little more love and care to arrive on the plate tender, moist, and perfectly grilled. Turkeys are available in smaller portions (especially as breast meat and as ground turkey, which is featured in Chapter 8), which are extremely versatile at any time of the year, so don't reserve turkey for holidays.

Grilled Turkey Tenderloins with Honey-Mustard Glaze

Tenderloins, from the breast of the turkey, are boneless, skinless, easily grilled, and less expensive than chicken breasts. Many of the marinades and basting sauces that are designed for chicken can be used to flavor turkey tenderloins. Watch the cooking time carefully — turkey tenderloins have little fat and dry out quickly. Try to remove them from the grill just at the point of doneness, when they are still moist and tender.

Preparation time: *25 minutes*

Marinating time: *4 hours or overnight*

Grilling time: *10 to 13 minutes*

Yield: *4 servings*

Honey-Mustard Glaze

$^1/_2$ *cup honey*   *Pepper to taste*

$^1/_4$ *cup plus 1 tablespoon Dijon-style mustard*

In a small bowl, whisk the honey and mustard until smooth; season the glaze with pepper. Cover and refrigerate until ready to use. (You can substitute a bottled honey-mustard glaze, if desired.)

(continued)

Grilled Turkey Tenderloins

4 boneless turkey tenderloins (about
1³/₄ to 2 pounds total)

6 tablespoons olive oil

Juice of 1 lemon

2 teaspoons Dijon-style mustard

1 tablespoon chopped fresh rosemary,
or 1 teaspoon dried rosemary

Salt and pepper to taste

1 large handful of presoaked hickory or
mesquite-flavored wood chips (optional)

1 Rinse the tenderloins under cold running water; pat dry with paper towels.

2 In a small bowl, whisk until smooth the oil, lemon juice, and mustard. Stir in the rosemary and adjust the seasoning with salt and pepper.

3 Place the turkey tenderloins in a shallow baking dish or a large resealable plastic bag. Add the lemon-mustard marinade and turn the tenderloins to coat. Cover the dish or seal the bag, pressing out any air; refrigerate for 4 hours or overnight.

4 Prepare a medium fire in a covered charcoal or gas grill. If desired, throw a large handful of presoaked wood chip onto the coals just before placing the tenderloins on the grill. If using a gas grill, wrap the chips in aluminum foil or place in a metal smoker box.

5 Remove the tenderloins from the marinade and place on an oiled grid. Discard the marinade. Grill, covered, for 8 to 10 minutes or until they are lightly browned on both sides, turning once.

6 Divide the Honey-Mustard Glaze in half. Baste the tenderloins on both sides, using half the glaze; reserve the other half as a finishing sauce. Grill the tenderloins, covered, for another 2 to 3 minutes or until done, turning once. Make a small incision in the center of each tenderloin to determine doneness. The meat is cooked when there is no trace of pink in the center or thickest part.

7 Transfer the tenderloins to a platter and let them stand, covered with aluminum foil, for 5 minutes before slicing across the grain. In a small saucepan, bring the remaining glaze to a boil; drizzle over the tenderloin slices.

Vary It! This recipe can be varied many ways by simply changing the basting sauce. Other sauce options are pesto (Chapter 6), a bottled barbecue sauce, or a chipotle sauce. Or omit the basting sauce completely and serve with a tomato or black bean salsa (recipes in Chapter 6).

If the wood chips flare up when you toss them onto a fire, spritz them lightly with a spray bottle filled with water. This dampens the flames and increases the smoke.

Grilled and Glazed Turkey Breast

We give the turkey breast the royal treatment in this recipe to retain its moisture and tenderness. First, it is brined and then foil-wrapped and grilled indirectly.

This recipe calls for one turkey breast half but yields enough marinade (or brine) to accommodate a whole breast if you want to feed 6 to 8 diners. Just be sure to split the breast (or have your butcher do this) into two pieces and double the ingredient amounts for the basting and glazing sauces.

Preparation time: *30 minutes*

Marinating time: *24 to 48 hours*

Grilling time: *1 hour*

Yield: *4 servings*

Brine

1 bone-in turkey breast half (about 2^1/$_2$ to 3 pounds)	*Grated peel of 1 large navel orange (about 1 tablespoon)*
7 cups water	*1 teaspoon whole black peppercorns*
^{1}/$_2$ cup kosher salt	*6 whole cloves*
^{1}/$_2$ cup light brown sugar, packed	*2 bay leaves*

Soy-Honey Glaze

2 scallions, cut into 1-inch pieces	*2 tablespoons honey*
2 large cloves garlic, peeled and crushed	*2 tablespoons soy sauce*
2 tablespoons chili sauce	*^{1}/$_4$ cup water*
2 tablespoons ketchup	*^{1}/$_8$ teaspoon crushed red pepper flakes*
2 tablespoons molasses	

Basting Sauce

1^1/$_2$ tablespoons vegetable oil	*2 tablespoons water*

1 Rinse the turkey breast half under cold running water. Combine the remaining ingredients for the brine in a large non-reactive container or 2-gallon resealable plastic bag (the large plastic liner of a salad spinner also works); stir for 3 to 4 minutes to dissolve the sugar and salt.

2 Place the turkey breast in the brine. If necessary, use a weight to keep the breast submerged. (Or squeeze the air out of the plastic bag as much as possible before sealing tightly.) Refrigerate for 24 to 48 hours, stirring occasionally.

(continued)

3 Several hours or a day before grilling the turkey, in a small bowl combine all the ingredients for the Soy-Honey Glaze. Cover and refrigerate the glaze until ready to use.

4 Prepare a medium fire in a covered charcoal or gas grill.

5 As the grill preheats, remove the breast from the brine and rinse it thoroughly under cold running water. Pat dry with paper towels.

6 Lay the breast on a long sheet of heavy-duty aluminum foil. Rub the breast with the 1¹/₂ tablespoons oil, covering all surfaces. Wrap the breast tightly, using a drugstore wrap (refer to Figure 10-2 in Chapter 10) and leaving one end of the foil packet open. Spoon the 2 tablespoons of water into the open end of the packet; seal the end tightly.

7 Place the packet on the grid, directly over the heat; cover and grill for about 15 minutes. Using tongs or a barbecue mitt, carefully turn the packet over and cook for another 15 minutes or until an instant-read thermometer registers between 150° and 160°.

8 Transfer the foil packet to a baking pan or large plate; carefully remove the aluminum foil, opening the packet so that the steam escapes away from you.

9 If you are using a charcoal grill, bank the hot coals to one side, adding additional coals to create an indirect, medium-hot fire. Place a drip pan, half-filled with water, next to the coals. If you are using a gas grill, increase the heat of one burner to medium-hot but leave the other burner off. Put a drip pan with water in place. (Check out Chapter 1 for directions on building an indirect fire.)

10 Baste the breast with the Soy-Honey Glaze, covering all surfaces. Place the breast on the grid on the side over the drip pan. Cover and cook indirectly, basting with the glaze and turning the breast every 10 minutes, for a total of 30 minutes or until an instant-read thermometer registers 170°.

11 Remove the breast from the grill. Cover loosely with aluminum foil and let rest for 10 minutes before carving. If desired, boil the remaining Soy-Honey Glaze and spoon over the meat slices.

Dale Curry's Hickory-Smoked Whole Turkey

To find out how to infuse a whole turkey with real smoked hickory flavors, we turned to Dale Curry, food editor of *The Times-Picayune* in New Orleans. Dale was born and raised in Memphis, where eating barbecue is an everyday experience. She says that everybody loves the following smoked turkey recipe.

This recipe shows you a very healthy way to cook a turkey. Slow-cooking and smoking over a very small fire of only about 30 briquettes allows the turkey meat to stay very moist and succulent without the addition of extra fat or butter-rich basting sauces. It's best to buy a turkey with a pop-up thermometer. Cooking the bird too long results in tough, dry meat. Be sure to check for doneness frequently, about every 15 minutes, towards the end of the cooking time.

Preparation time: *15 minutes*

Grilling time: *4 to 4 ¹/₂ hours*

Yield: *12 servings*

12-pound fresh or frozen and thawed turkey (preferably with a pop-up thermometer)	*Creole seasoning (store-bought variety)*
	6 heaping handfuls (about) presoaked hickory wood chips

1 Remove the giblet packages from the turkey cavities; rinse the turkey and pat dry. Sprinkle the bird all over with the Creole seasoning, inside and out. Let the turkey rest at room temperature as you prepare the charcoal fire.

2 Prepare a small charcoal fire, using about 30 briquettes, in a kettle grill with a lid. When the coals are hot, move them to one side of the grill. (See Chapter 1 for complete instructions on building an indirect fire.) Place a drip pan, filled about one-third with water, next to the coals. Sprinkle a large handful of presoaked hickory wood chips over the coals.

3 Place the turkey on the well-oiled grid, directly over the drip pan opposite the coals. Cover the grill. Open the vents directly under the fire and above the turkey to facilitate an even flow of smoke. Open the grill every 40 to 45 minutes, turn the turkey around or from side to side, and add 6 coals and another large handful of presoaked wood chips to the fire. Keep the grill lid closed between these times. Continue to cook the turkey in this fashion until the pop-up thermometer has sprung or until an instant-read thermometer in the inside of the thigh registers 180°. A 12-pound turkey will take about 4 to 4¹/₂ hours to cook, depending on the heat of the fire, the air temperature, the actual size of the turkey, and its distance from the fire. When done, the skin will look quite brown, but the inside meat will be moist and juicy. Remove the turkey from the grill and let it rest at least for 15 minutes before carving.

Creole seasoning is made by many commercial manufacturers, such as Zatarain's, McCormick, Tony Chachere, and Paul Prudhomme, and is commonly found in supermarket spice sections. It is a blend of salt, red and black pepper, garlic, and other spicy seasonings.

Game Birds Make for Healthy Eating

Aside from their wonderful, individual tastes, game birds are extremely healthy foods. They are lower in fat and cholesterol than chicken, and higher in protein — for instance, a 3.5 ounce portion of domestic quail with skin has about 133 calories, 21.7 grams of protein, and 2.8 grams of fat, compared with 193 calories, 29.2 grams of protein, and 7.6 grams of fat for the same amount of chicken. Because they use their muscles constantly, game birds burn off their fat. The feed of both wild and domestic birds tends to have more minerals and vitamins than poultry feed.

The wilder, the better

There are no two ways about it: Wild game has a flavor you just won't find in farm-raised game. Which is not to say that wild game is *game-y*, a term that's acquired the connotation of meaning strong-tasting, bitter, or like liver. Freshly killed wild game isn't game-y at all, unless the bird isn't dressed properly or is handled too long.

Not too long ago, wild game birds were a rarity at the market, but today they can easily be ordered from any good butcher with a few days' notice, and there are many sources for game by mail order and on the Internet.

Freshly killed game properly dressed and hung has absolutely wonderful flavor, much of which comes from the food the birds eat, which makes different species from different parts of the wild taste remarkably different. Farm-raised game has slightly more fat (though not as much as chicken), so you usually don't have to baste the birds.

Having said all that, we cannot wholly recommend going out and shooting your own wild birds for food unless you are, in fact, an experienced hunter or willing to become one. Aside from needing the knowledge of how to dress and prepare a bird, you need to know whether that bird is healthy, and only a trained inspector or experienced hunter can tell you that.

Fortunately, farm-raised game birds are now abundant, and although they do not possess the singular flavor of their wild cousins, birds like squab, quail, and pheasant offer superb grilling and dining possibilities. Therefore, we endorse the idea that farm-raised game birds are the safe way to go when it comes to grilling.

Getting to know game birds

You may think that anything you do with a chicken you can do with a game bird, but that's nowhere near the truth. Because of their unique textures, their difference in flavor, and their relative lack of fat, game birds must be treated differently than a chicken on the grill — the prep and the actual grilling differ a good deal. Yet in their own way — because game birds cook more quickly — they are wonderful options for a party or times when you don't want to spend even 30 minutes tending to the grill. You can find several varieties of game birds in Figure 15-2, and descriptions of each in the following list.

- **Rock Cornish game hen:** Many people who are squeamish about game birds but bored with chicken take advantage of the fine-flavored Rock Cornish game hen, which, despite its name, does not come from a rock nor from Cornwall, England. It is actually the result of an American breeding between a Plymouth Rock hen and a Cornish game cock. It weighs only 1 to 2 pounds — quite nice for one or two people. This is not a wild bird at all, and its popularity in the U.S. means that you almost always find it at the market. Rock Cornish game hens taste great when grilled. (Check out the recipe that follows.)

- **Grouse:** A very full-flavored red-meat bird with a pronounced taste, grouse is never farm-raised and is difficult to find. The best grouse come in from Scotland in the fall and usually get sold to restaurants. Because this bird feeds on evergreens, it can have a lovely sprucelike undertone. You need one grouse (about 1¼ pounds) per person for a dinner, and be prepared to pick out some of the buckshot from the meat! Grouse is best when roasted on a spit or grilled, split in half, to medium doneness. If cooked to a gray color, grouse loses its unique flavor.

- **Partridge:** This strong-flavored bird doesn't taste quite as much like liver as grouse does. Partridge is a good plump bird that's best when spit-roasted or grilled in halves. Serve one partridge per person. Partridge is wonderful with braised cabbage or wild rice.

- **Pheasant:** Farm-raised pheasant are becoming more available, and although they haven't quite the flavor of wild pheasant, they make for a delectable alternative to chicken. One bird will satisfy two healthy appetites. Pheasant takes well to light marinades.

- **Poussin:** Poussins — pronounced poo-SAHNS — are not really game birds, but rather small spring chickens that weigh about 1 pound. They have a sweet flavor and tender flesh. With about 25 percent less fat than commercially raised chickens, poussins should be marinated before grilling to ensure a moist bird.

Poussins are relatively expensive and may not be available in all supermarkets. Check with your grocer — or search the Internet — for sources.

✔ **Quail:** These tiny birds cook very quickly and have a delicate flavor, so they are best when simply grilled and served with marinades such as soy sauce and ginger. You can stuff them, but their size makes it difficult. A reasonable serving would be two to three quail per person, but one quail with greens can make a terrific appetizer.

✔ **Squab:** Squab is a nice name for a young pigeon, but then, we're not talking about those sooty urban rooftop dwellers. We're talking about a nice plump woodlands or farm-raised pigeon, which, like grouse, has a red meatiness and is delicious with lusty red-wine marinades. Actually, wild pigeons are exceedingly difficult to find, but the poultry industry has created a tender, delicious, featherless breed that also goes by the name rock dove. One bird per person is a good portion. Squabs are best when roasted on a spit and braised.

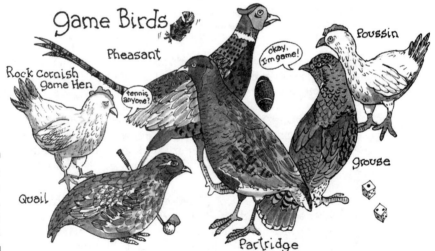

Figure 15-2:
If you're game, we're game!

As purveyors of fresh game and other gourmet products, a fast-growing family company, D'Artagnan, is seeing to it that Americans have a steady supply of fresh game birds at their local supermarkets and specialty grocery stores. D'Artagnan raises and distributes fresh quail, pheasant, squab, duck, and poussin. If you live in an area without a supermarket that carries fresh game, you can mail-order it direct from D'Artagnan at 1-800-327-8246.

Rock Cornish Game Hens with Molasses-Rum Marinade

Cook these lovely hens directly over the heat of the grill, basting frequently with the delicious Molasses-Rum marinade. A few wood chunks — mesquite, maple, pecan, or hickory wood — mixed into the charcoal briquettes can add a subtle layer of pleasant, smoky flavor.

Preparation time: *25 minutes*

Marinating time: *8 hours or overnight*

Grilling time: *25 minutes*

Yield: *2 to 4 servings*

2 Cornish game hens, each about $1^1/_4$ to $1^1/_2$ pounds, split in half

1 tablespoon butter

$1^1/_2$ teaspoons curry powder

$1/_4$ cup dark rum

2 tablespoons molasses

$1/_3$ cup fresh orange juice

Juice of 1 large lime (about 2 tablespoons)

$1/_2$ teaspoon grated lime peel

1 teaspoon kosher salt, or to taste

1 large clove garlic, peeled and crushed

1 teaspoon seeded and chopped jalapeño pepper

1 Rinse the hen halves thoroughly under cold running water; pat dry with paper towels. Place the hen halves in a large, resealable plastic bag or a non-reactive shallow container big enough to hold them snugly in one layer.

2 Melt the butter in a small saucepan, being careful not to let it brown. Stir in the curry powder and cook the mixture for 1 minute, stirring; remove the saucepan from the heat. Carefully add the rum and molasses.

3 Stir in the orange and lime juices, grated lime peel, salt, garlic, and jalapeño pepper; pour the marinade over the hens and refrigerate, covered, for 8 hours or overnight, turning the hens occasionally.

4 Prepare a direct, medium fire in a charcoal or gas grill.

5 Remove the hens from the marinade. Reserve the marinade.

6 Place the hens, skin side down on a well-oiled grid, directly over the heat. Cover the grill and cook for a total of 25 minutes, turning and basting with the marinade every 8 minutes during the first 16 minutes. The hens are cooked when an instant-read thermometer registers 180° or the juices run clear.

Splitting hens

Place the hen breast side up and using a pair of poultry shears, cut along the breastbone from the cavity to the neck end. Gently pry open the two sides. Turn the hen over and cut along one side of the backbone, cutting the hen in half. Cut along the other side of the backbone to remove and discard it.

How to Split a Rock Cornish Game Hen

Place the bird breast side up. Cut along the breast bone from cavity to neck end. Gently pry open.

Turn the hen over and cut along one side of the backbone, cutting the hen in half.

Cut along the other side of the backbone to remove and discard.

discard

Whole Game Hens with Asian Flavors

In this recipe, the hens are first grilled indirectly for about 1 hour and then shifted directly over the fire for a few minutes to nicely brown and crisp the skin. They are sauced twice — once with a sake-soy marinade and then again with a sweet-and-spicy basting sauce of honey, cloves, lemon juice, and Tabasco.

Preparation time: 25 minutes

Marinating time: 4 to 6 hours

Grilling time: 1 hour and 10 minutes

Yield: 2 to 4 servings

2 Cornish game hens, each about 1¹/₄ to 1¹/₂ pounds

¹/₂ cup sake or dry sherry

¹/₂ cup plus 2 teaspoons soy sauce, divided

¹/₄ cup honey, divided

¹/₂ teaspoon ground ginger

Pepper to taste

2 tablespoons fresh lemon juice

¹/₄ teaspoon ground cloves

Generous dash Tabasco sauce, or to taste

1 Remove the giblets from the cavity of the hens; wrap and freeze the giblets for adding to soups or stocks, if desired. Rinse the hens thoroughly in cold running water; pat dry with paper towels and place in a non-reactive shallow container that's large enough to hold them snugly side by side.

2 In a small bowl or measuring cup, combine the following marinade ingredients: sake or dry sherry, $1/2$ cup of the soy sauce, 2 tablespoons of the honey, the ginger, and pepper. Pour the marinade over the hens and refrigerate, covered for 4 to 6 hours.

3 Prepare a hot, indirect fire in a covered charcoal or gas grill, with a drip pan containing about 1 cup water. (Flip to Chapter 1 for instructions on building an indirect fire.)

4 Remove the hens from the marinade, discarding the marinade.

5 As the grill heats, in a small bowl combine the remaining 2 tablespoons honey and 2 teaspoons soy sauce, the lemon juice, cloves, and the Tabasco sauce to make a basting glaze.

6 Place the hens on the grid, over the drip pan, opposite the fire, breast side up; baste the hens with the glaze. Cover the grill and cook for 1 hour, turning the hens over and basting with glaze about every 20 minutes (but not during the last 20 minutes). (Be sure to add fresh briquettes about every 30 minutes to maintain the heat in a charcoal grill.)

7 Move the hens to the side of the grill directly over the fire; grill, breast side down, covered, for 3 to 5 minutes. Turn the hens breast side up and grill, covered, for 3 to 5 minutes more or until the juices run clear or an instant-read thermometer inserted between the breast and thigh reads 180°. (Watch the hens closely to avoid charring the skin over direct heat. Move them back to indirect heat, if necessary, to finish cooking.)

8 Let the hens rest about 5 minutes before serving. If desired, boil the drip pan juices for 1 to 2 minutes before spooning over the grilled hens.

Grilled Poussins with Mushroom-Butter Sauce

Most of the chopped herb and cracked pepper seasonings in this recipe will fall off into the fire unless they're firmly pressed into the skin and cavity of each poussin. Don't fret if the skin becomes very brown or even slightly charred. The underlying meat will remain moist and tender.

Preparation time: *30 minutes*

Marinating time: *8 hours or overnight*

Grilling time: *30 minutes*

Yield: *4 servings*

(continued)

4 poussins (each about 1 pound)

1/4 cup plus 1 tablespoon balsamic vinegar

3 tablespoons extra-virgin olive oil

3 tablespoons finely chopped fresh thyme, or 1 tablespoon dried thyme

2 tablespoons finely chopped fresh rosemary, or 2 teaspoons dried rosemary

2 cloves garlic, peeled and crushed

1 tablespoon plus 1 teaspoon cracked black peppercorns

Kosher or regular salt to taste

1 Rinse the poussins under cold running water and pat dry with paper towels. Using a sharp chef's or boning knife, cut the neck off each bird (where it is attached to the body) and trim any loose skin or fat. Place the birds in a large shallow, non-reactive baking dish.

2 In a medium mixing bowl or glass measuring cup, combine the remaining ingredients, except the salt, for the marinade. Pour the marinade over the poussins, turning to coat, rubbing the marinade and herbs into the skin and cavity of each bird. Cover and refrigerate for at least 8 hours, or overnight.

3 Prepare a medium fire in a charcoal or gas grill.

4 Sprinkle each poussin lightly with kosher or table salt. Brush each poussin generously with the marinade. Be sure to dab the herbs, crushed pepper, and garlic all over the skin and into the cavity of each bird. Reserve any remaining marinade.

5 Lay the birds on their sides, on a well-oiled grid, directly over the heat. Grill, covered, for 7 to 8 minutes. Baste the birds with marinade; give each a quarter-turn so that the breast side rests on the grid and cook for 7 to 8 minutes more, covered. Continue to baste and quarter-turn every 7 to 8 minutes, ending with the breast side up. (Do not baste during the last 8 minutes of grilling.) When the birds are done, an instant-read thermometer inserted between the breast and the thigh registers 180°, the juices run clear, and no trace of pink exists in the leg or thigh meat. Total cooking time is 28 to 32 minutes.

6 Place the poussins on a large serving platter and allow them to rest for about 10 minutes, covered with aluminum foil. Spoon the Mushroom-Butter Sauce (see following recipe) evenly over each bird and serve immediately.

Mushroom-Butter Sauce

2 tablespoons butter

1 tablespoon vegetable oil

3 tablespoons peeled and finely chopped shallots

1 1/2 cups chicken broth

1/3 cup finely chopped mushrooms (button, shitake, or a combination)

1 tablespoon finely chopped fresh parsley

1 In a small saucepan or skillet, melt the butter and oil over medium heat. Add the shallots and cook for 2 minutes or until they are softened and lightly browned.

2 Add the chicken broth and boil the mixture gently for 10 minutes, stirring occasionally. Add the mushrooms and cook for another 3 to 5 minutes or until the mixture is reduced by half and has thickened slightly. Remove the mixture from the heat and sprinkle with parsley. Spoon the sauce over the poussins. This sauce can be prepared ahead and held in the refrigerator for several hours or days. Reheat in a small skillet or saucepan, over low heat, just before serving.

Chef Frank Stitt's Grilled Carolina Quail with Corn and Arugula Salad and Molasses Vinaigrette

Frank Stitt is one of the South's most innovative chefs. Trained in French classic cooking techniques, he always adds a real touch of finesse to everything he cooks. This makes his restaurant in Birmingham, Alabama, — called Highlands Bar & Grill — one of the finest in the nation for both traditional Southern fare and modern twists on old favorites.

Squab and quail are often sold semiboneless or European style; by using the "gloved method" of boning, the breast cage is removed, leaving only the wing tips and leg bones. The boning decreases cooking time and ensures unbroken breast skin and a bird that's easier to eat. A metal clip or *grill pin* (as it's sometimes called) is set into the bird to help retain its shape, and is easily removed before serving.

Preparation time: *30 minutes*

Marinating time: *4 hours or overnight*

Grilling time: *6 minutes for quail, and 5 minutes for corn*

Yield: *4 appetizer servings or 2 main dish servings*

Quail

4 semiboneless quail

2 tablespoons olive oil

1 tablespoon molasses

2 cloves garlic, peeled and crushed

Several crushed juniper berries

3 to 4 long sprigs of fresh thyme, rosemary, or marjoram, cut into 1-inch lengths

1 Rinse the quail under cold running water. Pat the birds dry with paper towels and place in a large shallow baking dish.

(continued)

2 Combine the olive oil, molasses, garlic, juniper berries, and fresh herb sprigs in a small mixing bowl; rub the oil-herb mixture into the quail. Cover the quail or place them in a large plastic bag and seal, before refrigerating for 4 hours or overnight.

3 Prepare a medium-hot hardwood or charcoal fire or preheat a gas grill to medium-hot.

4 Prepare the Corn and Arugula Salad. (See the following recipe.)

5 Remove the quail from the marinade; discard the marinade. Place the quail on a well-oiled grid, breast side down. Grill until lightly charred. Turn and grill the quail, breast side up, until the meat between the breast and the leg has no trace of pink when cut, or an instant-read thermometer inserted between the breast and the thigh registers 180°.

Corn and Arugula Salad

3 tablespoons extra-virgin olive oil

1 tablespoon molasses

¹/₂ tablespoon fresh lemon juice

¹/₂ tablespoon sherry vinegar

1 shallot, peeled and finely minced

2 to 3 sprigs fresh herbs, such as thyme, parsley, or chives, finely chopped

Sea salt (or regular salt) and pepper to taste

2 bunches arugula or watercress (about 4 cups)

4 ears fresh sweet yellow corn, husked

Chopped fresh herbs, such as chives, parsley, or thyme, for garnish

1 In a medium mixing bowl, whisk together the olive oil, molasses, lemon juice, and sherry vinegar. Add the shallot and chopped herbs, stirring to blend well. Adjust seasoning with salt and pepper. Set the vinaigrette dressing aside. (You can make the dressing a day or two in advance and refrigerate it until ready to use.)

2 Rinse the arugula or watercress in several changes of cold water until it is free of all sand and grit, and spin it completely dry in a salad spinner.

3 Add the ears of corn, one at a time, to a large pot of boiling water. Cover and boil for 2 to 3 minutes. Drain well and grill the ears on an oiled grid, over a medium-hot fire, for about 5 minutes or until slightly charred, turning often. Cut off the top two-thirds of each ear. Shave the kernels off the larger pieces of corn. Reserve the smaller, bottom-third of the cobs for garnishing the serving platter.

To assemble the dish: Toss the arugula with the dressing in a large mixing bowl and arrange in the center of a large serving platter. Cut the grilled quail in half lengthwise along its backbone and "crisscross" the quail on top of the arugula. Scatter the corn kernels and cob pieces reserved for garnish on the platter. Sprinkle with chopped fresh herbs such as chives, parsley, or thyme.

Go-With: Chef Stitt recommends serving this dish as an appetizer for four and pairing it with a fruity red wine, such as Ravenswood Zinfandel.

Juniper berries — tiny, but pungent

Juniper berries, which are about twice the size of a small pea, grow in Europe and the U.S. on a prickly, evergreen shrub. They are too bitter to eat, so the berries are usually sold as a dried seasoning. The smooth, purple-black, soft berries are generally crushed before using with meat — game, pork, veal, or beef — or to season sauces, stuffings, pâtés, marinades, and brines. They are best known as the pungent ingredient that gives gin its distinctive flavor.

Chapter 16

The Gill and the Grill

Seafood makes a delicious feast for the grill. In this chapter, we introduce you to some delectable — and some unusual — ways to prepare seafood.

And by the way, the words *fish* and *seafood* are not interchangeable. Seafood encompasses all edible creatures that live in the sea, including shellfish and swimming fish. So, while all fish is seafood, not all seafood is fish. And there's another little twist: Even if the fish, mussels, or shellfish come from *freshwater* lakes, rivers, or streams, the term seafood still applies.

The Fish Story

Grilling fish is a job that causes many cooks to feel like, well, a fish out of water. This fear of fish is not surprising. The flesh of fish is very delicate, so you can overcook fish on the grill before you realize what's happening. In this section, we give you tips on how to know when fish is properly cooked and how to avoid having it dry out.

Grilling imparts a terrific flavor to the flesh of fish. Beyond that, the health benefits of eating fish are clear, from its low fat content to the omega-3 fatty acids in fish oil that can lower your cholesterol.

Start with fresh fish

Fish taken fresh from the sea or rivers has a taste unlike anything else. And anyone disliking fish because it is, well, fishy, just hasn't tasted a truly fresh fish. A fish just out of water, properly dressed and scaled and then grilled, is one of the purest of all culinary pleasures, and anglers take justifiable pride in bringing home fish of this quality.

The French have a saying about fish: If a fish smells like fish, it's not fresh fish. When shopping for fresh fish, here are some guidelines:

- Let your nose — not your eye — guide you. The one foolproof way to tell if a fish is fresh is to put your nose right up to it, especially near the gills. If you get a strong whiff of fishiness, move on.

- Don't buy fish that is stacked up on *top* of ice. A good fish seller buries the fish in ice.

- When poorly handled, frozen fish invariably loses its fresh smell and flavor, emerging from the freezer with a mushy or mealy texture and more than a whiff of fishiness. However, flash-freezing the fish — at –60 degrees right onboard gigantic trawlers — can maintain the freshness of fish much better than catching a fish and letting it sit around on ice for a few days.

- If you buy or store frozen fish, the best place to thaw it is in the refrigerator. Let it defrost slowly — 24 hours is best — and when the fish has come to refrigerator temperature, look for a nice plump, shiny appearance. Never, ever refreeze fish.

- Visit your seafood market frequently and get to know the owner. Let it be known that you expect good quality and good service. Show that you're serious about getting the best quality, and the owner will deliver the goods.

- For some examples of less-traditional fish that grill well, see Figure 16-1.

Thick and easy: Fish steaks

If you feel a little uneasy about your ability to grill fish, you really should have no problem with thick cuts of fish, especially steaks and kebabs.

If the fish steaks are sliced too thin, they will dry out on the grill and are likely to fall apart. Have them cut from 1 to 1 1/2 inches thick for best results. See the section "Be gentle with fillets" later in this chapter for tips on grilling thin fish fillets.

Figure 16-1:
Fishing
for great
grilling
ideas.

Timing is still important, but with fish steaks you can at least blink without worrying that your fish is going to overcook.

- ✔ Grill fish steaks directly over moderately hot coals, turning them only once. A moderately hot fire gives you plenty of heat to develop a nice brown sear and cook the fish thoroughly, but not so much that the surface blackens or burns.

- ✔ Most 1-inch steaks cook in about 8 minutes and continue to cook a little more after they're removed from the grill. However, cooking times vary according to wind, air temperature, and the heat intensity of your grill.

- ✔ Check the interior of the fish for doneness a few minutes before you expect it to be done. Use a thin-bladed knife to peek between the layers of flesh. Generally, when the flesh is no longer translucent, but rather opaque, and the knife meets no resistance, the fish is cooked.

- ✔ Fish will continue to cook after it's removed from the grill — you may want to remove it a few seconds shy of its fully-cooked time.

Fish steaks need little adornment in the way of seasoning. You can marinate or simply brush them with a little oil and seasonings before grilling. Throughout this book, we recommend using a large, resealable plastic bag to marinate food. However, fish is best marinated in a shallow non-reactive baking dish. With its very delicate flesh, fish should lie secure and flat in the dish, the marinade swirling around it. Tossing fish into a plastic bag may cause tender fillets to fall apart into small, impossible-to-grill pieces. Exceptions to this rule are, of course, shrimp and scallops.

Grilled Fish Steaks with Avocado and Citrus Salsa

Lime juice, orange sections, cilantro, and avocado give these grilled fish steaks refreshing flavor.

Preparation time: 25 minutes

Marinating time: 30 minutes

Grilling time: 8 to 10 minutes

Yield: 4 servings

4 salmon, halibut, swordfish, or shark steaks, cut about 1-inch thick, 6 to 8 ounces each

$^1/_4$ cup torn fresh cilantro or basil leaves

$^1/_4$ cup olive oil

$^1/_3$ cup peeled and chopped red onion, divided

2 tablespoons fresh lime or lemon juice

Grated peel of half a lemon or lime (about 1 teaspoon)

Salt and pepper to taste

1 large clove garlic, peeled and minced (about 1 teaspoon) (optional)

1 firm, ripe avocado, peeled, pitted, and finely chopped

1 navel orange, peeled, sectioned, and finely chopped

1 small jalapeño pepper, seeded and finely chopped

1 Prepare a medium-hot fire in a charcoal or gas grill.

2 Rinse fish steaks under cold running water; pat dry with paper towels. Place the steaks in a shallow, non-reactive baking dish, in a single layer.

3 In a blender container, combine the cilantro or basil, olive oil, 1 tablespoon of the red onion, the lime or lemon juice, grated lime or lemon peel, and salt and pepper. Whirl in the blender for a few seconds until the mixture is a coarse puree.

4 Remove $2^1/_2$ tablespoons of the mixture and reserve for making the salsa. Add the garlic to the remaining marinade (if desired). Pour the marinade over the fish steaks in the dish, turning to coat well. Cover and refrigerate for about 30 minutes, turning once.

5 Prepare the Avocado and Citrus Salsa: In a medium mixing bowl, combine the avocado, orange, jalapeño pepper, remaining red onion, and reserved $2^1/_2$ tablespoons marinade. Cover the salsa and refrigerate until ready to use.

6 When the fire is ready, remove the fish from the marinade. Place the fish steaks on a well-oiled grill grid, allowing some of the marinade to cling to each steak. Grill for about 8 to 10 minutes, turning once with a wide metal spatula. To check for doneness, make a small incision in the center of the steak with the tip of a thin-bladed knife. The flesh should be opaque, not translucent, when done. Spoon some of the Avocado and Citrus Salsa over each steak.

Grilled Tuna with Farfalle

This colorful combination of cold tuna and farfalle, seasoned with the unique, slightly salty flavors of olive, capers, and sun-dried tomatoes, makes a light and lovely summer meal. Serve with a loaf of Italian or French bread and a bottle of dry, crisp white wine like Sauvignon Blanc or a light red wine like Bardolino.

(continued)

Be sure to carefully plan the cooking steps so that the sauce and the grilled tuna are finished cooking just a few minutes before the pasta is drained. Pasta that isn't moistened with sauce soon after it's drained quickly gets unpleasantly sticky.

Preparation time: *30 minutes*

Grilling time: *8 to 10 minutes*

Yield: *4 servings*

Tuna Steak

1 pound tuna steak, about 1-inch thick, skinless

3 tablespoons olive oil

1 large clove garlic, peeled and minced

$1/4$ teaspoon red pepper flakes, or half a jalapeño pepper, seeded and minced (optional)

Salt and pepper to taste

Pasta

1 pound farfalle (bow-tie-shaped pasta)

Salt to taste

Sauce

$1/3$ cup extra-virgin olive oil

1 large red onion, peeled and thinly sliced

1 large clove garlic, peeled and thinly sliced

6 oil-packed sun-dried tomatoes, drained and chopped

12 kalamata olives, pitted and sliced

1 teaspoon capers, rinsed and drained (optional)

6 large basil leaves, cut into thin ribbons

$1/4$ cup chopped fresh parsley

Pepper to taste

1 Prepare a medium-hot fire in a charcoal or gas grill.

2 Rinse the tuna steak under cold running water and pat dry with paper towels. In a small bowl, combine the 3 tablespoons olive oil, garlic, red pepper flakes or jalapeño pepper (if desired) and salt and pepper. Brush both sides of the tuna steak with the flavored oil. Cover and refrigerate until the grill is ready.

3 As the grill heats, bring a large pot of water to a boil; salt lightly and add the farfalle. Stir a few times to prevent the pasta from sticking together. Boil according to package directions or until pasta is *al dente* — tender but not mushy, with some firmness remaining.

4 After starting the pasta water, make the sauce. In a large skillet or saucepan, heat the ¹/₃ cup olive oil over medium heat; add the red onion and garlic and cook, stirring occasionally, until the vegetables are softened, about 3 to 4 minutes. (Be careful not to let the garlic burn.) Add the sun-dried tomatoes, the olives, and the capers (if desired). Cover and set the sauce aside.

5 Place the tuna steak on a well-oiled grid. Cook for 4 to 5 minutes per side or until done. (Time is for medium tuna with an opaque center. For rare to medium-rare, reduce the cooking time as desired.) When done, remove from the grill to a cutting board and cut into bite-size chunks.

6 Add the grilled tuna with the basil and 3 tablespoons of parsley to the sauce; stir gently to combine.

7 Drain the cooked farfalle into a colander, setting aside ¹/₂ cup of the cooking water. Transfer the farfalle back to the pasta pot; add the tuna mixture and stir over low heat until thoroughly mixed and warmed through. If the mixture seems a little dry, add some of the reserved cooking water to moisten as necessary. Stir gently. Transfer the mixture to a large serving bowl. Add the remaining tablespoon of parsley and the pepper and serve immediately.

Grilled Swordfish Steak with Chipotle Salsa

Chipotles (chee-POHT-lehz) are smoked jalapeño peppers that are sold two ways: canned in adobo (ah-DOH-boh) sauce or dried. Dried chipotles require reconstituting in boiling water for about 40 minutes. Chipotles add bold smoky flavor to food and are a perfect seasoning ingredient for grilled fish, poultry or beef, salsas, salad dressings, mayonnaise, and compound butters. Here, canned chipotles are mixed into a tomato and onion salsa that's served over grilled swordfish. Make the salsa 1 to 2 hours before serving to give the flavors a chance to develop.

Preparation time: *30 minutes*

Marinating time: *15 minutes*

Grilling time: *8 to 10 minutes*

Yield: *4 servings*

(continued)

Chipotle Salsa

Yield: *2 cups*

2 cups cored, seeded, and diced plum tomatoes

1 small onion, peeled and diced (about ¹/₃ cup)

2 chipotle peppers (canned in adobo sauce), undrained and finely minced

2 tablespoons finely chopped fresh cilantro leaves

Juice of half a lime (about 2 teaspoons)

¹/₂ teaspoon salt, or to taste

¹/₂ teaspoon sugar

In a medium bowl, thoroughly mix all the ingredients. Cover and refrigerate for at least 2 hours. Spoon over grilled swordfish steaks.

Grilled Swordfish

1 swordfish steak, about 1 to 1¹/₄ pounds, cut 1-inch thick

Juice of 1 lemon

2 tablespoons olive oil

Salt and pepper to taste

1 Rinse the swordfish steak and pat dry with paper towels. Place the steak in a flat, non–reactive container.

2 In a small mixing bowl, combine the lemon juice, olive oil, and salt and pepper. Pour the mixture over the swordfish; cover and refrigerate for 15 to 20 minutes, turning once.

3 While the swordfish is marinating, prepare a medium-hot fire in a charcoal or gas grill.

4 When the fire is ready, place the swordfish on a well-oiled grill grid. Grill for 4 to 5 minutes per side or until done. To check for doneness, make a small incision in the center of the fish with the tip of a sharp, thin-bladed knife. The fish is cooked when the flesh is opaque and no longer translucent. Remove to a platter and spoon Chipotle Salsa over the top before serving.

Be gentle with fillets

Delicate whitefish fillets (like those from sole and flounder) are not the easiest cuts of fish to grill and need some special care. Grilling is a rough cooking method, so laying thin, skinless fillets directly on a grill grid may cause them to fall apart, as can excessive marinating. So follow these tips:

✔ Grill fillets on a perforated sheet of lightly oiled heavy-duty aluminum foil (simply puncture the foil with fork tines). The foil supports the fillets. However, be aware that you won't get that wonderful grilled, charred flavor — the whole point of outdoor cooking — when you use foil.

✔ A fish basket — a basket that's shaped like a fish — is the most useful basket that we've found. Buy fish baskets made of nonstick or stick-resistant material. Also look for baskets with long handles that make it easier to turn the fish. (See Figure 16-2.) Adjustable baskets conform to the shape and size of the fish, allowing them to hold the fish securely in place. These, too, should be oiled before placing the fish inside.

✔ Keep your grill grid clean. Fish can easily get stuck on the little particles of cooked food clinging to the rack.

✔ Coat the fish with a thin layer of oil before placing it on the grid. Be sure to gently shake off most of an oil-based marinade before placing fish on the grid to prevent flare-ups.

If you can't find your basting brush, cut an onion in half and coat the cut side lightly with oil. Stick a fork in the onion and rub the oil-coated side against the grid to oil it.

✔ Always be sure to oil the grid when it is cold to prevent dangerous flare-ups.

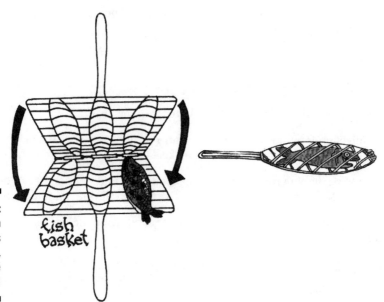

Figure 16-2:
Fish baskets are, well, shaped like a fish!

fish basket

✔ Don't overmarinate! Fish tissue starts to react to the acid in the marinade and will fall apart in an acid-based marinade. Thirty minutes is plenty of time to add sufficient flavor to most fish.

✔ After initially placing fish on the grid, resist any immediate attempt to move it around or turn it over. Letting it sear a little makes turning the fish easier.

Flatfish Fillets Grilled on Lemon Slices with Mediterranean Skillet Sauce

Want another way to protect delicate fish fillets from the harsh heat of the grill? Grill them on lemon slices as we do in this recipe. The thin fillets cook without needing a turn, and the lemons slices make a dramatic, copper-colored plate garnish (see the color photo section of this book). If you like, use thin slices of red or yellow onion rather than lemons.

Preparation time: *10 minutes*

Marinating time: *30 minutes*

Grilling time: *6 minutes*

Yield: *4 servings*

2 skinless flatfish fillets (cod, haddock, sea bass, or flounder, for example), about 8 to 10 ounces each

2 tablespoons olive oil

³/₄ teaspoon ground cumin

Salt and pepper to taste

16 lemon slices, thinly sliced about ¹/₄-inch thick (about 3 large lemons)

1 Prepare a medium-hot fire in a covered charcoal or gas grill.

2 Rinse the fillets under cold running water and gently pat them dry with a paper towel. Cut each fillet in half crosswise to make 4 pieces of fish, about equal in size.

3 In a small bowl, combine the olive oil, cumin, and salt and pepper. Brush both sides of the fillets with the mixture; cover and refrigerate for about 30 minutes to 1 hour.

4 Prepare the Mediterranean Skillet Sauce (see the following recipe) as the fish marinates.

5 When ready to grill, lay the lemon slices on the oiled grill, using 4 slices to make a square large enough to hold a piece of fish. (See Figure 16-3.) Repeat with remaining slices to make 4 squares directly over the heat. Set a piece of fish on top of each lemon square.

6 Cover and grill, without turning, for a total of 6 to 8 minutes or until the fillets are opaque in the center. To test for doneness, make a small incision with the tip of a sharp knife to peek into the center of each fillet. The flesh should be opaque and moist. Final cooking time will depend on the actual thickness of the fillets.

Laying Fish Fillets on Lemon Slices

Figure 16-3:
Grilling delicate fillets on lemon slices keeps them from falling through the grill grid as they cook.

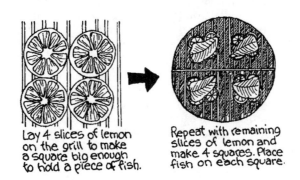

Lay 4 slices of lemon on the grill to make a square big enough to hold a piece of fish.

Repeat with remaining slices of lemon and make 4 squares. Place fish on each square.

7 Remove the fish to individual platters by sliding a wide metal spatula under the lemon slices and picking up the fish at the same time. Gently pull the lemon slices out from under the fish, inverting them on the platter, grilled side up. (They will have a bronzed, slightly caramelized look.) Spoon equal amounts of the Mediterranean Skillet Sauce over each fillet.

Mediterranean Skillet Sauce

Preparation time: *10 minutes*

Yield: *About 1 cup*

1 tablespoon butter

1 tablespoon olive oil

2 cups cored, seeded, and chopped ripe plum tomatoes

1 large clove garlic, peeled and minced

12 pitted black ripe olives, chopped

2 tablespoons rinsed and drained capers

Salt and pepper to taste

1 Combine the butter and olive oil in a medium skillet and cook over medium-high heat until the butter is melted. Add the tomatoes and garlic and cook for 2 to 3 minutes, stirring often. Add the olives and capers, and cook, stirring 1 minute more.

2 Remove from heat and season with salt and pepper. Cover and reserve. Just before serving, reheat, adding a little water or wine to the sauce if necessary, and spoon over the grilled fillets.

Vary It! You can substitute green olives or kalamata olives for the black olives, or add $^1/_4$ cup chopped, bottled artichoke hearts.

The biggest mistake people make when preparing fish — on or off the grill — is overcooking it. Hover over grilling fillets like a hen around her chicks. Check the interior for doneness. And don't forget this very important rule: You should never turn fillets on the grill more than once. In fact, you may not even have to turn the fillets at all: If the fillets are less than 1-inch thick and have their skin on, they will cook through with only small bits of skin clinging to the grid.

Fillets come dressed or undressed (so to speak). Flatfish like flounder, turbot, and sole is always skinless, as is mahi-mahi. But fillets with their skins on offer a natural barrier to the heat, which can prevent overcooking. The skin also holds the delicate flesh together as it grills. Bass, salmon, and bluefish fillets, for example, come with their skin intact.

Spice-Rubbed Catfish Fillets with Basil Mayonnaise

In this recipe, a bread crumb batter helps to keep the tender catfish fillets from burning on the grill, and a fresh basil and Tabasco sauce mayonnaise makes the perfect, assertive complementary sauce.

Preparation time: *20 minutes*

Grilling time: *8 to 10 minutes*

Yield: *4 servings*

Basil Mayonnaise (see following recipe)	*1 teaspoon dried basil*
1¹/₂ pounds catfish fillets	*¹/₂ teaspoon dried thyme, or ¹/₂ teaspoon ground cumin*
¹/₃ cup buttermilk	
¹/₄ teaspoon Tabasco sauce, or to taste	*Salt and pepper to taste*
¹/₂ cup fine dry bread crumbs	*4 sprigs of basil (optional)*
1 teaspoon grated lemon peel	*4 lemon wedges (optional)*

1 Prepare Basil Mayonnaise. Cover and refrigerate until ready to serve.

2 Prepare a medium-hot fire in a charcoal or gas grill.

3 Rinse the fillets under cold running water and pat dry with paper towels. Combine the buttermilk and Tabasco sauce in a shallow dish. Combine the bread crumbs, lemon peel, basil, thyme or cumin, and salt and pepper in a second shallow dish. Dip the catfish first in the buttermilk-Tabasco mixture and coat both sides lightly in the seasoned bread crumb mixture.

4 Place the fish on a well-oiled grid (directly over the heat) or in an oiled fish basket. Grill for about 4 to 5 minutes per side, turning once, until the fillets are opaque in the center and the crumb coating is lightly browned. To test for doneness, make a small incision with the tip of a sharp knife in the thickest part of each fillet. Catfish fillets vary, from $^1/_4$ to $^3/_4$ inches thick. Final cooking time depends on the thickness of the fillets.

5 Using a wide spatula, carefully transfer the fillets to individual plates. Top each with a generous dollop of Basil Mayonnaise. Garnish with a sprig of fresh basil and a lemon wedge (if desired).

Basil Mayonnaise

Yield: *About $^1/_2$ cup*

$^1/_2$ cup mayonnaise

$^1/_4$ cup packed fresh basil leaves

l teaspoon fresh lemon juice

$^1/_2$ teaspoon Tabasco sauce, or to taste

Puree all the ingredients in a blender container until smooth, stopping as necessary to scrape down the sides.

Vary It! For mouthwatering sandwiches, serve these fillets on slices of toasted sourdough or Italian bread with sprigs of tart, crisp watercress or arugula leaves.

For a lowfat dish, you can forgo the Basil Mayonnaise and serve these fillets with a simple drizzle of fresh lemon juice. Or use reduced fat mayonnaise, or fat-free yogurt combined with reduced-fat mayonnaise for fewer calories.

We generally advise you throughout this book to avoid using wood chips with foods that grill in less than 30 minutes. The smoke from chips, we feel, is too subtle to really have an effect on quick-grilling foods. However, the exception to this rule is grilling fish. Fish flesh, compared to beef, pork, poultry, and lamb, is so tender and delicate that it readily absorbs the gentle flavors of smoking wood chips. So, throw those presoaked chips into the fire (or place them in a smoke box if you have a gas grill). They have a very pleasant effect on all kinds of freshwater fish and seafood.

Asian-Style Salmon Fillets with Vegetables

Here's a recipe that tops lovely, center-cut, pink, grilled salmon fillets with thin red peppers, zucchini, and scallions — the color photo section shows a stunning example. Center-cut salmon fillets are about $1^1/_4$ to $1^1/_2$ inches thick. Thinner fillets, cut from the tail end of the salmon, can easily overcook and should not be used for this recipe.

Salmon skin grills to a tasty crispness, so purchase fillets with their skin intact. The fresh, thinly sliced vegetables are set on the grill, about 5 minutes before the fish, to steam in an aluminum foil packet.

Preparation time: *30 minutes*

Marinating time: *30 minutes to 1 hour*

Grilling time: *7 to 10 minutes for the salmon and 10 to 15 minutes for the vegetables*

Yield: *4 servings*

4 center-cut salmon fillets, about 6 to 7 ounces each and about $1^1/_4$ to $1^1/_2$ inches thick, with skin

2 tablespoons sesame oil

2 tablespoons light soy sauce

1 tablespoon water

$1/_2$ tablespoon balsamic vinegar

2 teaspoons peeled and minced fresh ginger

2 teaspoons light brown sugar, packed

1 clove garlic, peeled and minced

$1/_8$ teaspoon crushed red pepper flakes

1 zucchini, cut into strips about $1/_4$ to $1/_2$-inch wide and 3 to 4 inches long

1 red pepper, cored, seeded, and cut into $1/_4$ to $1/_2$-inch-wide strips

2 scallions, white and green parts, trimmed and sliced into 2-inch-long strips

$1/_2$ tablespoon vegetable oil

Salt and pepper to taste

1 Rinse the salmon fillets under cold running water and gently pat dry with paper towels.

2 Remove any pin bones in the fillets. (See Figure 16-4.)

3 In a shallow, non-reactive baking dish, mix the sesame oil, soy sauce, water, vinegar, ginger, brown sugar, garlic, and red pepper flakes. Add the salmon fillets and turn them to coat in the marinade. Cover and refrigerate, skin side up, for about 30 minutes to 1 hour, turning occasionally.

4 Prepare a medium-hot fire in a covered charcoal or gas grill.

Figure 16-4:
A pair of
tweezers
helps to
remove tiny
pin bones
from
salmon
fillets.

Remove any pin bones in the salmon fillets!

5 As the fire preheats, tear off a large piece of heavy-duty aluminum foil (or use a double thickness of foil), about 14 inches long. Arrange the zucchini, red pepper strips, and scallions in the center of the foil; season with salt and pepper. Bring the four corners of the foil together to make a packet. Starting at the bottom, crimp together the open edges, leaving a small opening at the top of the packet.

6 Using a metal spatula, lift the salmon fillets from the marinade to a clean plate, shaking off any excess marinade. Pour any remaining marinade into the foil packet over the vegetables. Add the vegetable oil and tightly crimp or close the opening in the top of the packet.

7 Place the packet on the grid. Cover and cook for 4 to 5 minutes *before* placing the salmon on the grill. (The vegetables need about 10 to 15 minutes total cooking time. Carefully peek into the packet to check for doneness after about 10 minutes; the vegetables should be crisp-tender. If necessary, set the packet on the edge of the grid to keep it warm until the fish is cooked.)

8 Place the salmon fillets skin side up, on the lightly oiled grill grid, over medium heat. Cover and grill for 7 to 10 minutes or until the salmon is done, turning once with a wide metal spatula. Insert a thin-bladed knife into the thickest part of each fillet to check for doneness; the fish is cooked when the pink flesh is almost opaque.

9 Use a wide spatula to remove the fillets to a serving platter. Use tongs or a mitt to carefully remove the foil packet from the grid. Open the packet — watch out for the hot steam. Pour the vegetables and juices over the salmon fillets on the platter and serve immediately.

Vary It! You can substitute 8 thin asparagus spears, cut into 2- to 3-inch lengths, or 24 snow peas (about 4 ounces), trimmed of stems, for the zucchini.

Attempting to guide people about how long to cook their fish is just as difficult as giving advice on how long to cook their steaks or hamburgers. Everybody has a preference for doneness. For example, some people like salmon well done, with no hint of pink in the center. Others like salmon deep pink and almost raw on the inside, with a sizzling, surface sear. That said, always treat our cooking times as guidelines. Peek into the flesh of the fish to test for doneness a few minutes before the estimated time. Fish, like other food, can be put back on the grid if it's underdone to your liking, but you can't reverse the grilling gears if it's overdone.

Holy smoked fish, Batman!

Lightly smoked fish, which can be made at home, using an ordinary covered charcoal grill and a steady supply of wood chips, has marvelous flavor that is well-worth pursuing. Here are several tips for smoking fish:

- ✔ High-fat and dark-fleshed fish are best suited for smoking because they are moist enough to slow-cook and smoke — fish with less fat may dry out on the grill.

- ✔ Fish that's ideal for smoking includes mackerel, salmon, tuna, swordfish, and marlin.

- ✔ Small fish, like mackerel and trout, can be left whole and should be wet-cured in a solution of water, salt, sugar, and seasonings of your choice.

- ✔ You can cut larger fish (such as salmon) into fillets, steaks, or chunks and dry-cure them with equal parts salt and sugar, and your choice of seasonings. Karen Homarus, owner and co-founder of Homarus, Inc. Smoked Seafood Mail Order in Mt. Kisco, New York, prefers the flavor of kosher salt and brown sugar — white sugar and regular table salt can work as well.

- ✔ Whenever possible, leave the skin on — it acts as a protective barrier to the fire. The skin isn't edible, however, so be sure to remove it after you've finished smoking the fish.

Smoked Salmon Fillet

A cloud of steady smoke, made by throwing handfuls of pre-soaked wood chips over the coals, permeates the delicate flesh of this dry-cured salmon, infusing it with incomparable flavor. If you love grilled salmon or smoked fish, you'll enjoy making (and eating!) this recipe on your covered charcoal grill. You can see an example of this dish in the color photo section of this book.

Preparation time: 15 minutes

Time needed to dry-cure salmon: 6 hours or overnight

Grilling time: 25 to 30 minutes

Yield: 6 main dish servings or 10 to 12 appetizer servings

2-pound salmon fillet with skin, about 1 inch at thickest point

$^1/_4$ cup coarse kosher salt

$^1/_4$ cup light brown sugar, packed

1 teaspoon garlic powder

1 teaspoon pepper

Oil for brushing the aluminum foil and the salmon

About 3 to 4 cups hardwood chips, presoaked

Lemon slices and watercress sprigs for garnish (optional)

1 Rinse the fillet and pat dry with paper towels. Check the salmon for any small pin bones and remove them. (Refer to Figure 16-4.)

2 Place the fillet completely flat in a non-reactive dish or container. Mix together the salt, sugar, garlic powder, and pepper and sprinkle the mixture onto both sides of the fillet. Let the fish sit in the refrigerator for at least 6 hours, or overnight. (The longer the fillet sits in the sugar-salt rub, the more intense and salty the flavor.)

3 Half an hour before smoking the fish, prepare a small fire in a covered charcoal or gas grill, using about 40 briquettes for a charcoal grill. A drip pan is not necessary. If using a gas grill, set the temperature to low, about 300°, and prepare an indirect fire in a gas grill, as explained in Chapter 1.

4 Rinse the fillet thoroughly under cold running water. Cut a piece of aluminum foil about 1 inch longer and wider than the fillet. Perforate the foil with a fork in about 6 to 7 places and oil it lightly. Place the fillet on the foil, skin side down. Brush the top of the fillet lightly with oil.

5 When the coals are hot, bank them to one side of the grill and top with 2 large handfuls of the presoaked wood chips.

6 Place the fillet on the grid, opposite the coals or heat. Cover the grill, half-closing the top vents, and cook, without turning, for about 25 to 30 minutes or until the flesh is firm and opaque but not dry. (The actual cooking time depends on the thickness of the fish and the intensity of the heat. An instant-thermometer will register 140° in the thickest part of the fillet when done. Start testing for doneness after 20 minutes.) Be sure to add more wood chips, after about 15 minutes and as necessary, to keep a steady supply of flavored smoke.

7 Remove the fillet from the grill and let stand 3 to 4 minutes. Carefully invert the fillet onto a large platter and peel off the aluminum foil. (The skin will stick to the foil and should be discarded.) Invert the skinless fillet onto a second platter with the colorful bright flesh facing up. Cover and refrigerate for several hours or until completely chilled.

8 If desired, garnish the platter with watercress and slices of fresh lemons.

Go-With: Serve as breakfast or brunch food with bagels, cream cheese, and sliced tomatoes, or as an elegant appetizer with plain crackers.

If you're not inclined to try curing and smoking fish yourself (and we certainly hope that you do), you can order preservative-free Norwegian smoked salmon, pastrami smoked salmon, and smoked trout from Homarus. Call 1-800-23-SALMON from October 1 to April 1.

Making heads and tails of whole fish

We believe that grilling a whole fish — head and tail intact — makes for some of the most delicious eating imaginable. Of course, we exempt from this discussion fish that may weigh several hundred pounds, like tuna, or fish that may take up half a backyard, like swordfish — both of which are sold as steaks. But grilling a beautiful smaller fish like trout, red snapper, bluefish, porgy, sea bass, or pompano (a fish Mark Twain said was as delicious as "the less criminal forms of sin") makes even the simplest recipe a feast.

A whole fish is a good grilling choice because the skin naturally protects the delicate flesh from falling apart as it grills. A whole fish stays juicier and is easier to turn if grilled with the head intact. We are not unaware, however, that many people don't much care for fish staring back at them while they're eating, so cutting off the head is okay. A whole, beheaded fish will still retain more succulence and flavor than a fillet. And you can always save the fish head to make a good fish stock.

Whole Grilled Trout with Thyme and Almond Butter Sauce

This is one of our favorite recipes in the book, and if you've never before grilled a whole fish, you are in for a pleasant culinary treat. (See the color photo insert for an example.) The skin grills to a crisp finish while the flesh stays moist and succulent. Slashing the fish along both of its sides allows the seasonings of olive oil, lemon juice, thyme, and garlic to permeate through the skin and into the tender flesh.

Preparation time: *15 minutes*

Marinating time: *30 minutes to 1 hour*

Grilling time: *10 minutes*

Yield: *2 servings*

1 rainbow trout, about $1^1/_4$ to $1^1/_2$ pounds, cleaned, gutted, and scaled, with head intact

2 tablespoons olive oil

2 teaspoons fresh lemon juice

2 medium cloves garlic, peeled and minced (about $1^1/_2$ teaspoons)

2 teaspoons minced fresh thyme, or $^3/_4$ teaspoon dried thyme

Salt and pepper to taste

3 to 4 fresh thyme sprigs, each about 2 to 3 inches long

Almond Butter Sauce (see following recipe)

1 Rinse the fish and pat dry with paper towels. Make 4- to 5 $^1/_2$-inch-deep slashes on each side of the fish, spaced about 2 inches apart. (See Figure 16-5.)

2 In a small mixing bowl, combine the olive oil, lemon juice, garlic, and the minced or dried thyme. Place the fish in a large, shallow, non-reactive dish or container. Rub the marinade into the slashes on both sides of the fish and into its *cavity* (the hollow area made by cleaning and gutting the fish). Sprinkle salt and pepper on both sides and in the cavity. Place the thyme sprigs into the cavity. Cover and refrigerate for 30 minutes to 1 hour.

3 Prepare a medium-hot fire in a charcoal or gas grill.

4 Generously oil both sides of a hinged, wire fish basket. Place the fish on one side of the basket with its head closest to the hinged end and its tail at the handle end. (This ensures that the thickest part of the fish is closest to the coals when grilling in a charcoal kettle grill, where the basket will not lay flat.) Close the basket.

(continued)

Figure 16-5:
Slash the fish to allow the seasoning to permeate through the skin and into the flesh.

5 Place the basket on the grid directly over the heat. Cover and grill for about 4 to 5 minutes or until nicely browned on one side. Turn the basket over; cover and grill for another 4 to 5 minutes or until the fish is done. Insert a thin-bladed knife or an instant-read thermometer into the thickest part of the fish. When done, the flesh near the bone will look opaque, and the thermometer will register 140°.

6 Open the basket; turn the fish onto a warm platter and drizzle the Almond Butter Sauce down the center of the fish. Serve by cutting down through the flesh to the backbone and lifting off sections between the slashes with a metal spatula or large spoon.

Vary It! To serve four, simply double the recipe and use two fish baskets or one large basket that holds two trout.

Almond Butter Sauce

It's best to chop and assemble the ingredients for this sauce while your grill pre-heats, and then finish making it just before the fish is grilled.

Preparation time: 5 minutes

Yield: Enough sauce for 1 1¹/₄- to 1¹/₂-pound trout

2 tablespoons butter

2 teaspoons lemon juice

2 tablespoons slivered almonds, coarsely chopped

Pepper to taste

In a small saucepan, melt the butter with the lemon juice; add the almonds and cook over low heat until the almonds are lightly browned. Season with pepper. Remove from heat immediately to prevent the almonds from overbrowning.

She Grills Shellfish by the Seashore

Grilling shellfish may sound like an odd idea, but you may be surprised to find out how tasty shellfish can be when cooked over an open fire.

Clams, mussels, and oysters

Mollusks such as clams, mussels, and oysters can be grilled directly on the grill or wrapped first in heavy-duty aluminum foil. Try to keep the delicious juices in each mollusk from spilling out into the fire. It helps to place them, with their cup side down, facing the fire. Or, better yet, place them in an aluminum pan and then on the grill. The pan catches any juices that may otherwise drip through the grid into the fire.

Grill only those clams, mussels, and oysters with tightly closed shells. Discard any with broken shells or those that do not close when tapped. And never store these live mollusks in water or a plastic bag because they will die and soon become toxic. Place them in a large bowl, uncovered, in the refrigerator and use within 24 hours of purchase.

Use a stiff brush to scrub clean hard-shell clams and oysters under cold running water. (Soft-shell clams, like steamers and razor clams, can hold large amounts of sand and grit. Soaking them in salted water with a handful of cornmeal for a few hours eliminates their impurities.) Mussels are a little harder to clean. Rinse them under cold running water and pull off the stiff, beardlike growth attached to each shell.

Be careful not to overcook naturally tender shellfish. Remove oysters from the grill when they open slightly. Clams and mussels will pop wide open when they're done.

Grilled Clams and Mussels with Fresh Tomato Sauce

This recipe is the perfect help-yourself party appetizer or light summer meal. Grilled mollusks are also popular with football tailgaters — a little portable grill or hibachi is all you need to get the shells to pop open. Prepare the simple lemon butter or the Fresh Tomato Sauce (recipe follows) before leaving home, and reheat in a small saucepan, right next to the shellfish. Don't forget to pack a loaf of crusty French or Italian bread to soak up the wonderful sauce.

Preparation time: *25 minutes*

Grilling time: *2 to 6 minutes*

Yield: *4 main dish servings or 6 to 8 appetizer servings*

36 to 40 hard-shell clams or mussels in the shell (or a combination of clams and mussels), all scrubbed clean

4 tablespoons butter

1 tablespoon olive oil

1 teaspoon Dijon-style mustard

1 tablespoon fresh lemon juice

Tabasco sauce to taste (optional)

Pepper to taste

Fresh Tomato Sauce (see following recipe)

(continued)

1 Prepare a hot fire in a charcoal or gas grill.

2 Combine the butter and oil in a small saucepan on top of the stove over low heat (or to one side of the grill). Heat until the butter is melted. Add the mustard and use a wire whisk or fork to incorporate it into the butter and oil. Add the lemon juice, Tabasco sauce (if desired), and the pepper; cook and stir over low heat for 1 minute. Cover to keep the sauce warm, and reheat if necessary.

3 Place mollusks in their unopened shells directly on the grill grid. (Or place them on a large metal baking pan to collect juices as the mollusks open.) Cover the grill and cook 2 to 6 minutes. Remove them as soon as their shells pop wide open, and place in a large bowl or platter. The actual cooking time depends on the size of each mollusk and intensity of the heat.

4 Move the mollusks that don't open after about 5 minutes to a hotter spot. Discard any that do not eventually open. The shells will be roaring hot! Use long-handled tongs or a barbecue mitt to remove them from the grill.

5 Twist off and discard the top shell, being careful not to spill the flavorful mollusk juice. (This is a good task for your guests!) Drizzle the melted butter mixture over them or serve with the Fresh Tomato Sauce. (See the following recipe.)

Vary It! For the flavors of fresh herbs, add $1/4$ cup chopped fresh cilantro, basil, or Italian parsley to the butter sauce.

Fresh Tomato Sauce

Preparation time: 20 minutes

Yield: $1^1/4$ cups

2 tablespoons olive oil

2 tablespoons butter

3 large cloves garlic, peeled and finely minced (about 1 tablespoon)

3 ripe plum tomatoes, seeded and finely chopped (about 1 cup)

$1/2$ cup bottled clam juice

Juice of half a lemon (about $1^1/2$ tablespoons)

$1/4$ teaspoon red pepper flakes

$1/3$ cup coarsely chopped fresh basil or Italian parsley

Black pepper to taste

1 Heat the oil and butter in a medium saucepan over medium heat. Add the garlic and cook briefly for 1 minute, until very lightly browned.

2 Add the tomatoes, clam juice, lemon juice, and red pepper flakes; simmer over medium heat for 4 to 5 minutes, stirring often. Remove from the heat.

3 Just before serving, add the chopped basil or parsley and the pepper. Pour the sauce over the grilled mussels and clams set into a large serving bowl. Serve immediately with crusty French or Italian bread.

Vary It! Serve the sauce over ³/₄ pound of steaming linguine, adding the clams and sauce as soon as the pasta is drained. If the sauce needs additional moisture, add ¹/₄ to ¹/₂ cup more bottled clam juice.

Soft-shell crabs

Soft-shell crabs do well on the grill. These days, frozen soft-shell crabs are readily available year-round — and they're not bad — but the best fresh soft-shell crabs start to come in mid-May, and the season is over before the end of summer.

Grilled Soft-Shell Crabs

We tested these crabs over a fire made of a combination of hardwood hickory chunks and charcoal. The hickory wood flavor was divine with the crab.

Preparation time: 10 minutes

Grilling time: 6 minutes

Yield: 4 servings

3 tablespoons butter	3 tablespoons finely chopped fresh basil, or 1 tablespoon dried basil
3 tablespoons olive oil	Salt and pepper to taste
Juice of half a lemon	Tabasco sauce to taste
Grated peel of half a lemon	8 soft-shell crabs, cleaned

1 Prepare a medium-hot fire in a charcoal or gas grill.

2 As the fire is preheating, melt the butter in a small saucepan; add the olive oil, lemon juice, lemon peel, basil, and salt and pepper. If you like a hot, spicy flavor, add Tabasco sauce. Brush the crabs with most of the butter sauce, coating both sides.

3 Place the crabs on a lightly oiled grid, directly over the heat. Turn and brush every 2 to 3 minutes with any remaining basting sauce. Cook for a total of 6 to 8 minutes. The crabs are cooked when they appear bright red and firm to the touch.

Go-With: Serve with Black Bean and Red Pepper Salsa (Chapter 6), or Grilled Tomatoes with Basil and Cornbread Stuffing (Chapter 17).

Shrimp

Shrimp is a classic grilled dish — especially in kebabs. (See Chapter 9.) In this section, however, we show you a unique way to prepare shrimp, stuffing them with pesto, and then share a famous chef's recipe that's out of this world!

Try not to buy shrimp that has already been shelled, deveined, and packaged. This shrimp will have lost some of its freshness. Practice deveining it yourself (see Figure 16-6) or have your fish handler devein fresh shrimp the same day you plan to grill it.

Cleaning and Deveining Shrimp

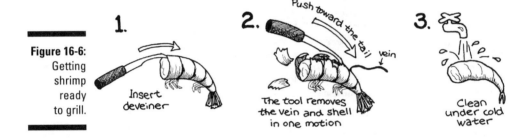

Figure 16-6: Getting shrimp ready to grill.

1. Insert deveiner

2. Push toward the tail — vein. The tool removes the vein and shell in one motion

3. Clean under cold water

Pesto Shrimp in the Shell

Grilling shrimp in their shells helps to keep the flesh moist and tender. A little pesto sauce, found in Chapter 6, stuffed into the shell adds flavor and color. If you have a wire basket, place the pesto-stuffed shrimp in the basket so that you can turn them over all at once. Purchase shrimp that is sized about 16 to 20 per pound, and sold as either extra-large or jumbo.

Although a little messy, this dish makes a terrific party appetizer; be sure to hand out plenty of napkins. Set the bright pink grilled shrimp on a large serving platter and garnish with lemon wedges.

Preparation time: *30 minutes (less if you start with cleaned shrimp)*

Grilling time: *4 to 5 minutes*

Yield: *8 to 10 appetizer servings*

1¹/₂ pounds extra-large to jumbo shrimp (about 24 to 28 shrimp), dark vein removed with shell intact

¹/₂ cup Pesto Sauce (recipe in Chapter 6)

Juice of 1 lemon

Salt and pepper to taste

8 to 10 lemon wedges, for garnish

4 sprigs of fresh basil, for garnish

1 Rinse and drain the shrimp under cold running water.

2 Stuff about ¹/₄ to ¹/₂ teaspoon pesto sauce into the vein cavity and between the shell and flesh of each shrimp. The shell holds the pesto stuffing in place as the shrimp grills.

3 Place the shrimp in a large, flat dish and drizzle the juice from the one lemon over them; season with salt and pepper. Cover and refrigerate 1 to 2 hours.

4 Prepare a medium-hot fire in a gas or charcoal grill.

5 Place the shrimp on an oiled grid or in an oiled wire basket, directly over the heat.

6 Grill for 4 to 5 minutes or until the shrimp are pink and opaque, turning frequently. Be careful not to overcook, or they will become dry and rubbery. Before serving, peel and taste a shrimp; serve with additional salt and pepper (if desired) on a large platter garnished with lemon wedges and fresh basil.

Jimmy Schmidt's Grilled Barbecued Shrimp

Jimmy Schmidt, owner of The Rattlesnake Club in Detroit, Michigan, is considered one of the fathers of New American Cuisine. Chef Schmidt can take a traditional dish and refine it to become something new and exciting, which is what he does here by adding sweet corn and peppers and the crunchy texture of jícama (pronounced HEE-kah-mah).

Chef Schmidt suggests skewering together raw shrimp to make them easier to turn on the grid, and to keep them from falling through the food grate. Lay 6 to 8 of the cleaned shrimp, side by side on your counter, but with heads and tails facing in opposite directions. Run 2 presoaked, wooden skewers parallel to each other, through the shrimp. Repeat with the remaining shrimp, and you're ready to grill.

Preparation time: *25 minutes*

Grilling time: *5 minutes*

Yield: *4 servings*

(continued)

³/₄ cup bottled or homemade barbecue sauce

¹/₄ cup fresh lime juice

3 tablespoons peeled and grated fresh ginger, divided

Tabasco sauce to taste

1¹/₂ pounds jumbo shrimp (16 to 20 shrimp per pound)

1 tablespoon olive oil

Paprika to taste

Salt and pepper to taste

¹/₂ cup chopped fresh cilantro leaves

Roast Corn, Peppers, and Jícama Slaw (see following recipe)

1 Prepare a hot fire in a charcoal or gas grill.

2 In a small bowl, combine the barbecue sauce, lime juice, 2 tablespoons of the ginger, and Tabasco sauce. Set aside.

3 Peel, devein, and rinse the shrimp (see Figure 16-6), leaving the tail shells intact.

4 In a medium bowl, toss together the shrimp, olive oil, and remaining 1 tablespoon grated ginger. Season with paprika and salt and pepper.

5 Place the shrimp on a well-oiled grill grid, (skewering, if desired, as described in the introduction to this recipe), directly over the heat. Grill for about 3 minutes; turn and brush with the barbecue-lime sauce. Grill for another 2 to 3 minutes or until the shrimp are pink. (Be careful not to overcook, or they will become tough and rubbery. If you wish, remove them from the grill just before they are fully cooked. The stored heat energy in each shrimp will finish cooking it.) Transfer the shrimp to the edges of a large serving platter and brush with more of the barbecue-lime sauce.

6 Mound the slaw (see following recipe) in the center of the platter. Arrange the shrimp around the slaw, slightly overlapping. Sprinkle the cilantro over the shrimp and serve immediately.

Roast Corn, Peppers, and Jícama Slaw

Preparation time: *25 minutes*

Yield: *4 servings*

2 ears fresh sweet corn, husks on, silk removed

2 red bell peppers, cut into fine julienne

1 jícama root, peeled and cut into fine julienne (about 2 cups)

¹/₂ cup extra-virgin olive oil

¹/₂ cup fresh lime juice

1 bunch scallions, green parts only, very finely chopped

1 clove garlic, peeled and finely minced

Salt and black pepper to taste

Red pepper flakes (optional)

1 Prepare a medium-hot fire in a charcoal or gas grill.

2 Place the ears of corn wrapped in their husks, with silk removed, on the grid (if necessary, see the recipe for Grilled Corn on the Cob in Chapter 17 for more specific directions on how to grill corn in its husk); cook until well browned on all sides, for 10 to 15 minutes. Remove from the grid and allow to cool.

3 Stand an ear of grilled corn upright on a flat dish and use a knife to scrape or cut the kernels off the cob. Repeat with the second ear. Transfer the kernels to a medium mixing bowl; add the peppers, jícama, olive oil, lime juice, scallions and garlic; stir until well combined. Season with the salt and black pepper and red pepper flakes (if desired). Cover and refrigerate at least 1 hour before serving.

If you have trouble locating jícama (see Figure 16-7), you can substitute a small green cabbage or head of bok choy.

Figure 16-7:
Although it's not the prettiest vegetable, jícama has a pleasant, crunchy texture and is good either raw or cooked.

Chapter 17

Not for Vegetarians Only

*T*hink "grilling" and you won't necessarily think of fruits and vegetables — but oh, are you missing something if you haven't tried grilling these fresh foods! In this chapter, you discover the vegetables and fruits that you can grill successfully — every time. From corn to summer squash, bananas to nectarines, we cover the gamut in here.

Veggies Not Like Mom Used to Make

Maybe if your mother had *grilled* your vegetables when you were a kid, she wouldn't have had to bribe you to clean them off your plate. Grilled vegetables take on the wonderful smoky flavors of the grill while retaining their natural sweetness and crunch. Boiling, on the other hand, robs vegetables of flavor and precious vitamins, while sautéing and deep frying can add unwanted fat and calories.

It's true that delicate veggies need tender loving care while grilling to keep them from charring, but the delicious end results are worth that little extra effort.

Here is a list of some vegetables that are particularly well suited for grilling. (See Figure 17-1 for examples of these cuts.)

- ✔ Asparagus
- ✔ Corn on the cob
- ✔ Eggplant
- ✔ Onions
- ✔ Potatoes
- ✔ Scallions
- ✔ Sweet peppers
- ✔ Tomatoes
- ✔ Zucchini

Simple seasoning (and brief marinating) is best

By far the simplest way to grill vegetables is to give them a brushing of oil — olive, peanut, corn, and safflower oils are all recommended — and a sprinkling of salt and pepper to taste. Other possibilities include:

Figure 17-1:
Slicing up veggies for the grill.

✔ Coarse kosher salt sprinkled to taste on any vegetable, before or after grilling, adds great flavor.

✔ Ground cumin or grated lemon peel is delicious with fresh tomato slices.

✔ Grated fresh ginger combined with grated lemon peel and garlic seasoned mushrooms and thin slices of acorn or butternut squash.

✔ Tarragon is terrific with eggplant and summer squash.

✔ Hot chili powder or Tabasco sauce livens up potato planks or wedges, or small new potatoes.

✔ Chopped fresh garlic, olive oil, and basil (mixed together) are good with just about any grilled, smoke-infused vegetable.

Many vegetables benefit from a little marinating before grilling. However, unlike meat or poultry, vegetables quickly absorb the flavors of the marinade and require only about 30 minutes to 1 hour of soaking — in fact, any longer may make them soft and mushy. If you don't have time to marinate vegetables, skip this step altogether and simply brush them with a little oil. Then after grilling, toss them in a lemon-herb vinaigrette, using a bottled dressing, if you like. (See Chapter 5 for loads of marinade recipes.)

Tossing vegetables with oil and seasonings in a large bowl before grilling is easier than brushing pieces individually. But don't try this with onions; they will separate from rounds into rings that are almost impossible to grill. Olive oils or vegetable oils, with their relatively high smoking point, are the preferred choices for brushing on vegetables before grilling.

Many vegetables can be seasoned and wrapped in aluminum foil packets before grilling. They steam in the packet, retaining color, moisture, and flavor. Be sure to pierce a few holes in the top of the packet so that the grill's smoke can penetrate and infuse the food with flavor. To make low-calorie vegetable packets, use canned broth, lemon juice, and fresh herbs as seasonings, omitting fats like butter and oil. Be sure to combine only those vegetables with the same cooking time. For example, don't mix snow peas with carrot pieces, unless the carrots are cut into thin julienne strips or parboiled until almost cooked through. Turn the packets occasionally to prevent the food inside from burning, especially if you are grilling the vegetables longer than 15 minutes.

You can't slough off while grilling vegetables — vigilance is important because vegetables can burn quickly. A slight char is very pleasing, but blackened, dried-out vegetables taste horrible.

Here are some more quick tips for grilling vegetables:

- ✔ Be sure that your grilling surface is scraped completely clean so that vegetables don't take on the flavors of other foods. Oil the grill grid well to prevent vegetables from sticking.

- ✔ Don't grill vegetables over too intense a fire, or they are sure to burn without cooking through. Most vegetables contain a fair amount of sugar, which sizzles beautifully into a light brown crust from the heat of the grill. But if cooked over too intense a heat, this natural sugar causes them to burn. A medium to medium-hot fire is plenty hot.

- ✔ A hinged wire basket or a grill topper (see Chapter 2) is a terrific grilling gadget to keep veggies, especially onions, from falling through the grid. If you're grilling directly on the grid, cut all vegetables large enough so that they don't slip through. Peppers can be halved or quartered before grilling and then sliced into smaller strips after.

- ✔ To determine doneness, use the skewer test: The vegetable is cooked if it can be easily pierced with a skewer. However, some people prefer a very crisp, almost raw, finish to their vegetables.

- ✔ When grilling vegetables with other long-cooking foods like chicken or beef, grill the vegetables first and move them to the outer edges of the grid or to a 300-degree oven to keep them warm.

You can save time by *parboiling* (boiling a few minutes to soften) thick, long-cooking vegetables like potatoes, hard-shell squash, and carrots before grilling, but they taste better if you take the time to grill them directly. Cut them into chunks or thin slices to shorten grilling time. Only vegetables with very thick, inedible skins need peeling.

Vegetables from A to T

In the following sections, we give you tips for grilling a range of vegetables — from artichokes to tomatoes!

Artichokes

Whole fresh artichokes should be parboiled for 20 to 25 minutes before grilling over a medium-hot fire. Slice the parboiled artichoke in half lengthwise and, using a spoon, scrape out the inedible, prickly choke. Brush generously with oil, flavored with garlic and lemon juice, or marinate in a lemon and mustard-flavored vinaigrette, before grilling. Bottled artichoke hearts, packed in oil and already cooked, are easily skewered with other foods before grilling. (Turn to Chapter 9 for Artichoke, Mushroom, and Cherry Tomato Kebabs.)

Asparagus

Grilled asparagus takes on the flavor of charcoal and develops a beautiful brown sheen. Trim off the woody ends and then peel the base to within 3 to 4 inches of the tip. Brush the stalks with oil that's flavored with a little crushed garlic and black pepper. Place the stalks perpendicular to the grill grid over medium-hot coals, turning so they brown on all sides. Pencil-thin stalks will be done in about 5 to 6 minutes, but thicker stalks can take up to 15 minutes. Stalks should be fork-tender before removing. Season with grated fresh pepper, kosher salt, and grated lemon peel.

Linguine with Goat Cheese and Grilled Asparagus

Steaming pasta and grilled vegetables are a dazzling combination. This dish tosses together grilled asparagus, tomatoes, linguine, and goat cheese for the perfect summertime appetizer or light dinner. The asparagus and tomatoes can be grilled ahead of time, if you wish, and held at room temperature before the pasta is cooked. Just be sure not to finish cooking the pasta without having the sauce ingredients ready to go. Cooked pasta needs sauce immediately to prevent its starch from gluing the strands together.

Preparation time: *25 minutes*

Grilling time: *10 minutes*

Yield: *4 servings*

1¹/₂ pounds fresh asparagus, trimmed

6 large ripe plum tomatoes, cored and halved

Olive oil for brushing vegetables

Salt and pepper to taste

1 pound linguine or fettuccine

1 tablespoon olive oil

1 tablespoon butter

2 shallots, peeled and finely chopped

2 cloves garlic, peeled and minced

6 ounces goat cheese, at room temperature

¹/₂ cup coarsely chopped fresh basil leaves

¹/₂ teaspoon red pepper flakes (optional)

1 Prepare a medium-hot fire in a charcoal or gas grill.

2 Brush the asparagus and tomato halves with oil; season with salt and pepper.

3 Place the vegetables on a lightly oiled grid. Grill asparagus for 10 to 15 minutes, depending on thickness, or until lightly browned on all sides and tender when pierced with the thin blade of a sharp knife, turning once or twice.

(continued)

Grill tomatoes for 8 to 10 minutes or until lightly browned on both sides, but still intact, turning once. Remove the asparagus to a cutting board; cut into 1$\frac{1}{2}$-inch pieces and place in a bowl. Chop the tomatoes coarsely (their skins will slip off easily and can be discarded) and place in the bowl with the asparagus. Be sure to include any tomato juices on the cutting board. Cover the bowl with foil to keep the vegetables warm.

4 When the asparagus and tomatoes are nearly finished grilling, bring 4 to 5 quarts of lightly salted water to a boil in a large covered pot; add the linguine or fettuccine. Stir thoroughly to separate the strands. Boil, uncovered, for 7 to 8 minutes or just until *al dente,* meaning the pasta still has some "bite" and is not overdone.

5 As the pasta cooks, heat the 1 tablespoon olive oil and butter in a small skillet; add the shallots and garlic and cook over medium heat, stirring occasionally, about 2 minutes or until the vegetables are wilted but not browned. (Be careful not to brown the garlic.)

6 Before draining the pasta, use a measuring cup to carefully scoop out and reserve about $\frac{1}{4}$ cup of the water. When it's ready, drain the pasta and return to the large pot.

7 Add the grilled vegetables, the goat cheese, the sautéed shallots and onion mixture, the basil, and the red pepper flakes (if desired). Toss well over medium heat for just 1 or 2 minutes, until warmed through, adding a little of the reserved cooking water if it needs more moisture. Adjust seasoning with additional salt and pepper and serve immediately.

Vary It! Almost any grilled vegetables can substitute for the asparagus in this dish. Try grilled cubes of eggplant, rounds of zucchini or yellow squash, broccoli or cauliflower florets, mushrooms, carrots, artichoke hearts, or bell peppers. If you don't like goat cheese, substitute 3 ounces each of ricotta cheese and grated Parmesan cheese.

For a dish that's not as rich in calories, omit the shallots and garlic sautéed in the butter and oil.

Belgian endive

When you think of endive, you probably think of elegant summer salads and English teas with watercress sandwiches. Think again. Endive is grillin' food. Its bitterness is mellowed when it's roasted over a charcoal fire. Cut endive heads in half lengthwise and marinate them in a good-quality bottled Italian dressing (or make up your own vinaigrette, using lots of lemon juice, olive oil, and garlic). Grill the endive halves, covered, over medium-high heat for 6 to 8 minutes or until tender, turning once and brushing frequently with marinade. Watch carefully so that the endive doesn't blacken or char.

Broccoli

Broccoli florets can be grilled, but they need to be blanched or parboiled before grilling. Trim the broccoli, cutting away the thick stalks to within 1 inch of the crown. (You can freeze the trimmed stalks and later add them to soups and stocks.) Cut the crowns into small clusters or florets. Place the florets in a covered pot with 1 inch of lightly salted boiling water; boil for about 3 to 5 minutes or until just crisp-tender. Drain and rinse under cold running water. Place the florets in a medium mixing bowl and cover with bottled salad dressing or your vinaigrette of choice. Grill, covered, on a lightly oiled grid or in a hinged wire basket over medium-high heat for about 8 minutes or until lightly browned. Turn and brush frequently with the marinade. Season with salt and pepper and serve hot or cold.

Broccoli florets can also be wrapped in heavy-duty foil with other vegetables that require the same amount of cooking time. For example, try pairing broccoli florets with cauliflower florets, sliced onion, bell pepper chunks, green beans, small cubes of potato, and rounds of zucchini and yellow squash. Add seasonings, butter or oil, and a little liquid such as broth or lemon juice to the foil packet; grill alongside other foods over direct heat. Open the packet carefully to check for doneness.

Brussels sprouts

The robust, cabbagelike flavor of Brussels sprouts stand up to smoky grilled flavors of the grill. Before grilling, parboil trimmed sprouts for about 7 minutes in lightly salted water. Drain and brush with olive oil or lemon butter and grill on skewers or in a hinged wire basket over medium-high heat for about 12 minutes, turning often and brushing with butter or oil.

Carrots

Grilling carrots brings out their natural sweetness. Cut each into 2- to 3-inch pieces, brush with oil and grill directly over medium-hot coals for about 20 minutes, until tender, turning as necessary to brown on all sides. You also can first parboil in $1/2$ to 1 inch of water for about 10 minutes; drain well and brush lightly with melted butter or oil before grilling for 10 to 15 minutes or until tender. Toss grilled carrots in a mixture of equal parts melted butter and brown sugar. Season with salt and pepper to taste. If desired, add a little Grand Marnier or other orange liqueur, or powdered ginger and crushed garlic. You can also wrap sliced carrots in heavy-duty foil with butter and seasonings and grill them (without parboiling first) over medium-high heat until crisp-tender.

Corn

When you're shopping for corn for the grill, always buy the freshest ears that you can find. As soon as corn is picked, its sugar begins to convert to starch, reducing its sweetness. Look for corn that is sold as fresh-picked or is at least kept cold to slow down the sugar to starch conversion. The green husks should look bright and fresh, and if pierced with a fingernail, the kernels should squirt out a milky-white liquid.

You can dress up melted butter for corn in endless ways. Add any of the following (to your taste) to melted butter for corn: lemon or lime juice, chili or curry powder, Tabasco sauce, cayenne pepper, soy sauce, minced garlic, finely minced dill, basil or cilantro, dry mustard, and ground ginger. For a butterless, fat-free, corn-eating experience, simply squeeze fresh lemon or lime juice over freshly grilled ears.

Grilled Corn on the Cob

Recipes for grilling corn often call for soaking the husks first in water for half an hour to prevent scorching as they grill. However, we find this extra step to be completely unnecessary. We show an example of this dish in the color photo section of this book.

Preparation time: 10 minutes for 6 ears

Grilling time: 20 minutes

6 ears fresh corn   Salt and pepper to taste

6 tablespoons butter, melted

1 Strip off 5 to 6 of the outer dark green corn husks.

2 Carefully peel back the remaining husks, leaving them attached at the base of the ear, and remove the silky threads. (See Figure 17-2.)

3 Pull the husks back up and wrap them securely in place, using kitchen twine or a thin strip of husk, as shown in Figure 17-2.

4 Place the ears on an oiled grid, over medium heat, and grill for 10 to 15 minutes, turning every 5 minutes. Peek beyond the husks at the kernels to determine doneness; the kernels should be golden yellow.

5 When the corn is cooked, remove the husks, brush the ears with melted butter (about 1 tablespoon per ear), and season with salt and pepper to taste.

6 Place the corn back on the grid (this time without the husks) and grill for 5 minutes more or until the corn is very lightly charred on all sides.

Figure 17-2:
Preparing
corn for
the grill.

If you want the corn to be served with other grilled foods, you can grill it in stages. Grill the ears in their husks until the kernels are golden yellow and then remove the ears from the grill. About 5 to 10 minutes before the rest of the food is ready, brush each ear with the melted butter and place back on the grid — without the husks — to finish cooking.

Eggplant

Some people say that eggplant is absolutely best when grilled, and boy, do we agree. Eggplant is a firm-textured vegetable that can be cut into large chunks for kebabs, sliced in half lengthwise, or sliced into rounds before grilling. Sautéing eggplant on the top of the stove requires a rich amount of high-calorie oil, but grilled eggplant needs only a thin coating of oil. Some controversy exists about whether the bitterness of eggplant is reduced by sprinkling cut slices with salt. If the eggplant is large, reduce the bitterness by sprinkling the cut rounds with salt and allowing them to drain for about 30 minutes. Before grilling, rinse the slices or wipe off the salt with paper towels. Smaller eggplants and Japanese-style eggplants have little bitterness and don't need this treatment.

To grill, cut eggplant into 1-inch-thick slices or cubes; brush with a flavored oil. (See Chapter 5 for ideas.) Grill over a medium-hot fire for 10 to 12 minutes, turning every 4 to 5 minutes until lightly browned on all sides. Toss grilled cubes into steaming pasta or mixed green salads or use them, along with sun-dried tomatoes and black olives, as a topping for pizza. Small grilled slices also can be wrapped around cubes of feta cheese or mozzarella cheese, secured with a toothpick into a roll, and served as an appetizer.

Baba Ghanoush

The grill's unique ability to impart rich, smoky flavor gives this popular Middle Eastern eggplant dip — pronounced bah-bah-gha-NOOSH — its very special taste. The thick tahini paste called for in this recipe is made from ground sesame seeds and is available in most supermarkets or specialty food stores.

Preparation time: *10 minutes*

Grilling time: *15 to 20 minutes*

Yield: *About 1¹/₂ cups*

1 large eggplant, about 1¹/₂ pounds

Olive oil for brushing eggplant

¹/₄ cup plus 1 tablespoon tahini

Juice of 1 large lemon (about 3 tablespoons)

3 tablespoons water

1 tablespoon extra-virgin olive oil

1 to 2 medium cloves garlic, peeled and crushed

¹/₂ teaspoon salt, or to taste

Pepper to taste

2 tablespoons chopped flat-leaf parsley

Warm pita triangles

1 Prepare a medium-hot fire in a charcoal or gas grill.

2 Cut the eggplant in half lengthwise; brush all over with oil. Place on a lightly oiled grid, cut side down. Grill, covered, for 8 to 10 minutes a side, turning once, until soft, blackened, and cooked through.

3 Transfer the eggplant to a colander over the sink, cut side down, and allow to cool and drain. When cool enough to handle, remove the charred skin, discarding any liquid and large clusters of seeds, and scoop out and reserve the remaining pulp.

4 In a food processor or blender, working in batches if necessary, add the eggplant pulp, tahini, lemon juice, water, 1 tablespoon olive oil, garlic, salt, and pepper; puree into a thick paste. Turn the dip into a bowl and garnish with parsley. Cover and let stand at room temperature for 1 hour. Or you can refrigerate the dip overnight and return it to room temperature before serving.

5 To serve, place whole pitas on the grid over moderate heat or in a 350° oven until warmed through, turning once. Cut into triangles and serve with the dip.

Garlic

Much of the world is obsessed with the incomparable power of garlic when it comes to enhancing grilled foods. Garlic makes just about every grilled food, except perhaps those with sweet flavors, taste better. A whole head of garlic is a cinch to grill and has dozens of delicious uses. Mix it into mayonnaise-based dressings or rub it onto thin, toasted baguette slices with goat cheese and sun-dried tomatoes for a simple appetizer. Add it to salad dressings or to marinated vegetables or whip it with milk and butter into mashed potatoes.

To grill a whole head of garlic (see Figure 17-3), remove any outer, loose, papery leaves. Slice across the top of the head, removing about $1/4$ inch and exposing the ends of the cloves. Drizzle with a bit of olive oil and then wrap in foil. (If desired, tuck sprigs of fresh herbs such as rosemary or thyme between the cloves.) Grill over medium-high heat for 45 minutes or until the cloves are soft and tender, turning occasionally. Squeeze out the roasted cloves. Individual cloves can also be oiled and grilled directly on the grid over medium heat for 6 to 7 minutes per side or until tender.

How to Trim and Grill garlic

Figure 17-3: Get great results with grilled garlic.

Trim one quarter off the top end of the head of garlic.

Pull off the papery, outside layer.

Wrap in foil and drizzle oil over the top and between the cloves.

After grilling, pull off the cloves and squeeze one end to pop out the insides easily.

Leeks

The leek, which looks like a giant scallion, makes a surprisingly good grilled side dish for a sizzling steak or lamb chop. Remove the green tops of the leeks to about 2 inches from the white base. Discard the base. Slice the leeks in half lengthwise and rinse thoroughly under cold running water. Gently pry apart the layers to clear out any sand or dirt. Drain well. Brush the leeks with olive oil, flavored perhaps with minced garlic and fresh or dried herbs, and sprinkle with salt and pepper; grill, cut side down, over medium-high heat for 7 to 8 minutes. Brush again with some of the oil mixture; turn and grill for another 7 to 8 minutes or until tender and lightly browned.

Mushrooms

All mushrooms, whether cultivated or plucked from the wild, can be grilled. Mushrooms should never be soaked in water to clean them. Wipe off any sand or grit with a damp paper towel, or rinse quickly and pat thoroughly dry. Button or white mushrooms are the most common. Before grilling, slice off their stems so that they lie flat — very large mushrooms can be halved or quartered before grilling. Set mushrooms directly on the grid over a medium-hot fire or skewer with pieces of fish, meat, or other vegetables. Baste them with an olive oil dressing before and during grilling. Grill about 5 minutes per side or until lightly browned. Overgrilling makes them dry and tough. Remove mushrooms from the grill when you can pierce their centers with a sharp knife or a skewer.

Garlic-Grilled Portobellos

Portobello mushrooms are huge, dark brown, umbrella-shaped mushrooms with meatlike texture and a woodsy taste that is enriched by the subtle smokiness of the grill. They are sold with or without their thick stems. Here's a simple recipe that bastes them with an olive oil, lemon juice, and garlic mixture. They are also delicious grilled and drizzled with pesto sauce. (See Chapter 6 for our Pesto Sauce recipe.)

Preparation time: *15 minutes*

Marinating time: *15 minutes*

Grilling time: *6 to 8 minutes*

Yield: *4 servings*

4 portobello mushrooms, each about 4 to 5 inches in diameter (about 1 pound)

¹/₃ cup extra-virgin olive oil

3 tablespoons lemon juice (about 1 large lemon)

2 cloves garlic, peeled and minced

Salt and pepper to taste

2 tablespoons minced fresh parsley

1 Prepare a medium-hot fire in a charcoal or gas grill.

2 Clean the portobellos by brushing off any dirt or grit with a damp paper towel. Remove the stems. (You can save them to flavor soups or stocks.)

3 In a small bowl, combine the oil, lemon juice, and garlic. Brush the caps on both sides with the flavored oil; sprinkle salt and pepper on both sides and let stand for 15 minutes, stem side up.

4 Place the caps on a well-oiled grid, stem side up; grill for 3 to 4 minutes. Turn the caps over and grill for another 3 to 4 minutes or until you can easily pierce them with a sharp knife. (Do not burn or overcook; the center should be tender and moist.)

5 Remove the caps to a platter and cut into thick slices. Garnish with parsley, and serve with grilled hamburgers, steaks, chicken, fish, or toss into salad greens.

Onions

Something about the taste of grilled onions is so appealing. Yellow, white, or red, onions have a natural sweetness that is released when they meet the heat of the grill. Yellow or red onions can be peeled and cut into 1/2-inch-thick rounds, quartered or halved. Brush the cut surface with any kind of marinade or dressing and grill over a medium-hot fire. Depending on the thickness, rounds need to cook for 5 to 6 minutes per side. Halves or quarters may take 12 to 15 minutes or more. Invariably, the rounds will separate into rings and fall through the grill grid. We recommend placing the onions in a grilling basket or on a grill topper. (Chapter 2 has the information about these grilling accessories.) Onion pieces are delicious skewered between pieces of beef, pork, or fish.

- ✔ Grilled red onions can be served as a side dish or as a colorful hamburger topping. Brush 3/4-inch-thick rounds with olive oil and grill for 5 to 6 minutes per side, until the onions are tender and lightly browned. Before serving, drizzle with a vinaigrette flavored with plenty of chopped fresh herbs.

- ✔ Small whole onions can be peeled and skewered or placed directly on the grid after being oiled or marinated. Grill for 15 minutes or until tender when pierced with a skewer. Serve with beef roasts (Chapter 12), rack of lamb (Chapter 14), or pork tenderloins (Chapter 13).

- ✔ Whole *shallots* look like baby onions and make a lovely garnish for other grilled foods. First, parboil the peeled shallots in boiling water for 2 to 3 minutes and then brush them with oil or a marinade; skewer and grill over medium heat for 10 to 15 minutes, until just tender.

- ✔ Green, leafy *scallions* can be successfully grilled with little fuss or preparation and served with grilled steaks, burgers, and chops. Trim off any roots at the base of the white bulb and remove any limp-looking green leaves. Slice off the tops, leaving 3 to 4 inches of green leaves. Brush with oil (flavored, if you want) and grill over medium-hot coals for 8 to 10 minutes, turning frequently to prevent them from charring; when done, the scallions will be lightly browned and tender through the bulb. Serve them whole or cut them diagonally into bite-size lengths. Scallions can also add flavor and decorative color to skewered kebabs of fish, shrimp, or chicken. (See Chapter 9.)

Parsnips

If you want to grill something different, try parsnips. Just like a carrot, a parsnip retains its sweet nutty flavor when grilled. Look for thick parsnips and scrub them clean (without peeling) under cold running water. Slice lengthwise or cut them into round chunks that can be skewered with other root vegetables. Brush them with oil or butter (flavored, if you want) and grill over medium-hot coals for 15 to 20 minutes, basting with additional oil or butter and turning every 7 minutes. (You can parboil them first to reduce the grilling time.) Check for doneness by piercing the thickest part with the tip of a sharp knife or a wooden skewer. Serve with additional melted butter, chopped fresh herbs, and salt and pepper. Parsnips are delicious with roasts, chops, or steaks.

A combination of grilled carrots and parsnips, garnished with chopped parsley, looks lovely on a platter of thin beef or pork slices.

Peppers

We can't heap enough praise on grilled peppers. A roasted pepper is a vegetable transformed to a smoky-flavored, velvet-textured delight. Whether red, green, yellow, or orange, roasted peppers can be used in the following ways. Keep in mind that this list is just for starters:

- For a simple, elegant appetizer, wrap roasted pepper strips around whole balls of fresh mozzarella cheese; secure with a toothpick.

- Serve strips as a salad with a balsamic vinegar dressing, black olives, artichoke hearts, and cubes of mozzarella cheese.

- Toss strips into steaming pasta with creamy goat cheese, or grilled sausages, olive oil, garlic, and herbs.

- Place on any kind of beef, pork, fish, sausage, or vegetable sandwich.

- Slice into omelets with grated fontina or mozzarella cheese.

- Place strips on toasted French bread with oil-packed sun-dried tomatoes, fresh garlic, and chopped basil for a hearty appetizer.

- Chop and combine with diced ripe tomatoes, black olives, and capers as a topping for grilled fish fillets and steaks.

- Puree into a smooth sauce and use as a colorful base for whitefish fillets or steaks. (See Chapter 16.)

Roasted Sweet Pepper Salsa

Make up a batch of this roasted pepper salsa on the weekend, so that you can serve it as a side dish for grilled meats, fish, and poultry the rest of the week. For an example, take a look at the color photo section of this book.

Preparation time: *15 minutes*

Marinating time: *1 hour*

Grilling time: *20 to 25 minutes*

Yield: *About 2 cups, or 4 servings*

2 red bell peppers

1 green bell pepper

1 yellow bell pepper

¹⁄₄ cup extra-virgin olive oil

1 tablespoon balsamic vinegar

1 to 2 tablespoons capers, rinsed and drained

1 tablespoon chopped fresh Italian parsley

1 large clove garlic, peeled and minced

Salt and pepper to taste

1 Prepare a medium-hot fire in a covered charcoal or gas grill.

2 Place the peppers on a lightly oiled grid. Grill, covered, for 20 to 25 minutes or until blackened all over, giving them a quarter turn every 6 to 8 minutes or when the side facing the heat blackens. Place the peppers in a paper bag; close the bag and let stand for 10 minutes to steam and loosen the skins.

3 Using a paring knife, core and seed the peppers; slice into thin strips about 2 inches long and ¹⁄₂-inch wide and place in a medium mixing bowl.

4 In a small mixing bowl, whisk together the olive oil and vinegar. Stir in the capers, parsley, garlic, and salt and pepper. Pour the dressing over the roasted peppers. Cover and refrigerate for at least 1 hour to mellow the flavors. (The peppers are best if made a day ahead.) Serve with everything from burgers to grilled fish.

Vary It! You can substitute 2 to 3 tablespoons chopped, oil-packed sun-dried tomatoes for the capers. You also can add 2 tablespoons pignoli, or pine nuts, that have been toasted in a dry skillet until lightly browned.

Potatoes

All kinds of white potatoes are appropriate for cooking on the grill. Scrub them without peeling, and then leave them whole or cut them into rounds, ovals, wedges, or chunks before grilling. Whole baking potatoes can be ember-roasted with or without a foil wrap. Wash and prick the potato with a fork in several places. Oil the skin and place the potato directly into the hot coals for about 40 minutes or until tender and the skin is completely charred. Pierce each potato with a skewer to check doneness. Cut in half and add butter, and salt and pepper. (Don't eat the skin!) To enjoy the skin of an ember-roasted potato, wrap raw, oiled-brushed potatoes in heavy-duty or double-thick aluminum foil and nestle in the hot coals until tender.

Individually foil-wrapped Idaho or other baking potatoes can also be placed directly above a medium-hot fire and cooked, covered, alongside a roast if desired, for 30 to 35 minutes or until tender, turning every 15 minutes. Remove the foil, brush the skin lightly with oil, and place the potatoes back on the grill grid for 10 minutes or until the skin is crisp, turning once. The potato is cooked when it can be easily pierced with the thin blade of a sharp knife, a skewer, or the tines of a fork.

Grilled Potato Planks

Sliced and grilled baking potatoes are a wonderful side dish for any type of grilled poultry, meat, or fish, and a healthy change from greasy french fries or pan-fried potatoes.

Preparation time: *15 minutes*

Marinating time: *30 minutes to 1 hour*

Grilling time: *15 minutes*

Yield: *4 servings*

4 medium potatoes (about 1¹/₂ pounds total), scrubbed	*1 teaspoon dried marjoram, oregano, or dill*
6 tablespoons extra-virgin olive oil	*¹/₂ teaspoon Tabasco sauce, or to taste*
1¹/₂ tablespoons white wine vinegar	*¹/₂ teaspoon kosher salt, or table salt to taste*
2 cloves garlic, peeled and finely minced	*Pepper to taste*

1 Cut the potatoes lengthwise into ¹/₃-inch-thick slices. Place the slices in a medium saucepan with enough lightly salted water to cover. Cover the pan and bring to a boil. Boil for 5 minutes or until nearly tender when pierced with the blade of a thin, sharp knife; drain thoroughly. Place the potatoes in a large, shallow baking dish.

2 Make the marinade by combining the remaining ingredients; pour the marinade over the warm potato slices, turning to coat. Cover and let stand for 30 minutes to 1 hour.

3 Prepare a medium-hot fire in a charcoal or gas grill.

4 Before grilling, brush both sides of the potatoes with the marinade, being sure to include bits of garlic and herb. Place the potatoes on a lightly oiled grid, grill until lightly browned, for 6 to 8 minutes. Turn and grill until lightly browned and crisp on the second side, 6 to 8 minutes more. If desired, season before serving with additional salt and pepper, and Tabasco sauce.

Go-With: These potatoes are delicious with steak, burgers, pork, or lamb, and ketchup makes a terrific dipping sauce.

Vary It! Brush parboiled potato planks with any tomato-based barbecue sauce before grilling.

When grilling hard, woody vegetables or potatoes, use metal skewers to shorten cooking times — the metal heats up to quickly cook the inside of the vegetable.

Grilled New Potato Salad with Fresh Mint

Small red potatoes, or *new potatoes,* as they are also called, are wonderful when skewered or randomly scattered on the grill to cook until browned and fork-tender. This recipe tosses them, after grilling, in a garlicky olive oil and mint dressing.

Preparation time: 20 minutes

Grilling time: 15 to 20 minutes

Yield: 4 to 6 servings

3 pounds new potatoes

2 tablespoons olive oil for coating the potatoes

¹/₄ cup olive oil

¹/₂ cup chopped fresh mint or basil leaves

3 to 4 cloves garlic, peeled and finely minced

Kosher or table salt to taste

Pepper to taste

(continued)

1 Prepare a medium-hot fire in a charcoal or gas grill.

2 Scrub the new potatoes under cold running water and pat dry with paper towels. Cut the potatoes in half and place in a large mixing bowl. Drizzle olive oil (use more than 2 tablespoons, if necessary) over the potatoes and toss with a spoon to coat on all sides.

3 Place the potatoes on a lightly oiled grid or in an oiled, hinged wire basket or grill topper (see Chapter 2); cover and grill for 15 to 20 minutes or until the potatoes are lightly browned on all sides and tender when pierced with the thin blade of a sharp knife. Turn as necessary to prevent the potatoes from charring.

4 Meanwhile, combine the ¼ cup olive oil, mint or basil, and garlic in a serving bowl. Transfer the grilled potatoes to the serving bowl with the dressing; toss to coat, and season with salt and pepper.

5 Serve immediately or at room temperature.

Go-With: This potato salad is delicious with pork, lamb, beef, or chicken.

Vary It! Revive leftover cooked vegetables by grilling them to perfection the next day. Slice boiled potatoes into planks or halves and then baste with a little butter before grilling. The same treatment works for hard-shelled squash, eggplant, summer squash, asparagus, and carrots. Cauliflower and broccoli are especially good when prepared this way. Grill each vegetable until lightly browned and enjoy what you might otherwise throw away!

Squash

Squash can be split into two types: hard-shelled and summer.

✔ **Hard-shelled squash:** Like potatoes, hard-shelled squash can be ember-cooked directly in the coals, with or without a foil wrapping. Be sure to oil the skins well before placing them in the coals. Depending on size, they need 40 to 60 minutes to grill, until fork tender. Butternut, a pear-shaped squash with deep orange flesh, can be cut into rounds or cubes for kebabs. If you are in a hurry, parboil the slices, cubes, or halves with or without the skin; brush them with oil and grill over a medium-hot fire for 15 minutes or until tender.

✔ **Summer squash:** Summer squash, like zucchini, yellow squash, crook-necks, and pattypans, are great candidates for the grill. They require no peeling and are delicious marinated, basted with a flavored oil, or even stuffed. Grilled rounds can be tossed into omelets, salads, or steaming pasta or served over couscous. Smaller vegetables are preferable because they have tender skin, few seeds, and fresh (some might even say sweet) flavor.

Cut zucchini and yellow squash into rounds or cubes for kebabs, or slice lengthwise into $1/2$-inch-thick strips. Grill over a medium to medium-hot fire for 10 to 12 minutes or until lightly browned on both sides.

Stuffed Summer Squash

This delicious recipe — shown in the color photo section of this book — stuffs summer squash with a mixture of cornbread, red peppers, and thyme. You can use your own cornbread recipe or a commercial mix, or you can buy corn muffins and break them apart into crumbs. If the cornbread is very moist and fresh, be sure to dry it out for 10 minutes in a 325° oven before adding it to the other stuffing ingredients. In this recipe, the heat of the grill is used both directly and indirectly. First, the empty squash shells are grilled for a few minutes over direct heat until lightly browned. Then they're stuffed and placed back on the grill where they finish cooking indirectly, without charring. They make lovely side dishes for any grilled meat, fish, or poultry.

Preparation time: *25 minutes*

Grilling time: *25 minutes*

Yield: *4 servings*

4 medium zucchini or summer squash or a combination of both, each about 8 to 10 ounces

$1/4$ cup olive oil, divided

$1/3$ cup peeled and finely chopped red or yellow onion

$1/3$ cup finely chopped red bell pepper

1 small jalapeño pepper, seeded and chopped (optional)

2 large cloves garlic, peeled and minced

1 cup crumbled, dried cornbread (see instructions at beginning of recipe)

$1^1/2$ teaspoons chopped fresh marjoram, or $1/2$ teaspoon dried marjoram

$1^1/2$ teaspoons chopped fresh thyme, or $1/2$ teaspoon dried thyme

Salt and pepper to taste

$1^1/2$ tablespoons butter

(continued)

1 Slice the squash in half lengthwise. Scoop out the pulp with a teaspoon, leaving a shell about $^{1}/_{4}$- to $^{1}/_{3}$-inch thick. Finely chop the scooped-out squash; set the shells and chopped pulp aside.

2 Prepare a hot, indirect fire in a charcoal or gas grill. (See Chapter 1 for complete directions.)

3 In a small skillet or sauté pan over medium heat, heat 2 tablespoons of the olive oil; add the chopped squash, onion, red pepper, jalapeño pepper (if desired), and garlic. Cook for 5 minutes or until the vegetables are tender, stirring occasionally. Remove from heat and add the cornbread, marjoram, thyme, and salt and pepper; stir to combine.

4 Brush the outsides of the squash shells with the remaining 2 tablespoons oil; sprinkle the inside lightly with salt and place the shells, cut side down, on a lightly oiled grill grid. Grill, uncovered, for 5 minutes or until the shell edges are lightly browned. Remove from the heat.

5 Spoon about 2 tablespoons of the squash mixture into each squash shell, mounding slightly. Dot the stuffing with butter. Place the stuffed squash on the side of the grid opposite the heat; cover the grill and cook for 20 to 25 minutes or until the squash is tender when pierced with the thin blade of a sharp knife. Serve hot or at room temperature.

Vary It! Add any one of the following to the stuffing mixture:

- ✔ $^{1}/_{3}$ cup chopped mushrooms
- ✔ $^{1}/_{3}$ cup cooked corn kernels
- ✔ $^{1}/_{3}$ cup finely grated Parmesan or Cheddar cheese
- ✔ $^{1}/_{3}$ cup finely chopped cooked shrimp or cooked ground sausage

Sweet potatoes

Delicious, vitamin-A-packed sweet potatoes are also superior grilling food. They can be sliced lengthwise into long ovals or wedges, cut crosswise into thin rounds, or cubed and grilled on skewers. Brush thin slices or cubes lightly with oil flavored with garlic, and salt and pepper. Grill over medium-hot coals for 15 to 20 minutes until tender. To reduce the grilling time, cook pieces in boiling water until nearly tender, 6 to 8 minutes; then grill an equal amount of time until nicely browned.

Wrap whole sweet potatoes, individually, in heavy-duty or double-thickness aluminum foil. Pierce the foil several times with a fork and grill for 40 minutes over a medium fire or until soft and tender. Serve with butter, a drizzle of maple syrup or honey, and salt and pepper to taste. Or complement the sweetness of the potato with a squeeze of lemon or lime juice and a pat of butter, forgoing the sweeteners.

Sweet potatoes can also be cooked directly in hot coals rather than over them. Scrub the potatoes clean and oil the skins lightly. Push them down into the coals; cook for 40 minutes or until tender, giving them a quarter turn every 15 minutes. The final result is a potato with completely blackened inedible skin and a fluffy interior. Grilled sweet potatoes are great for a camping trip, and are terrific with pork or turkey dishes.

Grand Marnier Grilled Sweet Potatoes

A splash of Grand Marnier (or other orange liqueur), a little brown sugar, a bit of allspice, and the heat of the grill flavor these wedges of sweet potatoes — see the color photo section for a sample.

Preparation time: 20 minutes

Grilling time: 10 to 12 minutes

Yield: 4 servings

$1^1/_2$ to 2 pounds sweet potatoes (about 3 medium)	$^1/_4$ cup Grand Marnier or other orange liqueur
$^1/_2$ cup butter (1 stick)	$^3/_4$ teaspoon ground allspice
$^1/_4$ cup light brown sugar, packed	Salt and pepper to taste

1 Prepare a medium-hot fire in a charcoal or gas grill.

2 As the grill preheats, peel the sweet potatoes and cut each into 6 wedges. (To cut them into wedges, slice the potatoes in half lengthwise and then slice each half into thirds.)

3 Place the potatoes in a medium saucepan with lightly salted water to cover. Cover and bring to a boil over high heat. Reduce the heat and simmer for about 5 minutes or until the potatoes are barely tender when pierced with the thin blade of a sharp knife. (Avoid overcooking or they will start to fall apart. You want them to finish cooking on the grill.) Drain immediately in a colander and run cold water over them briefly. Drain again and set aside.

(continued)

4 In a small saucepan, melt the butter over very low heat; add the brown sugar, Grand Marnier or other liqueur, and allspice. Whisk (or use a fork to stir the mixture) until the sugar is completely dissolved. Immediately remove from the heat and season with salt and pepper. Brush the sauce onto both sides of the sweet potato wedges. Reserve the remaining sauce.

5 Place the wedges on a lightly oiled grid. Grill for 10 to 15 minutes, brushing with the butter mixture and turning to expose each side to the heat of the grill. When done, the potatoes will be fork-tender and lightly charred at their ends and edges. Remove to a serving platter and drizzle with the reserved basting sauce.

Go-With: Serve these sweet potatoes with pork, chicken, beef, or lamb.

Tomatoes

Plentiful, ripe, and full of flavor in the summer when most of us cook outdoors, tomatoes are simple to grill. Red, round tomatoes — also known as globe tomatoes — are best when they're cored and sliced in half or into $1/2$-inch-thick rounds. Then simply brush them with oil or butter that's flavored with garlic and chopped herbs. Grill them over a medium-hot fire from 2 to 5 minutes, depending on thickness, turning once. Overcooking causes them to fall apart. Cook only until heated through and very lightly browned. Grilled tomatoes are a fine accompaniment to hamburgers, steaks, and any kind of chop or grilled fish.

Whole cherry and small plum or Roma tomatoes can be skewered and grilled until they're lightly browned and warmed through. Turn them often to keep them from charring and try to use square metal skewers to prevent the tomatoes from spinning uncontrollably when being turned. (See Chapter 9 for more tips on skewering.) Combine grilled cherry tomatoes with chopped fresh basil and grated Parmesan or Romano cheese to make a delicious, impromptu sauce for steaming pasta.

Grilled Tomatoes with Cumin Butter

For an easy, complete meal, combine these grilled tomato slices with burgers, juicy steaks, fish steaks, or kebabs. Change the seasoning any way you wish, substituting other herbs and spices for the cumin. Or simply oil the tomato slices before grilling, and spread with softened goat cheese and chopped fresh basil after grilling. Look for an example of this dish in the color photo pages of this book.

Preparation time: *10 minutes*

Grilling time: *5 to 6 minutes*

Yield: *4 servings*

$2^1/_2$ *tablespoons butter*

1 teaspoon ground cumin

Salt and pepper to taste

2 large, firm ripe tomatoes, sliced about $^3/_4$-inch thick

1 Melt the butter in a small saucepan; remove from heat and stir in the cumin and salt and pepper.

2 Brush the tomato slices on one side with half of the cumin butter. Place them, brushed side down, on a well-oiled grid (or on a grill topper, which is discussed in Chapter 2) and grill for 2 to 3 minutes or until very lightly browned on one side.

3 Brush the tops of the tomatoes with the remaining cumin butter. Turn and grill for 2 to 3 minutes more or until very lightly browned, but not falling apart. If the tomatoes brown too quickly, move them to the edge of the grill to finish cooking.

Grilled Tomatoes with Basil and Bread Crumb Stuffing

In this tempting vegetable side dish, you stuff ripe tomatoes with bits of tangy, grated lemon peel, basil, cornbread crumbs, shallots, and garlic. If it's more convenient, stuff the cored tomatoes several hours ahead of grilling time and refrigerate until you're ready to grill. However, chilled stuffed tomatoes may take slightly longer to grill.

Preparation time: *25 minutes*

Grilling time: *10 to 15 minutes*

Yield: *4 servings*

4 medium, ripe tomatoes, each about 6 ounces

2 tablespoons butter

2 large shallots, peeled and finely chopped, or 3 tablespoons chopped onion

2 large cloves garlic, peeled and finely chopped

$^1/_2$ cup day-old or oven-dried cornbread or white bread crumbs

2 tablespoons chopped fresh basil, or $1^1/_2$ teaspoons dried basil

1 teaspoon grated lemon peel

Salt and pepper to taste

Olive oil for brushing tomatoes

(continued)

1 Prepare a medium-hot fire in a covered charcoal or gas grill.

2 Slice off the top one-eighth of each tomato. Using a paring knife, remove the cores, cutting almost to the other end to make a narrow cavity for the stuffing mixture. Set the tomatoes aside.

3 In a small sauté pan or skillet, melt the butter over medium heat. Add the shallots or onion and garlic; cook, stirring, for 2 to 3 minutes or until the vegetables soften. (Do not let the garlic burn.) Remove from heat; add the bread crumbs, basil, and lemon peel; stir to combine. Season with salt and pepper. Set aside.

4 Brush the tomatoes on all surfaces and in their cavities with the olive oil; sprinkle lightly with salt and pepper. Place the tomatoes, cut side down, on a lightly oiled grid; cover and grill for 2 to 3 minutes or until the cut side is lightly browned. Remove the tomatoes from the grill to a flat baking sheet; spoon the stuffing into each cavity, mounding it over the top.

5 Place the stuffed tomatoes back on the grid. Cover and cook for another 5 to 10 minutes or until warmed through.

Vary It! If you don't have any dry bread crumbs, place fresh bread slices (or crumbled cornbread muffins) on a baking sheet and toast in a preheated 350° oven for 5 minutes or until dried and golden brown. Cornbread gives you better flavor than white bread crumbs for this recipe.

Grilled Fruit? Oh Yeah!

Grilling fruit takes a little more practice than grilling vegetables because the pulpiness of most fruits and the delicacy of their skin can be ruined by a grill that's too hot. Nevertheless, with a little care and imagination, most fruits come off the grill looking very luscious and toothsome — and they are definitely a surprise to most people at an outdoor party!

Don't think of grilled fruit only as a dessert choice, however — they can be dazzling side dishes as well:

- Toss grilled fruit into salads.
- Use grilled fruit as a garnish.
- Combine sweet fruit cubes with savory chunks of vegetable, fish, meat, or poultry on a skewer:

- Try mixing wedges of oranges with cubes of beef and red onion.
- Use pineapple wedges with cubes of smoked ham or fresh pork, and bell pepper strips.
- Combine apple wedges with chicken livers and bacon.
- Try using plum slices or halves and red onions with cubes of chicken or pork.

Here are some tips for grilling fruit:

✔ Be sure that the cooking grid is scrubbed completely clean. Leftover pieces of food clinging to the grid can make the delicate-flavored fruits taste like last night's dinner.

✔ Allow the natural sugar in fruits such as oranges and figs to brown slightly when grilling, to bring out their rich, sweet flavors.

✔ Brush fruit slices, cubes, or halves with melted butter and brown sugar before grilling over a medium to medium-low fire.

✔ Brush fruit with the same tangy lemon or balsamic vinegar marinade used for the main dish or salad and serve as a pretty plate garnish with savory grilled foods. Thick orange slices look especially attractive.

✔ An easy, fat-free basting sauce for any grilled fruits is dry white wine sweetened to taste with honey. For a savory glaze that's nice with pork or poultry, add Dijon-style mustard to taste,

✔ Half-inch slices or chunks of apples, apricots, bananas, cantaloupe — yes, cantaloupe — papaya, peaches, plums, nectarines, pineapple, and pears take about 10 minutes to grill; turn frequently to keep them from burning.

Grilled fruits are enhanced by the bold flavors of brandy, rum, and fruit liqueurs. Impress your guests with this simple dessert. Skewer together assorted fruit chunks (such as slices of plums, nectarines, and peaches), brushed first with a little melted butter and brown sugar syrup; grill until lightly browned and bring to the table on a warm platter. Pour $^1/_4$ cup of warmed brandy, rum, or fruit liqueur over the fruit and ignite the dish. Serve with vanilla or rum raisin ice cream. Ice cream is the best companion to grilled fruits.

Grilled Nectarines

Grilled nectarines make a colorful, tasty side dish for any savory beef, pork, or poultry roast. Set them on the grill while the roast is waiting to be carved. You can substitute peaches, but you'll first need to remove their skins.

(continued)

Preparation time: 10 minutes

Grilling time: 10 minutes

Yield: 4 servings

4 medium, ripe nectarines, halved and
pitted

2 tablespoons unsalted butter, melted

$1^1/_2$ tablespoons brown sugar, packed

1 Place the nectarine halves in a large bowl; drizzle with the butter and sprinkle with brown sugar. Toss to mix well. Cover and let stand for 30 minutes to 1 hour.

2 Place on a lightly oiled grid, over medium heat. Cook for 10 minutes or until tender and lightly browned, brushing and turning once with any remaining butter-sugar mixture.

Grilled Bananas with Caramel Sauce

Bananas on the grill are one of our favorite desserts. Because of their natural oils and sweetness, they need surprisingly little or no adornment in the way of fancy sauces or seasonings. In this dessert recipe (shown in the color photo section of this book), we grill bananas right in their skins to shield the soft, sweet, edible fruit from the harsh heat of the grill. After grilling the bananas, drizzle them with a lovely caramel sauce. However, you can forgo the rich caramel sauce and serve these bananas unadorned, alongside dishes like Satay (Chapter 9) or Jamaican Jerk Chicken (Chapter 15).

Preparation time: 20 minutes

Grilling time: 8 to 10 minutes

Yield: 4 servings

1 cup granulated sugar

$^1/_3$ cup water

$^1/_2$ teaspoon lemon juice

$^2/_3$ cup heavy cream

4 medium ripe but firm bananas

1 Prepare a medium fire in a charcoal or gas grill.

2 In a saucepan over medium-low heat, combine the sugar, water, and lemon juice. Stir with a wooden spoon for about 3 minutes, until the sugar dissolves.

3 Increase the heat to medium-high and cook, stirring occasionally, until the mixture reaches an amber color, about 3 to 4 minutes. (The mixture boils rather rapidly during these minutes.)

4 If you want a medium-colored caramel sauce, remove the mixture from the heat while it is still light golden; it continues to cook and darken from the heat. For a dark caramel color, remove when the mixture is medium golden-brown. Remove the pan from the heat and gradually pour in the heavy cream, stirring with a wire whisk. (Be careful; the cream bubbles wildly as you pour it into the mixture.)

5 When all is incorporated, return the saucepan to medium-low heat and stir for 2 to 3 minutes or until the mixture is velvety. After it cools, the sauce can be reheated in a microwave oven or over low heat on top of the stove.

6 Cut the bananas in half lengthwise without removing the peel; place on a lightly oiled grid, cut side up. Cover and grill for 8 to 10 minutes or until the flesh is warmed and slightly softened; spoon or cut away the flesh from the peel.

7 Place the bananas on four individual plates and spoon the hot caramel sauce over the bananas before serving.

Go-With: The best companion for this dessert is a rich and creamy vanilla ice cream.

Foil-Wrapped Baked Apples

Here's an easy dessert (shown in the color photo section of this book) that lets you complete most of the work before you get to the grill. Wrap the cored, nut-and-raisin-stuffed apples in sheets of foil and set them on the back of the grill behind other foods for your meal. If you plan it right, your baked apple dessert will be ready just as you finish the main course.

Be careful not to overcook these apples. Depending on the intensity of your grill's heat, they only need 20 to 25 minutes. Start testing their doneness with a skewer or the tines of a fork after 20 minutes and then every 5 minutes after that. They turn in an instant from cooked through — yet still shaped like an apple — to almost applesauce. Although the more done version is also delicious, it's not nearly as pretty.

Preparation time: 25 minutes

Grilling time: 20 to 25 minutes

Yield: 4 servings

(continued)

4 tart apples (such as Granny Smith or Macintosh), about 8 ounces each

¹/₄ heaping cup chopped walnuts or pecans

¹/₄ cup light brown sugar, packed

2 heaping tablespoons raisins

1 teaspoon cinnamon

¹/₄ teaspoon ground allspice

2 tablespoons butter

2 tablespoons apple brandy or rum (optional)

Vanilla ice cream or sweetened whipped cream (optional)

1 Core the apples (see Figure 17-4) and place each on a buttered 9-inch square of heavy-duty aluminum foil.

How to Core an Apple

Figure 17-4: The core of the matter.

Run a paring knife clockwise around the core (leaving ¼" at the bottom)...

...and pop out the core!

2 In a medium mixing bowl, combine the walnuts or pecans, brown sugar, raisins, cinnamon, and allspice; divide the mixture equally among the apples, packing into their hollowed centers. Top each with a half tablespoon of butter. Fold up the edges of the foil around the apples to make a tight package.

3 Prepare a medium fire in a charcoal or gas grill.

4 Place the foil packages on the grid; grill for 20 to 25 minutes or until the apples are tender when pierced with a fork. (Be careful not to overcook.) Rotate occasionally to different spots on the grid to ensure even cooking. Remove from foil and (if desired) pour ¹/₂ tablespoon brandy or rum over the top of each. If desired, serve with vanilla ice cream or whipped cream sweetened with maple syrup or maple extract and sugar.

Grilled Figs and Prosciutto

This dish makes a very impressive appetizer or — without the mustard — an interesting dessert. Thin slices of prosciutto, a salt-cured ham from Italy, are wrapped around fresh figs. The grilled figs caramelize slightly, and the ham loses most of its fat but none of its delicious saltiness. The recipe calls for 4 slices of prosciutto but works with twice that amount for prosciutto lovers.

Preparation time: 15 minutes

Grilling time: 6 minutes

Yield: 4 servings

2 tablespoons dry white wine

2 tablespoons honey

1 teaspoon Dijon-style mustard

4 large ripe fresh figs, quartered

4 (or 8, if desired) thin slices prosciutto or other spiced ham

Pepper to taste (optional)

1 Prepare a medium fire in a charcoal or gas grill.

2 In a small saucepan, combine the wine and honey; without allowing the mixture to boil, stir over low heat just until the honey blends with the wine. Remove from heat and stir in the mustard.

3 Thread 4 fig quarters and 1 slice (or 2 slices, if desired) of prosciutto on each of 4 skewers (see Figure 17-5). (If using wooden skewers, soak them in water for 30 minutes to prevent them from burning.)

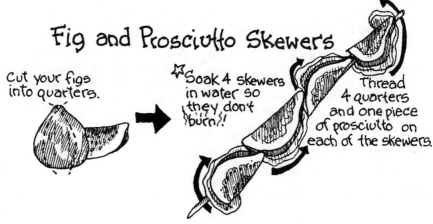

Fig and Prosciutto Skewers

Cut your figs into quarters.

☆Soak 4 skewers in water so they don't burn!!

Thread 4 quarters and one piece of prosciutto on each of the skewers.

Figure 17-5:
Go FIGure!

(continued)

4 Brush the figs and prosciutto with the wine-honey basting sauce and sprinkle each with pepper (if desired). Place the skewers on a lightly oiled grid, grill for 5 to 6 minutes, turning often and brushing with the basting sauce. Serve as a light appetizer over mixed salad greens or as a side for grilled duck, turkey, or pork.

Grilled Pound Cake and Fruit with Brandy Sauce

This dessert, shown in the color photo section of this book, brings together a heavenly combination of foods, sauces, and seasonings — grilled fruit and grilled pound cake, rum, brown sugar, orange peel, and vanilla ice cream. Slice the fruit as if you were preparing it for a pie filling; cut it first in half and then into slices about $1/2$- to 1-inch thick.

Preparation time: 20 minutes

Marinating time: 30 minutes

Grilling time: 12 to 14 minutes

Yield: 4 servings

2 tablespoons butter	Pinch of salt
$1/3$ cup dark rum or fruit-flavored brandy	1 teaspoon grated orange peel
4 medium nectarines, sliced 1-inch thick	8 slices frozen pound cake, thawed and cut $1/2$-inch thick
2 large ripe purple plums, sliced $1/2$-inch thick	1 pint vanilla ice cream, or 2 cups sweetened whipped cream
3 tablespoons brown sugar, packed	

1 In a medium saucepan, melt the butter over very low heat. Add the dark rum or the brandy, the nectarines, and the plums. Sprinkle with the brown sugar and salt; toss to mix well. Cook, covered, over low heat, for 1 minute or just until heated through; remove from heat and sprinkle with the orange peel. Set aside for 30 minutes or longer. (You may prepare the fruit to this point and keep it covered until ready to grill.)

2 Prepare a medium fire in a charcoal or gas grill. Be sure that the grill is thoroughly clean and free of any food particles.

3 Remove the fruit slices from the sauce, reserving the sauce.

4 Grill the fruit slices on a lightly oiled grid, for 7 to 10 minutes or until lightly browned on all sides, turning twice.

5 After the fruit has cooked for 5 minutes, brush both sides of the pound cake slices with the reserved sauce; reserve the remaining sauce. Grill for 4 minutes or until the cake is lightly toasted on both sides, turning once.

6 Transfer the grilled pound cake slices to individual serving plates, two to a plate, and top with grilled fruit slices and a scoop of vanilla ice cream or whipped cream. Drizzle any remaining brandy sauce over the fruit, cake, and ice cream.

Chapter 18

Grill to Go: Sandwiches, Pizzas, and Other Finger Foods

- -

In This Chapter

▶ Getting to know grilled pizza

▶ Introducing the best toast ever: bruschetta

▶ Grilling fajitas and quesadillas in style

▶ Experimenting with grilled open-face sandwiches

- -

*T*he idea of grilling sandwiches of any kind is of rather recent origin — which leads us to ask, "What took so long?"

In this chapter, you find out how to make crispy thin- and thick-crusted pizzas that invite people to join in the cooking process. You also discover how to prepare an easy alternative to pizza, called *bruschetta,* and, finally, how to make quesadillas, fajitas, and open-faced sandwiches — all on the grill.

Giving Pizza the Third Degree

Pizzas fresh off the grill can be a complete meal or a light appetizer. Your kids are sure to love them, and they're a nice change from all those hot dog dinners!

However, if at first, you're a little wary of attempting to grill a real pizza and feel that you need a little more experience to perfect your grilling skills, give this next recipe a try.

Thick-Crust "Pizza"

Instead of calling for fresh or frozen pizza dough, which can be a little tricky to work with, this recipe uses round, prebaked, pizza crusts that can be purchased in any major supermarket. (Boboli brand pizza crust styles have very nice flavor and are available in both thick and thin styles.) Technically speaking, it's really not pizza but rather a grilled flat-bread with pizzalike toppings. But who cares what it's called when the result is so quick and satisfying.

Preparation time: *15 minutes*

Grilling time: *15 minutes*

Yield: *4 main dish servings or 8 to 12 appetizer servings*

4 ripe Roma or other small tomatoes, cored and cut into ¹/₂-inch-thick slices (about 1 pound)

Extra-virgin olive oil for brushing tomatoes and pizza crusts

2 large cloves garlic, peeled and minced

4 small, round (6-inch) prebaked pizza crusts

6 ounces mozzarella cheese, finely diced (about 1 cup)

¹/₄ cup grated Romano cheese

¹/₄ cup chopped fresh basil

Garlic powder to taste

Salt and pepper to taste

1 Prepare a hot fire in a charcoal or gas grill.

2 Brush the tomato slices generously with olive oil; sprinkle the slices evenly on both sides with minced garlic and place on the edge of an oiled grid. Grill for 4 to 5 minutes, turning once, until softened and cooked through. Remove with a spatula to a cutting board and chop coarsely.

3 Brush the tops of the crusts generously with olive oil. Set the crusts on the grill, top side down; cover and grill for 1 to 2 minutes. Remove them to a flat cookie sheet, top side up. Evenly distribute the tomato over each shell; top each evenly with mozzarella cheese, Romano cheese, and basil; sprinkle with garlic powder and salt and pepper.

4 Cut 4 squares of heavy-duty aluminum foil, slightly larger than the crusts. Set a pizza on each square of foil; place on the grid, directly over the heat. Cover and cook for 10 to 15 minutes or until the cheese melts. About halfway through, move the pizzas to a different spot on the grill to promote even cooking and to prevent the bottoms from burning. Serve immediately as individual main dish servings or cut into wedges for appetizers.

Vary It! If you prefer, you can sauté the chopped tomatoes and garlic on top of the stove in 2 tablespoons olive oil.

Sun-Dried Tomato and Mozzarella Cheese Pizza

This recipe is the real thing — hot and crusty grilled pizza (shown in the color photo section of this book). In the section following this recipe, we give you tips for rolling out real pizza dough and a long list of mouth-watering toppings so that you can alter the main recipe many ways.

Although making pizza dough isn't difficult, it is time-consuming, and we find that very good, ready-to-use, commercial pizza doughs are now sold in the dairy or frozen food section of most supermarkets, and in authentic Italian delicatessens. Better yet, many local pizzerias will sell you fresh dough for pennies a pound.

Preparation time: *20 minutes*

Grilling time: *12 minutes*

Yield: *4 to 6 servings*

2 tablespoons plus 2 teaspoons olive oil, divided

2 cups chopped fresh tomatoes

2 large cloves garlic, peeled and minced

1 pound fresh (or frozen and thawed) pizza dough

Olive oil for brushing dough

1 cup shredded mozzarella cheese, packed (about 6 ounces)

¼ cup chopped oil-packed sun-dried tomatoes, drained

¼ cup chopped fresh basil

Garlic powder to taste (optional)

Salt and pepper to taste

1 Prepare a medium-low fire in a charcoal or gas grill.

2 In a small saucepan or skillet, heat 2 tablespoons of the olive oil over medium heat. Add the chopped tomatoes and garlic; cook for 1 to 2 minutes or just until the tomatoes are softened, stirring occasionally. Set aside.

3 Working on a well-floured countertop, pastry board, or inverted baking sheet, divide the pizza dough in half. Flatten or use a floured rolling pin to shape each half into free-form rounds, each 9 to 10 inches in diameter and about ¼-inch thick. Do not make a lip — the dough should be evenly thick right to the edge of each pie. Generously brush one side of each pizza with oil; place the pizzas, oiled side down, on a lightly oiled grid. (Transferring the dough from the counter to the grid is the toughest part of this recipe. See the "Play dough perfect" section for some help.)

(continued)

4 Cover and cook until very lightly golden and firm, about 2 to 5 minutes, depending on the heat of the grill. (Do not let the crust get too brown.) Remove from the grill to a large baking sheet. Brush the tops with oil and turn over, grilled side up.

5 Evenly spread the tomato-garlic mixture onto the grilled side of each crust; evenly distribute the mozzarella cheese, sun-dried tomatoes, and basil. Sprinkle each with garlic powder (if desired) and salt and pepper. Drizzle 1 teaspoon olive oil over each pizza.

6 Place the pizzas back on the grill. Cover and grill for 8 to 12 minutes, moving the pizzas to cooler spots if the bottoms get too dark. The pizza is done when the bottom of the crust is lightly browned and the top is hot and bubbly.

Vary It! You can substitute about $^1/_2$ cup homemade or bottled pasta or pizza sauce for the sautéed tomatoes and garlic.

Play dough perfect

On your first try making dough, you may feel like you've got the starring role in an *I Love Lucy* episode. Here are some tips on making pizza crust (see Figure 18-1), but the best advice is to practice. By the second or third try, you'll have the process down cold and be ready to invite the neighbors over for a very impressive pizza party.

- ✔ Be sure to work on a well-floured surface and to flour the rolling pin as well (if you use a pin) to shape the dough.

- ✔ Shape the pie as evenly and thinly as possible but not so thinly that holes appear in the dough. Some people like a crust that's less than $^1/_4$-inch thick; others prefer it a little thicker. When set on the grill, the dough gets firm immediately and also thickens slightly.

- ✔ Don't worry about making a perfectly round shape. Free-form shapes are perfectly acceptable. If on the first or even the fifteenth try your pie comes out looking like the boot of Italy, that's all part of the fun of making pizza.

- ✔ Transferring the dough to the grill is the most difficult part. If necessary, slide a long-handled spatula under the dough to gently loosen it from the countertop or work surface. You can drape the dough over a floured rolling pin and carry it to the grill, supporting any loose, hanging dough with your free hand. Unroll the dough onto the lightly oiled grid and repeat with the second piece. Or shape the dough on a flat, floured cookie sheet; then bring the sheet to the grill and slide the dough onto the grid.

Tips for Rolling Out Pizza Dough

1. Work on a well-floured surface.

2. Shape the pie EVENLY and THINLY (about ¼" thick)

3. DON'T worry about making a perfectly round shape! (uh oh)

4. Carefully loosen dough with a long spatula. Place on a cookie sheet or drape over a rolling pin and transfer to the grill.

5. If you don't get it right the 1st time, reshape the dough into a ball... (and try, try again)

6. Try 3 or 4 small pies instead of 2 big ones. (easier to manage)

Figure 18-1:
Did Lucy ever do it this well?

✔ You're not working with pie pastry, so you don't have to worry about overworking the dough. If necessary, reshape the dough into a ball and roll it out again.

✔ Smaller pies are easier to manage. On your first pizza-making attempt, you may want to take the Sun-Dried Tomato and Mozzarella Cheese Pizza recipe and roll out 3 or 4 individual pies rather than 2 large ones. Small pies make great individual party appetizers.

Can you top this?

Want to have a dinner party without endless fuss and preparation? Invite friends over for grilled pizza. Lay out an assortment of toppings so that guests can design their own individual pies. Don't worry about using exact measurements. Just don't pile on too much; overloading causes the thin crust to burn before the toppings are hot and cooked through.

As with the beloved hamburger (see Chapter 8), pizza has few topping restrictions; use whatever combinations you like, such as the following:

✔ Bottled artichoke hearts and grilled eggplant

✔ Pepperoni slices and mushrooms

✔ Black olives and capers

✔ Chopped anchovies or sardines, and roasted red peppers

✔ Sautéed peppers and onions

✔ Chopped cooked and drained spinach, and ground sausage or prosciutto

✔ Crisp bacon or grilled ham cubes, and bottled artichoke hearts

✔ Goat cheese and sun-dried tomatoes

✔ Smoked salmon, chives, and sour cream

✔ Pesto sauce, bottled salsa, or tomato sauce instead of fresh tomatoes and grated mozzarella cheese

✔ Grilled eggplant and goat cheese

✔ Grilled portobello mushrooms and asparagus

✔ Cooked ground meat, shrimp, scallops, or clams, and chopped fresh tomatoes and basil

Adding charcoal and hardwood to the mix

For really authentic wood-fired flavor, try grilling the pizzas over a combination of charcoal and hickory or other hardwood chunks. Here's how to prepare the fire by using these fuels together:

1. **Set several large hardwood chunks (do not presoak them) between the charcoal briquettes.**

2. **Ignite the wood chunks and coals together.**

3. **When the coals have burned to a medium-low (or when you can hold your hand above them for 4 to 5 seconds), move the chunks to the outer edges of the coals.**

   If the chunks continued to flame (rather that smolder), spritz them with a little water from a water bottle — not too much that the fire dies out, though.

Bring on the Bruschetta

Bruschetta is a lighter variation of warm garlic bread. In its most basic form, it is a grilled slice of crusty Italian or French bread that's rubbed with fresh garlic and coated with a good-quality olive oil. But that's just the beginning. Italian cooks pile all kinds of toppings onto this tasty morsel, turning *bruschette* (the plural of *bruschetta*) into more of an open-faced sandwich or hearty snack. Toppings can include chopped fresh tomato and basil, or grilled eggplant and goat cheese, or grilled zucchini and grated Parmesan cheese.

Oh where, oh where have the hardwood chunks gone?

Finding a source for a variety of hardwood chunks and chips can be anywhere from difficult to downright impossible. Hardware stores and other shops that sell grilling fuels don't always carry hardwood. Fortunately, some producers and packagers of these products now offer mail-order service. Peoples Woods, located in Cumberland, Rhode Island (800-729-5800), sells over 25 varieties of hardwood chunks and chips, including flavors like peach, cherry, hickory, oak, sweet birch, and apple. Owner Don Hysko encourages consumers to purchase "fresh-cut" hardwood. It's aged so long that it burns, but not aged so long that it loses its aromatic quality.

Try searching the Internet for additional sources.

Tomato Bruschetta

Here's a classic recipe for Tomato Bruschetta that requires a minimum of grilling — only the bread slices feel the heat of the grill. You can make the chopped tomato topping ahead of serving time — in fact it's preferable to do so. This recipe makes a terrific appetizer.

Preparation time: 15 minutes

Grilling time: 4 minutes

Yield: 6 to 8 appetizer servings

2 large red ripe tomatoes (about 1^1/$_4$ pounds), cored, seeded, and diced

^{1}/$_2$ cup coarsely chopped fresh basil

2 tablespoons peeled and diced red onion (optional)

About ^{1}/$_4$ cup extra-virgin olive oil, divided

1 clove garlic, peeled and minced

1 teaspoon balsamic or red wine vinegar

Salt and pepper to taste

12 slices crusty French bread, cut diagonally about ^{3}/$_4$-inch thick

3 cloves garlic, peeled and halved

1 In a small bowl, combine the tomatoes, basil, red onion (if desired), 2 tablespoons of the olive oil, the minced garlic, vinegar, and salt and pepper. Cover and let stand at room temperature for at least 30 minutes but not longer than 2 hours.

(continued)

2 Prepare a medium fire in a charcoal or gas grill.

3 Place the bread slices on an oiled grid. Grill for 4 to 5 minutes or until the bread is lightly toasted and golden on both sides, turning once.

4 Remove and immediately rub the edges and one side of each slice with a garlic clove half. (Use a half clove for every 2 slices.) Drizzle about $^1/_2$ teaspoon of olive oil onto the garlic-rubbed side of each slice.

5 Stir the tomato mixture with a large spoon to thoroughly moisten; top each bread slice with about $1^1/_2$ tablespoons of the tomato mixture. Place on a platter and serve immediately.

Vary It! Here are some other ways to add flavor to bruschetta: Add chopped black olives or finely chopped prosciutto to the tomato mixture; omit the tomatoes and spread the bread with soft goat cheese or Gorgonzola cheese; or top with pesto or grated Parmesan cheese rather than the tomato mixture.

Fixin' Fajitas and Fajita Fixin's

Along the Tex-Mex border of the United States, *fajita* (fah-HEE-tah) means "belt" and describes the look of a raw *skirt steak* — the diaphragm muscle of cattle originally used for fajitas.

A skirt steak can weigh from 1 to 2 pounds and is best grilled whole and then sliced into thin juicy strips. Slightly chewy but very tasty, skirt steaks benefit from a long marinating time. You can substitute less expensive flank steak: However, it's thicker and takes a few more minutes to grill.

Although they're not difficult to make, fajitas do require a game plan; you need to bring the meat, vegetables, and tortillas to the table all at once and sizzling hot. Mexican restaurants usually present fajitas on cast-iron skillets that retain the food's heat. Home cooks can use their ovens or the edges of the grill to accomplish the same thing:

- ✔ Grill the vegetables first, and place them in a low oven or move them to the edge of the grill where they will keep warm.

- ✔ Foil-wrap and keep the tortillas warm at the edge of the grill until you are ready to assemble the fajitas.

✔ Prepare the condiments, setting out bowls of sour cream, guacamole, salsa, and chopped cilantro on the table, before grilling.

✔ And if you can, have your guests waiting at the table for the meat to arrive hot and sizzling off the grill.

Best-Ever Fajitas

No one knows for sure who created the fajita, but a few stories worth their salt circulate about its origins. Ninfa Laurenza introduced an item similar to fajitas, called tacos al carbon, at her restaurant, Ninfa's, in Houston back in 1973. The creator of the first fajita must marvel today at the ingredients that go into fajitas. We've seen everything from grilled chicken to lobster in fajitas, with only the wheat tortilla as a constant. We still think they're best — and certainly most authentic — when made with skirt steaks, like this recipe. You can take a look at the finished product in the color photos near the center of this book.

Preparation time: *25 minutes*

Marinating time: *4 hours or overnight*

Grilling time: *12 to 14 minutes*

Yield: *4 servings*

$1^1/_4$ to $1^1/_2$ pounds skirt or flank steak	Salt and pepper to taste
1 small onion, peeled and chopped	2 medium green or red bell peppers
3 tablespoons vegetable oil	2 medium onions
2 tablespoons tequila (optional)	Vegetable oil for brushing peppers and onions
Juice of 2 limes	
Grated peel of $^1/_2$ lime (about 1 teaspoon)	8 large wheat flour tortillas, each about 8 to 9 inches in diameter
1 jalapeño pepper, seeded and diced	Fresh Tomato Salsa (optional — see Chapter 6)
2 cloves garlic, peeled and minced	
1 teaspoon ground cumin	Sour cream (optional)
1 teaspoon paprika	Guacamole (optional) (see Chapter 6)

1 Trim any loose pieces of fat from the steak.

2 In a non-reactive dish or a large, resealable plastic bag, combine the 1 chopped onion, 3 tablespoons oil, tequila (if desired), lime juice, lime peel, jalapeño pepper, garlic, cumin, paprika, and salt and pepper. Add the steak and turn, coating it in the marinade. Cover the dish or seal the bag, and refrigerate for at least 4 hours or overnight, turning occasionally.

(continued)

3 Prepare a hot fire in a charcoal or gas grill.

4 Meanwhile, core and seed the bell green peppers and cut each into strips about 1-inch thick. Peel the onions and cut crosswise into $1/4$-inch rounds. Brush the vegetables with vegetable oil.

5 Wrap the tortillas in 2 aluminum foil packages of 4 each; set aside.

6 Cook the onions and peppers on a lightly oiled grid. (Better yet, place them in a hinged wire basket or on a grill topper to keep them from falling through the grill grid and to make turning them easier.) Grill, uncovered, for 10 minutes, turning once, until tender and browned. When done, transfer the vegetables to a baking pan, cover with foil, and set on the edge of the grill or in a 300° oven to keep warm until ready to serve.

7 Remove the meat from the marinade and drain briefly, reserving the marinade. Place the meat on the center of the grid; grill for 6 to 7 minutes for rare to medium-rare, turning and basting once with the remaining marinade. (Actual cooking time depends on the thickness of the steak and intensity of the heat. Thicker flank steak takes a few minutes longer.) Use a sharp knife to make a small incision in the center of the steak to test doneness. The meat should be browned on the outside and pink and juicy inside. When done, move the steak to a carving board and cover with foil; let rest for a few minutes and then slice thinly across the grain. (See Figure 18-2.)

8 As the steak grills, place the tortilla foil packages on the edge of the grill for about 5 minutes to warm through, turning once. (Keep warm in foil until ready to serve.)

9 To assemble the fajitas, place a few slices of meat and some of the grilled peppers and onions on each tortilla; top with salsa, sour cream, and guacamole (if desired) before rolling them up.

Vary It! The fajita marinade is quite delicious if used to flavor other steak cuts such as top round or sirloin. For a vegetarian meal, skip the steak all together and serve the grilled peppers and onions in the warm tortillas with the salsa, sour cream, and guacamole. You can substitute corn flour tortillas for wheat flour tortillas.

Vary It! You need only a few ingredients — lime juice, oil, and some crushed garlic — to make the perfect fajita marinade. But a bottled Italian-flavored salad dressing makes a good marinade and saves you time. For fajitas with authentic Mexican flavor, be sure to add presoaked mesquite wood chips to a charcoal fire or, better yet, grill the meat over a mixture of mesquite wood chunks and hardwood charcoal.

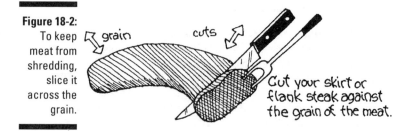

Figure 18-2:
To keep meat from shredding, slice it across the grain.

grain   cuts

Cut your skirt or flank steak against the grain of the meat.

Let Them Eat Quesadillas

A classic Mexican *quesadilla* (kay-sah-DEE-ah) is a gooey tortilla sandwich filled with a cheese stuffing (*queso* means "cheese" in Spanish), and usually fried in hot oil until crisp and bubbly. Grilling eliminates almost all the calories acquired through pan-frying, with identical results — a wafer-thin, crisp sandwich with a melted cheese filling.

Cheesy Quesadillas

This version of a quesadilla calls for cheese, beans, and salsa, but improvise to create up your own. Your kids will find these quesadillas irresistible. If you think they won't notice, add thinly sliced, quick-cooking vegetables, like bell peppers, mushrooms, and onions, to the cheese stuffing to get some vitamin-packed meals into those picky eaters. Adults might like to add chopped jalapeño or chipotle peppers.

Preparation time: *15 minutes*

Grilling time: *4 minutes*

Yield: *4 main dish servings or 8 to 10 appetizer servings*

8 large, wheat flour tortillas, each about 8 to 9 inches in diameter

Vegetable oil for brushing the tortillas

1¹/₃ cups refried pinto beans

¹/₂ cup bottled salsa, and more for garnish

1¹/₂ cups shredded cheese such as Monterey Jack, Cheddar, Gruyère, fontina, provolone, or mozzarella

Chopped fresh cilantro or parsley (optional)

Sour cream (optional)

1 Prepare a medium fire in a charcoal or gas grill.

2 Brush one side of 4 tortillas with oil; place the tortillas, oiled-side-down, on a large cookie sheet. Spread ¹/₃ cup refried beans over each tortilla. Spoon the salsa evenly over the beans, using 2 tablespoons per tortilla. Divide the cheese evenly and sprinkle over the salsa, covering to within ¹/₄ inch of edge.

(continued)

3 Top with the remaining 4 tortillas; brush with oil.

4 Using a wide spatula, carefully place the tortillas on a lightly oiled grid. Cover and grill until the bottoms are lightly browned, about 2 minutes. Using a spatula, carefully flip the tortillas over and grill, covered, for 2 minutes more or until the second side is lightly browned and the cheese is hot and melted. Rotate any quesadillas cooking too fast to cooler parts of the grill, if necessary, to prevent them from burning. Transfer to individual plates, cut into quarters, and serve with extra salsa, chopped cilantro or parsley (if desired), and sour cream (if desired). (Cut the quesadillas into smaller wedges if serving as hot appetizers.)

Tortilla Towers

If you like quesadillas, you'll love this multilayered version that uses ground meat, barbecue-flavored onions, Monterey Jack cheese, and chopped cilantro. After it's assembled, you grill the pancakelike stack to a crispy finish.

Preparation time: *20 minutes*

Grilling time: *6 minutes*

Yield: *4 servings*

³/₄ pound ground beef

¹/₂ to 1 jalapeño pepper, seeded and thinly sliced

Salt and pepper to taste

1 tablespoon vegetable oil, plus oil for brushing tortillas

2 medium onions, peeled, cut in half, and thinly sliced

¹/₂ cup favorite bottled or homemade barbecue sauce

12 6-inch flour tortillas

2 cups grated, loosely packed Monterey Jack cheese

Sour cream (optional)

¹/₄ cup chopped fresh cilantro, and extra for garnish

1 Prepare a medium fire in a charcoal or gas grill.

2 In a large heavy skillet or saucepan, cook the meat and jalapeño pepper over high heat until well browned. Use a wooden spoon to break up the ground meat, and stir often. Season with salt and pepper. Use a slotted spoon to transfer the meat mixture to a mixing bowl. Cover the bowl with foil to keep warm.

3 Add 1 tablespoon oil to the skillet and heat over medium heat. Add the onions; cook, stirring occasionally, until the onions are soft and translucent, 5 to 7 minutes.

4 Add the barbecue sauce and cook for 5 minutes more or until the onions are very tender, stirring and scraping the bottom of the pan often.

5 Assemble the quesadilla layers as follows: Brush one side of 4 tortillas with oil and place them, oiled side down, on a large cookie sheet. Spread the barbecued onions evenly over the 4 oiled tortillas. Using half the cheese, sprinkle equally over the onions. Sprinkle 1 tablespoon cilantro over the cheese. Cover with 4 more tortillas. Divide and spread the meat mixture over each tortilla. Sprinkle each with the remaining cheese and top with the remaining 4 tortillas. Brush the tops with oil.

6 Place the layered tortillas on a lightly oiled grid. Cover and grill for 2 to 3 minutes or until the side that's face down on the grill is lightly browned. Using a wide metal spatula, turn each tortilla carefully to avoid spilling out the ingredients, and grill, covered, for another 2 to 3 minutes.

7 Remove the layered tortillas to individual serving plates; cut each into quarters. Serve with a dollop of sour cream (if desired) and a sprinkling of chopped cilantro.

Vary It! You can substitute ground turkey, veal, pork, or even lamb for the ground beef.

Sandwich Face Off

When you eat a sandwich stuffed with your favorite foods, the experience can range from satisfying to heavenly. Grilling adds another dimension: Both the bread crust and the filling can be infused with smoky, grilled flavors. The sandwich recipes in this section are easy to make on a backyard grill or on a portable hibachi hauled out to the beach.

Vary It! Several recipes from other chapters can be quickly converted into grilled sandwiches and wraps. For example, use the Cajun-Style Steak Rub (Chapter 5) on thinly cut tender steaks or chicken breasts before grilling and then sandwich the meat between slices of grilled French or Italian bread. Or turn these dishes into sandwiches:

- ✔ Grilled Kielbasa with Creamy Mustard Sauce (Chapter 8)
- ✔ Jerk-Seasoned Chicken Breasts (Chapter 15) on grilled club rolls with shredded lettuce and slices of avocado and grilled tomato

Grilled Cheese Sandwich

When you make a grilled cheese sandwich, you usually reach for a griddle or a fry-pan. This recipe uses the grill with better results, and without the undesirable fat you get from pan-frying.

Serve these sandwiches as a light lunch or easy appetizers. To turn them into party hors d'oeuvres, cut the sandwiches into "fingers" about 2 inches long.

Preparation time: 5 minutes

Grilling time: 4 minutes

Yield: 1 serving

2 slices whole-wheat or whole-grain bread

Oil for brushing bread

3 to 4 thin slices Cheddar, Swiss, Monterey Jack, or other cheese

1 Prepare a medium fire in a charcoal or gas grill.

2 Brush one side of a slice of bread lightly with oil. Place the bread, oiled side down, on a flat plate; top with cheese. Place a second bread slice over the cheese; brush the top lightly with oil.

3 Place on a lightly oiled grid. Cover and grill 2 minutes per side or until the cheese is melted and the bread is lightly browned.

Vary It! Add an assortment of condiments and seasonings: Some of our favorites are chopped jalapeños; stuffed, chopped green olives; a slice of grilled tomato; crisp bacon; or avocado slices.

Open-Faced Grilled Eggplant and Goat Cheese Sandwiches

This healthy-hearty sandwich, shown in the color photo section of this book, stacks layers of smoky grilled eggplant, tomatoes, goat cheese, fresh basil, and olives on French bread. Cut into small 3-inch pieces, to make lovely appetizers for a summer party.

Preparation time: 20 minutes

Grilling time: 20 minutes

Yield: 4 main dish servings or 8 to 10 appetizer servings

2 small, long eggplants, about 1 pound each

4 medium, ripe tomatoes (about 1 pound total)

1 loaf French bread, about 24 inches long

$^1/_2$ cup olive oil, divided

2 large cloves garlic, peeled and forced through a press or finely minced

Salt and pepper to taste

2 teaspoons balsamic vinegar

4 ounces fresh goat cheese, at room temperature

2 tablespoons chopped fresh basil

Kalamata or other cured black olives (optional)

1 Prepare a medium-hot fire in a charcoal or gas grill.

2 Meanwhile, cut off the eggplant ends. Lay one eggplant on a cutting board and, with a sharp knife, cut off a thin slice lengthwise. Repeat on the opposite side. Discard these slices (they are mostly peel). Slice the remaining eggplant lengthwise into $^1/_2$-inch-thick slices. Repeat with the second eggplant. Core the tomatoes and slice crosswise into $^1/_2$-inch-thick slices. Place the vegetable slices on a large baking sheet. Slice the French bread in half lengthwise and then in half again crosswise, making 4 slices, each about 12 inches long.

3 In a small bowl, combine 6 tablespoons of the olive oil and the garlic. Brush the cut sides of the French bread and both sides of the vegetables with the oil-garlic mixture. Sprinkle the vegetables with salt and pepper.

4 Combine the remaining 2 tablespoons olive oil with the balsamic vinegar; season with salt and pepper and set aside.

5 Place the eggplant on a lightly oiled grid and grill for 6 to 7 minutes per side or until tender and lightly browned; move the eggplant to the edge of the grid to keep it warm. Grill the tomatoes until warmed through, 2 minutes per side. Place the French bread slices on the edges of the grid, cut side down; toast until golden brown, about 2 minutes; transfer, cut side up, to a serving platter or cutting board.

6 Spread the goat cheese on the toasted bread slices, dividing equally. Lay the eggplant and then the tomato on the bread slices, covering the bread completely; drizzle with the oil-vinegar dressing. Garnish with the chopped basil. Cut into main dish or appetizer servings. Serve with kalamata olives (if desired).

Vary It! Substitute chopped, oil-packed sun-dried tomatoes for the kalamata olives.

Warming up pre-baked breads is a cinch. Here are some ways to do it:

- ✓ **Garlic bread:** Slash a loaf of French bread almost through and at 1-inch intervals from end to end. Spread softened butter, flavored with chopped fresh garlic (or garlic salt) and chopped fresh herbs, between the slices. Wrap in aluminum foil and grill for 15 minutes over a medium-hot fire, turning often.

- ✓ **Grilled corn or bran muffins:** Slice the muffins in half, spread the cut sides with softened butter, and grill over medium heat until lightly browned.

- ✓ **Grilled polenta:** Cut off $1/4$- to $1/2$-inch thick slices. Oil them lightly on both sides and grill over medium-high heat, uncovered, for 5 minutes a side or until lightly browned and warmed through. Set the slices next to or under a piece of grilled chicken, lamb, or beef. These little grilled polenta rounds can transform a simple dish into something imaginative and elegant.

Part V:
The Part of Tens

The 5th Wave   By Rich Tennant

In this part . . .

In this part, we tell you where to find the best barbecue places in America and clue you in on how to throw an awesome outdoor party that fits your mood and your friends. And if you're happy with all this information, perhaps you'll invite us to come by for some ribs and a glass of wine!

Chapter 19

Ten of Our Favorite Barbecue Places in the U.S.

• •

In This Chapter

▶ Snooping out a good barbecue place

▶ Highlighting our top ten places

• •

*B*arbecue stands, shacks, Quonset huts, drive-ins, and family restaurants dot the country with encouraging regularity. Although you may find the greatest concentration of them in the American South, there are terrific barbecue eateries in New York, Los Angeles, St. Louis, Kansas City, Chicago, and just about everywhere else.

The key ingredient to a true barbecue place is long, slow grilling and smoking over hardwood — with no precooking or shortcuts. Some places that call themselves "barbecues" steam or precook their meat before tossing it on the fire, in order to cut the cooking time. What you get is a piece of mushy meat that tastes steamy with a little smokiness on the outside — that's definitely not good barbecue. Marinades, basting sauces, and dry spices can make some difference, but in the end, the talent, skill, and, more often than not, the secret ingredient of the pitmaster make one mess of ribs or beef better than the barbecue from the place down the street. (A *mess,* by the way, doesn't refer to the delectable sloppiness of eating barbecue with your fingers but to an old Latin word, *missus,* that means "a portion of food.")

Choosing a top ten is very tough for us, but here are our picks for the top ten barbecue places in the U.S.A. We've based our selection on regional variety as much as on good taste.

Tracking down the real McCoy

Good barbecue places are located down country roads, just off highways, in inner city neighborhoods, and in upscale shopping malls. So how do you tell if a place is any good or not? Here are some pointers — none of them foolproof!

✔ Look for a supply of split hardwood logs stacked somewhere on the premises. A good barbecue place may certainly use charcoal, but the authentic flavor comes from hardwood smoking.

✔ Look for smoke coming out of a chimney — a clear sign that the smoking is being done on the premises, not somewhere else.

✔ Sniff the air outside. It should smell like barbecue, and it should lure you in like a fish to the bait.

✔ Check the parking lot. Most good barbecue places draw a very diverse crowd. Good barbecue places are not secrets, and they're local hang-outs for everyone in town.

Arthur Bryant's

1727 Brooklyn, Kansas City, Missouri; 816-231-1123

Immortalized by author Calvin Trillin as one of the best restaurants in the world, Bryant's is indeed one of the great barbecue legends. Although Mr. Bryant has gone on to that big smokehouse in the sky, his legacy has been maintained, the lusciousness of his ribs, french fries, and iced beer lives on, the sauce has a flavor no one has ever pinned down, but the place is a lot cleaner than it used to be in the old days.

Charlie Vergos' Rendezvous

General Washburn Alley, Memphis, Tennessee; 901-523-2746

Although open only for dinner, dinner in Memphis begins at 4:30 p.m., and the Rendezvous is packed by 6 p.m. You'll get some dissenters who think that Charlie has gone commercial, but we find his unique, dry-rubbed, unsauced ribs absolutely addictive. The place has been open since 1948 (right across from the posh Peabody Hotel), and you could write a social and business history of the South from the calling cards and newspapers pinned to the wall here. After you've eaten here, you may also want to order from Charlie's mail-order catalog, which is what his detractors call "going commercial."

Dreamland Bar-B-Q Drive Inn

Jerusalem Heights, Tuscaloosa, Alabama; 205-758-8135

When you see the trailer park in Jerusalem Heights, glance on the other side of the road at the bunch of pine trees and then follow your nose to Dreamland. Opened in 1958, this wonderfully gregarious place draws everyone in town, from 10 in the morning to 9 or 10 at night. The pork ribs are a generous size, thick but very tender, with a good streak of fat and a subtle saucing. The beverage of choice here is beer, beer, and more beer.

Kreuz Market

208 South Commerce Street, Lockhart, Texas; 512-398-2361

About halfway between Austin and San Antonio, the little windswept, dusty town of Lockhart is home to one of the unique beef barbecue places in the country. A good deal of German and eastern European influence is in evidence here, and Kreuz Market (which sells its products directly to customers) has been here since 1924. You sit in a big open room at Formica tables, bring your beautiful beef brisket (no sauce) to the table on butcher paper, dig in with your fingers, nibble on white bread or saltines, and wash it all down with a pitcher of iced tea. You won't eat better or more simply in your life.

Lexington Barbecue No. 1

10 Highway 29-70 South, Lexington, North Carolina; 704-249-9814

You'll get a lot of argument about which is the best barbecue joint in Lexington, which likes to think of itself as the world capital of barbecue. But Lexington is certainly the capital of West Carolina-style barbecue. And you won't be disappointed at any of the dozen or more joints in this little town of about a thousand residents. You don't come here for ribs: You come for chopped pork on a warm bun, with a vinegary, peppery sauce with a touch of tomato (always made in small batches throughout the day) that makes this one of the essential stops on the 'cue tour.

Robinson's No. 1 Ribs

940 Madison Street, Clark Park, Illinois; 708-383-8452

Robinson's calls itself "No. 1" in the Chicago-style barbecue sweepstakes, and we have to agree that it edges out the competition by an inch or two. The baby back ribs are as good as you'll find in the Midwest — charred and crispy, juicy and tender — and the chicken is fine, the hot links wonderfully smoky, the black-eyed peas evocative, and the macaroni and cheese the ultimate comfort food. For a sweet ending, go for the sweet potato pie, which you can order with a scoop of Häagen Dazs ice cream!

Sconyers' Bar-B-Que

2511 Windsor Spring Road, Augusta, Georgia; 404-790-5411

Pray that you're not in Augusta on Sunday or Monday, because that's when Sconyers' is closed, and you wouldn't want to miss the experience of eating with the locals who pack this place the other five days of the week. It seats well over 400 ravenous eaters, who come not only for the superlative pork ribs and chopped pork sandwiches but for good chicken, too — all of it cooked upright so that the excess fat drips away. Sconyers' barbecue is so succulent that we have to use the cliché that it will "melt in your mouth."

Sonny Bryan's Smokehouse

2202 Inwood Road, Dallas, Texas; 214-357-7120

The original location (there are newer clones) doesn't look like much, which means it looks just the way you'd imagine a good Texas 'cue stand should. Low-lying, a little scuzzy inside and out, with schoolchildren's desks as tables, Sonny's has been here since 1958 and is a temple of fine barbecue cookery. (Sadly, Sonny is no longer with us.) The ribs are first-rate, but in Texas, the beef brisket is what counts, and Sonny's is fabulous. You line up at the counter, put in your order, and give your initials to the counter help. After a couple minutes, you hear your initials called out, and before you know it, you're in cow heaven.

Sylvia's Restaurant

328 Lenox Avenue, New York, New York; 212-960-0660

Great barbecue in New York? Well, of course: Sylvia's is in Harlem, one of the most soulful soul food neighborhoods in America, and Sylvia Woods has entertained every politician who ever wanted Harlem's vote, as well as a constant line of sports figures, movie stars, divas, and R&B singers. You can go for breakfast and have the light pancakes, or dig into a plate of Southern fried chicken at lunch, or stand in line for Sunday brunch, when all of Harlem seems to be knocking on Sylvia's door. But whatever you do, don't miss the pork ribs. They're very moist, kind of sweet, and absolutely delicious. Sylvia and her family have been slowly opening branches in other cities, but this is where it all began.

Tom's Place

7251 North Federal Highway, Boca Raton, Florida; 407-997-0920

Boca Raton may seem too upscale to have a good barbecue place, but Tom's is the real thing. Big, barnlike, and very friendly, it's a place where the ribs, which are pretty well sauced, are only the beginning. Tom's also serves up great chicken, hush puppies, and an array of Southern-style vegetables like okra, sweet potatoes, and corn on the cob that will make you very full and very happy.

Chapter 20

Ten Great Outdoor Party Tips

*D*on't overlook the details when you're giving an outdoor party. Your attention to the little things can guarantee the success of your barbecue. For example: Have you considered who is coming? What if it rains? What time of day is the party? Will you be involving your guests in the barbecuing? In this chapter, we answer these questions, along with some others that you may not have considered, especially if you're planning outdoors what you've previously done only indoors.

Plan for Rain

Few people can afford the luxury of having a tent constructed over a party, except at a wedding or other stellar event. So, if you're planning an outdoor party and rain looks imminent, make sure that you've made the inside of your house presentable for company.

Fortunately, rain does not usually affect grilling, unless the rain is truly torrential or an accompanying wind threatens to blow away your kettle grill. If such is the case or if you just can't stand grilling while getting soaked, consider canceling the whole outdoor grilling *idea,* but not the party itself. Remember, the same foods you can cook outside can be cooked inside, under the broiler.

If the rain is not too heavy, however, grilling can continue uninterrupted. Just make sure that you do not push the grill under any overhang that may catch fire when the grill is unattended.

Don't Guess Who's Coming to Dinner

You may be lucky enough to know and love each of your guests. On the other hand, maybe you must invite a few people you really don't care for, or maybe you have a mixed crowd of people who don't necessarily know each other. No matter what the situation, you may want to consider the following issues:

- Is this a fairly reserved crowd that probably won't want to help with the grilling? If so, you shouldn't plan on any help from them.

- If your guests are a dressy crowd, they're not going to want to eat much with their fingers, so plan your menu accordingly.

- If your guests are the casual type — shorts, T-shirts, and a keg of beer are their style — then you can probably coast through the grilling with the help of friends.

- Will your guests include children? They may be playing games in the backyard, so make sure that the grill is not positioned in the path of a football or soccer ball. Don't forget to fix some burgers and hot dogs for the kids in addition to the food you plan to serve to the adults.

- Do some of your guests have special diets? These days, it's a good idea to ask your guests in advance if they are vegetarians or on restricted diets so that you can plan accordingly to have something for them to eat.

Work on Your Timing

Nothing can spoil a party more than serving the food at the wrong time. Food that is cooked and ready to be served too soon — *before* all the guests arrive or *before* the appetizers and drinks are finished — is unappealing. On the other hand, don't take forever to bring out the main dishes.

- Prepare as much food as possible beforehand, especially appetizers and finger foods.

  - Dips are easy, salads are great, and good crusty breads are always welcome.

  - Make sure that desserts are ready before you serve the main course.

  - Cakes and pies are always welcome, and you can make them the day before.

- Depending on when your guests are due to arrive, get the fire going within minutes of the first guests' appearance. You can always add more coals to the fire later on, but you can't get a cold grill hot quickly enough if you've underestimated your guests' tolerance for small talk and cocktails. For this reason, you should always keep plenty of extra charcoal on hand.

Keep It Cool

Because most outdoor parties take place in warm weather, you need a lot of cold drinks. In order to make it easy for people to help themselves (you're going to be very busy cooking), always have two or more coolers filled with soft drinks and beer in a convenient location *outside* the house so that people can help themselves. Such a set-up also means less work for you.

Also, prepare cocktails, punch, or iced tea in big batches in advance and store as much as possible in the refrigerator. Have plenty of ice on hand if you don't have room to refrigerate all your cold drinks.

Think Buffet

Because you'll have your hands full with the grilling, opt for the buffet line for your guests. Set a pretty table, and gather a set of utensils and wrap them in a colorful napkin. Set out the glassware, fill the coolers with ice, beer, and soft drinks, and bring out a big festive punch bowl. Line up the spirits and wines, put out the appetizers on platters, and then, when the grilled foods are ready, either bring them to the buffet table or, better yet, serve people right from the grill.

Here are some of the buffet-style items (most recipes are in this book) that we think are excellent for outdoor service:

Antipasto platters of bite-size pieces of cheese, sliced sausages, and vegetable crudités in plastic bags

Spicy Chili Chicken Wings (Chapter 15)

Soups and chili, which can easily be reheated in big pots on the grills

Dips like Tapenade, Tabbouleh, Guacamole, Baba Ghanoush, Roasted Pepper, and Caper Salsa (Chapters 6 and 17)

Grilled Figs and Prosciutto (Chapter 17)

Cheesy Quesadillas (Chapter 18)

Tomato Bruschetta (Chapter 18)

Grilled Clams and Mussels with Fresh Tomato Sauce (Chapter 16)

Smoked Salmon Fillet (Chapter 16)

Grilled Kielbasa with Creamy Mustard Sauce or Grilled Italian Links with Caraway Sauerkraut (Chapter 8)

Three-Bean Bake (Chapter 7)

Orange-Ginger Coleslaw (Chapter 7)

Bow-Ties with Peppers, Peas, and Saffron Mayonnaise (Chapter 7)

Macaroni Salad with Sun-Dried Tomato Mayonnaise (Chapter 7)

Tomato and Red Onion Salad (Chapter 7)

Grilled Pizza with assorted toppings (Chapter 18)

Grilled Corn on the Cob (Chapter 17)

Garlic-Grilled Portobello Mushrooms (Chapter 17)

Marinated and Grilled Potato Planks (Chapter 17)

Foil-Wrapped Baked Apples (Chapter 17)

Grilled Bananas with Caramel Sauce (Chapter 17)

Tackle Tailgating

Sports fans have elevated tailgating to an elaborate event. Those pregame parking-lot meals are often served on tables decorated with linen cloths, candelabras, and crystal wine glasses. The menus are expanding, too. Portable gas and charcoal grills make it easier for tailgaters to serve hot foods — and a wider variety of foods — while waiting for the kickoff.

Major grilling manufacturers make portable gas and charcoal grills. CharBroil, Weber, Sunbeam, and Ducane all carry portable grills that retail from $20 to $200, depending on the features and the quality. We've also seen a Weber charcoal grill with the legs cut off so that the grill can fit into a car or van.

Tailgate treats

If you're having a tailgate party, think in terms of food that's going to cook fast. Here are some tips:

- ✔ Big, thick porterhouse steaks and massive pork chops are not a great idea because these meats need more grilling time than you may have.

- ✔ Thinly cut meats, cutlets, or scallops are great choices. A butcher can cut them uniformly, or you can buy $1/4$-inch-thick pieces and pound them at home between two pieces of waxed paper into thin cutlets.

✔ Another popular choice is flank or skirt steaks, marinated in teriyaki and soy sauces. These thin cuts carry certain advantages for tailgating: They cook very quickly, so you can feed a crowd in a hurry with a minimum of fuel, and they are boneless and perfect for sandwiches, eliminating the need for utensils. Tailgaters call them "flip-flops," because they cook in 1 to 2 minutes per side.

Tailgate tools

Food isn't all you need for your tailgate parties. Here are some items you should haul along with you:

✔ No matter what you may think about plastic kitchen supplies, they're ideal for portable parties. Plastic containers and zipper-type bags can transport food easily, safely, and without spilling. Tupperware containers can carry burgers, steaks, chicken cutlets, and kebabs. Plastic bags can keep foods marinating until grill time. You can also use plastic bags to store leftovers when you're cleaning up. Trash-can-size bags are good for disposing of your litter.

✔ Insulated coolers — some of which now come with wheels for easy moving — are extremely useful and come in every size. To make a portable cooler for beer, soda, and food, line a cardboard box or a recycling bin with a large garbage bag and fill it with ice. It will keep food and beverages cold for several hours.

✔ Foam containers, called Tuffoams, are useful for insulating cold drinks and to keep hands warm when drinking a cold beer in cold weather. The can sits in the foam holder.

✔ Portable bars. Every week, tailgaters haul the same set of liquor bottles, glasses, bar tools, and so on to the game. People build or buy their own wooden boxes for storing and carrying these items in their vans.

✔ Sterno cans are useful for warming hot food in steam-table pans.

✔ Hot water that you've brought from home in thermoses and insulated containers comes in handy when cleaning up.

✔ Don't forget the dish detergent.

Grilling in a parking lot can be safe, but only if you keep the grill far from anyone's vehicle, including your own. Never try to grill inside the back of a truck, station wagon, or recreational vehicle.

Themes Like Old Times

Call us sentimental, but every really good outdoor party we've ever been to has had some kind of theme, with appropriate music. Your theme can be as simple as a Fourth of July bash, where the tradition calls for barbecuing and hot dogs, or you can key the event to some local historic event.

✔ Ethnic-themed parties can be great fun, where, for instance, Middle Eastern lamb barbecue and shish-kebabs are featured along with hummus, tabbouleh, and other dishes of the area. You can play music from that region, too.

✔ Turn-of-the-century parties may offer homemade ice cream, a clambake, and old-fashioned pies and cakes. Good ragtime music or Sousa marches may be fun sounds to liven up the event.

✔ Decades parties can feature the clothing styles, foods ,and music of a particular recent period. For instance, you might ask guests at a "60s" party to show up in surfer shorts and other fashion artifacts. Your menu can include burgers, fries, onion dip, fondue, Brie cheese, and carrot cake. Play songs from the Beach Boys, Beatles, and Supremes.

Break Out the Marshmallows

Marshmallows? Yes, marshmallows. No good outdoor party ever took place without marshmallows roasted over a grill. Kids love them, and adults get all nostalgic for them. Just remember to offer people long skewers or branches and keep the number of people at the grill to a minimum.

As everyone knows, the best roast marshmallow has just the right proportion of black bubbles, a mix of toasty brown and white surfaces, a skin that has slight resiliency, and a center that oozes out warmly. And that's what grilling outdoors is all about.

For a twist on roasted marshmallows, make the Girl Scout classic — S'mores — as a tailgate dessert.

1. **Roast marshmallows on a stick or skewer at the edge of your gas grill or charcoal fire.**

2. **Place each hot marshmallow on top of a graham cracker square, cover with a 1-ounce piece of thin, dark chocolate, and then top with another graham cracker square.**

3. **Press together. Eat!**

Index

(continued)

• D •

• E •

• *H* •

(continued)

• *S* •

● *T* ●

• *U* •

• *V* •

(continued)

• W •

• Y •

• Z •

The BackYard BarbeQuer

is a 12-page, bi-monthly newsletter packed with barbecuing tips, trends, techniques and recipes. It's a perfect resource for beginner or master barbecuers. Regular features include what's new in equipment and foods, cookbook reviews, answers to barbecue questions, favorite recipes, and much more. Rate is $24 for a one-year subscription, and $44 for two years. International rate is $34 for a one-year subscription, $62 for two years.

Order your subscription today!

Save $4 off the regular rate of $24 for a one-year subscription (US)
and $6 off the regular rate of $34 for a one-year subscription (International)
by sending in the coupon below.

Name_____

Street Address_____ Apt.#_____

City /State/Zip _____

_____

Send Check payable to:
THE BACKYARD BARBEQUER, P.O. Box 767, Holmdel, NJ 07733

$4 OFF
a one-year
subscription
(US)

$6 OFF
a one-year
subscription
(Int'l)

IDG BOOKS WORLDWIDE
BOOK REGISTRATION

Register This Book and Win!

We want to hear from you!

Visit **http://my2cents.dummies.com** to register this book and tell us how you liked it!

✔ Get entered in our monthly prize giveaway.

✔ Give us feedback about this book — tell us what you like best, what you like least, or maybe what you'd like to ask the author and us to change!

✔ Let us know any other *...For Dummies*® topics that interest you.

Your feedback helps us determine what books to publish, tells us what coverage to add as we revise our books, and lets us know whether we're meeting your needs as a *...For Dummies* reader. You're our most valuable resource, and what you have to say is important to us!

Not on the Web yet? It's easy to get started with *Dummies 101*®: *The Internet For Windows*® *98* or *The Internet For Dummies*,® 5th Edition, at local retailers everywhere.

Or let us know what you think by sending us a letter at the following address:

...For Dummies Book Registration
Dummies Press
7260 Shadeland Station, Suite 100
Indianapolis, IN 46256-3917
Fax 317-596-5498

BESTSELLING BOOK SERIES